THE CAMBRIDGE COMPANION
TO THE ROMANTIC SUBLIME

This is the only collection of its kind to focus on one of the most important aspects of the cultural history of the Romantic period, its sources, and its afterlives. Multidisciplinary in approach, the volume examines the variety of areas of inquiry and genres of cultural productivity in which the sublime played a substantial role during the late eighteenth and early nineteenth centuries. With impressive international scope, this *Companion* considers the Romantic sublime in both European and American contexts and features essays by leading scholars from a range of national backgrounds and subject specialisms, including state-of-the-art perspectives in digital and environmental humanities. An accessible, wide-ranging, and thorough introduction, aimed at researchers, students, and general readers alike, and including extensive suggestions for further reading, *The Cambridge Companion to the Romantic Sublime* is the go-to book on the subject.

Cian Duffy is Professor and Chair of English Literature at Lund University, Sweden. He has published on various aspects of the cultural life and intellectual history of Europe in the Romantic period, including work on the Shelley circle, on the sublime, and on Romanticism in the Nordic countries.

A complete list of books in the series is at the back of the book.

THE CAMBRIDGE
COMPANION TO
THE ROMANTIC
SUBLIME

EDITED BY
CIAN DUFFY
Lund University

CAMBRIDGE
UNIVERSITY PRESS

Shaftesbury Road, Cambridge CB2 8EA, United Kingdom

One Liberty Plaza, 20th Floor, New York, NY 10006, USA

477 Williamstown Road, Port Melbourne, VIC 3207, Australia

314–321, 3rd Floor, Plot 3, Splendor Forum, Jasola District Centre, New Delhi – 110025, India

103 Penang Road, #05–06/07, Visioncrest Commercial, Singapore 238467

Cambridge University Press is part of Cambridge University Press & Assessment, a department of the University of Cambridge.

We share the University's mission to contribute to society through the pursuit of education, learning and research at the highest international levels of excellence.

www.cambridge.org
Information on this title: www.cambridge.org/9781316515914

DOI: 10.1017/9781009026963

First published 2023

A catalogue record for this publication is available from the British Library.

Library of Congress Cataloging-in-Publication Data
NAMES: Duffy, Cian, editor.
TITLE: The Cambridge companion to the romantic sublime / edited by Cian Duffy.
DESCRIPTION: Cambridge ; New York, NY : Cambridge University Press, 2023. |
Includes bibliographical references and index.
IDENTIFIERS: LCCN 2023014021 (print) | LCCN 2023014022 (ebook) | ISBN 9781316515914
(hardback) | ISBN 9781009013055 (paperback) | ISBN 9781009026963 (epub)
SUBJECTS: LCSH: Sublime, The, in literature. | Romanticism.
CLASSIFICATION: LCC PN56.S7416 C36 2023 (print) | LCC PN56.S7416 (ebook) |
DDC 111/.85–dc23/eng/20230505
LC record available at https://lccn.loc.gov/2023014021
LC ebook record available at https://lccn.loc.gov/2023014022

ISBN 978-1-316-51591-4 Hardback
ISBN 978-1-009-01305-5 Paperback

CONTENTS

FIGURES

CONTRIBUTORS

NINA AMSTUTZ is Associate Professor in the History of Art at the University of Oregon. Previously, she was a postdoctoral research associate at the Yale Center for British Art, where she co-curated the exhibition 'The Critique of Reason: Romantic Art, 1760–1860' (Yale University Art Gallery, 2015). She is the author of *Caspar David Friedrich: Nature and the Self* (Yale University Press, 2020) and co-editor of the volume *Das Bild der Natur in der Romantik: Kunst als Philosophie und Wissenschaft* (Brill, 2021).

SIMON BAINBRIDGE is Professor of Romantic Studies in the Department of English Literature and Creative Writing, Lancaster University. He has published several studies of Romantic-period writing, including the books *Napoleon and English Romanticism* (Cambridge University Press, 1992), *British Poetry and the Revolutionary and Napoleonic Wars* (Oxford University Press, 2005), and *Mountaineering and British Romanticism: The Literary Cultures of Climbing, 1770–1836* (Oxford University Press, 2022). He is a former president of the British Association of Romantic Studies and is currently a Trustee of the Wordsworth Trust.

CHRISTOPH BODE is Professor Emeritus at LMU Munich and was Visiting Professor at University of California, Los Angeles; University of California, Berkeley; and Tsinghua University Beijing (among others). He has published thirty books (e.g., *Romanticism and the Forms of Discontent* (Wissenschaftlicher Verlag Trier [WVT], 2017)) and some ninety scholarly articles, most of them in Romanticism, twentieth-century literature, poetics, narratology, and critical theory. A permanent Fellow of LMU's Centre for Advanced Studies and of the Academia Europaea, Bode is also the recipient of various substantial research grants, among them an ERC Advanced Investigator Grant. In 2013, he was awarded the Order of Merit of the Federal Republic of Germany.

TIMOTHY M. COSTELLOE is Professor of Philosophy at the College of William & Mary. His primary research and teaching interests are in aesthetics and history of philosophy. He is editor of *The Sublime: From Antiquity to the Present*

(Cambridge University Press, 2012) and the author of *Aesthetics and Morals in the Philosophy of David Hume* (Routledge, 2007), *The British Aesthetic Tradition: From Shaftesbury to Wittgenstein* (Cambridge University Press, 2013), and, most recently, *The Imagination in Hume's Philosophy: The Canvas of the Mind* (Edinburgh University Press, 2018).

CHRISTOPHER DONALDSON is Lecturer in Cultural History at Lancaster University, where he is also an associate of the Regional Heritage Centre. His recent publications include *Henry Hobhouse's Tour of Cumbria in 1774* (ed. with Robert W. Dunning and Angus J. l. Winchester; Cumberland and Westmorland Antiquarian and Archaeological Society, 2018).

CIAN DUFFY is Professor and Chair of English Literature at Lund University. His research has examined various aspects of the intellectual life and cultural history of Europe during the Romantic period, with particular interest in the Shelley circle, the sublime, travel writing, and Romanticism in the Nordic countries. Recent publications include *British Romanticism and Denmark* (Edinburgh University Press, 2022) and *Nordic Romanticism: Translation, Transmission, Transformation* (edited with Robert W. Rix; Palgrave, 2022).

CASSANDRA FALKE is Professor of English Literature at UiT – The Arctic University of Norway, where she also coordinates the English section and leads the Interdisciplinary Phenomenology research group. She is the author of *Literature by the Working Class: English Working-Class Autobiography 1820–1848* (Cambria, 2013), *The Phenomenology of Love and Reading* (Bloomsbury, 2017), and around forty articles and book chapters. She has edited or co-edited four essay collections including *Wild Romanticism* (with Markus Poetzsch, Routledge, 2021). Much of her work examines forms of human connectedness to each other and to the more-than-human world. New monographs are forthcoming on *Global Human Rights Fiction* (Routledge, 2023) and *Wise Passiveness: The Phenomenology of Receptivity in British Romantic Poetry* (Bloomsbury, 2024).

PATRICK GLAUTHIER is Assistant Professor of Classics at Dartmouth College. He has published on Ennius, Virgil, Manilius, Aratus and the Aratean tradition, the verse fabulist Phaedrus, and *Prometheus Bound*. His current book project is *The Scientific Sublime in Imperial Rome: Manilius, Seneca, Lucan, and the Aetna*, and he is co-editing a volume titled *The Sublime in the Ancient World*. Pieces on the sublime in Ovid, the Elder Pliny, and the early Christian *Proto-Gospel of James* are also in the works.

IAN N. GREGORY is Distinguished Professor of Digital Humanities at Lancaster University where he co-directs the Lancaster Centre for Digital Humanities. His main area of expertise is in spatial humanities, the use of geospatial technologies to understand the past. He has written or edited eight books on this subject, most recently *Deep Mapping the Literary Lake District: A Geographical Text Analysis* (with Joanna Taylor; Rutgers University Press, 2022). He has held grants from multiple funders including the European Research Council, Economic & Social Research Council, Arts & Humanities Research Council, and the Leverhulme Trust.

DAWN HOLLIS recently completed postdoctoral work at the University of St Andrews, during which she published on mountains and landscapes in a variety of contexts, including the classical 'reception of landscape' found in the travel writings of Christopher Wordsworth (1807–85) and the experience of the sublime in responses to Etna from the first century CE to 1773. She is co-editor of *Mountain Dialogues from Antiquity to Modernity* (with Jason König; Bloomsbury, 2021). Her monograph *Mountains before Mountaineering* will be published by History Press in 2024.

TATJANA JUKIĆ is Professor and Chair of English Literature at the University of Zagreb, where she teaches Victorian literature and arts, film studies, and in the doctoral programs of Comparative Literature and of Croatian Language and Literature. She is the author of two monographs, *Zazor, nadzor, sviđanje: Dodiri književnog i vizualnog u britanskom 19. stoljeću* [Liking, Dislike, Supervision. Literature and the Visual in Victorian Britain] (Zagreb, 2002) and *Revolucija i melankolija* [Revolution and Melancholia] (Zagreb, 2011), as well as of essays in, amongst other journals and collections, *The Henry James Review*, *Orbis Litterarum*, *Neue Rundschau*, and the *European Journal of English Studies*.

ANDREW MCINNES is Reader in Romanticisms at Edge Hill University. From 2020 to 2022, he was an Arts and Humanities Research Council Early Career Researcher Leadership Fellow on 'The Romantic Ridiculous' project. He has published widely on Romantic-period women's writing, gothic fiction, and children's literature, including the monograph *Wollstonecraft's Ghost: The Fate of the Female Philosopher in the Romantic Period* (Routledge, 2017). He is co-director of EHU19: Research Centre in Nineteenth-Century Studies.

LIS MØLLER is Professor of Comparative Literature at Aarhus University and president of the Nordic Association for Romantic Studies (NARS). Her most recent book publication is *Middelalderisme I dansk romantisk litteratur* [Medievalism in Danish Romantic Literature], written in collaboration with Hjort Møller, Grosen Jørgensen, Zetterberg-Nielsen, and Kjærulff (Aarhus University Press, 2023). Her current book project is tentatively entitled *Ballads across Borders*.

NORBERT LENNARTZ is Professor of English literature at the University of Vechta. Previous publications in English include the edited collections *Lord Byron and Marginality* (Edinburgh University Press, 2018) and *The Lost Romantics: Forgotten Poets, Neglected Works and One-Hit Wonders* (Palgrave, 2020), and the monograph *Tears, Liquids and Porous Bodies in Literature across the Ages: Niobe's Siblings* (Bloomsbury, 2022). He is currently working on a book examining open and submerged discourses of Germanophilia and Germanophobia in nineteenth-century British literature.

ROBERT W. RIX is Associate Professor at the University of Copenhagen. He has published widely in several areas relating to the eighteenth and nineteenth centuries: politics, religion, language, nationalism, Nordic antiquarianism, and print culture/book history. One area of interest has been the circulation of Scandinavian texts in Anglophone contexts. In recent years he has also written on perceptions of the Arctic. His next monograph, *The Vanished Settlers of Greenland: In Search of a Legend and Its Legacy*, is forthcoming with Cambridge University Press.

MATTHEW SANGSTER is Professor of Romantic Studies, Fantasy and Cultural History at the University of Glasgow. He is the author of *Living as an Author in the Romantic Period* (Palgrave, 2021) and co-editor (with Jon Mee) of *Institutions of Literature, 1700–1900* (Cambridge University Press, 2022) and *Remediating the 1820s* (Edinburgh University Press, 2023). His digital project Romantic London (www.romanticlondon.org/) explores how different genres represent the metropolis; he has published on this research in *Life Writing*, the *Journal of Victorian Culture*, *Romanticism on the Net*, and the *Keats Letters Project*.

RICHARD C. SHA is Professor of Literature and Affiliate Professor of Philosophy at American University, Washington. He is the author of three books: *Imagination and Science in Romanticism* (Johns Hopkins University Press, 2018), *Perverse Romanticism* (Johns Hopkins University Press, 2008), and *The Visual and Verbal Sketch in British Romanticism* (Penn Press, 1998). *Imagination and Science* won the Jean-Pierre Barricelli Prize in 2018. Most recently, he has co-edited *Romanticism and Consciousness, Revisited* (with Joel Faflak; Edinburgh University Press, 2022). He is currently working on two projects: one on the ethics of uncertainty and another on models of emotion today, and how they make deliberation seem impossible.

TESS SOMERVELL is a lecturer in English at Worcester College, University of Oxford. Her research interests include the literature of the long eighteenth century and the literary and cultural history of weather and climate change. She is the author of *Reading Time in the Long Poem: Milton, Thomson, and Wordsworth* (Edinburgh University Press, 2023) and co-editor of *Georgic Literature and the Environment: Working Land, Reworking Genre* (Routledge, 2023).

MIRANDA STANYON is a Senior Research Fellow in English at the University of Melbourne, where she currently holds an ARC Discovery Early Career

Researcher Award exploring Romantic-period receptions of Andromache (DE200101675). Her publications include *Resounding the Sublime: Music in English and German Literature and Aesthetic Theory, 1670–1880* (University of Pennsylvania Press, 2021) and the edited collection, with Sarah Hibberd, *Music and the Sonorous Sublime in European Culture, 1680–1800* (Cambridge University Press, 2020).

JOANNA E. TAYLOR is Presidential Fellow in Digital Humanities at the University of Manchester. Her research explores the uses of digital technologies at the intersection between literary geographies, cultural heritage, and environmental studies, using digital methodologies to extend the reach of this work. She is the author of *Deep Mapping the Literary Lake District: A Geographical Text Analysis* (with Ian Gregory; Bucknell University Press, 2022) and has published widely in leading journals across literary studies, digital humanities, and geographical information science.

PATRICK VINCENT is Professor of English at the University of Neuchâtel. He recently authored *Romanticism, Republicanism, and the Swiss Myth* (Cambridge University Press, 2022) and edited *The Cambridge History of European Romantic Literature* (Cambridge University Press, 2023). Other publications on the Alps include a critical edition of Helen Maria Williams' *A Tour in Switzerland* (Slatkine, 2011), a co-edited collection of essays entitled *Romanticism, Rousseau, Switzerland: New Prospects* (Palgrave, 2015), and a special issue of *Studies in Travel Writing* on visitors' books and travel culture (2021).

ABBREVIATIONS

The following abbreviations and standard editions are used throughout this Companion.

Byron
: George Gordon, Lord Byron, *A Critical Edition of the Major Works*, ed. Jerome J. McGann, Oxford, Oxford University Press, 1986.

Coleridge
: Samuel Taylor Coleridge, *The Complete Poems*, ed. William Keach, London, Penguin, 1997.

COPJ
: Immanuel Kant, *Critique of the Power of Judgment* (1790), trans. Paul Guyer and Paul Wood, volume 5 of *The Cambridge Edition of the Works of Immanuel Kant*, Cambridge, Cambridge University Press, 2000. All references are to the section number or General Remark (GR) and pagination of the Akademie der Wissenschaften edition of Kant's Complete Works.

Costelloe
: Timothy M. Costelloe (ed.), *The Sublime: From Antiquity to the Present*, Cambridge, Cambridge University Press, 2015.

Cultures
: Cian Duffy and Peter Howell (eds.), *Cultures of the Sublime: Selected Readings, 1700–1830*, London, Palgrave, 2011.

Discourse
: Peter De Bolla, *The Discourse of the Sublime: Readings in History, Aesthetics and the Subject*, London, Blackwell, 1989.

Doran
: Robert Doran, *The Theory of the Sublime from Longinus to Kant*, Cambridge, Cambridge University Press, 2015.

Enquiry
: Edmund Burke, *A Philosophical Enquiry into the Origin of Our Ideas of the Sublime and the Beautiful*, London, 1757. All references are to part and section numbers.

Hertz
: Neil Hertz, *The End of the Line: Essays on Psychoanalysis and the Sublime*, New York, Columbia University Press, 1985.

Hipple
: Walter John Hipple, *The Beautiful, the Sublime, and the Picturesque in Eighteenth-Century British Aesthetic Theory*, Carbondale, University of Illinois Press, 1957.

Keats
: John Keats, *The Major Works*, ed. Elizabeth Cook, Oxford, Oxford World's Classics, 2001.

Landscapes
: Cian Duffy, *The Landscapes of the Sublime, 1700–1830*, London, Palgrave, 2013.

Longinus	*On the Sublime*, trans. William Smith, London, 1739.
Monk	Samuel Holt Monk, *The Sublime: A Study of Critical Theories in XVIII-Century England*, Ann Arbor, University of Michigan Press, 1960.
Nicolson	Marjorie Hope Nicolson, *Mountain Gloom and Mountain Glory: The Development of the Aesthetics of the Infinite*, Ithaca, NY, Cornell University Press, 1959.
Reader	Andrew Asfhield and Peter De Bolla (eds.), *The Sublime: A Reader in British Eighteenth-Century Aesthetic Theory*, Cambridge, Cambridge University Press, 1996.
Richardson	Alan Richardson, *The Neural Sublime: Cognitive Theories and Romantic Texts*, Baltimore, MD, Johns Hopkins University Press, 2015.
Shelley	Percy Bysshe Shelley, *Selected Poems and Prose*, ed. Jack Donovan and Cian Duffy, London, Penguin, 2016.
Weiskel	Thomas Weiskel, *The Romantic Sublime: Studies in the Structure and Psychology of Transcendence*, Baltimore, MD, Johns Hopkins University Press, 1976.
Wordsworth	William Wordsworth, *The Major Works*, ed. Stephen Gill, Oxford, Oxford World's Classics, 2000.

CIAN DUFFY

Introduction

The Romantic Sublime, Then and Now

In September 1846, Thomas De Quincey invited the readers of *Tait's Edinburgh Magazine* to view 'the famous nebula in the constellation of Orion' through what was then the most powerful telescope in the world: 'Come', De Quincey says, 'and I will show you what is sublime!'[1] Scarcely less sublime than the 'frightful' nebula itself, De Quincey thought, was the 'almost awful telescope', the so-called Leviathan of Parsonstown, which had 'inaugurated' a 'new era for the human intellect' by making it possible to see 'effectively into the mighty depths of space', into 'the abyss of the heavenly wilderness' (403, 400). Published in a mainstream periodical well beyond the high tide of the Romantic period in Britain, De Quincey's claim for the twin 'magnitudes' of the night sky and human endeavour wouldn't have struck any of his readers as particularly original (403). As many as forty years earlier, as William Wordsworth records in his poem 'Star Gazers' (1807), 'Show men' in London's Leicester Square (and in other cities around Europe) had been charging passers-by to look through a telescope at the 'resplendent vault' of the 'heavens' or at 'the silver Moon with all her Vales, and Hills of mightiest fame' (lines 5, 7, 12, 15). What is significant about De Quincey's invitation is that it reveals how the sublime had become, over the course of the previous hundred years, a key component of an extraordinarily diverse range of areas of enquiry and genres of cultural productivity in Europe and America, from philosophical aesthetics to Gothic novels, and a key motivator of emergent cultural practices like commercial tourism and the kind of commodified popular science exemplified in De Quincey's own essay.[2]

This widespread engagement with the sublime first became the subject of sustained academic interest in the early twentieth century, when cultural historians in Europe and America began to speculate about its origins and to examine how it was manifested in philosophical aesthetics, in literature, in painting and in music. The most studied aspect of it remains the extensive theoretical speculation about the nature and causes of sublime experience in eighteenth-century philosophical aesthetics, what Peter De Bolla calls 'the discourse on the sublime'.[3] But it is undoubtedly the case that the engagement with the sublime remains (for better or for worse) a major emblem and archetype – arguably *the* emblem and archetype – of the wider cultural movement that scholars have called 'Romanticism'. The image that most often serves to represent Romanticism, and which provides the cover for this *Companion*, Caspar David Friedrich's *Der Wanderer über dem Nebelmeer* (Wanderer above the Sea of Fog) (c. 1818), is an image of the sublime. Canons of national Romanticisms consistently foreground engagements with the sublime, whether it be Victor Frankenstein's encounter with his creature on the Mer de Glace; Thomas Cole's paintings of the American wilderness; the Gothic forests and mountains of Ann Radcliffe's novels and the plays and poems of Friedrich Schiller and Gottfried Bürger; Wordsworth's account of crossing the Alps in *The Prelude* (1805); the Italian vistas described by Madame De Staël, Ugo Foscolo and Giacomo Leopardi; the Swiss landscapes of Jean-Jacques Rousseau's *Julie* (1761) and Adam Mickiewicz's *Lausanne Lyrics* (c. 1839–40); the Nordic scenes from Mary Wollstonecraft's *Letters Written during a Short Residence* (1796) and the paintings of Knud Baade and J. C. Dahl; the symphonic poems of Franz Liszt and the symphonies and concertos of Ludwig van Beethoven; or the apocalyptic canvases of John Martin, J. M. W. Turner and Joseph Wright. Historians of culture, too, still routinely use the development of interest in the sublime to describe a perceived transition from eighteenth-century Neoclassicism to Romanticism.

Hence, when Philip Shaw wrote that 'the sublime has a history', he might more properly have written that it has *two*.[4] There is the history of the sublime as it was engaged, experienced, mediated and commodified during the eighteenth century and Romantic period; and then there is the much more recent history of the sublime as part of the wider academic study of Romanticism, the history of what scholars, following Thomas Weiskel's landmark study, have called 'the Romantic sublime'. Both these histories, and the complex and often contradictory relationship between them, are explored in this Companion.

Reapproaching 'the Romantic Sublime'

In his essay 'On Goethe' (1798), the German poet and philosopher Novalis argues that the idea of a 'classical literature', presented by his contemporaries as a gold standard to be imitated, is less a fact of history than an invention of modern scholarship. 'Classical literature', Novalis writes, 'is not a given, it is not there already, but it has first to be produced by us. We can bring a classical literature – which the ancients themselves did not possess – into existence only by keen and intelligent study of the ancients.'[5] *The Cambridge Companion to the Romantic Sublime* starts from a similar provocation: what has been called 'the Romantic sublime' is not a concrete historical phenomenon, of which Romantic-period writers and thinkers were purposively aware, but rather an academic *construct*: a conceptual tool formulated by historians of literature and culture in the twentieth century to describe various tropes and practices visible in cultural texts from across late eighteenth- and early nineteenth-century Europe and America.[6]

As a *construct*, the Romantic sublime has evolved to include four key assumptions. First: that it is actually possible to detect and to describe a uniform 'Romantic' configuration of the sublime in late eighteenth- and early nineteenth-century responses to a wide variety of different experiential contexts. Second: that this uniform Romantic sublime broadly coincides with the paradigm described by Immanuel Kant in the 'Analytic of the Sublime' from his *Critique of the Power of Judgement* (1790). Third: that discussions in (a few, supposedly key) works of eighteenth-century British and German philosophical aesthetics were the primary context for the generation and motivation of ideas about the sublime in the Romantic period, typically including Edmund Burke's *Philosophical Enquiry into the Origins of Our Ideas of the Sublime and the Beautiful* (1757). Fourth: that explanations of 'sublime' experience should be sought primarily in psychology rather than in physiology or other embodied phenomena. Each of these assumptions is subjected to sustained criticism in *The Cambridge Companion to the Romantic Sublime*: a key aim of our essays is to question the extent to which the Romantic sublime as a construct is still adequate (if it ever was adequate) to describe the multifaceted engagement with the sublime during the late eighteenth century and Romantic period.

Two influential early studies of the history of the aesthetic in the eighteenth century laid the groundwork for the construct of a uniform Romantic sublime: Samuel Holt Monk's *The Sublime* (1935, 1960) and, to a lesser but still significant extent, Marjorie Hope Nicolson's *Mountain Gloom and Mountain Glory* (1959). Monk and Nicolson posit different, though not incompatible, hypotheses for what they see as the emergence of a new interest in the sublime in the eighteenth century and both identify the Romantic period as the culmination of that process. From different starting points, and for different reasons, both also argue that Romantic-period writers and thinkers agreed in understanding the sublime as a property and product of the human mind rather than of the external world, and therefore aligned with idealist rather than empiricist philosophies.

For Monk, the rediscovery and making available in French and English translations, in the early eighteenth century, of the first-century CE treatise *Perì hýpsous* (On the Sublime), attributed to Longinus, led to a renewed interest in how certain forms of language could generate an extreme affective response in the reader or listener, the so-called rhetorical sublime. From the 'fountain-head' of Longinus, Monk claims, the understanding of the sublime in British eighteenth-century philosophical aesthetics 'slowly develops ... into a subjective or semi-subjective concept'; there is a 'transition', Monk says, from 'the idea that sublimity in some way depends upon qualities residing in the object' to a 'psychological or even physiological investigation into the origin of aesthetic experience' (*Monk*, 10, 4, 86). Monk points to certain works of philosophical aesthetics as especial motivators of this 'transition', notably including Burke's *Enquiry*, which (in a now routinely quoted passage) insists on the centrality of the *vicarious* experience of 'terror' to the sublime:

> Whatever is fitted in any sort to excite the ideas of pain, and danger, that is to say, whatever is in any sort terrible, or is conversant about terrible objects, or operates in a manner analogous to terror, is a source of the *sublime*.... When danger or pain press too nearly, they are incapable of giving any delight, and are simply terrible; but at certain distances, and with certain modifications, they may be, and they are, delightful. (*Enquiry* I viii)

According to Monk, this teleological 'growth' of the aesthetics of the sublime 'toward a subjective point of view reaches its fulness in Kant' and his 'Analytic of the Sublime' (*Monk*, 9). Kant's *Critique*, Monk says, is the 'unconscious goal' of eighteenth-century philosophical aesthetics, 'the great document that coordinates and synthezises the aesthetic concepts which had been current throughout the eighteenth century' by concluding that 'sublimity as an aesthetic concept is ... entirely subjective' (4, 8).

From a different starting point and using a different hypothesis, Nicolson outlines a similar trajectory towards a subjectivist aesthetics of the sublime reaching its apex in the Romantic period. According to Nicolson, a second revolution in astronomy, enabled by advances in optical technology in the late seventeenth century, started a cultural process by which the affective responses previously occasioned by the idea of a creator-god came progressively to be transferred to the most awe-inspiring phenomena of the natural world, now increasingly understood as manifestations of divine power, the so-called natural sublime. Like Monk, Nicolson points to certain texts as having had a decisive influence on this process, but while Monk focuses on works of philosophical aesthetics like *Perì hýpsous*, Burke's *Enquiry*, and Kant's *Critique*, Nicolson emphasizes, rather, the role of writings in natural philosophy, particularly Thomas Burnet's *Sacred Theory of the Earth* (1681, 1684). 'Basic and radical changes' took place in 'theology, philosophy, geology, astronomy', Nicolson argues, in order to drive interest in and develop understanding of the sublime (*Nicolson*, 3).

From this broader cultural-historical perspective, then, Nicolson, reads *Perì hýpsous* less as a 'fountain-head' (Monk's word) for new attitudes than as providing a glossary of terms for describing those new attitudes. Monk and Nicolson agree, however, in reading William Wordsworth's account of crossing the Alps in Book VI of *The Prelude* (1805) as the 'apotheosis' of 'the experience that lay behind the eighteenth-century sublime', as Monk puts it (*Monk*, 231). Monk argues for 'a general similarity between the point of view of the *Critique of Judgement* and the *Prelude*' and uses this 'analogy' to bolster his reading of the *Critique* as 'the book' in which the discussion of the sublime in eighteenth-century philosophical aesthetics was 'refined and re-interpreted' (5, 10). Nicolson, as we have seen, downplays the significance of philosophical aesthetics – barely mentioning either Burke or Kant – but she, too, reads the engagement with the sublime in Book VI of *The Prelude* as 'the perfect expression' of what she calls 'the aesthetics of the infinite', an aesthetics predicated on an understanding of the sublime as evidence of the 'workings of one mind', be it divine or human.[7]

In *The Romantic Sublime* (1976), Thomas Weiskel followed Monk and Nicolson in reading Book VI of *The Prelude* as what he calls a 'set piece of the sublime' (*Weiskel*, 196). 'The essential claim of the sublime', so Weiskel begins, 'is that man can, in feeling and in speech, transcend the human' (3). Weiskel's subsequent interrogation of this 'claim' agrees with what he calls Monk's 'classic history of the sublime' and the 'precision' of its core argument that 'Kant established decisively the discrimination of the aesthetic boundary' while 'at the same time he located the judgements of the sublime and the beautiful in a network of a priori relations to the cognitive and ethical dimensions of the mind' (5, 13, 38). Reading from a psychological perspective, Weiskel adds post-Freudian ideas to the Kantian paradigm, a move later extended by Neil Hertz in *The End of the Line* (1985), arguing that 'the sublime moment recapitulates and thereby reestablishes the oedipus complex' and that both 'positive' and 'negative' versions of 'the Romantic sublime' are therefore visible in works like *Prelude* VI, involving successful or interrupted 'transcendence' of a subject-object/mind-world dichotomy (*Weiskel*, 94, 103, 135).

This supposed trajectory of engagements with the sublime during the eighteenth-century towards a uniform Romantic configuration of the experience, broadly consistent with the transcendental idealist paradigms of Kant's 'Analytic' and visible in an array of late eighteenth- and early nineteenth-century cultural texts from various national contexts, is the 'history' of 'the sublime' to which Shaw points. And it has been a remarkably influential history, informing many engagements with the sublime after Weiskel, including single-author studies, wider-scale histories and surveys, and even works rightly critical of the biases implicit in the Romantic configuration of the sublime, such as Barbara Freeman's *The Feminine Sublime* (1995). As Adam Potkay puts it in his thoughtful essay on 'The British Romantic Sublime', which is not so well known as it should be, 'subsequent criticism on the Romantic and post-Romantic sublime has drawn heavily on [Weiskel's model], more often than not accepting its main points uncritically'.[8] But from the outset, there have also been dissenting voices and those voices have grown louder in recent years. Not least amongst them is Potkay himself, who opens his essay with thought-provoking questions about the relationship between how 'the Romantics conceive[d] of the sublime' and how 'critics conceived of the Romantic sublime'.[9]

The Romantic Sublime and the Sublime in the Romantic Period

Let's pause, for a moment, to specify the precise nature of the problem here. The question is not whether the analysis of the sublime offered by Kant in his *Critique of the Power of Judgement* is accurate, which is irrelevant. The question is not the extent to which Kant's 'Analytic of the Sublime' influenced the subsequent history of the aesthetic in the global North, which is indisputable. The question is to what extent the critical construct of the Romantic sublime is useful, accurate or effective as a conceptual tool for describing the place of the sublime in the cultural history of late eighteenth- and early nineteenth-century Europe. Or, to put that same question another way: To what extent has the construct of the Romantic sublime been imposed upon and distorted the discursive and experiential history of engagements with the sublime during the Romantic period?

As a representative case-in-point here we might consider the place of the sublime in the genre of 'Gothic' literature that emerged and flourished in the late eighteenth and early nineteenth centuries, in the hands of influential, internationally known and commercially successful practitioners like Ann Radcliffe. Gothic writing is often indebted, explicitly or implicitly, to discussions in philosophical aesthetics, of the connection between terror and the sublime, of what Anna Aikin calls 'the Pleasure derived from Objects of Terror'.[10] Gothic narratives frequently feature the kinds of landscapes and persons increasingly being denominated as 'sublime': mountains, forests, oceans, tyrants and monsters, the mentally ill. Gothic writing very often also engages with the link between sublime landscapes and religious experience, theorized by philosophers like Archibald Alison and Thomas Reid. And yet Gothic literature – which, on account of its runaway popularity, was one of the most prominent and accessible cultural contexts in which sublime affects could be encountered – exhibits little of the Romantic Sublime, as that construct has been traditionally defined by academic histories. This is not, of course, to say that what scholars have called the Romantic configuration of the sublime played no part in the cultural history of late eighteenth- and early nineteenth-century Europe. But it certainly does recommend caution about any claim that the Romantic Sublime was the primary or even a dominant contemporary mode of the sublime, supposedly spanning national traditions and borders.

The first scholar to question the 'summary proposition' of Monk's narrative history of the sublime was Walter Hipple, who observes, in his unjustly neglected study *The Beautiful, the Sublime, and the Picturesque in Eighteenth-Century British Aesthetic Theory* (1957) that 'it seems doubtful that the intellectual history of any age can be viewed, without distortion, as a progression towards some one culmination' (*Hipple*, 284). Accordingly, Hipple argues against the possibility of 'narrative propositions' about eighteenth-century philosophical aesthetics that 'will neither conflict with the data nor be so vaguely general as to be nugatory' (5). 'Not finding a history in the subject, and not desiring to superimpose one', Hipple focuses instead on 'the analysis of texts, interposing historical conjectures only where clear-cut intellectual causes appear' (6).

In *The Sublime: A Reader in British Eighteenth-Century Aesthetic Theory* (1996), Andrew Ashfield and Peter Bolla also critique the 'scholarly tradition', deriving from Monk, 'that has repeatedly told a story about the beginning of aesthetics in eighteenth-century Britain in terms of a gradual shift towards the Kantian critique of judgement' (*Reader*, 2). Ashfield and De Bolla outline two problems with this 'tradition'. First: it distorts the relationship between investigations of the sublime in different national contexts around Europe by 'explicitly casting the British discussion as a kind of dress rehearsal for the full-fledged philosophical aesthetics of Immanuel Kant and his heirs' rather than considering the full variety of aesthetics across the continent (3). Second: in its emphasis on subjectivity, this 'tradition' also distorts and simplifies the British enquiry into the sublime. 'While parts of the British tradition can be seen in terms of ... the gradual development of "subjectivism"', Asfhield and De Bolla remark, 'the vast bulk of discussion and debate is not exclusively concerned with "autonomous subjectivity" at all' – and so, in histories like Monk's, 'much is left out or to one side' (3).

Many of the essays in Timothy Costelloe's collection *The Sublime: From Antiquity in the Present* (2012) also query what Costelloe calls in his introduction, following Ashfield and De Bolla, the 'common lore' about the place of the sublime in the history of aesthetics (*Costelloe*, 2). Ashfield and De Bolla note how 'the aesthetic, at least since Kant, has been understood as without political or ethical motivation since its *affective* registers are, according to the Kantian model, disinterested' – although they also point out that this is partly a 'misreading of the Kantian text, where the political and ethical constantly impress themselves' (*Reader*, 2–3). In a similar vein, Adam Potkay's essay in Costelloe's collection notes how, in academic studies of the sublime, an emphasis on 'the mind's transcendence of a natural or social world' and 'the rigorous exclusion of ethics' has obscured the extent to which 'the sublime and morality' are intertwined, not just in Kant's text but also in a much wider range of British Romantic-period engagements with the sublime (*Costelloe*, 203, 207). 'We need', Potkay concludes, 'to move beyond the way the Romantic sublime has been thought of in the past' (*Costelloe*, 216).

Alan Richardson, in *The Neural Sublime* (2015), also takes issue with the dominance of Kantian paradigms in academic histories of the sublime following Monk and Weiskel, arguing: 'We need to reconsider the competing accounts [of the sublime] of Burke and others in the British tradition not so much as stepping stones to Kant but as intriguing constructions in their own right that, after all, would have been more familiar to British Romantic-era writers than would have been Kant, then only known to a few' (*Richardson*, 25). Doing so, Richardson writes, 'disrupts teleological readings of the sublime tradition, such as Samuel Holt Monk's, that trace the growing internalization or psychologizing of the sublime to its culmination in Kant's *Critique of Judgement*' and allows us to recognize the more embodied configurations of the sublime in eighteenth-century philosophical aesthetics, notably including the physiological arguments of Burke's *Enquiry*, which Kant (and Monk) dismissed, but which others, like Thomas Reid in Scotland and Johann Gottfried Herder in Germany, embraced (*Richardson*, 24–5; *Monk*, 96).

My own earlier work on the sublime – in *Shelley and the Revolutionary Sublime* (2005), *Cultures of the Sublime* (2011) and *The Landscapes of the Sublime, 1700–1830* (2013) – has likewise sought to examine how an 'uncritical acceptance' (to use Potkay's phrase) of the idea of a uniform and essentially Kantian Romantic sublime has often obscured, if not altogether misrepresented, the place of the sublime in various aspects of the cultural history of the Romantic period, from the poetry of Percy Bysshe Shelley to the manifold literary and scientific responses triggered by dramatic natural phenomena in different cultural and geographical contexts. Most recently, in my chapter on 'The Romantic Sublime' in *The Cambridge*

History of European Romantic Literature (2023), I return again to the Gordian relationship between two histories of the sublime, between what I call there 'the history of the sublime *at* the time' and 'the history of the sublime *since* the time', and explore the extent to which the latter has been imposed upon the former and the consequences of this imposition for our understanding of the Romantic period.

In each of their various ways, the essays in *The Cambridge Companion to the Romantic Sublime* continue this reassessment of the Romantic sublime. The topics we cover by no means exhaust the extraordinary range, diversity and complexity of Romantic-period engagements with the sublime. But they do provide a good indication of the scope and significance of this cultural phenomenon and its subsequent legacy to some of today's most pressing concerns about the relationship between humans and the non-human world.

Structure and Scope

The essays in *The Cambridge Companion to the Romantic Sublime* are grouped in three, loosely chronological parts, pitched before, during and after the Romantic period, broadly defined. But the essays themselves often challenge received teleologies and demarcations of period and national boundaries, mindful, like Hipple, of 'not finding a history in the subject, and not desiring to superimpose one' (*Hipple*, 6). This is especially true of the four essays in Part 1, 'The Sublime before Romanticism', each of which not only refuses to conceptualize the sublime it describes as 'pre-Romantic', or intelligible only in relation to Romanticism, but also extends our understanding of the range of different 'sublimes' available to eighteenth-century and Romantic-period writers around Europe. In Chapter 1, 'The Classical Sublime', Patrick Glauthier addresses what he sees as the overemphasis on Longinus in traditional histories of classical and eighteenth-century aesthetics, making clear that eighteenth-century and Romantic-period writers who were well versed in classical literature would have had access to a much greater diversity of engagements with the sublime than has usually been recognized by academic studies, following Monk, which assume Longinus to have been their primary interlocutor. In a similar move, Dawn Hollis, in Chapter 2, 'The Natural Sublime in the Seventeenth Century', returns to Thomas Burnet's *Theory of the Earth* (1681), which has often been read as 'an early precursor to the Romantic Sublime'. Rereading Burnet alongside contemporaries like Athanasius Kircher and William Lithgow, however, Hollis argues that rather than viewing the natural sublime as an *invention* of the Romantic period, we should instead understand eighteenth-century and Romantic-period writers to have developed a new vocabulary and a new conceptual framework for describing affective responses with a far longer history and a far wider visibility in seventeenth-century cultural texts. My own essay, Chapter 3, 'The Sublime in Eighteenth-Century English, Irish and Scottish Philosophy', challenges the still influential narrative, deriving ultimately from Monk, which reads accounts of the sublime in eighteenth-century British and Irish philosophical aesthetics as moving progressively closer to the transcendental idealist paradigms set out by Kant in his *Critique of the Power of Judgement*. I map, instead, a thriving, empirical and associationist aesthetics that has often been left out of academic accounts of the Romantic sublime but which was much more immediately accessible to Romantic-period writers in Britain and Ireland than German philosophy. Lis Møller's essay, Chapter 4, 'The Nordic Sublime', brings Part I to a close. Møller explores the still relatively undocumented role of the 'landscapes, climates, peoples and creatures of Norse myth' – newly accessible outside Scandinavia through eighteenth-century antiquarian scholarship, through travel writing, and through classical and contemporary Nordic poetry circulating in translation across national and linguistic borders – as repertoires of sublime tropes, narratives and settings for an array of Romantic-period cultural texts from around Europe.

The essays in Part II, 'Romantic Sublimes', explore a representative, though certainly not exhaustive, selection of themes and contexts that became major focal points for engagements with the sublime during the Romantic period. Some of these are very familiar; others are areas of historical significance to which scholars have only recently begun to turn their attention, armed with new understandings of the wider cultural history of Romantic-period Europe. Christoph Bode opens Part II with Chapter 5, 'German Romanticism and the Sublime', and leads us on a grand tour through philosophy, literature, painting and music, from Goethe to Beethoven. In Chapter 6, 'The Romantic Sublime and Kant's Critical Philosophy', Timothy Costelloe keeps us in Germany with his reappraisal of the place of the sublime in Kant's aesthetics, looking before and after, at Kant's indebtedness to earlier eighteenth-century works of philosophical aesthetics and at responses to Kant's 'Analytic' by writers like Coleridge, Ahrendt and Lyotard.

In Chapter 7, 'Alpine Sublimes', Patrick Vincent takes us back to some of the most familiar landscapes of the Romantic sublime: the Alps. Vincent considers why the Alps became so central to interest in the sublime; offers fresh readings of key Romantic-period responses, such as Book VI of Wordsworth's *Prelude*; and sketches the afterlife of the Alpine sublime in the later nineteenth century. While engagements with the sublime during the Romantic period have often been understood as concerned, primarily, with non-human landscapes, Matthew Sangster, in Chapter 8, 'Urban Sublimes', reminds us that cityscapes, too, were thought sublime. Concentrating on London, but glancing also at Paris and Rome, Sangster tests the notion of the Romantic sublime against some canonical and lesser-known Romantic-period writings about the city.

From the streets of Europe's capitals, Simon Bainbridge leads us upwards once more, in Chapter 9, 'Highlands, Lakes, Wales', to some of the most celebrated peaks of British Romanticism, exploring anew the connection between the mountain sublime and the rise of domestic tourism and showing how that link was represented in a range of letters, journals, notebooks and poems. Richard C. Sha, in Chapter 10, 'Science and the Sublime', shows how ideas about the sublime were often integrally related to the theory and practice of science in the Romantic period, in various disciplines and national contexts – giving the lie to John Keats' claim, in *Lamia* (1820), that 'the mere touch of cold philosophy' would 'unweave' the 'awful rainbow' (Part 2, lines 229–38). In Chapter 11, 'Musical Sublimes', Miranda Stanyon surveys the complex relationship between music and the sublime during the Romantic period: her essay introduces the variety of music bound up with the sublime, from Covent Garden musicals to the symphonies of Beethoven, and outlines the centrality of music to debates in philosophical aesthetics and the broader cultural imaginary of the Romantic period.

In Chapter 12, 'The Arctic Sublime', Robert W. Rix guides us on an expedition through the frozen wastes of the northern polar regions, showing how a discourse of the Arctic sublime, often cultivated by those who knew the landscapes only vicariously, emerged in parallel with attempts, motivated by scientific, political and commercial interests, to explore and map the Arctic wilderness. Moving from the icy to the corporeal, Norbert Lennartz's essay, Chapter 13, 'The Body and the Sublime', extends the attention recently shown by scholars such as Alan Richardson to how eighteenth-century thinkers addressed the embodied aspects of the experience. Lennartz documents how the body, in a range of European Romanticisms, is understood to be in a relentless transition from short-lived Promethean sublimity to abjection, or from fire to dust (as Byron would have it). In Chapter 14, 'The Sublime in Romantic Painting', Nina Amstutz examines the influence of philosophical descriptions of the sublime, by thinkers like Burke and Kant, on theorists of visual art such as Uvedale Price and Richard Payne Knight, as well as on Romantic-period paintings of dramatic landscapes and natural phenomena, of animal violence, and of emergent industrialization. Andrew McInnes, in Chapter 15, 'From the Sublime to the Ridiculous', uses the well-known aphorism, which has its roots in the Romantic-period, as the touchstone for examining the complex relationship between sublimity and humour in a selection of English and German Romantic-period writings, with special focus on the German novelist and philosopher Jean Paul Richter. Cassandra Falke closes Part II with Chapter 16, 'The Sublime in American Romanticism'. Falke takes as her focus the nature writing of William Bartram, which she identifies not only as an influence on subsequent representations of the sublime in English and American Romanticisms but also as offering a philosophically distinctive model of sublime experiences in wild ecosystems.

Part III, 'Legacies', explores the afterlife of engagements with the sublime during the Romantic period, new methodological approaches to those engagements, and the cultural impact of the Romantic sublime as a critical construct. In Chapter 17, 'The Victorian Chthonic Sublime', Tatjana Jukić reads altered attitudes to the sublime as a key component of the Victorian response to Romanticism, arguing that a revision of Romantic-period ideas about the natural sublime was a necessary condition for the emergent modernity visible in some Victorian literature and painting. In Chapter 18, 'Mapping the Nineteenth-Century Sublime', Joanna Taylor, Christopher Donaldson, and Ian Gregory use state-of-the-art methodologies in digital humanities to trace occurrences of the term 'sublime' in a corpus of 10,000 Anglophone texts from the 1890s; doing so allows them to map geographical hot-spots for the sublime at the end of the nineteenth century and also to chart correspondences and deviations from how and where 'sublime' was being used during the Romantic period. In Chapter 19, 'The Romantic Sublime and Environmental Crisis', Tess Somervell brings our volume to a close on an urgent note. Noting how an aesthetics of the sublime continues to shape representations of, and responses to, environmental catastrophe in the global North, Somervell queries whether the concept of the Romantic sublime, based on Kantian paradigms of transcendence, is either possible or desirable in the current crisis. Understanding environmental catastrophe as in various ways the product of the early nineteenth century, Somervell's essay looks again at Romantic-period engagements with the natural sublime to assess the role they might play in helping us to rethink our relationship to the non-human world.

NOTES

1 Thomas De Quincey, 'System of the Heavens as Revealed by Lord Rosse's Telescopes' (1846), quoted from Grevel Lindop (gen. ed.), *The Works of Thomas De Quincey*, 21 vols., London, Pickering & Chatto, 2000–3, vol. 15, 403.
2 For the sublime and popular science in De Quincey's 'System of the Heavens', see *Landscapes*, 174–90.

3 De Bolla contrasts this analytical discourse with what he calls 'the discourse of the sublime', 'a discourse which produces, from within itself, what is habitually termed the category of the sublime' (see *Discourse*, 2; see also Chapter 3 in this Companion).

4 Philip Shaw, *The Sublime*, 2nd edition, London, Routledge, 2017, 5.

5 Novalis, 'On Goethe', quoted from Jay Bernstein (ed.), *Classic and Romantic German Aesthetics*, Cambridge, Cambridge University Press, 2002, 227–34 (229).

6 In this distinction between historical phenomena and conceptual tools, I draw in part on Christoph Bode's discussion of European Romanticism in Nicholas Roe (ed.), *Romanticism: An Oxford Guide*, Oxford, Oxford University Press, 2015, 126–36 (126).

7 *Nicolson*, 231, quoting William Wordsworth, *The Prelude* (1850), VI, 636.

8 Adam Potkay, 'The British Romantic Sublime', in *Costelloe*, 203–16 (207).

9 Ibid., 203.

10 Anna Laetitia Aikin, 'On the Pleasure Derived from Objects of Terror', in John and Laetitia Aikin, *Miscellaneous Pieces, in Prose*, London, 1773, 119–27.

PART I

The Sublime before Romanticism

I

PATRICK GLAUTHIER

The Classical Sublime

Any consideration of the classical sublime is bound to start with Longinus, whose *On the Sublime*, mostly likely written in the first century CE, is the only extant ancient treatise expressly dedicated to the topic.[1] For Longinus, sublimity is an experience of unrivaled intensity, and to call an object "sublime" is to indicate its incomparable value. At the same time, the treatise interweaves several core themes: the overwhelming power of language, which manifests itself as an irresistible force of nature and as an extension of the divine; a fervent belief that the human mind is summoned to greatness, which requires it to push both language and thought to their limits; and a relentless drive to connect with something that transcends the here-and-now, from the distant past to the furthest reaches of the cosmos to God himself. Longinus's vision is striking for its compelling vividness and sustained drive, but as recent scholarship has made clear, this treatise stands at one end of a long tradition. A deep interest in the boundaries of human achievement and in the vital potency of nature, language, the mind, and the gods motivate a wide range of poets, philosophers, literary critics, and other intellectuals, from Homer and Hesiod through Plato and Aristotle right down to Longinus and his Greek and Roman contemporaries. A critical discourse devoted to the sublime appears to have emerged in the mid-fifth century BCE, and while its terminology remained fluid, its way of conceptualizing the sublime proved relatively stable and made its presence felt in a wide variety of genres – on the comic stage, for instance, the Athenian general Pericles can be imagined to hurl rhetorical thunderbolts from the heights of Olympus centuries before Longinus compares the power of sublime speech to lightning.[2] By the end of the fifth century, the sublime had become a recognizable phenomenon, an ethical stance, a marker of ideology and value, and a topic of debate, and so it remained. Thanks to an overemphasis on Longinus, however, the striking variety of contexts within, and ends to, which ancient writers cultivate the sublime have only recently begun to receive adequate critical attention. By adopting an expansive understanding of sublimity, from the beginning of antiquity to its end, and by decentering Longinus from the plot, we can better appreciate the multiple and often contested nature of the classical sublime.

An expansive understanding of the sublime still requires a definition. I rely on Robert Doran's treatment of the sublime as an experience of affective intensity that exhibits a dual structure, that of being simultaneously overwhelmed and elevated, overpowered and uplifted (see *Doran*, 4, 10–11). This state is often described as wonder, amazement, stupefaction, terror, or dread, and it registers a moment of or aspiration towards transcendence, broadly construed. To pass beyond the limits of everyday sense-perception; to become suddenly aware of nature's vastness, might, or order; to be transported mentally through space or time; to come into contact with the divine – such are the experiences of the classical sublime and such is the legacy that would have been available to those eighteenth-century and Romantic-period writers versed in the classical tradition, a legacy that extended well beyond the work of Longinus. Edmund Burke, for instance, to take the most obvious example, makes frequent references to classical sources in his *Enquiry into the Origins of Our Ideas of the Sublime and the Beautiful* (1757).

Sublime Spectacles

The ancient terms most frequently translated as "sublimity" or "sublime" literally mean "height, elevation" (Greek *hypsos*, Latin *sublimitas*), and "on high, elevated, lofty" (Latin *sublimis*). Objects and phenomena that are physically located or take place "on high," such as celestial bodies and meteorological phenomena, are consistently represented through the logic of the sublime, from the beginning of the written record onward. Often, the sublime reflects the physical might of the natural world in exceptional bursts of energy, anticipating eighteenth-century and Romantic-period engagements with the so-called natural sublime – a sudden crash of thunder, the explosive fire of a volcanic eruption, the seismic jolt of a devastating earthquake. All three of these phenomena shake the stage simultaneously at the conclusion of the tragedy *Prometheus Bound*, attributed to Aeschylus and produced in the mid-fifth century BCE. But the sublime is not always so violent. In *Iliad* 8, Homer compares the number of fires in the Trojan camp to the panoply of stars:

> Just as in the sky about the gleaming moon the stars
> shine clear when the air is windless,
> and into view come all mountain peaks and high headlands

and glades, and from heaven breaks open the infinite air,
and all the stars are seen, and the shepherd rejoices in his heart;
in such multitudes between the ships and the streams of Xanthus
shone the fires that the Trojans kindled before Ilios. (8.555–61)[3]

The shepherd's joy names the affective intensity of the sublime. The illuminated calm of the night sky, the landscape's towering heights, the limitless or literally unspeakable expanse of dark air (*aspetos aithēr*), and the totality of stars are both beyond comprehension and a source of profound delight, pulling the gaze of the shepherd and audience skyward, where the Homeric gods move unseen. The sublimity of that show, however, imbues the world down below with a similarly breathtaking quality. The infinite air with its multiplicity of stars transforms the plain full of Trojan fires into the mirror image of heaven. The sublimity of the night becomes the sublimity of the camps and of the poem itself, as the shepherd's joy becomes the joy of the audience contemplating the multitude of warriors in anticipation of the fighting yet to come. Similes in the *Iliad* typically provide relief from the harsh realities of battle while reminding the audience of the world that the war has disrupted, potentially irreversibly. The shepherd's vision is out of reach for those who are engulfed in the conflict at Troy – the sublimity of a nighttime spectacle is set against the devastation of war and the loftiness that comes from the demonstration of greatness in combat.

Although the natural world remains a constant source of sublimity, as it did during the eighteenth century and Romantic period, the logic of the sublime can shape practically any area of human experience. In his *Histories*, composed in the second half of the fifth century BCE, Herodotus applies this logic to the Egyptian labyrinth (2.148). Stressing that he has personally seen the labyrinth, Herodotus declares that it is greater than *logos* ("speech, language, calculation, reason"), represents a larger expenditure of labor and money than all the architectural accomplishments of the Greek world, and outstrips even the Egyptian pyramids, which are collectively greater than *logos*. The sheer excess of the labyrinth, which frustrates human comprehension, is the manmade equivalent of Homer's dark air, which is itself unspeakable; through the labyrinth, the human viewer passes beyond the merely human world. Not to leave the reader in doubt, Herodotus relates that the structure's 3,000 rooms were divided into two, the subterranean and the "elevated" or "lofty" (*ta meteōra*). Herodotus was allowed to tour only the latter, which were "greater than manmade structures" and whose winding corridors and passageways were a source of "infinite wonder." Herodotus's wonder telegraphs the affective intensity of the sublime, and the adjective with which he describes the elevated half of the compound is an early term for sublime objects. Ancient Greeks and Romans were keenly interested in marvels, but a more self-reflective impetus is at work here: the labyrinth's endless series of rooms and passageways figure the numerous stories and intricate patterning that constitute Herodotus's expansive narrative. According to Herodotus, the Egyptian pharaohs constructed the labyrinth to be a monument for posterity, and Herodotus himself, in his preface, frames his own enterprise as a similar act of monument building. Reflections on sublimity often imply the sublimity of the text in which they appear; as Pope remarks of Longinus, in *Essay on Criticism* (1711), he 'Is himself that great Sublime he draws' (line 680).

Of course, the classical sublime cannot be reduced to mere height. Book 8 of Virgil's *Aeneid*, set in Rome's prehistory, contains a haunting description of a numinous landscape and ominous ruins at the site of what would eventually be the civic and religious heart of the imperial capital (lines 347–58). Here, a wooded hill emanated a "dreadful awesomeness" that left the locals trembling and afraid, suspecting that a god – which one, they did not know – inhabited the spot. Nearby, lay the crumbling walls of two long-vanished towns, "the remnants, and a reminder (*monimenta*), of ancient men." The scene creates sublimity, not out of Olympian gods and soaring architecture, but from something much more ineffable and intangible, an unsettling aura of divinity and the inscrutable signs of what might have existed long ago. A triumphalist reading concludes that Virgil's contemporaries are not as naive as their ancestors; the Romans have cleared the woods, built a temple, and founded a city that will last forever. But monuments (*monimenta*) crumble, turning into reminders of the impermanence of human achievement, and the sophisticated elite ignore the "dreadful awesomeness" of their city's native gods at their own peril. Virgil's poem reverberates with such competing voices; the sublime contributes to the chorus.

The classical sublime also thrives in unexpectedly small spaces. Near the end of his encyclopedic *Natural History*, written in the first century CE, the Elder Pliny discusses the gemstone, in which "nature's grandeur is gathered together within the narrowest limits": the variety, colors, texture, and elegance of such stones make them "more wondrous" than any other part of nature's creation; they seem "to be beyond price and to defy evaluation in terms of human wealth"; many consider it sacrilegious to violate them with engravings; "very many people find that a single gemstone alone is enough to provide them with a supreme and perfect vision of nature."[4] The compressed dimensions of an individual gemstone paradoxically bring into focus the vastness of the natural world, and it is that dynamic tension between the unfathomably large and the incredibly small that quivers with the energy of the sublime. Such objects lie beyond all ordinary categories of human reckoning, literally crystallizing that which is truly magnificent and thereby bringing us into contact with something greater than ourselves.

Sublime Subjects

Implicit in Pliny's hymn to the gemstone is the idea that nature is infinite and infinitely powerful, a byword for the cosmos as a whole and the divinity that pervades, orders, and animates it. But to recognize nature as such and to see its distillation in a gemstone, one must have the right intellectual outlook and moral character – one must possess a certain high-mindedness or greatness of soul.[5] This is what it means to be a sublime subject, the kind of person who experiences the sublime and inspires it in others. Pliny's remarks unobtrusively demonstrate how to play the game, but others are more explicit and more urgent, including Longinus, for whom moral and artistic excellence are correlates.

In numerous works of classical philosophy, the exemplarity of the sublime subject serves a protreptic function. In Plato's *Symposium*, for instance, the sublime vision of a life lived in contemplation of beauty, virtue, and truth is a powerful force that sweeps the reader into the study of philosophy. In the dialogue's penultimate movement, Socrates relates a conversation he had with a woman named Diotima who explained how one's desire for physical beauty can be refined and redirected toward abstract ideas. Eventually, "the lover is turned to the great sea of beauty, and, gazing upon this, he gives birth to many gloriously beautiful ideas and theories, in unstinting love of wisdom, until, having grown and been strengthened there, he catches sight of such knowledge, and it is the knowledge of such beauty."[6] The "love of wisdom" is philosophy (*philosophia*), and through philosophy the lover finds himself physically and morally fortified, to the point that he can finally know beauty absolutely. Later, Diotima frames the journey as an ascent that resembles the revelation of esoteric knowledge in a mystery cult:

> "This is what it is to go aright, or be led by another, into the mystery of Love: one goes always upwards for the sake of this Beauty, starting out from beautiful things, and using them like rising stairs: from one body to two and from two to all beautiful bodies, then from beautiful bodies to beautiful customs, and from customs to learning beautiful things and from these lessons he arrives in the end at this lesson, which is learning of this very Beauty, so that in the end he comes to know just what it is to be beautiful. And there in life, Socrates, my friend," said the woman from Mantinea, "there if anywhere should a person live his life, beholding that Beauty…. The love of the gods belongs [to this kind of person], and if any human being could become immortal, it would be he."   (*Symposium*, 211b–d, 212a)

Diotima's speech is an exhortation to philosophy that mesmerizes the reader through a sublime vision of true beauty, conceptualized as the boundless sea that encircles the Mediterranean world and the end point on a journey that takes us to a new and objectively better reality. Crucially, Diotima speaks as one who has undergone initiation and made the journey. Her experience, mediated through Socrates, is an open invitation to initiate oneself into the mystery of Love and to extend oneself beyond what is human, toward immortality, which is reconfigured as the life of the mind. After Socrates finishes, a crowd of drunken revelers bursts onto the scene, suggesting the difficulty of sustaining such a sublime project amid the hubbub of everyday life; the world that we inhabit is not well suited for such elevation of spirit.

At the risk of understatement, the Platonic ascent has a long afterlife. To cite one example, some 700 years after Plato's death, Augustine easily repurposes the imagery and basic idea of Diotima's speech in the service of Christianity. At a pivotal moment in *Confessions* (IX.24), Augustine remembers an ecstatic vision he and his mother shared in Ostia: fired by love of God, they made a gradual ascent through the physical world up to heaven, marveling at his works as they climbed, transcending the limits of their minds, only to return to the clamor of everyday speech. After all his false starts, Augustine has finally become the kind of person who can experience, at least fleetingly, the sublimity of God, and the reader is summoned to share the affective intensity of the moment and to strive to make it their own. The intellectual history of the ascent – its history as a sublime experience – marks its value in a radically new cultural context.

Just as they would in the eighteenth century and Romantic period, in the classical tradition the sublime and the sublime subject also play central roles in texts devoted to the scientific explanation of natural phenomena. Lucretius's poem *On the Nature of the Universe*, written in the 50s BCE, has emerged as a central document in this tradition and, indeed, in the history of the sublime more generally.[7] The poem is an extended exposition of the materialist physics of the Greek atomist Epicurus, and Lucretius's ultimate goal is to eradicate the related fears of death, the afterlife, and the gods. Near the beginning, Lucretius describes the terrifying stranglehold that Religion, monstrously personified, used to hold on humanity, until Epicurus ("a man of Greece") discovered the atomic structure of reality and proved the soul's mortality and the gods' disinterestedness in human affairs:

> The first who dared
> raise mortal eyes against [Religion], first to take
> his stand against it, was a man of Greece.
> He was not cowed by fables of the gods

or thunderbolts or heaven's threatening roar,
but they the more spurred on his ardent soul
yearning to be the first to break apart
the bolts of nature's gates and throw them open.
Therefore his lively intellect prevailed
and forth he marched, advancing onwards far
beyond the flaming ramparts of the world,
and voyaged in mind throughout infinity.
Whence he victorious back in triumph brings
report of what can be and what cannot. (I. 66–76).[8]

The narrative enacts the dual experience of the sublime, moving from terror through bold action to intellectual triumph. Within this drama, Epicurus plays the role of a Homeric hero, physically and morally superior to ordinary mortals, and a Roman general, backed by and invested with all the majesty of empire, and it is his indomitable character and high-minded response to Religion's threat that enable the elevating upswing of the sublime to redeem the terror with which the vignette begins. Epicurus's intellectual adventure also plugs into long-standing narratives of philosophical enlightenment that are closely connected to the Platonic ascent: the "flight of the mind" and "the view from above," whereby a subject travels around the earth or up to heaven, leaving behind the biases of terrestrial life, and thereby gains a new perspective on reality.[9] This trope would become commonplace in the eighteenth century and Romantic period, and is visible, for instance, in Volney's *Les ruines* (1791) and Percy Shelley's *Queen Mab* (1813). In the classical context, the tradition marks Epicurus as a sublime subject, and we are summoned to reenact his dramatic adventure through submission to Lucretius's potent words and irrefutable logic. As the poem unfolds, relentlessly plunging the reader into the chaos of atomic motion, it challenges us to demonstrate the "ardentness of soul" that defines Epicurus. Lucretius knows that many will fall short; the ecstatic experience of recognizing atomic truth is no more lasting than the visions of Plato or Augustine.

On the flip side, greatness of spirit all too easily comes unhinged, and when it appears to dive deep into darkness and depravity, it problematizes the orientation of our own moral compass. Tragedy offers numerous examples of this mode of sublime subjectivity. A powerful instance is Clytemnestra in Aeschylus's *Agamemnon*, produced in the mid-fifth century BCE – as she recounts how she has just now killed her husband in the name of justice, a blood-spattered Clytemnestra glories over the corpse and exalts in her triumph, leaving the Chorus to gaze in amazement at her boldness (lines 1372–400). In the Roman world, Lucan's historical epic *Civil War* contains multiple characters who embody this tradition. Lucan's poem dates to the mid-first century CE and tells the story of the conflict between Julius Caesar and Pompey the Great. That Caesar himself exemplifies this morally ambivalent mode of the sublime becomes clear in a prominent simile that compares the general to a thunderbolt (1.146–57).[10] Both an unstoppable force of nature and the terrifying instrument of a god, Caesar strikes repeatedly, leaving a trail of wreckage in his wake. He is simultaneously hero and villain, a source of admiration and panic, who blinds onlookers – and readers – with his brilliance even as he leaves them trembling and brings the world crashing down upon itself. The line that separates Lucan's Caesar from Lucretius's Epicurus is difficult to establish. They are revolutionaries who transform their surroundings and alter how others perceive the world. Lucan's relentless denigration of Caesar as a maniacal tyrant bent on universal destruction only sets him further apart from the rest of humanity. He is a sublime subject precisely because he embodies Roman imperial magnificence and inaugurates the death of freedom, thereby transcending the limits of ordinary human behavior and exceeding the moral criteria by which we evaluate one another. Accounts of the sublime in eighteenth-century philosophical aesthetics would often similarly struggle to unpack the complex relationship between sublimity and morality that figures like Lucan's Caesar bring to life.

The Fall

Ancient writers are keenly aware that the sublime is a momentary sensation, a thrilling rush that recedes. For Plato, Lucretius, and Augustine, the very possibility of experiencing the sublime is evidence of the human race's exceptional status, but the baggage of our earthly lives always drags us back down, one way or another – and therein lies a significant point of interest. While Augustine and his mother, for example, return to ground level calmly, other narratives place great weight on the failure to persist in a state of sublimity, and this failure is itself a source of the sublime. In Ovid's shape-shifting epic *Metamorphoses*, written early in the first century CE, the story of Phaethon brings this phenomenon into sharp relief (1.748–2.400).[11] Although entirely unqualified, Phaethon secures the opportunity to drive the chariot of his estranged father, the Sun. While guiding the physical sun through the heavens, Phaethon wonders in amazement at the constellations up close. Unfortunately, the sight of the earth from such a high altitude unnerves him; he grows fearful and loses control of the horses. The team careens wildly across the sky, a great conflagration engulfs the world, and Jupiter feels compelled to shatter the carriage with a thunderbolt, checking the spread of the flames and sending Phaethon tumbling to earth. The first half of Phaethon's journey is easily read through the logic of the sublime, a paradigmatic instantiation of both "the flight of the mind" and "the view from above" – the subject, claiming his birthright, elevates himself to the level of the divine and is filled with wonder as he gazes at the universe, clear eyed.[12] But Ovid is interested less in the ascent itself or what one sees from the pinnacle of heaven than in Phaethon's inability to maintain that state of serene insight. In his headlong plunge, Phaethon resembles a shooting star, and when a group of minor divinities buries him, they affix the following epitaph to his tomb: "Here lies Phaethon, driver of this father's chariot. / Although he could not control it, nevertheless he fell amidst deeds of great daring" (*Metamorphoses*, 2.327–8). The magnificence of the undertaking redeems Phaethon's failure and excuses the catastrophe he has unleashed. Human beings may be related to the divine and able to transcend moment- arily their earthly limits, but we are still fundamentally earth-bound; the sublimity of a fall amid deeds of great daring bears witness to our own limitations and is a source of consolation.

The sublime fall appears in various contexts.[13] For instance, writing at roughly the same time as Ovid, Horace uses the conceit to think about the dangers and rewards of poetic imitation. In *Odes* 4.2, Horace compares Pindar, the incomparable master of Greek lyric, to a river that crashes down a mountain and spills over its banks; Pindar is sublime. The poem begins, however, with the suggestion that anyone who tries to write like Pindar will play the role of Icarus, "destined to give his name to the glassy sea" (lines 3–4). To attempt Pindaric elevation is to court disaster, and yet it is disaster that ends in everlasting fame, since Icarus's name lives on, with the Icarian Sea attesting to his flight. In the first half of the poem, Horace tries out this precarious mode of grandeur, setting himself up for the thrill and attendant approbation of a sublime fall, before transitioning to an ostensibly lower, less dangerous register. Similarly, the paradigm of the sublime fall lies behind Longinus's preference, in *Sublime* 33–6, for flawed sublimity over technical perfection. "Perhaps," writes Longinus, "it is also certain that inferior and middling natures will remain practically flawless and secure because they avoid risks and do not aim for the highest goals, while great talents are liable to stumble precisely because of their greatness."[14] Longinus is thinking of literature, but his discussion of flawed sublimity contains the famous passage in which he writes of the spectacle of nature, the erotic passion that draws humans toward grandeur, and our inborn desire to mentally cross all boundaries.[15] The natural world, philosophical speculation, and artistic potential merge, reinforcing one another's claims to sublimity. Ovid, Horace, and Longinus are all thinking with the same intellectual tool kit – failure to maintain a sublime subjectivity is no failure at all.[16]

Pushback

The sublime was also a source of controversy. At a relatively early date, Aristophanes's satirical depiction of Socrates in *Clouds*, staged in 423 BCE, draws on the popular conception of philosophers as subversive hacks who preposterously lay claim to sublime subjectivity. Related but fundamentally different are those passages where Horace heaps disdain and abuse, tinged with irony, upon intellectuals whose sublime utterances are not worthy of the name.[17] In such texts, Horace positions himself as a guardian of the sublime, and such policing of sublimity is common in the imperial period – it is, after all, a major preoccupation of Longinus. Seneca the Younger, a rough contemporary of Longinus, is similarly invested in maintaining the integrity of the sublime in his *Natural Questions*, a text devoted to the physics of celestial and meteorological phenomena. Modeling himself partially on Lucretius, Seneca presents the study of nature as a sublime enterprise that elevates and fortifies the mind, even if it is highly contingent and often leads to spectacular falls.[18] The sublimity of this project contrasts starkly with other sources of sublimity that Seneca deems morally problematic, such as the intoxicating grandeur of Roman political power and the depraved ecstasy of unrestrained sexual adventure.[19] For Seneca, to allow oneself to be carried away by thoughts of empire or the pleasures of the flesh is to lose perspective, to mistake the earthly semblance of grandeur for true grandeur. Seneca vividly demonstrates the sublimity of such concepts and behaviors only to reject their value for those who dedicates themselves to the pursuit of virtue and knowledge; as I have already noted, eighteenth-century philosophical aesthetics would struggle with similar tensions.

A final example comes from poem 51 of Catullus. The mid-first century BCE text is a Latin translation of a poem by Sappho, happily preserved by Longinus.[20] In the original, Sappho describes the physical breakdown of her body when she beholds "you," an unnamed woman – Sappho's voice, tongue, and eyes fail her, a flame runs through her limbs, her ears thunder, she sweats and shivers and turns pale, she is close to death. The text breaks off in mid-sentence: "all must be dared." The devastating sight physically overwhelms and psychologically emboldens Sappho; her experience is sublime. From our perspective, Catullus alters Sappho's text in two significant ways. First, Catullus names his addressee, using the familiar pseudonym of his most prominent love interest, Lesbia. In the present context, however, "Lesbia" ceases to be a known character in Catullus's dramatic soap opera and takes on its literal signification, "woman from Lesbos." The "woman from Lesbos," of course, is Sappho herself. The substantivized adjective stands metonymically for Sappho's poetry, and suddenly the sublime experience of erotic longing figures the sublime experience of reading poetry and trying to connect with the literary past, all of which teeters thrillingly on the brink of collapse. As Sappho's sublime subjectivity becomes Catullus's own, the Roman poet anticipates and literalizes Longinus's dictum (in *Sublime* 7.2) that sublime literature makes us feel as if we ourselves have produced the very text that we have encountered. Second, although we do not know how Sappho's poem ended, Catullus takes a different tack. In the final strophe, he pulls himself back from the brink:

> Leisure, Catullus, is dangerous to you:
> in leisure, you run riot and exult extravagantly:
> leisure, in time gone by, has ruined kings and
> prosperous cities (51.13–16).[21]

Catullus equates the passionate excesses of the sublime with leisure (*otium*), which stands in implicit contrast to the political and financial business (*negotium*) in which young Roman aristocrats are supposed to engage and that Catullus continually resists; leisure, love, and literature are sublime, and that is where Catullus longs to spend his time, and where he feels he cannot. Through the swift pivot from erotic breakdown to moralizing soliloquy, the sublime emerges as a role, a *persona* ("actor's mask") that Catullus puts on and takes off. While that does not make it any less compelling, it reveals that the sublime is part of a cultural performance that signals value and communicates ideology. In the elite and highly educated contexts within which we have been moving, the classical sublime is never a simple expression of unmediated emotional truth; it is always deployed for a reason, and those reasons bear interpretation.

NOTES

1 For introduction, text, translation, and commentary, see Stephen Halliwell, ed., *Pseudo-Longinus: On the Sublime*, Oxford, Oxford University Press, 2022. For more discussion, see *Doran*, 27–94, and James Porter, *The Sublime in Antiquity*, Cambridge, Cambridge University Press, 2016, 57–177. Unless otherwise indicated, translations of Greek and Latin are my own.

2 See Aristophanes, *Acharnians* 530–1, produced in 425 BCE, and Longinus, *Sublime* 1.4, 12.4, 34.4.

3 Translation by A. T. Murray and William F. Wyatt, *Homer: Iliad, Books 1–12*, Cambridge, MA, Harvard University Press, 1999, 393.

4 Pliny, *Natural History* 37.1. Translation based on D. E. Eichholz, *Pliny: Natural History, Books 36–37*, Cambridge, MA, Harvard University Press, 1962, 165.

5 For greatness of soul, see Porter, *Sublime*, 195–201.

6 *Symposium* 210d–e. Translation by Alexander Nehamas and Paul Woodruff, *Plato: Symposium*, Indianapolis, IN, Hackett, 1989.

7 See Gian Biagio Conte, "Instructions for a Sublime Reader: Form of the Text and Form of the Addressee in Lucretius' *De rerum natura*," in *Genres and Readers: Lucretius, Love Elegy, Pliny's Encyclopedia*, trans. Glenn W. Most, Baltimore, MD, Johns Hopkins University Press, 1994, 1–34; Porter, *Sublime*, 445–73 (463–73 on Lucretius and Kant); and Philip Hardie, *Lucretian Receptions*, Cambridge, Cambridge University Press, 2009, 65–228. Cf. Burke on Lucretius in *Enquiry* II v and V v.

8 Translation from Ronald Melville, *Lucretius on the Nature of the Universe*, Oxford, Oxford University Press, 1997, 5.

9 See, succinctly, Pierre Hadot, *Philosophy as a Way of Life*, trans. Michael Chase, Malden, MA, Blackwell, 1995, 238–50. For a comprehensive account of these tropes and their reception, see Philip Hardie, *Celestial Aspirations: Classical Impulses in British Poetry and Art*, Princeton, NJ, Princeton University Press, 2022.

10 See Henry J. M. Day, *Lucan and the Sublime*, Cambridge, Cambridge University Press, 2013, 106–78 (107–16).

11 For Ovid's Phaethon and the sublime, see Alessandro Barchiesi, "Phaethon and the Monsters," in Hardie, ed., *Lucretian Receptions*, 163–88.

12 Cf. Longinus, *Sublime*, 15.4.

13 See Matthew Leigh, "Statius and the Sublimity of Capaneus," in M. J. Clarke, B. G. F. Currie, and R. O. A. M. Lyne, eds., *Epic Interactions*, Oxford, Oxford University Press, 2006, 217–41 (233–41); Hardie, *Paradox*, 212–17; and Patrick Glauthier, "An Image Sublime: The Milky Way in Aratus and Manilius," in Jenny Strauss Clay and Athanassios Vergados, eds., *Teaching through Images*, Leiden, Brill, 2022, 82–104 (96–100).

14 Longinus, *Sublime*, 33.2; translation from Halliwell.

15 See Longinus, *Sublime*, 35.2–5. For this chapter, see Stephen Halliwell, *Between Ecstasy and Truth*, Oxford, Oxford University Press, 343–67, and Porter, *Sublime*, 175–7.

16 It should be noted that throughout antiquity poetic inspiration, often termed "madness," is regularly represented according to the logic of the sublime. Two particularly influential ancient discussions of this experience are Plato, *Ion* 533d–536d and *Phaedrus* 245a–c. For inspiration in Longinus, see Halliwell, *Pseudo-Longinus*, xlvi–li.

17 For *Clouds*, see Porter, *Sublime*, 434–43. For Horace, see Hardie, *Lucretian Receptions*, 197–202.

18 For the sublime in the *Natural Questions*, see Gareth D. Williams, *The Cosmic Viewpoint*, New York, Oxford University Press, 2012, 213–57. At 224–5, Williams tentatively connects Lucretius, Seneca, and Kant.

19 *Natural Questions* 4a praef. 20–2 on empire and 1.16 on Hostius Quadra's sexual transgressions.

20 Longinus, *Sublime*, 10.2. For Longinus's analysis, see Porter, *Sublime*, 118–24. For the relationship between the two texts, the cultural contexts of which differ significantly, see Paul Allen Miller, "Sappho 31 and Catullus 51: The Dialogism of Lyric," in Julia Haig Gaisser, ed., *Oxford Readings in Classical Studies: Catullus*, Oxford, Oxford University Press, 2007, 476–89.

21 Translation based on Peter Green, *The Poems of Catullus*, Berkeley, University of California Press, 2005, 99.

2

DAWN HOLLIS

The Natural Sublime in the Seventeenth Century

There are some phrases that stick with you. Several years ago, I came across a comment by Richard W. Bevis, who observed that 'sublimity has become a modern academic hobby horse whose meaning varies with the rider'.[1] In this essay, it is my turn to take a mount, in considering 'the natural sublime' in the seventeenth century, and laying out how it both differed from and paved the way for the Romantic sublime.[2] The basic shape of my hobby horse is this: that conversations regarding the sublime are frequently complicated by the fact that 'the sublime' can be taken to refer to (at least) two different things. On the one hand, 'the sublime' is a philosophical concept that was largely developed during the eighteenth century. On the other, it refers to a type of aesthetic experience and to expressions *of* that experience, often relating to the 'natural world' in particular. These two things are not unrelated: the philosophical concept of the sublime could be described as the aesthetic experience made self-conscious. Likewise, visitors to – for example – the Alps today are the inheritors of those Romantic-period engagements with the sublime, and the sublime experiences that they enjoy continue to be shaped by them.

However, the distinction between the two senses of the sublime is important when considering the 'prehistory' of the Romantic sublime. By the first definition, it would be anachronistic to speak of 'the Romantic sublime in the seventeenth century' since Romantic-period configurations of the experience did not yet exist. By the latter definition, however, it would be problematic to suggest that people did *not* experience the affective response that would later be described as sublime simply because that response had yet to become the subject of formal theorization.

How, though, to identify an experience of the sublime before it would have been deliberately labelled as such? In exploring the imaginary of the north Daniel du Chartier has proposed the construction of a 'grammar of the idea of north'.[3] Through studying descriptions of a place identified as 'north', he argues, you can construct a 'grammar' of the characteristics that evoke a sense of nordicity (regardless of the actual latitude of a place). A grammar of the natural sublime might note that it is generally felt in response to the sight of spectacular natural phenomena and that the experience can be described in terms of awe, fear, horror, inspiration, or of being overwhelmed.

In what follows I consider three seventeenth-century examples that match this 'grammar'. The example of William Lithgow demonstrates the basic point that experiences of what would come to be called the sublime occurred and were recorded in the seventeenth century. That of Athanasius Kircher highlights the specifically early modern significance of a belief in the divine that underpinned (some of) those experiences. My third example provides a more in-depth case study. Thomas Burnet, thanks to his commentary on mountains in his *Theory of the Earth* (1681), has often been proposed as an early precursor of the Romantic sublime. By my reading, Burnet certainly does not represent the first or a unique early modern example of sublime *experience*, but it is possible to see his work as a lynchpin in the development of the eighteenth-century *concept* of the sublime.

'High stands thy top': Poetry of Etna

We know relatively little of William Lithgow other than what he tells us of himself in his travel writings. If these are to be believed, he 'attracted adventures to himself like iron filings to a magnet' during the course of his journeys across Europe, the Middle East, and Africa.[4] Lithgow often frames his physical engagements with nature as (exaggeratedly) fraught and heroic: ascending the dizzy heights of Mount Quarantine, in Palestine (approximately 360 metres high), Lithgow endured 'diverse dangers, and narrow passages'; on his way down, a friar in his company slipped, and would apparently 'have fallen five hundred fathoms' had Lithgow himself not 'rashly and unadvisedly endangered my own life for his safety'.[5]

It comes as no surprise then, that when travelling home from Africa via Sicily in 1615, Lithgow paused to climb Mount Etna, undertaking 'tedious toil, and curious climbing' in order to regard the 'terrible flames, and cracking smoke' of the crater.[6] This experience inspired him (or so he tells us) to write a poem on the spot:

> High standes thy toppe, but higher lookes mine eye,
> High soares thy smoake, but higher my desire:
> High are thy roundes, steep, circled, as I see,
> But higher farre this Breast, whiles I aspire:
> High mountes the furie, of thy burning fire,

But higher farre mine aymes transcende aboue:
High bendes thy force, through midst of *Vulcanes* ire,
But higher flies my sprite [spirit], with wings of loue:
High preasse thy flames, the chrystall air to moue,
But higher farre the scope of my engine:
High lies the snow, on thy proude toppes, I proue,
But higher vp ascendes my braue designe.
   Thine height cannot surpasse this clowdie frame,
   But my poore Soule, the highest Heauens doth claime.
   Mean-while with paine, I climbe to view thy toppes,
   Thine hight makes fall from me, ten thousand droppes.[7]

This poem shows us how a 'grammar of the sublime' can be used to assess the relationship between pre-Romantic engagements with sublime land-scapes where the specific vocabulary of 'sublimity' that developed during the eighteenth century is absent. Lithgow's poem certainly contains a sense of awe at the enormous volcano he seeks to ascend. But Lithgow's assertion of first the grandeur of Etna and then the greater nature of his own strength and spirit resonates not only with ideas of transport found in Longinus's treatise *On the Sublime* but also with eighteenth-century British and German debates about transcendence and the sublime. But this confidence is then reversed (albeit only partially) in the closing lines of the poem, where Lithgow admits that while his soul might claim the 'highest Heavens', his body is forced to pain and sweat by the effort of ascent.

I do not want to suggest that this eccentric Scottish traveller in any way anticipated later formulations of the natural sublime, or that he should be considered in any way a 'predecessor' whose writings influenced, either directly or indirectly, eighteenth-century or Romantic-period constructions of the sublime. What I do want to say is that there are marked similarities between the experience of nature reflected in Lithgow's sonnet and the experience of nature that was formally theorized by eighteenth-century philosophers and writers, and which in turn continues to provide the vocabulary for many modern-day experiences of nature. By this token, then, Lithgow's experience, when assessed according to a grammar of the sublime, can be read as a sublime experience by another name.

Athanasius Kircher: The Eschatological Sublime

Another eccentric traveller; another visit to Mount Etna, this time by the Jesuit Athanasius Kircher in 1638.[8] A voracious seeker of knowledge, Kircher's opening comments on the size of the volcano noted its troublesome tendency to change; past writers had variously recorded the crater as two miles, thirty miles, or even 400 miles wide. Although Kircher thought the last figure a printer's error, he also considered it entirely reasonable that 'in an Orifice, expos'd to so many great tumultations, and continually agitated and tossed, with so many assaults, fits, and convulsions of ferocious, and raging nature', measurements might find it to be 'sometimes larger, sometimes streighter; according to the condition of the Times' (47). The volcanic nature of Etna defies any definitive, empirical classification.

Kircher proceeds to describe the volcanic activity by which the crater, and the sides of the volcano itself, continually changed their scale and form: the 'horrible Tempests of burnings' of lava that spewed out of it at all levels. Such eruptions represented a 'spectacle so formidable, that there is none so stout-hearted, that can look into it without fear; and, as we say, his Hairs standing an [sic] end, and his head turning round with giddness': a description of the physical effects of a sublime experience (48). On his return journey from Sicily, Kircher was forced by a series of earthquakes to make landfall in southern mainland Italy. This tectonic activity gave him the unexpected opportunity to also visit Vesuvius, where he described his personal, haptic response to the volcano in greater detail:

> I saw what is horrible to be expressed, I saw it all over of a light fire, with an horrible combustion, and stench of Sulphur and burning Bitumen. Here forthwith being astonished at the unusual sight of the thing; Methoughts I beheld the habitation of Hell; wherein nothing else seemed to be much wanting, besides the horrid fantasms and apparitions of Devils. There were perceived horrible bellowings and roarings of the Mountain; An unexpressible stink; Smoaks mixt with darkish globes of Fires; which both the bottom and sides of the Mountain continually belch'd forth ... and made me in like manner, even and anon, belch, and as it were, vomit back again at it.   (35)

As would later be experienced by celebrated eighteenth-century natural philosophers exploring volcanoes and alps, the rational collector of data is here, briefly, overwhelmed by the volcano, to the extent that his body begins to demonstrate in microcosm the behaviour of Vesuvius in macrocosm: both are belching, gasping, the mountain with fire and the man for air.[9] Kircher, however, is not so entirely overwhelmed that he does not pause to observe and describe that which is still visually beautiful about the volcano, and to theorize as to its cause. Looking at the lava flowing from the crater, he theorizes that it must contain various minerals in order to exhibit every colour of the rainbow, such as 'yellow ... from Sulphur', 'red; from Cinnabar', and 'black; from Vitriol mixt with Water' (36).

However, the height of Kircher's sublime experience is neither in his physical response to the horror of the volcano nor in his detailed enjoyment of the colour-shifting lava. In viewing both Etna and Vesuvius, he is driven to cite Romans 11.33: 'O the depth of the Riches and Wisdom of God!' (49, 35). At Etna, he specifically instructs any person who 'desires to behold the power of the only Great and Good God' to visit a volcano (49). At Vesuvius, he goes even further, associating the sight of the volcano with thoughts of the end-times: 'If thou [God] shewest thy power against the wickedness of mankind in so formidable and portentous Prodigies and Omens of Nature; What shall it be in that last day, wherein the Earth shall be drown'd with the Ire of thy Fury, and the Elements melt with fervent heat?' (35).

Kircher's sublime experience, then, is intensified by thoughts of God. Initially, this is simply in what might be called general terms: the grandeur of Creation leads naturally to thoughts of the Creator. However, it also leads more specifically to thoughts of the end times. A volcano is not merely astonishing in itself, and does more than just reflect back the immense power of God; it stands as a symbol of the apocalypse, a microcosm of the fires that will (according to Christian tradition) destroy the world. Of course, where a volcano – both terrible, frightening, but also inspiring of awe and wonder – is a sublime object, to someone such as Kircher the apocalypse is a sublime concept to dwell upon. The thought of the end of days is a horrifying one in terms of the destruction involved, but also marvellous, representing the fulfilment of prophecies for this Earth and the promise of a newly made, sinless world for the redeemed after its passing. Kircher's experience is not just of the natural sublime but of what might be termed the eschatological sublime.

So, where William Lithgow demonstrated that the general 'grammar' of the sublime was extant in seventeenth-century experiences, Kircher's experiences of Etna and Vesuvius highlight more specifically the space filled by the divine in early modern sublime experiences. Connections between religion and the sublime were indeed drawn out both in Longinus and in later eighteenth-century philosophical aesthetics, but I believe that a belief in God's role in designing the world inhabited a particular, foundational position in seventeenth-century responses to nature. However, as my final example will show, this position did not remain unquestioned.

Thomas Burnet: Lynchpin, Not Originator

Burnet's *Sacred Theory of the Earth* (published in two volumes in Latin in 1681 and 1689, and in English in 1684 and 1690) represented an attempt to explain both the origins and future dissolution of the Earth – both cosmogony and eschatology – from solely rational, or natural, causes. He was troubled simultaneously by the doctrine of the Universal Flood and by the current form of the world. Looking at the world as it currently exists, he observed that there was not enough water in it to cover the tops of the highest mountains, as Genesis reported had occurred.[10] He was also displeased with the natural world that he saw around him. It had to him 'the true aspect of a World lying in its rubbish', and this was exactly what the first book of his *Theory* proposed it to be (110–11). The original Earth, he claimed, had been a perfectly smooth ovoid, with water lying underneath its outer shell of land. Over time the sun heated this water, and at the 'appointed time ... that All-wise Providence had design'd for the punishment of a sinful World', this water broke the egg-shell of the Earth, simultaneously causing the Flood *and* creating the irregular mountains, valleys, and seas of the present Earth (72–3). Thus, the conundrum of the water overtopping the highest mountains was solved: the mountains were created by the flood, and so only revealed as the roiling waters receded.

In the midst of his lengthy explication of the above narrative, Burnet produced a stirring passage that has almost certainly been quoted more frequently than any other sentence he wrote, in the *Theory* or otherwise. It seems at first glance to be an encomium on mountains:

> The greatest objects of Nature are, methinks, the most pleasing to behold; and next to the great Concave of the Heavens, and those boundless Regions where the Stars inhabit, there is nothing that I look upon with more pleasure than the wide Sea and the Mountains of the Earth. There is something august and stately in the Air of these things that inspires the mind with great thoughts and passions; We do naturally upon such occasions think of God and his greatness, and whatsoever hath but the shadow and appearance of INFINITE, as all things have that are too big for our comprehension, they fill and over-bear the mind with their Excess, and cast it into a pleasing kind of stupor and admiration. (139–40)

Burnet's language ticks many boxes in terms of the 'grammar of the sublime'; excess, stupor, and admiration are all recurrent tropes in eighteenth-century formulations, making it seem quite reasonable for modern commentators to read Burnet as 'anticipating' later writings. However, sentences later Burnet reveals that he considers this pleasure to be deceptive, and that 'these Mountains ... to confess the truth, are nothing but great ruines; but such as show a certain magnificence in Nature; as from old Temples and broken Amphitheaters of the *Romans*' (140). His tone becomes even more critical, as he seeks to remove from his reader's eyes the illusion of mountainous beauty: 'There is nothing in Nature more shapeless and ill-figur'd than an old Rock or a Mountain', and newly made after the Flood they 'would have appear'd very gastly and frightful' (144–5). For all this, it is

Burnet's deliberately misleading praise that has earned him a place in histories of the sublime.

Since the Romantic period, writers have attempted to trace the development of the apparently modern 'feeling for nature', to which a sense of the natural sublime is central, and have presented Burnet as an early outlier. William Wordsworth, for instance, asserted that, before Thomas Gray, Burnet was the only 'English traveller' who wrote of mountains with anything approaching 'admiration' rather than 'dislike and fear'.[11] Wordsworth's goal in claiming this was, specifically, to demonstrate that 'a vivid perception of romantic scenery is ... [not] inherent in mankind'; he would disagree strongly with any discussion of the prehistory of the Romantic sublime (342–3). In 1871, Leslie Stephen, mountaineer, clergyman, and literary critic, offered both Kircher and Burnet as early examples of a modern appreciation of mountains as 'intensely interesting and suggestive of elevating thoughts'.[12] Then, in 1959, the literary scholar Marjorie Hope Nicolson cast Burnet as a central figure in her monograph *Mountain Gloom and Mountain Glory: The Development of the Aesthetics of the Infinite*. Despite its age, Nicolson's work continues to shape historical understandings of the Western relationship with landscape through time, and sought to address what Nicolson saw as 'a basic problem in the history of taste: why did mountain attitudes change so spectacularly in England [during the seventeenth and eighteenth centuries]?' (*Nicolson*, iv). Although *Mountain Gloom and Mountain Glory* has largely been cited for the dichotomous narrative inherent in its (main) title, Nicolson's overarching point is in fact more complex: as her subtitle elaborates, she argued that the eighteenth century saw the creation of 'the Aesthetics of the Infinite', which might also be termed the natural sublime. Her epilogue dwells upon canonical expressions of sublime experiences, focalized upon mountains, as recorded by English Romantic poets: Byron, Shelley, Wordsworth (*Nicolson*, 371–93). Throughout, Nicolson characterizes Burnet as *of his era* in his denigration of mountains as irregular and unappealing, and as heterodox and unusual in his praise of them as inspiring of 'great thoughts and passions' (*Nicolson*, 207–17).

Since Nicolson, Burnet has firmly belonged within the canon of modern histories of the sublime. Bevis, in his *Road to Egdon Heath*, notes that while the title alludes to Thomas Hardy, whom he identifies as standing at the 'midpoint' between the origin of the 'great in nature' and the modern day, he might just as easily have started with 'Longinus or Thomas Burnet'. The passage quoted above, Bevis suggests, was 'seminal' in the history of aesthetics, although he does acknowledge the ambivalence of Burnet's overarching view of mountains.[13] A few years later, in illustrating that 'the sublime has a history' Philip Shaw moves from Longinus to Burnet to Burke, and later treats Burnet as the earliest of five 'influential theorists' (including John Dennis and Joseph Addison) whose work developed upon the ideas of Longinus.[14]

However, as an episode in the history of aesthetics, Burnet's *Theory* does not stand alone; his attempt at rationalizing the biblical narrative of creation and the Flood sparked a flurry of responses. The passage quoted above had excited just as much comment from his seventeenth-century critics as it would in later centuries, but not because they found it to be anything out of the ordinary; rather, because they agreed with it. For example, his first published respondent, Herbert Croft (the octogenarian Bishop of Hereford), protested that 'surely all men who behold these things have the same delightful contemplation, as he acknowledges to have felt', while implying that it is in viewing them 'as broken ruined fractions of a former Structure' that Burnet is heterodox.[15]

Other respondents took issue with Burnet's denigration of mountains as misshapen and unappealing, further suggesting that it was this side of his contradictory response which set him against the general attitudes of his day. According to Erasmus Warren, mountains, along with the other irregularities of form to which Burnet objected, represented the 'Tornings, and Carvings, and ornamental Sculptures' of the Earth, reflecting the 'marvellous and adoreable Skill of her *Maker*', and gestured to passages from the Psalms in which thoughts of 'the *Mountains*, the *high Hills*, the *Rocks*, and the *great and wide Sea*' led in turn to thoughts of God's wisdom and power in creating them.[16] The current, irregular form of the Earth was read by some as 'admirable variety', with John Beaumont citing earlier humanist writers to assert the 'Ornament, Use and Delight' of the world 'set forth the Wisdom, Power and Goodness of the Creator'.[17] Almost all of Burnet's respondents emphasized the *utility* of the Earth in its current form: the mountains that Burnet deemed to be irregularities were in fact vital to the world as the source of the rivers that fed valleys and the metals which, in being turned into tools, enabled the development of human civilization.[18]

An obvious response to the above is that ornament or beauty is a category distinct from the sublime, and that 'usefulness' seems positively faint praise to the point of scarcely being relevant in a discussion of aesthetics.[19] I suggest that the distinction between beauty, sublimity, and utility represents a modern, anachronous lens. It was only with the later *theorization* of the sublime that 'beauty' came to be seen as a distinct category from 'the sublime'. Moreover, I believe that when Burnet's respondents spoke of usefulness, they were in fact gesturing towards something very great indeed, namely, their innate belief in God's role as the creator of nature. When a seventeenth-century clergyman such as Croft or Warren looked at a mountain and thought, 'This pleases my eye, and is of use to the Earth', the subtext was, 'This was deliberately created *for* my enjoyment and *for* its usefulness to the Earth by God.' And to such a person, could there be anything greater than the thought of an all-powerful God and his act of creation? Nature was sublime because God was sublime, and God had created nature.

It is here, then, that I think Burnet was a lynchpin. His *Theory* caused enormous controversy because it essentially said that the world in its current form was *not* created by God, that the world as God had originally designed it no longer existed. Worse, the event that transformed the original, perfect Earth into the current, flawed Earth was God's act of punishment, the Flood, against the sinfulness of mankind. Contemporaries of Burnet who looked upon mountains and thought with pleasure of the divine and of his benevolence in making the world in such a form could no longer do so, if they accepted his *Theory*. Instead, they should look on them and think of punishment and sin. Leslie Stephen observed that mountains were never viewed so poorly in English literature as in the early eighteenth century, when they stood merely as 'big chaotic lumps'.[20] Daniel Defoe, for example, found the land now treasured as the Lake District to be 'the wildest, most barren and frightful of any' he had ever passed over.[21] It is no coincidence that Defoe was also familiar with Burnet's *Theory* (59).

At the same time, it is no coincidence that Burnet was also read (and lauded) by authors who would contribute to the eighteenth-century formalization of the sublime. For example, Joseph Addison, years before writing 'The Pleasures of the Imagination' in 1712, composed a Latin ode to that 'famous man' Thomas Burnet, summarizing and celebrating his *Sacred Theory*.[22] Burnet's *Theory*, then, simultaneously did two things in terms of the history of the sublime. First, it effectively removed the theological foundation of many early modern sublime experiences. If you accepted Burnet – and, despite the initial controversy surrounding his work, it was his *Theory* and none of the many animadversions that went on to be republished and remembered – you could no longer look at a mountain, feel awed, and know this to be an entirely theologically correct experience, nor could you look at a volcano, reflect on its divinely designed end, and feel uplifted. Before Burnet, the assumption that the world was as God had created it both produced and justified sublime experiences of the natural world. By the end of the eighteenth century, the idea of divine creativity would again be incorporated into articulations of the sublime, but now in terms of the sublime response as providing evidence for original design and thus for the grandeur of God; Creation thus being the end-point *proven* by a sense of sublimity rather than the uncontested fact upon which it was based.

Second, after Burnet (and it is important to acknowledge that Burnet *was* 'of his time' in that he represented, rather than created, a general intellectual shift away from biblical literalism and towards increasingly 'rational' attempts at explaining natural history), there existed a sort of aesthetic vacuum, at least in English literature and natural philosophy. It is that vacuum which, I believe, formed the preconditions for the slow development, over the course of the eighteenth century, of various formal articulations of a theory of the sublime that could (and often did) include an acknowledgement of the divine, but did not rely upon a foundational belief in the literal interpretation of Genesis in order to explain sublime experiences. It was not in recognizing the grandeur of mountains that Burnet 'anticipated' the natural sublime of later centuries. Instead, it was in divorcing them from the awe-inspiring fact of divine creation that he served to effectively change the terms upon which sublime experiences could be enjoyed.

Conclusion

My arguments above are by no means radical departures from previous perspectives. The general idea that, in the words of Philip Shaw, 'the sublime has a history' predating the Romantic sublime of the eighteenth and nineteenth centuries is widely acknowledged in most studies of the subject. Nor is my specific reading of Burnet a world away from the narrative set forth by Nicolson who (as summarized by Cian Duffy and Peter Howell) 'suggests that … [the] early eighteenth-century interest in the *natural* sublime stemmed from the gradual transfer of the emotional responses previously evoked by the idea of God to those aspects of the natural world which seemed to reflect or partake of divine grandeur' (*Cultures*, 2). However, I would nuance both of these ideas. The shift between the early modern and the Romantic sublime was not, I think, one of *transferral* of emotions evoked by God onto the natural world; as shown by the examples discussed in this essay, nature was inspiring of sublime experiences long before the eighteenth century. Rather, it was a shift from a natural sublime that frequently (though not always, as the complicating example of Lithgow demonstrates) *started* with the grandeur of God to one which had the potential to encompass and even move beyond it. In terms of generalities, I would prefer to see it said that the sublime *is* a history, and to see more emphasis on the need to distinguish between the sublime as a specific moment of philosophical and terminological development and the sublime as a class of aesthetic experience of the natural world. There is always, of course, a risk of anachronism, but I think it is worth the risk, for the language and grammar of sublime experience has great value for the study of pre-modern engagements with nature. It provides a vocabulary that captures for modern-day readers both the quality of those historical engagements and the common ground between past 'sublime' experiences and those which we might have today.

NOTES

1 R. W. Bevis, *The Road to Egdon Heath: The Aesthetics of the Great in Nature*, Montreal, McGill-Queen's University Press, 1999, 11–12.

2 This essay represents the culmination of many years of work and thinking on this topic, and thus synthesizes research and ideas found elsewhere in my unpublished and published writings. See Dawn Hollis, 'The "Authority of the Ancients"? Seventeenth-Century Natural Philosophy and Aesthetic Responses to Mountains', in Dawn Hollis and Jason König, eds., *Mountain Dialogues from Antiquity to Modernity*, London, Bloomsbury Academic, 2021, 55–73; 'Aesthetic Experience, Investigation and Classic Ground: Responses to Etna from the First Century CE to 1773', *Journal of the Warburg and Courtauld Institutes*, 83, 2020, 299–325; 'Mountain Gloom and Mountain Glory: The Genealogy of an Idea', *ISLE: Interdisciplinary Studies in Literature and Environment*, 26.4, 2019, 1038–61; and 'Re-Thinking Mountains: Ascents, Aesthetics, and Environment in Early Modern Europe', PhD thesis, University of St Andrews, 2017.

3 Daniel Chartier, 'Towards a Grammar of the Idea of North: Nordicity, Winterity', *Nordlit*, April 2007, 35–47.

4 Clifford Edmund Bosworth, *An Intrepid Scot: William Lithgow of Lanark's Travels in the Ottoman Lands, North Africa and Central Europe, 1609–21*, Aldershot, Ashgate, 2006, xvi.

5 William Lithgow, *A most delectable, and true discourse, of an admired and painefull peregrination from Scotland, to the most famous kingdomes in Europe, Asia, and Affricke* (London, 1614), sig. P4v.

6 William Lithgow, *The Total Discourse, of the rare aduentures, and painefull peregrinations of long nineteene years trauayles*, London, 1632, 390.

7 William Lithgow, *The Pilgrimes Farewell, to his natiue countrey of Scotland*, Edinburgh, 1618), sig. Fr.

8 Kircher's observations of volcanoes were published first in his *Mundus subterraneus* (1665), but are cited here from an anonymous early modern translation, *The Vulcano's; or, Burning and Fire-vomiting Mountains* (1669).

9 The belching of the volcano has classical precedent; see Cian Duffy, '"Famous from all Antiquity": Classical Myth and Romantic Poetry', in Dawn Hollis and Jason König, eds., *Mountain Dialogues from Antiquity to Modernity*, London, Bloomsbury, 2021, 40.

10 Thomas Burnet, *The Theory of the Earth*, 2 vols. (London, 1684), vol. 1, 9–20.

11 Wordsworth, letter to the editor of the *Morning Post* published 11 December 1844, in W. J. B. Own and Jane Worthington Smyser, eds., *The Prose Works of William Wordsworth*, 3 vols., Oxford, Clarendon, 1974, vol. 3, p. 342.

12 Leslie Stephen, *The Playground of Europe*, London, Longman 1871, 23–7. For more on Wordsworth's and Stephen's reflections on the (supposedly) modern appreciation for mountains, see Hollis, 'Mountain Gloom and Mountain Glory'.

13 Bevis, *Road to Egdon Heath*, xi, 33–4.

14 Philip Shaw, *The Sublime*, London, Routledge, 2006, 4–5, 27–30.

15 Herbert Croft, *Some Animadversions upon a Book Intituled the Theory of the Earth*, London, 1685, 142.

16 Erasmus Warren, *Geologia; or, A Discourse Concerning the Earth before the Deluge*, London, 1690, 143, 147 (citing Psalms 104).

17 John Beaumont, *Considerations on a Book, entituled the Theory of the Earth*, London, 1693, 57, citing, for example, Johannes Reuchlin's *De verbo mirifico* (1494) and George Hakewill's *Apologie or Declaration of the Power and Providence of God* (1627).

18 These examples from John Bentley, *A Confutation of Atheism from the Origin and Frame of the World*, London, 1693, 36–9; Warren also expands at length upon the utility of mountains in *Geologia*, 148.

19 Bevis argues that Warren's writing acknowledges the beauty of the present form of the Earth but does not, as Burnet's does, reflect a sense of 'the Great' (35).

20 Stephen, *Playground*, 30.

21 Daniel Defoe, *A Tour Thro' the Whole Island of Great Britain, divided into Circuits or Journies*, 3 vols., London, 1727, vol. 3, 223.

22 Joseph Addison, 'Ad Insignissimo Virum D. Tho. Burnettum, Sacræ Theoriæ Telluris Autorem', in *Musarum anglicarum analecta*, 3 vols., Oxford, 1699, vol. 2, 284–6.

3

CIAN DUFFY

The Sublime in Eighteenth-Century English, Irish and Scottish Philosophy

In his introduction to *The Sublime*, Monk suggests that while 'a study of the sublime in England' in the eighteenth century 'comes very near being a study of English thought and arts', the widespread engagement with the subject 'has its roots in the psychology and the philosophy of the times' (*Monk*, 3). Monk's claim that the 'roots' of the Romantic sublime are to be found in eighteenth-century philosophical discourse has, like much else in his study, been robustly contested. Scholars such as Nicolson and Hollis, for instance, have shown that extended responses to the sublime in English cultural texts considerably predate the flowering of philosophical aesthetics in the early eighteenth century.[1] Others, including Howell and myself, have shown that during the late eighteenth century and Romantic period, philosophical aesthetics was only one of a dizzying array of discursive and experiential contexts in which one might encounter the sublime, and very far from the most prominent of such contexts (see *Cultures*). But all this granted, it is undoubtedly also the case that discussions of the sublime constitute an extensive, even ubiquitous, strand of eighteenth-century English, Irish and Scottish philosophy. Those discussions, and twentieth-century academic responses to them, are my subject here.

Philosophical Questions about the Sublime

Eighteenth-century English, Irish and Scottish philosophical aesthetics focuses, in the main, on two distinct species of the sublime, although discussion of the two frequently overlaps. The first is the ability of speech or writing to generate sublime affect; academic historians usually trace interest in this so-called rhetorical sublime to the re-introduction to European thought, in the late seventeenth century, of the treatise *Perì hýpsous* (On the Sublime), attributed to the first-century CE author known as Longinus, which was first translated into French in 1674 and into English in 1739. The second is the ability of certain kinds of landscape or other natural phenomena to generate sublime affect; although now largely synonymous, in academic and popular discourse, with 'the Romantic sublime', engagements with this so-called natural sublime in Anglophone thought predate interest in the rhetorical sublime, and are also visible in the classical tradition, including *Perì hýpsous*.

An early debate between Monk and Nicolson, those pioneering historians of the topic, sought to establish where and why eighteenth-century interest in the sublime originated. For Monk, the rediscovery and extensive analysis of *Perì hýpsous* constituted the 'fountain-head of all ideas' about the sublime in Anglophone philosophical aesthetics (*Monk*, 10). For Nicolson, conversely, *Perì hýpsous* rather provided Anglophone writers with a vocabulary for expressing the new admiration for the natural world that arose from scientific enquiry, and from astronomy in particular, during the late seventeenth century (*Nicolson*, 3, 29n.39). Nicolson might have drawn support for this argument from Adam Smith, whose essay 'The Principles Which Lead and Direct Philosophical Enquiries; Illustrated by the History of Astronomy', published in the posthumous *Essays on Philosophical Subjects* (1795), traces the origins of scientific enquiry to the wonder provoked by sublime natural phenomena. But the whole question remains intractable and ultimately serves to illustrate how academic histories of eighteenth-century interest in the sublime often become mired in the difficulties of retrospectively imposed chronologies. Hipple sounded an early note of caution here, 'not finding a history in the subject, and not desiring to superimpose one' (*Hipple*, 6).

Armed with this caution, what we can with confidence say, however, is that eighteenth-century philosophical investigations of both the rhetorical and the natural sublimes, and of the relationship between them, consistently address, while often making very different answers to, some recurrent questions: How can the experience of the sublime be defined? What exactly *do* we experience? Is it a physiological response or a psychological response or some combination of the two? What triggers the experience? Is sublimity a property of certain objects or phenomena or situations, which we can perceive, or is it a function of *how* we perceive those objects or phenomena or situations? Is the experience produced by external objects or by the mind itself? How can visual representations of those external phenomena that generate sublime affect (e.g., a painting of a volcanic eruption) trigger the same response as the phenomena themselves? By extension (and perhaps most perplexingly), how can textual descriptions produce the same response as the phenomena or moral situations described? How can *reading* generate an experience of the sublime? How is the sublime to be distinguished from other affective responses and aesthetic modes like 'the beautiful' or, later in the century, 'the picturesque'?

These questions make apparent how and why philosophical investigation of the sublime readily spilled over into much more fundamental questions about perception and ontology. Thinking about the sublime in English, Irish and Scottish philosophy frequently intersected with contemporary constructions of gender, race and physical and mental health. The sublime, for instance, is routinely associated with the masculine, and the beautiful with the feminine, as in an often-quoted passage from *Enquiry* III xv, where Burke points to 'the smoothness; the softness; the easy and insensible swell' of 'the neck and breasts' of a woman as exemplary of the characteristics of that 'beauty' which he (like many writers) distinguishes from the more angular, masculine 'power' of the sublime. Through the stadial theory of sociocultural development associated with Scottish Enlightenment philosophy, and particularly with Ferguson's *Essay on the History of the Civil Society* (1767), the sublime is often also associated in Anglophone philosophical aesthetics with the primitive or the Oriental. In his *Critical Dissertation* (1763), for example, Blair, reasoning by analogy, explains the sublimity of the Ossian poems (ostensibly the work of a third-century Scottish bard), by arguing that just as 'the powers of imagination' are 'most vigorous' in 'youth', so 'poetry, which is the child of imagination, is frequently most glowing and animated in the first stages of society'.[2] In the descriptions of the sublime energies of genius given by, for example, Young in his *Conjectures on Original Composition* (1759) and Duff in his *Essay on Original Genius* (1767), the 'irregular greatness of imagination' by which 'original genius' is said to be characterized is often represented as dangerously close to insanity.[3] And while the extreme affective response produced by the sublime – called 'enthusiasm' by Dennis in *The Grounds of Criticism in Poetry* (1704) and by Shaftesbury in *Characteristicks* (1714), and linked by both to religious fervour – was often presented as a form of (potentially misleading) intoxication, other writers, such as Hartley in his *Observations* (1749), argue that the ability to experience such affect was entirely dependent 'upon Health, and the Integrity of our bodily Faculties'.[4] Burgh, in *The Art of Speaking* (1761), emphasizes how the completely controlled 'movement of limb, or feature' is a prerequisite of sublime oratory, when the auditors are left 'unable to resist' by the combination of gesture and content.[5]

Eighteenth-century philosophical investigations of the sublime in English, Irish and Scottish thought also frequently posed ethical and political questions, since explanations of the experience very often turned (as we shall see later) upon why, under certain circumstances, we seem to take pleasure in ostensibly unpleasant situations and phenomena. Equally, while instances and descriptions of personal and civic virtue were often praised as sublime by the moral sense philosophy that finds its early, eighteenth-century expositions in Shaftesbury's *Characteristicks* and Hutcheson's *Inquiry into the Original of Our Ideas of Beauty and Virtue* (1725), later thinkers came increasingly to grapple with morally problematic instances of sublimity. How, for example, might one account for the sublimity of Milton's characterization of Satan in *Paradise Lost* (1667), a work often cited as a pre-eminent example of the rhetorical sublime? Beattie poses the problem succinctly when discussing Milton's Satan in his *Dissertations Moral and Critical* (1783): 'a character may be sublime, which is not completely good, nay, which is upon the whole very bad. For the test of sublimity is not moral approbation.'[6] In his *Theory of Moral Sentiments* (1759), Adam Smith wonders in a similar vein how we might account for the sublimity of 'mighty conquerors' like 'a Caesar or an Alexander ... an Atilla, a Genghis': they are 'violent' and 'brutal' and yet 'the great mob of mankind' regard them 'with a wondering'.[7] Hume asks in his *Treatise of Human Nature* (1739–40) why markers of social injustice such as 'power and riches' are 'associated with height and sublimity' when 'poverty, slavery, and folly are conjoined with descent and lowness'.[8] And of course Burke, in *Enquiry* II iii, argues that sublimity can actually shore up oppressive political power, noting that 'heathen' religions use 'darkness' and 'obscurity' to augment the affective power of their ceremonies and that 'those despotic governments, which are founded on the passions of men, and principally upon the passion of fear, keep their chief as much as may be from the public eye'.

The remarkably broad scope and no less remarkably porous discursive boundaries of the investigation of sublimity explain why it became such a ubiquitous component of English, Irish and Scottish philosophy during the eighteenth century: simply put, myriad discursive threads led to and from it. It is no exaggeration to say that philosophical enquiry into the different species of the sublime not only stands at the head of modern formulations of literary criticism and of the aesthetic more generally, but also constitutes a key moment in the formation of modern constructions of subjectivity, that is to say, in the Romantic re-negotiation of Enlightenment understandings of the self. There is now widespread acceptance amongst scholars that 'the sublime', as Peter Otto summarizes, emerges from eighteenth-century philosophy as 'a technique used for producing the self discovered by Romanticism'.[9] Peter De Bolla, the earliest scholar fully to articulate this idea in a discussion of eighteenth-century Anglophone aesthetics, does so by mapping the transition from what he calls the 'discourse on the sublime' to the 'discourse of the sublime': from an 'analytic discourse' concerned to explain *how* sublime experience is generated to a 'self-transforming' discourse that actually 'produces from within itself sublime experience' (*Discourse*, 12).

Arguably, it is the investigation of the sublime in the German philosophical tradition, and in the work of Kant in particular, which has left a more substantive and enduring legacy to the *subsequent* history of the aesthetic and the subject. But eighteenth-century English, Irish and Scottish thinking about the sublime, with its distinctively empirical, associative and analogical emphases, had a much more direct and immediate influence on British Romanticism than German philosophy. Many academic historians of the sublime have accepted, explicitly or implicitly, Monk's early claim for a teleological relationship between Anglophone and German philosophical investigations of the sublime, that 'eighteenth century aesthetic has as its unconscious goal the *Critique of Judgement*, the book in which it was refined and re-interpreted' (*Monk*, 6). Hipple was the first to question this idea that English, Irish and Scottish thinking about the sublime should be seen as 'an unconscious prolegomenon' to Kant's 1790 'Analytic of the Sublime' in the *Critique of the Power of Judgement* (*Hipple*, 284). Ashfield and De Bolla, too, insist on the need for a 'detachment' from 'a scholarly tradition which has repeatedly told a story about the beginnings of aesthetics in eighteenth-century Britain in terms of the gradual shift towards the Kantian critique of judgement' (*Reader*, 2). We can better understand the relationship between the two traditions as an instance of what Christoph Bode, in a discussion of European Romanticism, calls 'family likenesses': Anglophone and German philosophical investigations of the sublime overlap on certain points of terminology and argument not because they have a teleological relationship to each other, but because they constitute, to borrow Bode's terminology, 'diverging responses' to 'the same set' of questions about the aesthetic and the subject – and, in particular, about the boundaries of rationalism and the role of the imagination in perception, cognition and creativity.[10] An especially signal difference between the German and the Anglophone traditions is the emphasis that the latter places on the role of the association of ideas, through the agency of the imagination, in the experience of the sublime: unlike Kant's insistence, in *Critique of the Power of Judgement*, on the disinterestedness of the aesthetic response to the sublime, the Anglophone tradition is, with some few exceptions, much more alert to the importance of the personal and cultural contexts for sublime affect.

Defining the Sublime

In his *Essay on the Sublime* (1747), Baillie suggests that Longinus 'has entirely passed over the inquiry of what the Sublime is . . . and is principally intent upon giving Rules' for what Dennis describes, in a notoriously problematic expression, as writing of such 'invincible force' that it 'commits a pleasing Rape upon the very soul of the Reader'.[11] However, many eighteenth-century Anglophone thinkers advance some variant of the two-phase paradigm that Longinus develops for explaining how the rhetorical sublime produces the intense affective response which he calls 'Transport' (*Longinus*, 12). In the first phase, Longinus suggests, the mind is over-whelmed by the 'Strength irresistible' of the sublime, but in the second phase it somehow recovers: 'for the mind is so naturally elevated by the true Sublime', Longinus writes, 'that it swells in Transport and an inward Pride, as if what was only heard had been the product of its own Invention' (*Longinus*, 14). The precise means by which the mind somehow takes pleasure in the recovery from an initially overwhelming affect, through a (possibly mistaken) recognition of its own capacities, becomes a recurrent focus of eighteenth-century English, Irish and Scottish enquiries into the sublime, with the key question remaining whether the sublime itself should be understood as a property of certain things or a property of how the mind responds to those things.

One of the earliest eighteenth-century attempts to produce a systematic account of the sublime as an experiential phenomenon, within the context of what we would now call philosophical aesthetics, can be found in Addison's essays on the 'pleasures of the imagination', which ran in *The Spectator* from 21 June until 3 July 1712 (nos. 411–21) and which, in Addison's own opinion, constitute an 'entirely new' kind of enquiry.[12] Addison categorizes the 'pleasures of the Imagination' as 'primary' and 'secondary': those 'which arise from the actual view and survey of outward Objects' and those we experience when 'the Idea[s] of visible Objects' that 'are not actually before the Eye' are raised in 'our Minds by Paintings, Statues, Descriptions, or any the like Occasion' (no. 412, 92; no. 411, 89). In other words, Addison locates the cause of aesthetic affects not only in the properties of external objects but quite specifically in *visible* properties: in 'the Sight of what is *Great, Uncommon,* or *Beautiful*' (no. 412, 93). These visible properties produce 'pleasure' in the imagination, Addison argues, 'because it loves to be filled with an object or to grasp at anything that is too big for its capacity. We are flung into a pleasing astonishment ... and feel a delightful stillness and amazement' (no. 412, 93). Artistic representations, by extension, afford only second-order experiences that function via *association*, when images or words bring to our minds the affective properties of the actual things represented.

Addison's explanation for how this associative process functions develops a notion of aesthetic distance that would remain influential in eighteenth-century Anglophone accounts of the sublime and which is quite distinct from the idea of disinterested aesthetic judgement later put forward by Kant in his *Critique of the Power of Judgement*. The crux of the matter for Addison is a matter of ethics as much as of aesthetics. Noting that 'the two leading passions which the more serious parts of poetry endeavour to stir up in us are terror and pity', he wonders 'how it comes to pass, that such passions as are very unpleasant at all other times, are very agreeable when excited by proper descriptions' (no. 418, 136). To explain this, Addison notes how 'we are delighted with reflecting upon dangers that are past, or in looking on a precipice at a distance, which would fill us with a different kind of horror, if we saw it hanging over our heads' (no. 418, 137). In a similar vein, Addison argues, the 'pleasure' that we derive from, for example, the evocation of terror through representation is produced not so much by 'the description of what is terrible' as from the 'reflection' that we are not in any real danger (no. 418, 136). For the same reason, we can derive pleasure from reading about human suffering that would not be felt were we confronted with an actual suffering human when the experience 'bears so hard upon us, that it does not give us time or leisure to reflect' on our own safety (no. 418, 138). The rhetorical sublime functions, in other words, by offering a *vicarious* experience of terror or pity that is entirely different from what we experience when a terrible or pitiful 'object presses too close upon our senses' (no. 418, 138).

The connection between the vicarious experience of terror (in particular) and the sublime is a recurrent theme of eighteenth-century Anglophone philosophical aesthetics. The most familiar (but by no means the only) statement of that connection is *Enquiry* I vii, where Burke suggests that 'terror', 'pain', and 'danger', if experienced vicariously ('at certain distances, and with certain modifications') generate sublime affect ('the strongest emotion which the mind is capable of feeling'). And of course that same connection becomes an important component of eighteenth-century 'grave-yard poetry' and central to the 'Gothic' literature that became popular across Europe in the late eighteenth century.[13] Hartley, Burke and a number of others trace the role of terror in generating sublime affects to the *physiological* responses of the human body to certain properties of external objects and the ideas or sensations that those properties evoke. Perception, for Hartley, involved 'vibrations' in the cerebral nervous system occasioned by the proper-ties of nearby objects, while for Burke, the experience of the sublime was closely connected to the biological instinct for 'self-preservation', which, he says, generates 'the most powerful of all the passions' (*Enquiry* I iv).

The attempt to provide *physiological* as well as psychological explan-ations for what *Enquiry* IV i calls the "efficient cause" of the sublime is one of the most distinctive elements of the Anglophone tradition, albeit one that has often been ignored by subsequent historians of the aesthetic. Even Monk, though, grants that it is 'at this point' that Burke is 'most original' and exhibits 'remarkable "modernity" of thought', while Alan Richardson goes further, suggesting that the physiological arguments of Burke and Hartley form 'part of a revisionary countertradition' within Anglophone philosophical aesthetics that 'understands the sublime less as divine rapture than as physical rupture', a tradition continued by Priestley, Duff and Reid, who use 'metaphors of enlarging, stretching, dilating, and swelling' to describe the effect of the sublime on the mind (*Monk*, 96; *Richardson*, 25–6). The recovery of this 'countertradition', Richardson explains, permits and requires us to 'reconsider the competing accounts [of the sublime] of Burke and others in the British tradition not so much as stepping stones to Kant but as intriguing constructions in their own right that, after all, would have been more familiar to British Romantic-era writers than would have been Kant, then known to only a few' (*Richardson*, 25).

The Sublime and the Association of Ideas

Burke continues the physiological basis of his arguments into the final section of *Enquiry*, where he examines the rhetorical sublime. 'The effects of poetry', he suggests, 'are by no means to be attributed to the images it raises' but rather to the ability of words to evoke the 'passions' when the author or speaker invokes 'those modes of speech that mark a strong and lively feeling in himself' (*Enquiry* II iv, V vii). The rhetorical sublime is thus generated by 'sympathy' rather than 'description' and indeed it is *feeling* that, for Burke, precisely marks the distinction between mimesis and poiesis, that is, between what he calls a 'clear expression' and a 'strong expression', or between describing 'a thing as it is' and a thing 'as it is felt' (*Enquiry* V vii).

While Burke identifies the rhetorical sublime as a response to 'ideas which present no distinct image to the mind', or to 'ideas which are not presentable but by language' (*Enquiry* V vii), however, for many other Anglophone theorists of the sublime it is the principle of the association of ideas that not only explains how the sublime works but which also forms the common ground between the rhetorical and the natural sublimes. The emphasis on the association of ideas in English, Irish and Scottish philosophical aesthetics is visible from early in the eighteenth century. It forms the basis for the religious interpretation of the sublime that later finds expression, during the Romantic period in, for example, the novels of Ann Radcliffe or the responses to the Alps which Percy Shelley critiques in 'Mont Blanc' (1816). Both Shaftesbury and Dennis, for instance, link the affective power of the sublime to its ability to evoke 'religious ideas', from which, Dennis suggests, 'the greatest sublimity is to be derived' (76). According to Shaftesbury, the natural sublime (the 'spectacle' of 'mighty Nature!') derives its impact precisely from being a 'substitute of Providence!', that is, from evoking the idea of 'the Sovereign Mind' of the *Deity*' assumed to have created it.[14] But more secular accounts, too, emphasize the association of ideas. In his *Course of Lectures* (1777), for instance, the radical philosopher and chemist Joseph Priestley insists that 'in all sublime conceptions, there is a kind of secret retrospect to preceding ideas and states of mind', and hence the rhetorical sublime, as a 'species' of what Priestley calls 'transferred sublimity', can 'raise sensations similar to those which are excited by objects which have corporeal magnitude and elevation'.[15]

The centrality of the principle of the association of ideas to eighteenth-century Anglophone accounts of the sublime is most prominent, however, in the response of Scottish 'common sense' philosophers like Alison, Reid and Stewart to the scepticism of Hume and the idealism of Berkeley, and especially so in Alison's *Essays on the Nature and Principles of Taste* (1790), the second edition of which would 'revolutionize aesthetic speculation in Britain' and become one of the most widely read and widely referenced works on the subject during the Romantic period (see *Hipple*, 158–9).

For Reid and for Alison, the association of ideas by the imagination is fundamental to the experience of the natural and the rhetorical sublimes: both thinkers insist that aesthetic effects are produced, as Alison puts it, 'when the Imagination is employed in the prosecution of a regular train of Ideas'.[16] Reid and Alison firmly reject any material or objectivist explanation for *how* such associative 'trains' are triggered, arguing that neither natural phenomena nor cultural texts can have any aesthetic value in themselves but can only acquire such value by becoming associated with 'the attributes of mind', through what Reid, in his *Essays on the Intellectual Powers of Man* (1785), describes as a 'stretch of the imagination'.[17] 'When we ascribe grandeur to any portion of matter', Reid argues, this 'quality' is actually 'borrowed' from 'something intellectual' of which this material phenomenon 'is the effect, or sign, or instrument, or to which it bears some analogy' (735–6). Or, as Alison puts it: 'matter itself is unfitted to produce any kind of emotion' and can become 'sublime or beautiful only as it is significant of mind' (vol. 1, 176; vol. 2, 436). In sum, then, for Alison and for Reid, the affective response to the natural sublime is triggered by the perception of *material* qualities that are capable, by virtue of association, of suggesting the *mental* qualities ('the attributes of mind') which they consider to be the true sources of aesthetic affect.[18] 'The beauty and sublimity which is felt in the various appearances of matter', Alison writes, 'are finally to be ascribed to their expression of mind; or to their being, either directly or indirectly, the signs of those qualities of mind which are fitted, by the constitution of our nature, to affect us with pleasing or interesting emotion' (vol. 2, 423).

Hence, while neither Alison nor Reid offers an empirical account of the sublime, neither has recourse to an idealist account since neither understands aesthetic affects to be produced by the experiencing subject's awareness of the capacities of their *own* mind. Quite the contrary, in fact: Alison, for example, argues that the 'delight' occasioned by the sublime comes from our being 'unable to trace either the progress or connection of those thoughts which have passed with such rapidity through our imagination' (vol. 1, 5–6). Reid's account of the rhetorical sublime provides, perhaps, the readiest means of grasping the key conceptual move here. If we experience a work of literature as sublime, Reid argues, the sublimity that we experience is a property not of the work itself but rather of the conception embodied in the work. 'By a figure', Reid explains, 'we ascribe to a work that grandeur which is properly inherent in the mind of the author . . . the grandeur is ascribed to the work, but is properly inherent in the mind that made it' (731, 732). And in his account of the natural sublime, Reid argues along similar lines: 'we assign to the effect a quality which is inherent only in the cause' (732). Ultimately, then, the origin of the affective response to the natural sublime is, in Reid's analysis, the idea of God since 'the Deity is of all objects of thought the most grand', something which, he says, even 'Longinus, a heathen critic', had recognized (730). Alison follows suit, concluding that 'all the works of human art or design, are directly significant to us of the wisdom, the invention, the taste, or the benevolence of the artist; and the works of nature, of the power, the wisdom, and the beneficence of the Divine artist' (vol. 2, 418).

For Alison and for Reid, then, the affective response to the natural sublime is evidence of intelligent design, not just of the physical universe but also of the ability of the human mind to recognize sublime natural phenomena as 'signs . . . conducting us . . . to the throne of the Deity'.[19] Consequently, both thinkers argue that the associative 'trains of pleasing or of solemn thought' which trigger the affective response to the sublime arise 'spontaneously within our minds': 'even upon the man of the most uncultivated taste', Alison argues, 'the scenes of nature have some inexplicable charm' (vol. 2, 437). Other late eighteenth- and early nineteenth-century Anglophone writers, however, increasingly emphasize the personally and culturally deter- mined aspects of aesthetic experience. To an extent, of course, that emphasis had always been present within the Anglophone tradition as part of the discourse of *taste* that is visible from Hutcheson and Shaftesbury onwards. But a significant and high-profile instance of it during the Romantic period is the emergence of the aesthetics of the picturesque developed by Gilpin, Price and Repton: an aesthetics that not only rejects any rigid dichotomy between the sublime and the beautiful but which also understands that the aesthetic response both can and arguably *needs* to be learned and refined, that is to say, that it is an acquired rather than an innate response. Within the Scottish associationist tradition, this position is most visible in Stewart's account of the aesthetic, where he argues that central to the affective response is not just the imagination in general but rather specifically what he calls 'a *cultivated imagination* ... an imagination which has acquired such a degree of activity as to delight in its own exertions'.[20] And a 'cultivated imagination', in Stewart's analysis, is explicitly the result of what he calls (by no means unproblematically) 'culture' and 'civilisation' (544–5). Rejecting the link between the sublime and early or so-called primitive societies that had been visible, in the Anglophone tradition, since at least the emergence of the Ossian poems, Stewart affirms that 'of this activity and versatility of imagination, I find no traces among rude tribes' (544–5).

Conclusion

Arguably, it is the emphasis on the association of ideas that most clearly distinguishes eighteenth-century Anglophone, and especially Scottish, philosophical descriptions of the natural and rhetorical sublimes from the German idealist tradition that came, following Monk, to dominate academic constructions of 'the Romantic sublime' in the twentieth century. Associationist accounts such as those formulated by Alison, Reid and Stewart not only offer an alternative, and more culturally and historically immediate, paradigm to the transcendental idealism of Kant's 'analytic of the sublime' but also offer an alternative to the Kantian idea of the *disinterestedness* of aesthetic judgement. In so doing, Scottish associationist accounts allow, in particular, for a greater recognition of the role of personally- and culturally-specific elements in the response to the natural and rhetorical sublimes, a role to which recent critical histories of the place 'Romantic sublime' in the cultural history of the period have increasingly drawn attention.

NOTES

1 For Nicolson, Monk and others who prioritize philosophical aesthetics in the cultural history of the sublime 'have their cart before their horse' (see *Nicolson*, 29n). See also Chapter 2 in the present volume and Dawn Hollis, '*Mountain Gloom and Mountain Glory*: The Genealogy of an Idea', *ISLE: Interdisciplinary Studies in Literature and Environment* 26.4, Autumn 2019, 1038–61.
2 Hugh Blair, *A Critical Dissertation on the Poems of Ossian*, London, 1763, 3.
3 William Duff, *Essay on Original Genius*, 2nd edition, London, 1767, 63.
4 David Hartley, *Observations on Man*, London, 1749, 423.
5 James Burgh, *The Art of Speaking* (London, 1761), 28–9.

6 James Beattie, *Dissertations Moral and Critical*, 2 vols., Dublin, 1783, vol. 1, 367.

7 Adam Smith, *The Theory of Moral Sentiments*, 2nd edition, London, 1761, 448.

8 David Hume, *A Treatise of Human Nature*, ed. L. A. Selby-Bigge, Oxford, Clarendon, 1888, 435–6.

9 Peter Otto, 'The Sublime', in Iain McCalman, ed., *An Oxford Companion to the Romantic Age*, Oxford, Oxford University Press, 723.

10 Christoph Bode, 'Europe', in Nicholas Roe, ed., *Romanticism: an Oxford Guide*, Oxford, Oxford University Press, 2005, 126–36 (134–5).

11 Samuel Holt Monk, ed., *John Baillie: An Essay on the Sublime*, Augustan Reprint Society, No. 43, Los Angeles, CA, Clark Memorial Library, 1953, 2; John Dennis, *The Grounds of Criticism in Poetry*, London, 1704, 79.

12 Joseph Addison, *The Spectator: Volume the Sixth*, London, 1789, 81 (no. 409). Addison never actually uses the term 'sublime', perhaps, as Hipple suggests, because of its contemporary connection to rhetoric rather than natural phenomena (16).

13 For more on the relationship between the sublime and the Gothic, see, for example, *Cultures*, 121–50; David B. Morris, 'Gothic Sublimity', *New Literary History* 16.2, 1985, 229–319; and Andrew Smith, 'The Gothic and the Sublime', in *Gothic Radicalism*, London, Palgrave, 2000, 11–37.

14 Anthony Ashley Cooper, Earl of Shaftesbury, *Characteristicks of Men, Manners, Opinions, Times*, 3 vols., London, 1714, vol. 2, 345–6.

15 Joseph Priestley, *A Course of Lectures on Oratory and Criticism*, London, 1777, 151, 158, 156.

16 Archibald Alison, *Essays on the Nature and Principles of Taste*, 3rd edition, 2 vols., Edinburgh, 1812, vol. 2, 104.

17 Thomas Reid, *Essays on the Intellectual Powers of Man*, Edinburgh, 1785, 731, 730.

18 Ibid., 731.

19 Alison, *Essays*, vol. 2, 442.

20 Dugald Stewart, *Philosophical Essays*, 2nd edition, Edinburgh, 1816, 541 (original emphasis).

4

LIS MØLLER

The Nordic Sublime

In 1790, the Anglo-Swiss artist Henry Fuseli submitted as his reception piece for the Royal Academy of Arts in London a grandiose painting, *Thor Battering the Midgard Serpent* (see Figure 4.1). Fuseli's painting shows a towering nude male figure in a small boat on a stormy sea. Emerging from an inky background, his muscular torso is almost luminescent against the enwrapping darkness. From an equally dark sea rises his opponent, a huge, black, water serpent glistening with moisture. The rendition of the torso is a vestige of classical sculpture. The artist has drawn on the "established iconography" of Greco-Roman mythology, the pose of the male figure vis-à-vis his adversary recalling depictions of Heracles/Hercules raising his attribute, the club, to strike the Hydra.[1] Yet Fuseli's motif is Nordic. The male figure is Thor, Norse god of thunder and lightning and famed for his great physical strength, and the sea monster is his archenemy, the Midgard serpent. Thor has caught the monster in a chain and is wielding his attribute, the powerful hammer Mjolnir, ready to strike. The serpent, writhing with agony and fury, is whipping the sea into tempestuous waves. At the stern, a smaller figure is couching in terror, the giant Hymir. In the upper left corner of the painting, one spots a diminutive white-bearded figure looking down on the scene, presumably Odin, the supreme god of Asgard and the father of Thor. The scene itself is quintessentially sublime but Fuseli's canvas also epitomizes how the sublime landscapes, climates, peoples, and creatures of Norse myth came to provide a rich, new source of imaginative material for the eighteenth century and Romantic period.

Fuseli was a "literary" artist who often found his subjects in works of literature. According to his biographer Peter Tomory, his source for *Thor Battering the Midgard Serpent* was "Hymiskviða" (the Lay of Hymir) in the *Poetic Edda*. In December 1788, Fuseli had reviewed for the *Analytical Review* a bilingual, Old Norse and Latin, edition of this work.[2] Furthermore, one must assume that Fuseli was familiar with the *Prose Edda*'s version of story of Thor's fishing expedition as retold by his

Figure 4.1 Henry Fuseli, *Thor Battering the Midgard Serpent*, 1790. Royal Academy of Arts, London.

compatriot, the Swiss historian Paul-Henry Mallet. With the express intention of improving Denmark's reputation internationally, the Danish king Frederik V had commissioned Mallet to write a history of the ancient Danes. Mallet's *Introduction a l'histoire du Dannemarc* (Introduction to the History of Denmark), introducing among other things the main gods in Nordic mythology, was published in Copenhagen in 1755, followed by a supplementary volume, *Monuments de la mythologie et de la poésie des Celtes* (Memorials of the Mythology and Poetry of the Celts) (1756), containing retellings of stories from the *Prose Edda* as well as translations of specimens of Old Norse poetry. Mallet's two volumes, which for the first time made Old Norse texts available in a major modern language, were soon translated into Danish, German, and English, sparking off a new interest in Nordic mythology and its sublimities. The English translation by Thomas Percy was published in 1770 in two volumes under the title *Northern Antiquities*. The *Prose Edda* tale of Thor's fishing expedition to catch the Midgard serpent is included in volume 2 ("The Twenty-Seventh Fable. Of the Journey Undertaken by Thor, to Go to Fish for the Great Serpent").[3] Whereas the account in the *Poetic Edda* leaves much out, the *Prose Edda* tells a full story with many details. We hear that Thor pulled so hard on the line that he drove both his legs through the planks of the boat and that the terrified Hymir (Eymer, in Percy's translation), seeing the water pouring into the vessel, cut the line just as Thor was about to strike the Midgard serpent, allowing the monster to escape.

The *Prose Edda* story of Thor's unsuccessful fishing expedition with Hymir might lend itself to a humorous rendition. However, there is nothing comic in Fuseli's interpretation. The artist has chosen to represent the most pregnant and terrifying moment, as rendered by Mallet (in Percy's translation): "It is impossible to express the dreadful looks that the God darted at the Serpent, whilst the monster, raising its head, sprouted out venom upon him" (vol. 2, 36). As noted, his depiction of the scene – the blackened sky, the heavy seas threatening to sink the small vessel, Thor's muscular body bespeaking superhuman strength, and his awful antagonist rising from the deep – is firmly set within the aesthetics of the sublime. The figure of Thor is seen from a frog's eye view, making him look even grander and more terrible, and his torso is illuminated from below by an invisible and non-natural light source, creating the dramatic contrast between darkness and white light that according to Burke is conductive of the sublime (see *Enquiry* II xiv).

Presenting *Thor Battering the Midgard Serpent* to the Royal Academy as his admission piece, Fuseli was breaking new ground. Fuseli and the Danish painter Nicolai Abildgaard, whom Fuseli had befriended during his years of study in Rome (1770–8), were among the first visual artists to depict motifs from Norse mythology and to raise iconographically the Northern gods to the dignity of the gods of classical mythology.[4] In the light of the recent events in France and Fuseli's well-known enthusiasm for the French revolution (1789), it is not too far-fetched to view his choice of motif and his idealizing representation of the Norse god as a political statement. The French political philosopher Charles-Louis Montesquieu had pronounced the people of the North the source of liberty in Europe, and the association of the ancient North with freedom was well established by the end of the eighteenth century. Accordingly, *Thor Battering the Midgard Serpent* has been interpreted as an allegorical representation of the French people's struggle for freedom against the *ancien régime*.[5]

Whereas depictions in the visual arts of topics from Norse mythology were still comparatively scarce, Danish poets were already mining the sublimities of this hitherto unused treasure. In May 1802, two fifth-century gold drinking horns were stolen from the Royal Collection in Copenhagen. The horns, which had been discovered near the village of Gallerhus in southern Denmark in 1639 and 1734, respectively, were richly decorated with mysterious images, and one bore a runic inscription. In November the same year, the Danish poet Adam Oehlenschläger made the finding of the gold horns and their recent purloining the subject of a poem, "Guldhornene," first translated into English by George Borrow as "The Gold Horns." Written in imitation of the meter of Eddaic poetry and admired for its grand and sublime imagery, "Guldhornene" is widely regarded as the poem that inaugurated Romanticism in Scandinavian literature. Oehlenschläger's poem interprets the finding of the two horns as a gift from the Norse gods, who subsequently, as the sacredness of these relics was not reverenced, retrieved their offering.

"The Gold Horns" begins with antiquarians blindly groping for relics from the ancient North. Perplexed by the mystery of inscriptions on jumbled "Rune-stones," they pray for a "glimpse" of the days long past "When the North was uplighted / And with earth heav'n united."[6] In response to this prayer, the gods assemble above, pledging that a relic displaying the stamp of "the times most olden" shall be found, not by the antiquarians but by a "maiden" (173). Borrow's translation mistakenly interprets the giver of the golden horn as the ghosts of the dead rising from their burial mounds, yet Oehlenschläger's poem expressly speaks of "de … Höie" (the High Ones), that is, the Norse gods.[7] The High Ones, however, are not rendered as anthropomorphic figures; they are present in the poem in the form of a solemn voice from above and as sublime forces of nature, "bustling" clouds, "night blasts," and "Thunder" (172–3). As the finding of the first horn elicits nothing but a greedy search for more gold, the gods, a century gone by, assemble above, their presence announced by howling winds and furious bursts of rain. The gods agree to bestow a second relic, this time intended only for the chosen few, who behold the divine creator in nature and "tremble adoring, / 'Fore the rays of His power / In the sun, in the flower" (175). A shudder rushing through nature followed by "Holy silence" accompany the finding of the second golden horn (176). However, once again the mysterious holiness of the ancient relic goes unappreciated. Displayed in a museum as "spectacles" to "the silly and the prying," the gold horns are appreciated only for their "lustre" (177). In sublime rage, the ancient gods take back their sacred gifts:

> Storm-winds bellow, blackens heaven!
> Comes the hour of melancholy;
> Back is taken what was given, –
> Vanished is the relic holy.   (177)

Oehlenschläger's poem decries the dull mindlessness and materialism of his own age, pitting it against the sublimity of the ancient North. Not long after the publication of "The Gold Horns," the man who had stolen the horns was apprehended. Incidentally, the thief lived only a few doors away from the lodgings where Oehlenschläger composed the poem. The golden horns, however, were irrecoverably lost. The thief had melted them down, using the gold to manufacture pieces of jewelry and false coins – and thus ironically confirming the critical tenet of Oehlenschläger's poem.

The lust for gold is also a main theme in the German composer Richard Wagner's (1813–1883) monumental *Gesamtkunstwerk*, *Der Ring des Nibelungen* (The Ring of the Nibelung), a cycle of four grandiose operas of about sixteen hours of music, bringing the sublimity of the Old Norse pantheon onto stage. Wagner based his operatic tetralogy on the Middle High German epic poem *Das Nibelungenlied* (c. 1200), which in the early nineteenth century had acquired the status of the German national epic. However, though having some of its origin in historic events of the fifth and sixth centuries, the *Nibelungenlied* had adopted a courtly setting where "greed, lust, and treachery predominate and God is strangely absent."[8] Aspiring to create a Germanic mythology, Wagner turned to Old Icelandic versions of the Nibelungen story in the *Poetic Edda*, the *Prose Edda*, and the *Völsunga Saga* (The Saga of the Volsungs), assigning principal roles to Wotan (Odin) and his Valkyrie daughter, Brünnhilde, sung by a dramatic bass-baritone and a dramatic soprano, respectively. The gods are predominant particularly in the tetralogy's first two operas, *Das Rheingold* (The Rhinegold) and *Die Walküre* (The Valkyrie). The ring from which the cycle derives its title is a ring of power, forged by the dwarf Alberich, a Nibelung, from gold taken from the Rhine-daughters. Subsequently, Wotan lures the gold and the ring from Alberich in order to pay off the two giants, who have erected Valhalla, the dwelling of the gods. Wotan reluctantly parts with the ring. In handing over the ring of power to the gods, Alberich has cursed it, and the curse is released as the giants come into possession of it: quarreling over the ring, one clubs the other to death. The story of the ring of power will be known to readers of J. R. R. Tolkien's epic fantasy novel *The Lord of the Rings* (1954–5), a work heavily indebted to the sublimities of Norse mythology as well as to Wagner's rendition of the Nordic sublime.

As upholder of the Law, Wotan is unable to retrieve the ring, which he himself has given in payment. His design is to act by proxy: he has fathered a human hero, Siegmund, strong enough to take possession of the ring. Siegmund has fallen in love with his own twin sister, Sieglinde, married to the evil brute Hunding, and while Siegmund is preparing to meet Hunding in battle, the Valkyries, "choosers of the slain," are preparing to grant the victory to Siegmund. The goddess Fricka, however, outraged at the incestuous love between brother and sister, demands that Siegmund must die. Wotan reluctantly complies, but Brünnhilde, sympathizing with the lovers, disobeys her father's order, granting Siegmund the upper hand. At that point, Wotan, magnificent and terrible in all his might, enters the battle and breaks Siegmund's sword. Allowing Hunding to slay Siegmund, Wotan himself strikes down Siegmund's slayer. In the third and final act of *Die Valküre*, featuring the famous "Ride of the Valkyries," Wotan must punish his favorite daughter, the disobedient Brünnhilde. Stripped of her Valkyrie status, Brünnhilde shall sleep on the mountaintop until woken by a mortal man.

Compelled to sacrifice his son and his daughter, Wagner's Wotan is a tragic as well as a sublime figure, yet he is also morally tainted and incapable of righting the wrongs that he himself has instigated. Much like Fuseli's *Thor Battering the Midgard Serpent*, Wagner's *Ring* had as its backdrop a revolutionary upheaval, in this case the revolutions of 1848, which, spreading to the German kingdoms, called for the abolition of old monarchial structures and a new united Germany. First performed as a cycle in 1876 and written (the libretto and the music) over the course of twenty-six years, the conception of the *Ring* was intimately associated with the Dresden uprising in 1849, in which Wagner took an active part on the side of the rebels.[9] The *Ring* is an explicitly revolutionary and anticapitalist drama. The greedy lust for gold and power as symbolized by the ring draws a bloody trail through the four operas. Alberich abjures love in order to possess it; the giant Fafner kills his brother and is subsequently (in the third opera) killed by the son of

Siegmund and Sieglinde, Siegfried, the hero who wakes Brünnhilde; Siegfried kills Mime, who wanted to kill *him* and take the ring; and finally the ring leads to the betrayal and killing of Siegfried and to the death of Hagen, the son of Alberich. However, the *Ring* is also an attack on obsolete authorities, including the gods. In Fuseli's painting, the sublime Norse god may be construed as a symbol of freedom; in Wagner's work, freedom is freedom *from* the gods. Henrik Nebelong refers to the *Ring* as the first great atheist drama in European literature.[10] In the final scene of the last opera, *Götterdämmerung* (Twilight of the Gods), the flames from Siegfried's funeral pyre rise to Valhalla, and as the ring is returned to the Rhine-daughters, the gods of Valhalla perish in the fire. The age of the gods is over; the age of humankind has begun. The tenet of the *Ring* is humanistic, yet Wagner was never a democrat. The dissolution of obsolete divine authority is due not to the people but to the exceptional hero. In the twentieth century, Wagner's hero worship was taken up by the Nazis, who explicitly drew on his version of the Nordic sublime.

Legendary Heroes Revisited

One of the first Old Norse poems to be translated into modern European languages was the twelfth-century Old Icelandic *Krákumál*, or the Death Song of Ragnar Lodbrog. Via a Latin translation by the Danish antiquarian Ole Worm, the poem was translated into English by Thomas Percy to appear in his *Five Pieces of Runic Poetry* (1763) under the title "The Dying Ode of Regnar Lodbrog." Extracts had also been included in the second volume of Mallet's history of Denmark.[11] In his headnote, Mallet explains that Ragnar was a "celebrated Warrior, Poet, and Pirate" who "reigned in Denmark about the beginning of the ninth century" (vol. 2, 226). After many years of successful expeditions and raids, Ragnar's luck ran out. He was captured by the English King Ella and thrown into a snake-pit, facing a slow and painful death. The ode was purportedly composed by the dying Ragnar himself. Two passages from this poem came to define the late eighteenth-century conception of the sublime Norse warrior – or Viking, as we would say today. In the ode's final line, Ragnar declares (in Percy's translation) that "I die laughing."[12] Dying laughingly – the so-called *ridens moriar* motif – epitomized the idea of the Vikings' death-defying courage in battle. Believing that dying in combat would win them a seat at Odin's table in Valhalla, they unflinchingly looked death in the face. In a previous stanza, Ragnar looks forward to his reception into "the splendid hall of Odin," where "we shall drink Beer out of the skulls of our enemies" (40). The image of the dead heroes drinking from the skulls of their departed enemies – actually deriving from a mistranslation of these lines (which refer to drinking from animal horns) on the part of Worm, perpetuated in subsequent translations, and not corrected until the nineteenth century – placed the Viking warrior culture within the bounds of the sanguinary sublime.[13]

Hugh Blair, in his *Critical Dissertation on the Poems of Ossian* (1763), famously contrasts the barbarian spirit of Ragnar Lodbrog's death song with the noble sentiments of the poems of Ossian, the late eighteenth-century epitome of "the poet of the Sublime":[14]

> This is such poetry as we might expect from a barbarous nation. It breathes a most ferocious spirit. It is wild, harsh, and irregular; but at the same time animated and strong.... But when we open the works of Ossian, a very different scene presents itself.... We find tenderness, and even delicacy of sentiment, greatly predominant over fierceness and barbarity. Our hearts are melted with the softest feelings, and at the same time elevated with the highest ideas of magnanimity, generosity, and true heroism. When we turn from the poetry of Lodbrog to that of Ossian, it is like passing from a savage desart into a fertile and cultivated country.[15]

In his 1800 prize essay on the question, "Would it be fruitful for Scandinavian literature to replace Greek mythology with the ancient Nordic?," Oehlenschläger counters this supposed barbarism of Old Norse poetry, taking as his point of departure the conception of Nordic mythology as "poor and raw" (*fattig og raae*).[16] According to Oehlenschläger, the first half of this statement is easily refuted. Norse mythology is anything but poor; on the contrary, it is immensely rich. As to the second half, he tends to agree – provided that "raw" is understood to mean "crude" rather than "brutish." Nordic mythology is no savage desert, but unlike Greco-Roman mythology, Nordic mythology has not yet been adapted and polished by poets and artists. In Oehlenschläger's metaphor, Old Norse mythology is an open garden still waiting to be cultivated. As a model for its poetical cultivation, Oehlenschläger explicitly proposes the poetry of Ossian.

An Ossianized version of the ancient Nordic hero is precisely what one encounters in the Swedish poet Esaias Tegnér's *Frithiof's Saga* (1825), an epic poem in twenty-four cantos. Based on an Old Icelandic saga, *Friðþjófs saga hins frœkna* (c. 1300), Tegnér's poem was soon translated into other languages and became extremely popular not only in Scandinavia but also in Germany, Britain, and North America. Set on the rough West Coast of Norway, *Frithiof's Saga* tells the story of the brave and fearless Viking, Frithiof, and his faithful love for Ingeborg, the king's daughter. Unwilling to marry their sister to a commoner, Ingeborg's brothers set Frithiof a test, sending him off on a difficult and perilous mission to the Orkney Islands.

Returning against all odds, Frithiof finds that he has been betrayed by the brothers: Ingeborg has been married off to the aging King Ring. In anger, he accidentally sets fire to the temple of the god Balder and is consequently banished from Norway. Although Frithiof wins glory and riches at sea, he never forgets Ingeborg and his fatherland. In the end, his faithful love is rewarded. After King Ring's death, he wins Ingeborg and is elected the leader of his people. Canto X of *Frithiof's Saga*, "Frithiof at Sea," may illustrate the hero's noble mindset. Setting out for the Orkney Islands, Frithiof's ship runs into a terrible storm, conjured up by his enemy, King Helge:

> Gloomy is the heaven growing,
> Through desert skies the thunders roar,
> In the deep the billows brewing
> Cream with foam the surface o'er.
> Lightnings cleave the storm-cloud, seeming
> Blood-red gashes in its side;
> And all the sea-birds, wildly screaming.
> Fly the terrors of the tide.[17]

Not only must Frithiof brave the sublime elements; like Thor in Fuseli's painting, he must also fight the monsters of the deep.[18] What stands out, however, is not just Frithiof's superb boatmanship and his death-defying courage as he stands at the helm, "delighting / In the tempest's stormy play," but also his concern, in this hour of peril, for his crew (79). Taking off his heavy golden arm ring, Frithiof chops it up and distributes the pieces among his men, "none forgetting / Unto every man a part," so that no one shall meet "Ran" empty-handed (81, 82). In Norse mythology, Ran is the cold and terrible goddess of the sea. Thus Frithiof incarnates a kind of moral sublimity, the "highest ideas of magnanimity, generosity, and true heroism" that Hugh Blair had found in the poems of Ossian. Like Macpherson's heroes, the exiled Frithiof is capable of tender feelings and elegiac sentiments: "They are happy from home who have never departed, / Ne'er banished afar from their ancestor's graves!" (129).

Andrew Wawn speculates that the international success of *Frithiof's Saga* was in part due to the "lingering popularity" of Ossian: "Those drawn to the misty melancholy of the Ossianic corpus would also enjoy the Frithiof romance."[19] Apparently, Tegnér himself was well aware of the association with the Ossian poems. William Strong, the first English translator of *Frithiof's Saga*, cited these words by Tegnér on the front page of his translation, linking the poem to the sublime:

[I]f you delight in the gigantic, but pale forms, which float upon the mist, and darkly whisper of the world of spirits, and of the vanity of all things save true honour: – then must I refer you to the hoary – to the Saga-stored North, where Vala chanted the key-tone of creation, whilst the moon shone upon the cliffs, the brook trilled its monotonous lay, and, seated on the summit of a gilded birch, the night-bird sang an elegy upon the brief summer – a dirge over expiring nature.[20]

A very similar mood is evoked by the Norwegian artist Knud Baade (1808–1879) in his 1850 painting *Scene from the Era of Norwegian Sagas* (see Figure 4.2). As a painter, Baade excelled in sublime Northern land- and seascapes. Rough and inaccessible coastlines, moonlit ragged clouds, tempestuous waves, and perhaps a shipwreck or a vessel distressed – all key tropes of the sublime – were among his favorite subjects.

Scene from the Era of Norwegian Sagas belongs within this category, yet adds an elegiac dimension. The painting shows a wild and rugged Norwegian coastal landscape. A full moon shining palely from behind towering dark clouds displays the silhouette of a male figure standing on a tall projecting rock, leaning on his long pointed spear. Who is this lonely warrior? A watchman scanning the horizon for hostile ships or gazing out over the empty sea for kinsmen who may never return? Singlehandedly

Figure 4.2 Knud Baade, *Fantasibilde fra den norske Sagatid* (Scene from the Era of the Norwegian Sagas), 1850. Nordnorsk Kunstmuseeum, Tromsø.

braving the vastness and emptiness of the landscape, the lonely warrior is a noble but melancholic figure. Perhaps he is the last of his kind, soon to be engulfed by the ominous darkness encroaching the scene. The Norwegian title of Baade's painting, *Fantasibilde fra den norske Sagatid* (Fantasy Image from the Age of the Norwegian Sagas), suggests that the warrior by the coast belongs to a lost heroic age – a bygone era only to be (re)imagined from the remains of the Old Norse sagas and poems.

Old Nordic Poetry and the Aesthetics of the Sublime

Norse mythology provided eighteenth- and nineteenth-century poets and artists with stories, motifs, and characters (supernatural or human) that readily lent themselves to adaptations in the sublime mode. However, one might also argue that the aesthetics of the sublime was a contributory factor in creating a new taste for the style of ancient Scandinavian poetry, a new appreciation of its aesthetical and not just antiquarian merit. Old Norse poetry is not conventionally pleasing; it is rough, forceful, and passionate. Measured with the yardstick of the beautiful or neoclassical standards of taste, it falls short and seems deficient. In the light of the cultivation of everything grand and terrible, however, it assumed a new value. Commenting on the poetry of the ancient Scandinavians, Mallet writes (in Percy's English translation):

> The stile of these ancient poems is very enigmatical and figurative, very remote from the common language, and for that reason, grand, but tumid; sublime, but obscure. If it be the character of poetry to have nothing in common with prose, if the language of the Gods ought to be quite different from that of men, if every thing should be expressed by imagery, figures, hyperboles, and allegories, the Scandinavians may rank in the highest class of poets. (vol. 1, 393)

In his assessment of Old Norse poetry, Mallet comes close to endorsing an idea that in the course of the late eighteenth century was becoming increasingly prevalent, namely, that the progress of civilization had been damaging to imaginative poetry. Compared with Old Norse poetry, modern poetry, according to Mallet, is nothing but "reasoning in rhime" (vol. 1, 394).

The taste for Skaldic poetry extended to other forms of old Scandinavian poetry. In 1811, Wilhelm Grimm, one of the famous Brothers Grimm, put out a German translation of selected legendary ballads from the Danish language. A distinguishing feature of the numerous ballad collections that saw the light of day during the second half of the eighteenth and the beginning of the nineteenth centuries is the learned introductions and copious notes framing the ballads. Believing the heroic ballads to be truly ancient, contemporary with or even older than Old Norse skaldic poetry, Grimm in his lengthy introduction to *Altdänische Heldenlieder* (Old Danish Heroic Ballads) presents the ballads as a hitherto neglected treasure: "Little thought has been given to the ancient poetry [of Scandinavia], yet Homer's sun also shone over these icebergs and disseminated its gems on the frost-covered valleys."[21] The invocation of the Nordic (if not Arctic!) sublime is characteristic of Grimm's rhetoric in the introduction. Scandinavia is represented as the region of ice and snow. The poetry fostered in this climate, it is implied, is not beautiful and pleasing, but rough, fierce, and strong. Commenting on the form and style of the heroic ballads, Grimm describes them as devoid of ornament; they "disdain all outer gloss" (xxxi; my translation). In these ballads, everything is about event and action, and due to the brevity of the ballad format, only the most important events are included. Comparing the ballad narrative to a mountainous Nordic landscape where the sunlight does not reach down into the valleys, he writes: "Everything that lies in between [the important events] and links together is left out. Actions stand rigorously next to each other like mountains where only the summits are illuminated" (xiv; my translation).

Conclusion

As a challenge to neoclassical standards, the aesthetics of the sublime encouraged an expansion of the poetical canon, allowing for the inclusion of the anonymous poetry of the Middle Ages, which the previous generation had scorned. The revived interest in the Danish legendary ballads, which had first been collected and printed by the renaissance antiquarian Anders Sørensen Vedel in 1591, both drove and reflected this new taste in poetry. Following Grimm's German translation, a large number of these ballads were translated into English, first by Robert Jamieson in his *Illustrations of Northern Antiquities* (1814) and subsequently by George Borrow in *Romantic Ballads, Translated from the Danish* (1826). In the passage from Mallet cited above, sublimity is opposed to obscurity ("sublime, *but* obscure"). To Burke, however, "obscurity," that is, everything "dark, uncertain, confused, terrible" (*Enquiry* II iii), is a major source of the sublime. The extreme obscurity of some of the old legendary ballads made them attractive to a new readership championing the aesthetics of the sublime. In the words of August Wilhelm Schlegel, a leading figure of Jena Romanticism, the ancient ballads possess a captivating "incoherence ... that holds us tight with inexpressible magic" and leave the impression of something "unfathomable deep and divinely noble."[22] Schlegel does not use the term "sublime," but the word readily comes to mind.

NOTES

1 Knut Ljögodt, "'Northern Gods in Marble': The Romantic Discovery of Northern Mythology," *Romantik. Journal for the Study of Romanticisms* 1, 2012, 141–65 (146).

2 Peter Tomory, *The Life and Art of Henry Fuseli*, London, Thames and Hudson, 1972, 102.

3 Paul-Henri Mallet, *Northern Antiquities*, trans. Thomas Percy, 2 vols., London, 1770, vol. 2, 134–7.

4 See Kasper Monrad and Peter Nørgaard Larsen, *Mellem guder og helte. Historiemaleriet i Rom, Paris og København 1770–1820*, Copenhagen, Statens Museum for Kunst, 1990, 9–18.

5 See, for instance, the website of the Royal Academy: www.royalacademy.org.uk/art-artists/work-of-art/thor-battering-the-midgard-serpent (accessed 9 December 2021).

6 I use George Borrow's translation as given in *The Songs of Scandinavia and Other Poems and Ballads*, 2 vols., London, Constable, 1923, 172–7 (172).

7 Adam Oehlenschläger, "Guldhornene," in *Digte*, ed. Johan de Mylius, Copenhagen, Det Danske Sprog- og Litteraturselskab/Gyldendal, 2019, 68–73 (69). For the term "de[n] Höie," see also the Eddaic poem "Hávamál," literally "The Speech of the High One" (Odin).

8 Gregers Einar Forssling, *Nordicism and Modernity*, London, Palgrave, 2020, 56.

9 Henrik Nebelong, *Richard Wagner*, Copenhagen, Forlaget Vandkunsten, 2008, 130–7.

10 Ibid., 167.

11 According to Rix, the seventeenth-century linguist Robert Sheringham was the first English antiquarian to quote extensively from Old Norse texts, including Ragnar Lodbrog's death song, and based on his work selected stanzas were translated into English by Aylett Sammes in 1676. See Robert W. Rix, "The Afterlife of a Death Song: Reception of Ragnar Lodbrog's Poem in Britain until the End of the Eighteenth Century," *Studia Neophilologica* 81.1, 2009, 53–68 (55).

12 Thomas Percy, *Five Pieces of Runic Poetry Translated from the Islandic Language*, London, 1763, 42.

13 Andrew Wawn, *The Vikings and the Victorians: Inventing the Old North in 19th-Century Britain*, Cambridge, D. S. Brewer, 2002, 22–3.

14 Fiona Stafford, *The Sublime Savage: A Study of James Macpherson and the Poems of Ossian*, Edinburgh, Edinburgh University Press, 1988, 173.

15 Hugh Blair, *Critical Dissertation on the Poems of Ossian* (1763), in *The Poems of Ossian and Related Works*, ed. Howard Gaskill, Edinburgh, Edinburgh University Press, 2003, 349.

16 Adam Oehlenschläger, *Æstetiske Skrifter 1800–1812*, ed. F. J. Billeskov Jansen, Copenhagen, Oehlenschläger Selskabet, 1980, 7; my translation.

17 Esaias Tegnér, *Frithiof's Saga*, trans. William Lewery Blackley, ed. Baynard Taylor, New York, Leypoldt & Holt, 1867, 77.

18 A painting of this scene (*Frithjof Slaying Two Trolls at Sea* [1826]) by Tegnér's contemporary, the Danish-Swedish artist Carl Peter Lehmann (1794–1876), shares its iconography with Fuseli's painting: the storm-swept sea, the inky sky, sea monsters rising from the deep, and the dramatic contrast of bright light and darkness.

19 Wayn, *Vikings*, 130.
20 Esaias Tegnér, *Frithiof's Saga; A Skandinavian Legend of Royal Love*, trans. William Strong, London, J. Wacey, 1833, n.p.
21 Wilhelm Carl Grimm, *Altdänische Heldenlieder, Balladen und Märchen*, Heidelberg, 1811, vi. My translation.
22 A. W. Schlegel, "Bürger" (1800), in *Über Literatur, Kunst und Geist des Zeitalters*, Stuttgart, Reclam, 1994, 148–215 (164). My translation.

PART II

Romantic Sublimes

5

CHRISTOPH BODE

German Romanticism and the Sublime

Prior to Immanuel Kant's *Critique of the Power of Judgement* (1790), there is no specifically German concept of the sublime. When writers, critics, or philosophers spoke of "das Erhabene," they either meant (in the French tradition of Nicolas Boileau-Despréaux) a certain *rhetorical* quality, an elevated style, or (in the British tradition of Thomas Burnet, John Dennis, and Edmund Burke) a certain greatness and vastness in *natural objects* (e.g., high mountains, the sea, the starry night sky) or a violence and force in *natural events* (thunderstorms, gigantic avalanches, erupting volcanoes) that could trigger the characteristically mixed feeling of "delightful horror" in the beholder. Of course, when writers patently dealt with sublimity, they did not always use the word for it (e.g., Johann Joachim Winckelmann, Johann Jacob Bodmer, Johann Jakob Breitinger, Johann Georg Sulzer), nor did they always have a fully fledged concept in mind when they occasionally used it (e.g., Friedrich Gottlieb Klopstock, Christoph Martin Wieland, Karl Philipp Moritz). But this is evidently not a German problem alone, nor is it period-specific: generally, the history of the sublime (as *subject matter*) does not always coincide with that of the *word* "sublime," nor do these two histories always coincide with the third, the history of the sublime as a *philosophical concept* of aesthetic, ethical, and epistemological dimensions. There is therefore good reason to keep in mind this differentiation between *Sachgeschichte*, *Wortgeschichte*, and *Begriffsgeschichte*.[1]

But these three histories do coincide in Kant and it is in his *Critique of the Power of Judgement* – not Mendelssohn's "Betrachtungen über das Erhabene und das Naïve in den schönen Wissenschaften" (Reflections on the Sublime and the Naïve in the Fine Arts) (1758) or Kant's own "Beobachtungen über das Gefühl des Schönen und Erhabenen" (Observations on the Feeling of the Beautiful and the Sublime) (1764), neither of which goes substantially beyond Burke's *Enquiry* – that we find the first original German contribution to the established and highly varied European discourse of the sublime. This chapter will first walk the reader through

Kant's thinking in the third *Critique* and show that it does indeed constitute no less a Copernican revolution with regard to the sublime than his *Critique of Pure Reason* (1781) had been with regard to pre-critical epistemology, so that it was not entirely without reason that Monk controversially remarked that "it may be said that eighteenth-century aesthetic has as its unconscious goal the *Critique of Judgment*, the book in which it was to be refined and re-interpreted" (*Monk*, 6). I will then show that the Kantian sublime, although it deals almost exclusively with nature, does have its application to the arts as well; for this purpose I will discuss one of Caspar David Friedrich's most famous paintings, *Der Mönch am Meer* (The Monk by the Sea) (1808–10) and Heinrich von Kleist's equally awesome review of it. After that, the chapter will explain how Kant's radical and indeed revolutionary redefinition of the sublime was first popularized, but then decisively reinterpreted by Friedrich Schiller in four essays composed between 1792 and 1796, whose idea of the "pathetic-sublime" makes the concept amenable to poetics and productive for literature again, particularly so with respect to tragedy. The chapter then closes with a brief discussion of sublimity in romantic-period musical composition, taking, perhaps not surprisingly, as its examples Ludwig van Beethoven's *Fidelio* and his Ninth Symphony, with the words of the final chorus from Schiller's *Ode an die Freude* (Ode to Joy), although there is a deeper, less obvious current connecting the poet and the composer, namely, a specific idea of the sublime.

Kant's famous discussion of the sublime in §§23–9 of *The Critique of the Power Judgement* begins with some similarities and differences between the beautiful and the sublime. When Kant says that the sublime – contrary to the beautiful, which produces *direct* pleasure – is attended by "a pleasure that only arises *indirectly*, being generated, namely, by the feeling of a moment-ary inhibition of the vital powers and the immediately following and all the more powerful outpouring of them," then Burke's influence is palpable (*COPJ* §23 245; emphasis added). Burke had explained the delightful horror we experience in the sublime as the effect of a physiological tension and then relaxation of our blood vessels and nerves – a decidedly *bodily* experience, which made August Wilhelm Schlegel joke that Burke's sublime was nothing but "a noble laxative."[2] Kant keeps the Burkean idea that the experience of the sublime is essentially a two-phase phenomenon, but he goes beyond the "psychological empiricism" of his predecessor by asking the *philosophical* question: What are the conditions of the possibility of this experience?[3] The decisive difference between the beautiful and the sublime, argues Kant, lies in the fact that natural *beauty* conveys a *Zweckmäßigkeit* (purposefulness or finality) in its form, "through which the object seems as it were to be predetermined for our power of judgment, and thus constitutes an object of satisfaction in itself," whereas "that which ... excites in us the feeling of the *sublime* may to be sure appear in its form to be contrapurposive for our power of judgment, unsuitable [or inappropriate, CB] to our faculty of [re]presentation, and as it were doing violence to our imagination, but is nevertheless judged all the more sublime for that" (*COPJ* §23 245; emphasis added). This is indeed puzzling. These objects are an affront to our sensuous facilities and to our imagination. From which it follows – and here Kant formulates his revolutionary turn for the first time –

> that we express ourselves on the whole incorrectly if we call some *object of nature* sublime ... For how can we designate with an expression of approval that which is apprehended in itself as contrapurposive? We can say no more than that the object serves for the [re]presentation of *a sublimity that can be found in the mind*; for what is properly sublime cannot be contained in any sensible form, but concerns only ideas of reason, which, though no [re]presentation adequate to them is possible, are provoked and called to mind precisely by this inadequacy, which does allow of sensible [re]presentation.   (*COPJ* §23 245; emphasis added)

That is the core of Kant's theory of the sublime: the sublime resides in our becoming aware of an *idea of reason*, to which we are provoked by the experience of the ultimate *inadequacy* of our sensuous faculties and the imagination. It is the failure of these powers that reminds us we are bigger than that, for it directs us to the superior instance that can record this very failure: *reason*. It is not, Kant maintains, in provocative opposition to the established discourse on the sublime, the objects themselves that are sublime:

> Thus the wide ocean, enraged by storms, cannot be called sublime. Its visage is horrible; and one must already have filled the mind with all sorts of ideas if by means of such an intuition it is to be put in the mood for a feeling which is itself sublime, in that the mind is incited to abandon sensibility and to occupy itself with ideas that contain a higher purposiveness.   (*COPJ* §23 245–6)

Sublimity resides *in us* as beings of reason, and this becomes apparent the moment we realize we are not just physical, sensuous beings, but there is something higher in us that transcends nature.

This becomes even clearer in §24, where Kant explains the necessity of differentiating between, on the one hand, the "mathematically ... sublime," which we encounter when we are confronted with "what is great beyond all comparison," and, on the other, the "dynamically sublime," or "nature as might" (*COPJ* §24 131; §28 260). In the former it is again our insight into the inadequacy of any standard of our senses or the imagination that points to a superior faculty – "That is sublime which even to be able to think of demonstrates a faculty of the mind that surpasses every measure of the senses" – and beyond that to our destination or vocation (*Bestimmung*) as beings whose *proprium* lies beyond the merely sensuous (*COPJ* §25 250). The classical formulation by which Kant stands the established theory of the sublime on its feet (his second Copernican revolution after the epistemological one in the *Critique of Pure Reason*) follows in §27:

> our imagination, even in its greatest effort with regard to the comprehension of a given object in a whole of intuition (hence for the [re]presentation of the idea of reason) that is demanded of it, demonstrates its limits and inadequacy, but at the same time its vocation for adequately realising that idea as law. Thus the feeling of the sublime in nature is respect for our own vocation, which we show to an object in nature through a certain subreption (substitution of a respect for the object instead of for the idea of humanity in our subject), which as it were makes intuitable the superiority of the rational vocation of our cognitive faculty over the greatest faculty of sensibility.   (*COPJ* §27 257)

The experience of the sublime is a displeasure/delight mix, a dialectical tipping-point that highlights "the supersensible vocation in us" as it were by detour, through an exposition of the limitations of our sensuous and imaginative faculties (*COPJ* §27 257). Neither by our senses nor by our imagination can we comprehend as a whole what is great beyond measure – its very magnitude baffles us – but we can form an *idea* of infinity.

After this, Kant needs far less room to explain the corresponding experience of the dynamically sublime in §28. Here, the feeling of sublimity sets in once we realize that although as physical, mortal beings we should be entirely impotent and helpless if directly exposed to "nature as a power," there is yet something in us that allows us to see us apart from the physical world, to see that in us *the idea of humanity* cannot be harmed or annihilated even if our individual bodily existence were taken from us. We realize the sublimity of our own vocation, even over nature.

Summing up, Kant says at the end of §28 that "sublimity is not contained in anything in nature, but only in our mind, insofar as we can become conscious of being superior to nature within us and thus also to nature outside us (insofar as it influences us)" (*COPJ*, §28 264). According to Kant, then, the sublime is the dialectical self-recognition of man as a rational being in confrontation with its Other, the otherwise humanely incommensurable. His only instances of a manmade sublime are the Egyptian pyramids and St. Peter's in Rome, seen from inside (see *COPJ*, §26 252). The sublime is an act of appropriation, even of subjugation of the Other, an act in which initial impotence is transformed into eventual omnipotence. We glory in our superiority over anything that is merely physical, within us and without us. Pace Crowther, this is not so much a "self-transcendence from the sensuous level of our being to the universal" but from the sensory to the super-sensory.[4] But this self-empowerment also places man into a potentially indifferent, vacant universe. For when Kant introduces, at the end of §28, the idea of God (a regulative idea in any case), he makes it clear that we owe this Being respect not so much for "his power, which he displays in nature" as for "the capacity that is placed within us for judging nature without fear and thinking of our vocation as sublime in comparison with it" (*COPJ* §28 264). God receives an honourable mention. He is of no systematic import-ance to Kant's theory of the sublime.

Johann Gottfried Herder was shocked to read this and rejected Kant's "Analytic of the Sublime" as leading man into "vacancy": without Christian revelation, Herder thought, the sublime would be the quintessence of human self-glorification, without measure and end.[5] And it is true: in Kant, the sublime is redefined as the moment of self-recognition in opposition to the radically nonhuman, to the absolutely great and immeasurably powerful: we realize who we are in confrontation with what we are definitely not. It is in that very moment that we defiantly claim our status as beings who invest an ostentatiously indifferent, potentially meaningless universe with our own, human meaning, because there is no other. Beauty there may be. But there is no natural sublime after Kant. It is always us, and only us.

The representation of any object formerly known as sublime unavoidably suffers from the necessary diminution of its size. Measuring 110.6 by 171.4 centimeters, Friedrich's *The Monk by the Sea* (actually, not a monk, just a lonely human figure in long, brown cloak – the title is not Friedrich's) is not even a large-format painting (see Figure 5.1). Still, its effect is stunning and breathtaking. Why? In the foreground, we see some sandy dunes. Beyond that, an agitated, but not stormy sea, whose almost black waves are some-times crested with white surf. And beyond that, in turn, the sky, which covers four fifths of the canvas. At the horizon, the sky has a very dark coloring, which, however, brightens up: in the upper half, the clouds become translucent and then disappear entirely to reveal a light-blue sky, blending into dark again. Except for the human figure and some seagulls, this sea-scape is entirely empty. "But there is nothing to be seen!" exclaimed a friend of Friedrich's when she first saw the painting.[6] Exactly. Nothing. To be seen. That sums it up.

In the process of its restoration (2013–16) it was discovered by X-rays and infrared reflectography that Friedrich systematically eliminated, painted over, all other objects initially in the painting: two or three sailing boats on the water and fishing nets hung up to dry on scaffolding.[7] No picturesque diversions: he deliberately emptied out the painting to leave only nature – and the contemplating man (the figure is slightly arched backward and has

Figure 5.1 Caspar David Friedrich, *Der Mönch am Meer* (The Monk by the Sea) (1808–10).
Alta Nationalgalerie, Berlin.

put his chin into his right hand). Just man, confronting nature, this figure gives us the only scale, or measure, in the whole painting (the seagulls hovering over the water do not). But ironically, he offers no physical scale to measure, by comparison, the extension of the sea – true, it ends at the horizon, but that is no objective limitation. And the sky? Measureless to man. Boundless and bare is all we see. In fact, the organization of the painting makes it impossible for us, even in this representation, to make any reliable estimate of the extension and the depth of that space. We are dumbfounded as sensuous beings. And yet: by the *Rückenfigur* we are reminded that at the same time we *are* the sole measure in this vacant universe.

Nobody captured the shock of the painting better than Heinrich von Kleist, who found Achim von Arnim's and Clemens Brentano's copy so inadequately frivolous that he, as editor, wrote his own review instead:

How magnificent it is to gaze, in an infinite loneliness at the coast, under overcast skies, at the unlimited wastes of water. Admittedly, you must have gone there, you must return, you want to cross over, you can't, you lack everything you need for life, and yet you harken to the voice of life in the roaring of the tide, in the blowing of the wind, in the passing of the clouds, the lonely cries of the birds. It takes a demand made by the heart and a rupture, as it were, inflicted by nature. But this is impossible in front of this painting, for what I should have found in the painting itself, I only found between myself and the painting, namely a demand which my heart made on the painting and a rupture which the painting inflicted upon me; and thus I myself became the Capuchin friar, the painting became the dune – but that upon which I should have gazed with longing, the sea, was missing entirely. Nothing can be sadder and more uncomfortable than this position in the world: the only spark of life in the wide realm of death, the lonely centre of a lonely circumference.... And since this painting, in its monotony and its boundlessness, has nothing but its frame as foreground, it is, when you look at it, as if your eyelids had been cut off.[8]

For Kleist, the painting refuses all metaphysical consolation, offers no beyond. (The fictional equivalent to my reading of Friedrich's painting is Jean Paul's 1796 "Speech of the Dead Christ from the Edifice of the Universe That There Is No God.") The spectators are entirely thrown back upon themselves, at once framed and deframed, held captive by the view they try to avoid. To be forced to see something horrific, nonhuman, to look into a void: the spectator's situation in front of *The Monk* becomes itself iconic in Stanley Kubrick's *Clockwork Orange*. You cannot, you must not avert your eyes.

No matter what Friedrich's own interpretation of his painting might have been, *Der Mönch am Meer* is one of the most radical instances of the Kantian sublime in art history. It is a climax of the German romantic sublime and the beginning of a new, modern tradition (James Abbott McNeil Whistler, *Trouville*; Gustave Courbet, *Le bord de mer à Palavas*; Edvard Munch, *The Scream*; Barnett Newman's and Mark Rothko's large formats; Gerhard Richter). After this, it would be impossible, anachronistically impossible, "to maintain 'the sublime' / In the old sense. Wrong from the start," as Pound puts it in "Hugh Selwyn Mauberley" (3–4). It is awesome; it is also frightening, depending on whether you regard this radical redefinition of the sublime as liberating or as annihilating: dreadful freedom. In any case, it would only be fitting if it left you with mixed feelings.

There are two reasons why the Kantian sublime remained dominant in Germany even after the younger generation of idealist philosophers had tried to replace "'[den] alleszermalmende[n]Kant' [thus Mendelssohn], i.e. the all-becrushing, or rather the *all-to-nothing-crushing* Kant" as Coleridge puts it in *Biographia Literaria* (1817).[9] First, in none of their own systems did the sublime play a key role. For instance, in his *System of Transcendental Idealism* (1800), Friedrich Wilhelm Joseph Schelling (in this like Herder) denies that there is a qualitative or essential difference between the beautiful and the sublime – they are basically the same, he claims. And Georg Wilhelm Friedrich Hegel relegates the sublime from aesthetics altogether and treats it under "philosophy of the history of religion" instead: for him, the sublime stands for a historically obsolete form of trying to understand the world, namely, in terms of the Mosaic, Jewish faith.

The other reason for Kant's continuing prevalence is that none other than Friedrich Schiller becomes his torchbearer. In his essays on the pathetic, the tragic, and the sublime (1792–6), Schiller paraphrases and explicates Kant, but he also gives the Kantian sublime a decisive twist – curiously enough by tapping other Kantian sources: in the first two *Critiques*, but also as early as in the *Grundlegung zur Metaphysik der Sitten* (Groundwork of the Metaphysics of Morals) (1785), Kant had stated that if you observe mankind only from outside nothing gives reason to assume that we are not subject to natural causality (just like all other living beings and the rest of inanimate nature), but that this changes radically once you take an interior point of view. For if we observe ourselves from within, we realize we have a sense of right and wrong, of good and bad; we have different options to act, and some of them are ethically less questionable than others (to put it mildly), and it is this feeling of morality that presupposes or points to a freedom of the will (typically for Kant, it only points to it; it does not prove it exists – free will, like "God," is only a regulative idea, a reasonable assumption). It is by exercising free will in our actions that we rise above natural causality (that still governs us as physical, sensuous beings) and prove ourselves to be moral and rational beings with a super-sensuous side (exercising a higher kind of causality, "causality through freedom" or "causality of reason," for in our moral-rational decisions we are not chaotic, but guided by reason). Our freedom is of a transcendental kind in the sense that it transcends the limits of our animal existence.

Schiller takes this as the core of his philosophy: he is *the* philosopher of inner, moral freedom (*Sittlichkeit*). As physical beings, we are dependent; as moral, rational beings, we become independent and free. Nature may determine our physical state, but not our will, by which we set ourselves apart from nature, transcend it. Sublimity thus resides in being conscious of our own free, rational will, and to watch somebody rise above mere nature is always sublime.

It takes but one step to reveal why sublimity in human action should be at the very center of Schiller's thinking about the arts and drama in particular: Why is it uplifting to watch a noble character suffer and ultimately fail in their battle against unsurmountable obstacles? Because in suffering we show our inner moral independence, the triumph of the will over nature: we are free. The measure of our sublimity is the greatness or magnitude of adversity we have to overcome: our physical being has to suffer, and suffer greatly, so that we can see how great and sublime the resistance of man as a free moral being is – even to the point (and this recalls Kant's dynamic sublime) that our physical annihilation cannot harm the idea of mankind. The idea abides. Our freedom shows in adversity. It is evident that no art serves this purpose better than tragedy, because (different from painting or sculpture) it can represent human suffering as *action* and because, as art, it provides the necessary *distance* to lift mere compassion and empathy (which we experience when we witness *real* suffering) to the level of an aesthetical-rational recognition of human superiority over mere circumstance. Schiller shifts the Kantian sublime to the sphere of human action.

Schiller's sublime is therefore the pathetic-sublime: "the idea and representation of somebody else's suffering, linked with emotion and with the consciousness of our inner moral freedom, is *pathetic-sublime* ... From this, the two fundamental laws of all tragic art derive. They are, *first*: representation of suffering nature; *second*: representation of moral independence in suffering," which is synonymous with "representation of moral *resistance* to suffering."[10] It is true to say that the sublime, if not in Schiller's overall aesthetics, then surely with regard to his idea of humanity and our destination, is more important than the beautiful.[11] In his own dramatic works, this concept of the sublime is arguably best realized in his tragedies *Mary Stuart* (1800) and *The Maid of Orleans* (1801).

In German literature, instances of the Kantian sublime (moments of realization of who we are in opposition to what is overwhelmingly big or powerful), or of Schiller's pathetic-sublime, can be found in Friedrich Gottlieb Klopstock; in some tragedies of Johann Wolfgang von Goethe (e.g., *Torquato Tasso*, *Iphigenia in Tauris*) and Heinrich von Kleist; in the lyrical poetry of Friedrich and August Wilhelm Schlegel; in the poems of Joseph von Eichendorff, Wilhelm Heinrich Wackenroder, Ludwig Tieck, Achim von Arnim, and Clemens Brentano; and in the lyric and epic poetry and novels of Novalis and Friedrich Hölderlin. In a way, even the "black," or Gothic romanticism, in the tales of E. T. A. Hoffmann can be regarded as a chapter – the last – of the history of the sublime in German romanticism, with the decisive difference that the confrontation with the supernatural (as opposed to the super-sensuous in ourselves), or the look into the magnitude of the abyss within ourselves, offers no delightful, uplifting relief. These are comparatively cheap thrills, characterized by an absence of sublimity. They highlight the sublime *ex negativo*.

Ludwig van Beethoven's only opera, *Fidelio* (final version 1814), is incontestably the finest example of the pathetic-sublime in the field of musical compositions of the era. But the opera is not exclusively about Florestan's, the secret prisoner's, sufferings and his eventual liberation by his faithful wife Leonore (a.k.a. Fidelio) – with dramatic suspense, Florestan remains a conspicuous absence until Act 2. *Fidelio* is not only a celebration of conjugal love ("Wer ein holdes Weib errungen" ["Who calls a faithful wife his own"] – Beethoven's first quote from Schiller's "Ode to Joy"). At the same time it offers a more general, universal message, a utopian vision of the liberation of all prisoners – by implication, of all mankind – from the confinement imposed upon them by lawless despotism. This is underscored by the most moving scene of Act 1 (and, as has been argued, one of the most famous and greatest moments in all the history of opera), the so-called *Gefangenenchor* (Prisoners' Chorus). Fidelio has successfully pleaded with Rocco, the warden of the prison, to temporarily release the prisoners from their dark cells into the garden of the garrison. As they slowly step into the warm and bright sunshine, they sing, first hesitantly and with quiet and subdued voices, "Oh, welche Lust, in freier Luft / Den Atem leicht zu heben! Nur hier, nur hier ist Leben. Der Kerker eine Gruft" ("Oh what joy, in the open air / Freely to breathe again! / Up here, up here alone is life! / The dungeon is a grave"). This theme of universal, not just individual, liberation is taken up again, and with a vengeance, in the grand finale of *Fidelio*, when after the saving of Florestan's life and his freeing from the deepest dungeon of the prison, *all* political prisoners are freed for good, and the chorus of "prisoners and the people" join Florestan and Leonore in jubilantly praising the day of universal liberation: "Heil sei dem Tag, Heil sei der Stunde" ("Blessed the day, blessed the hour"). As Ernst Bloch, the Marxist philosopher of utopian hope, has argued, the utopian pervades and abides in *Fidelio*, "the most powerful opera ever."[12] But it is a powerful utopian vision that has its deep roots in the sublime: for the dignity of humankind resides in its capacity to act freely – take that core away and you deny their humanity. Any such degradation and humiliation cry out for restitution: sublimity resides in the moment when the doors of all prison cells are opened and the "conditions of possibility" for humankind as a confederation of free, moral, and rational beings are won.

Schiller, initially, like so many others of his generation, a supporter of the ideas of the French Revolution (and honorary citizen of the French Republic!), became increasingly skeptical as to whether the liberation of mankind could be achieved by political means. From the mid-1790s onward, he argued for an *aesthetic* education of mankind instead, particularly of the lower orders (with the stage as a "moral institution"), because they were not yet mature enough for political freedom. But curiously enough, it was one of Schiller's early poems (1785), originally words for a drinking song with strong masonic undertones, which served Beethoven to compose in 1824 what is arguably the most sublime piece of music ever written: the Fourth Movement of his Ninth Symphony with Schiller's "Ode to Joy" as final chorus. Beethoven had been familiar with Schiller's ode for decades and had always wanted to set it to music. For his Ninth, he chose only a few selected lines, but had these repeated over and over again. This is not the time and place for a musicological analysis of this Fourth Movement; suffice it here to say that Beethoven makes use of *all* possible compositional parameters – instrumentation, tempo, volume, reinforcement through repetition, and so on – to build up a gigantic climax, which few, if any, can resist. The effect is at one and the same time overpowering and uplifting – it is, in one word, sublime. Beethoven himself adds only a few words of his own by way of introduction ("O Freunde, nicht diese Töne" ["Oh friends, not these sounds"]) before he ingeniously plunders Schiller's ode. Few will deny that the oft-repeated lines "Alle Menschen werden Brüder" ("All humanity become brothers and sisters") and "Seid umschlungen, Millionen! / Diesen Kuss der ganzen Welt!" ("Be embraced, ye millions! / This kiss is for all mankind!") are key drivers toward the ecstatic climax, when the consummation of earthly joy in universal brotherhood finds its apex in the tentative recognition of something bigger and higher above us: "Brüder, überm Sternenzelt / muss ein lieber Vater wohnen" ("Brothers, above the canopy of stars / There must reside a benevolent father"). With this musical vision, Beethoven had opened the door to a utopia for all mankind.[13]

Neither Schiller nor Beethoven lived to hear this. Schiller had died in 1805 – and in 1824 Beethoven was stone deaf. The immediate response after the first performance was enthusiastic beyond measure; the audience went wild. But Beethoven, having turned his back upon them, did not notice any of this; he had to be turned around to face them and so get an idea of their frenetic applause and endless jubilations. He bowed. Yet another triumph over the merely sensory. At the end of his second critique (1788), Kant had written: "There are two things that fill the mind with ever new and increasing admiration and reverence: the starry sky above me and the moral law within me."[14] Placed as we are between these two infinities – the infinity of the physical cosmos and the infinity of my own invisible self – we are forced to recognize our own utter insignificance as physical beings and, at the same time, allowed to imagine that we are possibly the only point in this immensity that can invest this vacant universe with any meaning. The realization of the correlation of these two infinities constitutes the sublime in German romanticism.

NOTES

1 See Karl Viëtor, "Die Idee des Erhabenen in der deutschen Literaturgeschichte," in *Geist und Form: Aufsätze zur deutschen Literaturgeschichte*, Bern, Francke, 1952, 234–266; *Ästhetische Grundbegriffe*, ed. Karlheinz Barck et al., Stuttgart,

Metzler, 3 vols., 2010, vol. 2, s.v. "Erhaben," 275–310; *Historisches Wörterbuch der Philosophie*, ed. Joachim Ritter, 13 vols., Darmstadt, WBG, 2019, vol. 2, s.v. "Erhaben, das Erhabene," 623–36.

2 Carsten Zelle, *"Angenehmes Grauen": Literaturhistorische Beiträge zur Ästhetik des Schrecklichen im achtzehnten Jahrhundert*, Hamburg, Meiner, 1987, 194.

3 Viëtor, "Die Idee," 255.

4 Paul Crowther, *The Kantian Sublime*, Oxford, Clarendon, 1989, 15.

5 Cf. *Ästhetische Grundbegriffe*, 296.

6 Michel Le Bris, *Die Romantik in Wort und Bild*, Stuttgart, Klett-Cotta, 1981, 77.

7 *Der Mönch ist zurück: Die Restaurierung von Caspar David Friedrichs* Mönch am Meer *und* Abtei im Eichwald, ed. Kristina Mösl and Philipp Demandt, Berlin, Nationalgalerie, 2016 (bilingual edition).

8 Heinrich von Kleist, "Empfindungen vor Friedrichs Seelandschaft," in *Sämtliche Werke und Briefe*, ed. Helmut Sembdner, 2 vols. in 1, Munich, dtv, 2013, vol. 2, 327–8, my translation.

9 Samuel Taylor Coleridge, *Biographia Literaria*, 2 vols., London, 1817, vol. 2, 93n.

10 Friedrich Schiller, *Theoretische Schriften*, ed. Rolf-Peter Janz, Munich, dtv, 2008, 419, 422, 426. My translation, last emphasis added.

11 See Viëtor, "Die Idee," 261.

12 Ernst Bloch, *Das Prinzip Hoffnung*, 3 vols., Frankfurt/M., Suhrkamp, 1959, 1974, vol. 2, 974, my translation; cf. also vol. 3, 1295–7, "Marseillaise und Augenblick in Fidelio."

13 See Jan Caeyers, *Beethoven: A Life*, Oakland, University of California Press, 2020, part 5, chapter 9.

14 Immanuel Kant, *Kritik der praktischen Vernunft*, ed. Karl Vorländer, Hamburg, Meiner, 1985, 188; my translation.

6

TIMOTHY M. COSTELLOE

The Romantic Sublime and Kant's Critical Philosophy

Immanuel Kant's mature treatment of sublimity is contained primarily in the 'Analytic of the Sublime', which forms part (§§23–9 and General Remark, 244–78) of the *Critique of the Power of Judgment* (1790). Kant himself declares the 'theory of the sublime' a 'mere appendix' to aesthetic judgment since it indicates 'nothing purposive in nature', making it less important and 'rich in consequences' than what is revealed in the 'Analytic of the Beautiful' (*COPJ* §23 246); there is evidence that its inclusion was 'last-minute'; and despite Kant's official method of proceeding, there might be less 'structural parallelism' between the two kinds of judgments than he realized.[1] Whatever the final word, Kant's treatment still stands as an important application and extension of his Critical Philosophy to a specific domain of aesthetic experience, the results of which proved the most influential treatment of the subject since Burke's *Enquiry*, to which, along with other eighteenth-century works of philosophical aesthetics, Kant is heavily indebted.[2]

In the context of 'Romanticism', Kant's treatment of the sublime has an ambiguous appearance. In content, style, and organization, the views Kant expresses are inseparable from the European tradition of eighteenth-century philosophical aesthetics of which his 'Analytic' is both part and outcome, and only retroactively and anachronistically might one identify it with a movement that took shape in the century after his death. At the same time, Kant takes up and develops themes destined to become defining features of the Romantic conception of sublimity, and, seen in that light, one might classify him as a Romantic philosopher and the 'Analytic of the Sublime' as a Romantic text. This might seem at odds with the long-standing and prevailing treatment of Kant as a paragon of Enlightenment thought. However, the suggestion that elements of his system anticipate the Romantic movement to come is not unfamiliar.[3] His treatment of 'imagination', in particular, provides rich ground for unearthing such connections, an observation supported by the fact that Samuel Taylor Coleridge appropriated the third *Critique* early for the Romantic cause, thereby introducing it, almost single-handedly, to the English speaking-world.[4] Debates over the appropriateness of reading Kant in this way notwithstanding, in the present context I assume it as a point of departure and background against which to identify three dominant themes in 'Kant's Critical Sublime' that – to draw on the trope of echoes – are sounded loudly and distinctly in the Romantic tradition that follows: 'transcendence and the phenomenal self', 'the moral subject within', and 'the "objects" of nature and art', each of which I consider in turn.

Transcendence and the Phenomenal Self

A central characteristic of the Romantic sublime is transcendence, that is, the sense that the self we experience – the phenomenal self – cannot be contained by the worldly home it ordinarily inhabits; one has the feeling, at once uncanny and liberating, that full realization and true contentment lie beyond empirical objects or real events, which stand merely as signs to a signified. Following Thomas Weiskel's influential treatment, one might characterize this experience as 'positive', 'egotistical', or 'metonymical', defined by a heightened awareness of the self as it appears to extend into all things; alternatively, one might consider it 'negative' or 'metaphorical', where the self dissipates into and merges with something greater. In this division, Weiskel categorizes the Kantian sublime as negative, since it suggests, he says, that the experience 'conducts us ... to the frontier of the "invisible world" but leaves us as soon as that world is consciously represented or given any positive content'; its structure is thus an 'indeterminate relation' – a 'movement between two states' – and denies precisely what the 'positive' sublime asserts, namely, that the self can 'subsume all otherness' such that the 'phenomenal or sensible ego is aggrandized in place of the self-recognition of the noumenal reason' (*Weiskel*, 41, 43, 49). Wordsworth's lines from *The Prelude* (1805) in praise of the imagination and yearning for 'infinitude' (he had, famously, failed to gain the actual prospect of the Alps he had anticipated) have often been read by scholars as the paradigm – even the 'apotheosis', as Samuel Monk describes it – of the 'positive' alternative (Book VI, lines 538–48; *Monk*, 5).

It is unclear whether there is a strict division between a 'Kantian' and 'Romantic' sublime; Wordsworth himself considers the resistance found in negative 'humiliation and submission' a more powerful route to the 'intense unity' of sublime experience than the more positive participation through 'union and communion'.[5] Whatever the final word on this question, Weiskel's otherwise instructive terminology fails to reflect the complexity of Kant's discussion, which includes both 'positive' and 'negative' elements, transcendence involving the 'self-recognition' of noumenal reason *and* 'aggrandizing' the phenomenal self. The first is perhaps the most characteristically Kantian part of Kant's account. Whether incomprehension in the face of magnitude that is 'absolutely great' ('mathematically sublime') or feeling overwhelmed by the power of nature ('dynamically sublime'), one *abandons* the sensible for the supersensible, turning to the 'higher purposiveness' contained in the 'ideas of reason' provoked, albeit paradoxically, by the very 'inadequacy' of the imagination to present them sensibly (*COPJ* §23 246).

Kant's language reflects the confusing, disorienting, even disturbing quality of the experience – he speaks of 'formlessness', 'indeterminacy', 'separation', 'inhibition', 'limitation', the 'abyss' (*Abgrund*) of 'excess' (*COPJ* §27 258), all expressions of fear, anxiety, suffering, and loss – with the precise moment of transcendence occurring when the 'mind is put in the mood for a *feeling* which is itself sublime' (*COPJ* §23 245–6); only at this point does one gain the ineffable sense of movement upward and beyond oneself, of merging with something greater in the course of which one discovers one's rational nature and value as a moral being. In the process, Kant says, the 'mind makes palpable to itself' its superiority over nature, manifest in such familiar but heightened emotional states as 'self-esteem', the 'incoercibility of mind' manifest in the warrior and general, the courage of a people at war to defend its rights, reverence for the Divine, and humility in facing one's failings. Kant also characterizes it as a shift of perspective that reveals the 'trivial' character of everyday concerns – 'goods, health and life' – in comparison to the 'highest principles' of one's humanity (*COPJ* §28 262–4).

As these examples suggest, in Kant's account, any loss of self in the recognition of reason at once belies a simultaneous and closely connected aggrandizement of the phenomenal self that Kant also isolates as a crucial component of the sublime. One might characterize this as a return to or affirmation of the self in and at the very moment of loss, a state made manifest most tangibly in the profound *pleasure* (*Lust*) that Kant diagnoses in the experience, which is, after all, *aesthetic*, involving the presentation of an object to the human faculties (imagination and understanding or reason), and thus, to borrow a phrase from Jacques Derrida, defined by the 'being-pleasure of pleasure'.[6] Pleasure thus conceived defines aesthetic experience in general, but in sublime experience its specific form is strange and singular, posing, as eighteenth-century writers conceived it, a 'problem' in need of a solution: Why should, and precisely how does, one find pleasing the obviously painful experiences of being threatened and overwhelmed?

Both Burke and Joseph Addison had captured the phenomenology of this complex feeling through 'astonishment', which they parse as 'delightful terror' and 'delightful stillness and amazement', respectively.[7] Kant uses the same term (*Verwunderung*) (*GR* 269), but attempts other routes to its mystery through, variously, the language of absence ('negative' satisfaction born of the imagination's loss of freedom [*GR*, 269]), paradox (a 'pleasure which is possible only by means of a displeasure' [*COPJ* §27 260]), and metaphor (a 'movement of the mind' that 'may be compared to a vibration ... a rapidly alternating repulsion from and attraction to one and the same object' [*COPJ* §27 258]). Inevitably, perhaps, variety of expression produces instability of conception, which at bottom might reflect a personal confession and 'product' of an 'inveterate tendency to evaluate everything by reference to moral value'.[8] Be this as it may, Kant himself is convinced that sublime pleasure is distinct – 'very different in kind' (*sehr unterschieden*) (*COPJ* §23 244) – from what follows upon the harmony of imagination and understanding that underly judgments of beauty, and over which we are disposed to 'linger' (*COPJ* §12 222).[9]

In fact, Kant's clearest exposition emerges when he juxtaposes sublime pleasure with its counterpart in the beautiful. Judgments of beauty, Kant thinks, involve 'purposiveness' because apparently 'predetermined for our power of judgment' (*COPJ* §23 245) and bring a light-hearted feeling of delight in the 'promotion of life' (*COPJ* §23 244) arising directly from the imagination 'at play' (*COPJ* §23 245); those of the sublime, by contrast, are 'contrapurposive' and reflect a 'serious activity of the imagination' that does 'violence' to the very faculty it engages. Within the experience of the sublime, one appears to feel pain and pleasure 'at the same time' (*zugleich*), though Kant deciphers its temporal dimensions, there being *first* pain from the 'momentary inhibition of the vital powers' and *then* pleasure from the 'all the more powerful outpouring of them' (*COPJ* §23 245). This feeling might be complex and difficult to describe, but its foundation lies firmly with the phenomenal self.

The Moral Subject Within

If transcendence and the phenomenal self each figure prominently in Kant's Critical Sublime, so does their condition and corollary in the notion of an autonomous being aware of itself as the subject undergoing the experience in question, the 'modern' self and a candidate reason why the eighteenth century witnessed a sudden, widespread, and subsequently sustained reflection on aesthetic value and its manifestation in art. This conception is not Kant's alone, of course, but he assumes and articulates it, and in so doing adumbrates what was to become a central tenet of Romanticism, namely, the conviction that the primary locus of value is not to be sought in the external world and its qualities, which (as the eighteenth-century 'science of man' had it) somehow affect the faculties intrinsic to human nature, but in the *subject* who is at once engaged in and undergoing the experience. The immediate and direct object of consciousness is the self, with objects playing an auxiliary role, merely the *occasion* for aesthetic value to arise.

The appearance of this element in the Critical Sublime takes shape as the 'moral subject within', a phrase intended to capture two salient features of Kant's thinking. First, he conceives sublimity as primarily 'self-regarding', not in the form of self-interest but as it reveals and makes palpable something *in ourselves*; this distinguishes it from the 'other-regarding' direction that dominates in the case of beauty, where we discover something outside ourselves, 'nature', that is purposive for our power of judgment.[10] Kant's language is, correspondingly, of inwardness and revelation, the experience showing something that would otherwise remain hidden: 'becoming conscious' of our superiority to nature (*COPJ* §28, 264), of our extra-natural 'power' being called forth (*COPJ* §28 262), of 'elevat[ing] the strength of our soul' that allows us to 'discover within ourselves a capacity' (*COPJ* §28 261) or that 'demonstrates a faculty of mind that surpasses every measure of the senses' (*COPJ* §23 250). From such descriptions Kant draws the conclusion that what we call 'sublime' is really a 'disposition of the mind', of discovering the 'supersensible faculty in us' (*COPJ* §25 250). This is not to say that certain (paradigmatically) natural objects are not required for the experience (of which more below). However, Kant insists, because it 'concerns only ideas of reason', the 'properly sublime cannot be contained in any sensible form' (*COPJ* §23 245). It is a deeply personal experience, trades on annihilating distance, and moves the subject away from the public space that Kant associates with taste to a private one that reflects the complexity and ineffability of the feeling that is involved.

Second, what is discovered from this movement within is reason in its 'practical' mode; sublime experience is ultimately and irremediably 'moral' since it concerns the *Bestimmung* – 'vocation', 'calling', or, more generally, 'determination' – of the human mind and human capacities in which the subject recognizes its superiority to the phenomena that occasion, through incomprehensible magnitude and overwhelming power, the pain of inadequacy. Sublime feeling is the function of repulsion and attraction, inhibition and outpouring, but it involves 'another feeling' (*COPJ* §39 292), 'respect' (*Achtung*), which, though one might regard it as a 'mode of the Kantian sublime,' is not, strictly speaking, sublime at all.[11] It is simply *painful*, the 'feeling of the inadequacy of our capacity for the attainment of an idea that is a law for us' and 'makes intuitable the superiority of the rational vocation of our cognitive faculty over the greatest faculty of sensibility' (*COPJ* §27 258), the basis upon which Kant urges that sublime experience has universal validity, albeit, as an aesthetic judgment, one that is based in the subject. In recognizing this connection between sublimity and morality, Kant at once affirms the self-regarding character of sublime experience and denies that the feeling involved is 'communicable' in the way that applies in the case of beauty. One might refer sublime communicability, as does Jean-François Lyotard, to reason 'inscribed in the form of the moral law' – but this does not alter Kant's claim that the experience does not demand universal agreement in any obvious or direct way, something that Lyotard does not, in the final analysis, appear to deny.[12]

One might also note Kant's more explicit claim to discover a 'ground of necessity' for sublime judgment (the counterpart of the 'Fourth Moment', 'modality', of a judgment of taste in the 'Analytic of the Beautiful' [*COPJ* §§18–22 236–40]) in 'human nature' and the 'predisposition' it contains to the 'feeling for (practical) ideas' such that we can expect in our own judgment the 'assent of the judgment of other people' (*COPJ* §29 265). This presupposes the 'refinement' of the cognitive faculties – 'culture' (*Kultur*) – and thus a 'sensitivity' to the ideas in question (*COPJ* §29 264), a requirement that surely undermines the expectations one might reasonably have of other people; the response of the Savoyard peasant in the form of distress, danger, and need to the Alps is likely the rule rather than the exception [*COPJ* §29 265]). More importantly, it does not touch in any substantial way the self-orientated nature of the experience that Kant takes as a central desideratum, the main reason, one assumes, that Hannah Arendt effectively banishes the sublime from her project of finding in the third *Critique* clues for Kant's 'nonwritten political philosophy'.[13] As a citizen and social being, one is '*not* as a member of a supersensible world' where '*I obey law given to myself* regardless of what others may think of the matter'.[14] Only under the auspices of taste does one find solid ground for the 'universal communicability' of the pleasure that arises when an object is judged beautiful (*COPJ* §§6–8), 'taste as a kind of common sense' (*sensus communis*), an 'extra' sense that 'fits us into a community' where individuals are connected through mutual need, independent critical thought, and, most significantly, the interdependence between subjective pleasure with the pleasure of others.[15] Even the genius of the artist must be combined with taste, Kant insists, because the latter 'polishes' and gives 'guidance' to the former, imposing order on and ensuring clarity of the aesthetic ideas being expressed, helping guarantee that its products are 'capable of an enduring and universal approval, of enjoying a posterity among others and in an ever progressing culture' (*COPJ* §50 319). The aspects of sublime experience celebrated by Romanticism stand, in almost every respect, opposed to the very publicness that judgments of beauty demand and require.

The 'Objects' of Nature of Art

If Kant's Critical Sublime finds later Romantic echoes in the form of transcendence and the moral subject within, one might wonder about the 'other regarding' dimension of the sublime, its outwardness or the fact that external (paradigmatically) natural objects are required for the experience to arise. What is the status of 'nature' and its 'objects' if these are merely the 'occasion' for an experience that is fundamentally private and self-regarding? Iconic examples of the Romantic sublime – Caspar David Friedrich's *Wanderer above the Sea of Fog* (Der Wanderer über dem Nebelmeer) (1818) or Wordsworth's descriptions of the Alps – suggest not only the *existence* of natural objects, either real or represented, but ones either with or suggestive of sufficient size and scope to render the human individual insignificant, humbled by something primordial, wild, vast, and untamed. In a moral idiom, these scenes often portray simplicity, purity, and innocence, places if not entirely unblemished by human interference, then at least with the marks of such presence rendered decisively moot – made small or blasted to ruin – by overwhelming and irresistible forces.

There is a paradox coded from the outset in such images of sublimity, of course. One must be in the presence and proximity of the phenomenon, but encounter it at a distance in order to guarantee that any real and present danger is mitigated or removed altogether. Friedrich's wanderer is *above* the sea of fog, not lost in its obscure depths, as Wordsworth views the Alps from *afar*, unconcerned with their treacherous paths and gaping ravines (he is unaware of even having crossed them!). Here, we might say, is the external analogue of internal transcendence, the individual physically distanced from the object as the self is psychically distanced from the subject who is transcended. As such, one might conclude, the Romantic vision of nature involves paying attention less to the objects per se than to the *relationship* one takes to them, captured phenomenologically in the act – to us a Kantian term – of aesthetic 'contemplation' (*Kontemplation*).

Kant's approach captures perfectly the complex relationship that obtains among natural objects, physical distance, and psychological proximity, something that emerges in his discussion both of the mathematically sublime and, especially, of the dynamically sublime, where the origin of the experience requires the presence of phenomena capable of facilitating the requisite discovery that nature is a 'power that has no dominion over us', 'power' (*Macht*) being the 'capacity to overcome great obstacles' and 'dominion' (*Gewalt*) meaning that it cannot resist, in turn, the power it calls forth in response (*COPJ* §27 260). First, Kant emphasizes that the experience requires being safe from any *actual* danger. This appears as a purely psychological thesis about the emotional state the experience involves, which, Kant's explicit rejection of Burke's *Enquiry* notwithstanding (he dismisses it as 'empirical psychology' and poor substitute for a 'critique of taste' [*GR*, 277–8]), puts him in close company with Burke, who had emphasized how only the threat of danger 'at certain distances' and thus pain 'with certain modifications' could produce the delightful terror underlying the passion of sublimity (see *Enquiry* I vii).

Kant too describes the sublime in terms of 'astonishment bordering on terror' where one only need 'involve' oneself to feel the 'power' of the imagination and the sense of superiority to nature that results; this is 'not *actual* fear' (*GR* 269, emphasis added), which would alter the balance of such involvement (comparable to being in the 'grip of inclination and appetite' when judging things beautiful [(*COPJ* §28 261]) and risk 'under-distancing' the observer, as Edward Bullough was to express the thought more than a century later.[16] The demand for distance reflects how judgments of sublimity are aesthetic, involving 'merely' the presentation of an object to the imagination and reason. As such, objects are and only need be '*represented* as arousing fear' (*COPJ* §28 260, emphasis added); the 'sublime state of mind' and subsequent insight into one's moral and spiritual vocation (*COPJ* §28 263–4) means that the object as such – the phenomenon – is nugatory. For this reason an object might be 'fearful' without causing 'fear', a point Kant exploits in reference to the virtuous individual who recognizes God as a fearful Being, but not one of whom anybody in a 'God-pleasing disposition' would be afraid (*COPJ* §28 260).

This Critical thesis also explains, second, how Kant can treat the sublime aesthetically while also speaking of 'nature outside us' (*COPJ* §28 264) and even compiling a lengthy list of *real* phenomena that are directly involved in the experience, each exhibiting sufficient 'power' to cause the required effect: 'Bold, overhanging, as it were, threatening cliffs, thunder clouds towering up into the heavens, bringing with them flashes of lightning and crashes of thunder, volcanoes with their all-destroying violence, hurricanes with the devastation they leave behind, the boundless ocean set into a rage, a lofty waterfall on a mighty river, etc.' (*COPJ* §23 261).

As Kant emphasizes, however, such objects are not sublime *qua objects*, and one should not take them (as did Burke) to contain sublime qualities ('threatening', 'violent', 'all-destroying', and the like) because the 'properly sublime' (as noted above) is a feeling connected with a state of mind and not contained in any 'sensible form'. All we can claim is that the 'object serves for the presentation of a sublimity that can be found in the mind' (*COPJ* §26 254), but to predicate 'sublimity' in any other way would be to express oneself 'incorrectly' and commit a *vitium subreptionis* ('vice of subreption').

We 'gladly call these objects [of nature] sublime because they elevate the strength of our soul above its usual level', but this is really to recognize in ourselves a 'capacity' for another kind of 'resistance' (*COPJ* §23 261). One might press Kant here and ask precisely *what* about the phenomenally yet not 'properly sublime' object accounts for the experience in question. One answer, emphasized by Lyotard, is by way of the noumenal 'other object', not itself an object of possible experience but encountered *through* the phenomenal object.[17] The real object – the actual mountain or storm at sea – is not so much lost as revalued in a shift of perspective so that it becomes a sign or indicator of something more, a reference of the unpresent-able, presented (albeit impossibly) in and through the phenomenal object, even though the 'elevating sentiment' of the sort felt by Herr de Saussure at the foot of Alpine glaciers requires time and cultivation to realize (*COPJ* §29 265). As such, Kant's real focus is less on objects as the 'ground' for the experience than on the subject 'for whom' such a judgment and the corres-ponding feeling is possible by virtue of one's 'identity as a moral being'.[18]

In addition, and while his final position on the matter is open to debate, Kant more than hints that such sentiments need not require the presence of original objects, such that one might be moved by representations of them, seeing Friedrich's painted *image* or reading Wordsworth's literary *sketch*.[19] Admittedly, Kant does omit sublimity from his discussion of the arts, and he excludes explicitly any productions – 'buildings, columns, etc.' – where the form and magnitude are designed for specific human ends, such teleology contaminating the 'pure' character of an aesthetic judgment (*COPJ* §26 252); the same principle applies to any part of nature that 'brings with it a determinate end', that is, a biological function – 'animals with a known natural determination' (*COPJ* §26 252–3) – as well as objects that charm or elicit fear (*COPJ* §26, 253). At the same time, Kant acknowledges that while one might turn first to the sublime in nature since (one assumes) this is where the power of objects is most keenly felt, it does not exclude the possibility of the sublime 'in art', though it would be 'restricted to the conditions of agreement with nature' (*COPJ* §23 245).

In his exposition of the mathematical sublime, moreover, Kant refers to the Pyramids of Egypt and St Peter's Basilica in Rome (*COPJ* §26 252), objects of human origin that (apparently) reveal at least as well as natural ones the inadequacy of the imagination to comprehend a whole. For this reason, one might speak of an 'artefactual' sublime in Kant or even, if all that is required is the presentation of an object, an 'expressive' sublime as well, when artists evoke in an audience a sense of the universal significance of the subject matter and make vivid the scope of the artistic expression in ques-tion.[20] This seems in keeping with Kant's conviction that it is not the *actual* 'violence' of volcanoes or 'devastation' wrought by hurricanes that is important, but the ideas that 'fill the mind' as a result (*COPJ* §23 245–6). Sublime feeling follows from the intentional status of the object rather than its real presence, something that might have been raised in Kant himself should he have lived to see a Friedrich painting or read the poetry of Wordsworth.

Conclusion

It is worth noting, by way of brief conclusion, how later in the *Critique of the Power of Judgement* (§§43–53), Kant treats (what we now consider) the 'fine arts' under the auspices of beauty, 'beautiful art' (*schöne Kunst*) being the expression, through the 'spirit' of genius, of 'aesthetic ideas,' representations produced by the imagination that inspire thought but without a concept that is adequate to them. Kant there relegates music to the 'beautiful play of sensations' (*COPJ* §51 324) but sees in poetry an unparalleled power to 'expand' the mind and 'set free' the imagination to connect the presentation of its object 'with a fullness of thought to which no linguistic presentation is fully adequate' (*COPJ* §53 326). It is surely but a shift of perspective in the Romantics that allows them to connect these and other arts to the *sublime* instead, finding in them ways of conveying meaningfully a feeling and experience that cannot easily or obviously be put into words.[21]

NOTES

1 See Henry Alison, *Kant's Theory of Taste*, Cambridge, Cambridge University Press, 2001, 304–7; and Rodolphe Gasché, *The Idea of Form*, Stanford, CA, Stanford University Press, 2003, 119–54.

2 On Kant's debt to eighteenth-century philosophical aesthetics, see Donald W. Crawford, 'The Place of the Sublime in Kant's Aesthetic Theory', in Richard Kennington, ed., *The Philosophy of Immanuel Kant*, Washington, DC, Catholic University of America Press, 1985, 161–84; Paul Crowther, *The Kantian Sublime*, Oxford, Oxford University Press, 1989, 7–18; and Melissa Merritt, *The Sublime*, Cambridge, Cambridge University Press, 2018, 11–27.

3 Jane Kneller, *Kant and the Power of the Imagination*, Cambridge, Cambridge University Press, 2007, 20–37; Emily Brady, *The Sublime in Modern Philosophy*, Cambridge, Cambridge University Press, 2013, 90–114; and Karl Ameriks, 'Hölderlin's Path: On Sustaining Romanticism from Kant to Nietzsche', in Elizabeth Millán Brusslan and Judith Norman, eds., *Brill's Companion to German Romantic Philosophy*, Leiden, Brill, 2019, 258–79.

4 See Rudolf A. Makkreel, *Imagination and Interpretation in Kant*, Chicago, University of Chicago Press, 1990, esp. 67–107; and the 'philosophical chapters' (5–13) of Samuel Taylor Coleridge, *Biographia Literaria*, London, 1817.

5 See William Wordsworth, *The Sublime and the Beautiful*, in W. J. B. Owen and Jane Washington Smyser, eds., *The Prose Works of William Wordsworth*, 3 vols., Oxford, Clarendon Press, 1974, vol. 3, 349–60.

6 Jacques Derrida, *The Truth in Painting*, trans. Geoff Bennington and Ian McLeod, Chicago, University of Chicago Press, 1987, 43–4.

7 See *Enquiry* II i; and Joseph Addison, *The Spectator*, ed. Donald F. Bond, 5 vols., Oxford, Clarendon Press, 1965, vol. 3, 540 (essay no. 412).

8 On the former, see Paul Guyer, 'The Beautiful and the Sublime', in Paul Guyer, *Kant and the Experience of Freedom*, Cambridge, Cambridge University Press, 1993, 203–5, 211–14, and, on the latter, Malcom Budd, 'The Sublime in Nature', in Paul Guyer, ed., *Kant's Critique of the Power of Judgment: Critical Essays*, Lanham, MD, Rowman & Littlefield, 134.

9 On Kant's view of pleasure as a 'disposition' to continue in a certain state of mind, see Paul Guyer, 'What Is It Like to Experience the Beautiful and Sublime?', in Kelly Sorensen and Diane Williamson, eds., *Kant and the Faculty of Feeling*, Cambridge, Cambridge University Press, 2018, 147–65.

10 See Brady, *The Sublime*, 67–89; Katerina Deligiorgi, 'How to Feel a Judgment: The Sublime and Its Architectonic Significance', in Sorensen and Williamson, eds., *Kant*, 166–83; and Merritt, *The Sublime*, 7–11.

11 For a defense of this view, see Melissa M. Merritt, 'The Moral Source of the Kantian Sublime', in Timothy M. Costelloe, ed., *The Sublime: From Antiquity to the Present*, Cambridge, Cambridge University Press, 2012, 37–49, and Merritt, *The Sublime*, passim.

12 Jean-François Lyotard, *Lessons on the Analytic of the Sublime*, trans. Elizabeth Rottenberg, Stanford, CA, Stanford University Press, 1994, 231, 225.

13 Hannah Arendt, *Lectures on Kant's Political Philosophy*, ed. Ronald Beiner, Chicago, University of Chicago Press, 1982, 9.

14 Ibid., 67–8, emphases added.

15 Ibid., 70–1.

16 Edward Bullough, '"Psychical Distance" as a Factor in Art and as an Aesthetic Principle', *British Journal of Psychology* 5, 2 (1912), 87–117.

17 See Lyotard, *Lessons*, 232–3.

18 See Deligiorgi, 'How to Feel', 176–9.

19 See the discussion in Robert Clewis, *The Kantian Sublime and the Revelation of Freedom*, Cambridge, Cambridge University Press, 2009, 116–25.

20 Crowther, *Kantian Sublime*, 152–74. See also Brady, *The Sublime*, 64–6 and 117–47.

21 I would like to thank Rachel Zuckert for valuable comments on an earlier draft of this chapter.

7

PATRICK VINCENT

Alpine Sublimes

The Alpine sublime contributed to the Romantic vogue for mountains and for mountaineering, but also to the development of modern aesthetics and subjectivity.[1] As with the sublime in general, the Alpine sublime varied depending on one's class and gender; the discourses, genres, or art forms though which it was mediated; and whether it was experienced from the summit or from below. This chapter can only provide a selective overview of the many aesthetic, scientific, and literary texts that address the Alps, briefly touching on more ephemeral documents such as travel journals, visitors' books, and visual media. Proceeding chronologically, it argues that the Alpine sublime served as an expression of authority and, conversely, of moral, political, and creative autonomy, but also, more prosaically, as a form of social distinction.

The Alps and the Enlightenment

In a letter to his mother describing his 1739 horseback ride with Horace Walpole along the winding mountain road leading to the convent of the Grande Chartreuse, Thomas Gray recounts that it was 'one of the most solemn, the most romantic, and the most astonishing scenes I ever beheld', drawing on the new diction of the sublime to describe their terrifying ascent into the clouds.[2] In his own account, however, Walpole transforms the same experience into something closer to parody: 'Precipices, mountains, torrents, wolves, rumblings, Salvator Rosa ... Here we are, the lonely lords of glorious desolate prospects!'[3] In a lilting rhythm that reproduces their feeling of dizziness, the author deploys the sublime as a marker of upper-class taste, playing on the popularity of Rosa's gloomy landscapes and anticipating the frequent recourse to Alpine scenery in the Gothic novels of Ann Radcliffe and others that he would himself initiate.

Walpole's outburst indicates how fashionable, if not formulaic, the association between the sublime and the Alps was fast becoming in eighteenth-century culture. Starting with Joseph Addison, aesthetic theory and travel writing both began linking mountain scenery with the 'pleasures of the imagination'.[4] Although Edmund Burke never mentions the Alps in *Enquiry*, for example, his chapter on 'Vastness' (II vii) makes it clear that the experience of mountains, in the form of rough, perpendicular masses and the sensation of depth, are eminently suited to produce a strong physiological effect. For theoreticians of the Picturesque, the Alps' irregular forms and pointed summits were viewed as 'objects of singularity rather than beauty'.[5] By the time William Coxe published his popular *Sketches of the Natural, Civil, and Political State of Switzerland* (1779), 'sublime' had become the stock epithet to describe the Alps: not known to be an original writer, Coxe uses it twenty-one times. Even Kant, who never set eyes on the Alps, relies on them to argue his case in 'Analytic of the Sublime' (1790), notably when explaining the dynamically sublime as 'Bold, overhanging, as it were, threatening cliffs' viewed from a position of 'safety' (*COPJ* §28 261), when citing the 'Savoyard peasant' to demonstrate that culture is necessary to experience the natural sublime (*COPJ* §29 265), or when concluding that the 'astonishment bordering on terror' felt when observing 'mountain ranges towering to the heavens' makes us feel our imagination's power and 'assert our independence in the face of the influences of nature' (*COPJ* §29 269). For Kant, mountains are the ideal emblem of a chastening power (stemming from God, Nature, or Monarchy) that human subjects must imaginatively overcome to become aware of their moral freedom.

To understand the conventional nature of the Alpine sublime, one may compare Kant's description of mountains with that of Lady Mary Wortley Montagu. Reaching the top of Mont Cenis in September 1718, she anticipates and implicitly invalidates Kant's notion of aesthetic disinterestedness: 'The prodigious prospect of mountains covered with eternal snow, of clouds hanging far below our feet, and of vast cascades tumbling down the rocks with a confused roaring, would have been entertaining to me, if I had suffer'd less from the extreme cold that reigns here.'[6] Lady Montagu's account reminds us that aesthetic conventions were not just artificial but also gendered, and that if women were just as capable as men of deploying the new discourse of the sublime, many chose not to.[7] The few who did, including Margaret Cavendish Spencer in 1763, Lady Anna Riggs Miller in 1770, and Hester Lynch Piozzi in 1784, often paid more attention than their male counterparts to the material conditions of travel, offering versions of the sublime that are closer to Burke's physiological than to Kant's disembodied aesthetics. By century's end, some writers were even satirizing the sublime, a sure sign that it had become overly fashionable. In 'A Tour to the Glaciers of Savoy' (1796), for example, Esther Milnes Day gives a comic account of the uncomfortable travelling conditions in Chamonix, which impact her enjoyment of the scenery: 'Yet though 'twas enchantingly fine, / *Très superbe, magnifique*, the rude murmur, / Still the part I thought nearest divine, / Was when my feet touched *terra firma*.'[8]

The Alpine sublime did not limit itself to philosophical aesthetics or picturesque tourism. Indeed, the Enlightenment was primarily interested in mountains for scientific purposes. Yet its emphasis on vision and development of new optical technologies, such as the camera obscura, panorama, and relief model, allowed for aesthetic as well as empirical observations. In *Voyages dans les Alpes* (1779–96), for instance, the century's most authoritative publication on the Alps and a source for Kant, Horace Bénédict de Saussure describes his experiences of the sublime in various places, including on the summit of Mont Blanc, which he reached in 1787. There he expresses his satisfaction at dominating the surrounding peaks and being able to understand their structure in one glance, yet remains more concerned with his scientific experiments than with the view.[9]

Many writers, artists, and simple tourists also presented their aesthetic experiences in the Alps as something supplemental to their scientific interests. Goethe, who visited three times in 1775, 1779, and 1797, left several sublime descriptions, notably at the Furka Pass, as well as detailed renderings of geological formations and of the effect of light, both of which informed his later scientific writings.[10] Crossing the St Gotthard Pass in 1793, Georgiana, Duchess of Devonshire, wrote in a letter-journal to her mother that 'our expectations of Grandeur & horror were alone justified', but was more interested in collecting crystal specimens, studying Pfyffer's relief map of central Switzerland (qualified as sublime by Coxe), and walking on the Bernese glaciers, all of which inform her didactic poem, 'The Passage of the Mountain of St Gothard' (1799).[11] Glaciers were a particular source of fascination during the eighteenth century. In 1741, William Windham and Richard Pococke had conducted the first organized ascent to Chamonix's Mer de Glace. In his *Account of the Glaciers or Ice Alps of Savoy* (1744), Windham evokes his 'Pleasure of beholding Objects of an extraordinary Nature' and his inability to describe them, a typical trope of the sublime, yet his curiosity outweighs any feeling of terror.[12]

By the time Alsatian writer and geologist Louis Ramond de Carbonnières published his own 'Observations of the Glacieres and the Glaciers' in his 1781 French translation of Coxe's *Sketches*, several natural historians, including Albrecht von Haller, Jean-André Deluc, and Saussure, had made significant progress in explaining their mysteries, and hundreds of visitors began exploring the valleys of Grindelwald and Chamonix each summer, among them the painters Caspar Wolf, William Pars, and John Robert

Cozens in the 1770s and 1780s, and J. M. W. Turner in 1802. Combining the traditional view of the Alps as a figure of God's grandeur with their more modern identification with imaginative power, Ramond first describes a bird's-eye view of the mountains, then the 'enormous masses of ice' coming down like 'ruins' into the cornfields, a vivid contrast that allows the 'Imagination' to 'catche[s] a glimpse of the image of eternity, which she hails with religious terror'.[13] The passage is inspired as much by Jean-Jacques Rousseau as by a peak in the Little Ice Age, explaining why Ramond and his contemporaries believed glaciers to be inexorably expanding, despite Saussure's claim to the contrary.

With the advent of the French Revolution, itself often represented as sublime, glaciers and the Alps in general became powerful political metaphors. Early Modern writers had begun mythologizing the descendants of William Tell as hard working, virtuous, and free.[14] Haller's *Die Alpen* (1732) contributed to this myth by idealizing a Golden Age still surviving high up in the Alps, as did a number of British writers. Personifying liberty in his eponymous Whig progress poem, for example, James Thomson makes it halt in Switzerland, where 'The mountains then, clad with eternal snow, / Confessed my power.'[15] Many other mid-eighteenth-century British poets, including Collins, Keate, and Goldsmith, similarly identified the Alps with classical republicanism. It was Rousseau, however, who most successfully disseminated the Alpine myth around Europe. His 'Letter on the Valais', in *Julie, or the New Heloise* (1761; Book I, Letter XXIII), not only describes the experience of ascending a mountain, but also idealizes the happy, virtuous community that lives there. Likewise, Rousseau's account of a popular assembly in the Alps in *The Social Contract* (1762: Book IV, Chapter I) served as a model for democratic republicanism. Drawing on both Ramond and Rousseau, William Wordsworth could thus depict a Swiss mountain shepherd, in his early *Descriptive Sketches* (1793), who 'marches with his flute, his book, and sword', and whose 'eye sublime, and surly lion-grace' mark him out as a true republican (lines 530–5).

The appropriation of the Alpine sublime in the iconography of the French Revolution led to an ideological struggle over mountains' political and religious significance. In 1793, revolutionary troops annexed Savoy and transformed it into the department of Mont-Blanc. That same year, Robespierre and the most radical faction of the French national assembly, known as the *Montagne*, seized power and started usurping Rousseau and the Alps in the name of the Revolution. In the civic festivals inspired by the Genevan philosopher, artificial mountains were erected and celebrated as symbols of liberty, but also of a rational God. Paradoxically, the spiritual significance of the Alps did not just survive the Revolution but arguably grew stronger, both augmenting and adding a newly politicized inflection to accounts of the relationship between religion and sublime experience already developed in eighteenth-century Anglophone and German philosophical aesthetics. In texts such as Coleridge's 'Hymn before Sunrise, in the Vale of Chamouni' (1802), for instance, mountains served as expressions not just of Christian piety but also of political legitimacy as both poets and tourists admired the peaks from below.[16]

The Alps and Romanticism

In *The Prelude* (1805), Wordsworth registers the French Revolution's usurpation of the Alpine sublime as well as his own and Coleridge's turn away from their former radicalism when he laments that 'the lordly Alps themselves' are no longer the 'gladsome image' they used to be, and that 'Freedom now / Stands single' in Great Britain (Book X, lines 990, 994, 981–2). From the beginning, Wordsworth had associated mountains with both political and creative freedom, theorizing the mountain sublime as the effect of three component parts: individual form, duration, and power.[17] Yet if the Alps after 1800 continued to exert a liberating power, that liberty was now more private than public. Friedrich Schiller's historical drama *Wilhelm Tell* (1804), for example, celebrates the Alps as a bastion of Christian faith and heroic resistance rather than of democracy. Likewise, Germaine de Staël's account of an alpine festival in *De l'Allemagne* (1810) imagines the living and the dead forming an organic community that corresponds more closely to Burke's 'little platoon' than to Rousseau's social contract.[18] It was Napoleon's crossing of the Great St. Bernard Pass in May 1800, however, that most immediately transformed the Alps' symbolism, linking the mountain chain with the French ruler's outsized ambition.

Composed between 1799 and 1804, the Simplon Pass episode in Book VI of *The Prelude* transforms what William Wordsworth conventionally called 'the more awful scenes of the Alps' during his 1790 tour into a secular epiphany, but also, as some have argued, into a form of political retreat. In the critical tradition of A. C. Bradley, influential readings by Geoffrey Hartman and Thomas Weiskel, among others, have interpreted the apostrophe to the imagination as an idealist set piece mirroring the Kantian model of the sublime.[19] An initial blockage ('I was lost as in a cloud, / Halted without a struggle to break through') is compensated by the speaker's intimation of an 'invisible world', leading to a triumphant self-vindication when the poet-speaker recognizes that the sublime lies in his own mind: 'Our destiny, our nature, and our home, / Is with infinitude – and only there' (Book VI, lines 525–48). Since Alan Liu's groundbreaking historicist study, on the other hand, critics have also understood this passage of the poem as the product of the Alps' shifting historical and political representations, and viewed the poem's idealism as paradigmatic of what both Liu and Jerome McGann consider Romantic ideological praxis. Arguing that the apostrophe to the imagination relies on diction associated with the Napoleonic wars ('struggle', 'usurpation', 'banners militant', 'spoils', 'Nile'), Liu claims that Wordsworth seeks to conceal and displace history in order to assert his imaginative ascendancy over Bonaparte.[20]

What is striking is how the Simplon episode relies on a wholly conventional description of the pass and on well-established associations with Napoleon to make the case for the poet's primacy. Beginning with John Evelyn in 1646, the Gondo ravine in particular had awed travellers with what Heinrich Reichard in 1785 described as its 'deepest precipices', 'impetuous torrents', and 'crosses and chapels': the pioneer German guidebook writer recommends it to all those 'who like Rousseau love to contemplate the dizzy heights.'[21] Unsurprisingly, travellers' accounts of the Simplon's strongly contrasted scenery closely resemble Rousseau's fictional 'Letter on the Valais', as does Wordsworth's splendid Miltonic depiction of Gondo's 'narrow chasm', first published separately as 'The Simplon Pass' in 1844 (Book VI, line 553). A carefully equipoised assemblage of contraries that expresses the imagination's attempt to unite mind and nature, the passage leads to the by then commonplace analogy between the Alps and God (Book VI, lines 565–72).

Wordsworth and his companion had failed to 'contemplate the dizzy heights' when facing the Mont Blanc two days earlier, explaining their desire to reach what Hansen calls a 'summit position', and their intense disappointment upon realizing 'that we had crossed the Alps' (Book VI, line 525).[22] Whereas idealist critics interpret this moment of bathos and the epiphany it triggers as a form of Kantian negative transcendence, the passage may equally be read as a response to the more material instantiations of the sublime in travelogues and in Rousseau, as Cian Duffy has noted (*Landscapes*, 34, 66–7). The fact that some French troops crossed the pass in 1800 and that Bonaparte's road over the Simplon was completed in 1805 suggests furthermore that Wordsworth was not trying to conceal history when writing about the Simplon. Indeed, the pass very quickly came to be seen by tourists as a 'noble monument of Napoleon's genius and enterprise', and the poet continued to struggle with its Bonapartist associations when he returned to the Alps in 1820.[23]

The Romantic fashion for the sublime, together with the end of hostilities and new travel infrastructure, including steamboats and the Simplon road, abetted a post-Napoleonic rush on the Alps. Many prominent British poets toured Switzerland during this period: Samuel Rogers left a journal account of the Simplon very similar to Wordsworth's, then transformed it into a historical set piece in *Italy* (1822).[24] Robert Southey expressed his preference in his journal for the Lake District over the Alps, by then a commonplace comparison.[25] And Thomas Moore claimed with feigned horror in 'Rhymes on the Road' (1823) that all of London would soon be seeking the sublime on the Simplon.[26] Fiction writers also met the new demand for vicarious sublimity, following the seminal example of Rousseau's *Julie* by casting the Alps as a setting for sentimental or gothic romances.[27] The best known of such novels, Mary Shelley's *Frankenstein* (1818), came into existence during the legendary Geneva summer of 1816, which, because of the Tambora eruption a year earlier, was particularly cold and rainy, making the glaciers appear more threatening than ever.

In *History of a Six Weeks' Tour* (1817), Percy and Mary Shelley combine the journal account of their ill-planned elopement to Switzerland in 1814 with four letters describing their second visit in 1816, including Percy Shelley's and Lord Byron's week-long Rousseau pilgrimage around Lake Geneva, and the Shelleys' four-day tour of Chamonix, closing the volume with one of the Romantic period's most familiar poems about the Alpine sublime: 'Mont Blanc, Lines Written in the Vale of Chamouni'. Both Byron and Shelley hated to be mistaken for tourists, whom they saw as corrupting local manners, profaning the landscape, and disturbing their sense of class distinction.[28] Unlike their idealized accounts, Mary's journal provides a more honest testimony, stating for example that they were at the Mer de Glace with 'Beaucoup de Monde'.[29] Yet she transforms this same glacier into the 'sublime and magnificent' setting for her novel's second volume, in which 'the presence of another would destroy the solitary grandeur of the scene', and where Victor encounters his Creature at the very height of his experience of the sublime and transcendence of his sorrows.[30] For Mary Shelley, the Alpine sublime is a figure of Romantic selfishness and solipsism, but also of revolutionary politics, generating a vengeful Creature implicitly identified with Rousseau and the angry *peuple*.[31]

Mary Shelley's distaste for revolutionary violence may explain why her journal remains silent regarding her husband's much commented inscriptions of 'democrat', 'philanthropist', and 'atheist' in Chamonix's visitors' books.[32] Here and in his poem 'Mont Blanc', begun in Chamonix, Percy Shelley was reasserting the sublime as a progressive Enlightenment trope rather than as the pious expression of divine order. After the Restoration, there was a deliberate effort in Chamonix and elsewhere to re-sacralize the Alps, exemplified in Coleridge's 'Hymn', and conventional examples of the religious sublime filled visitors' albums and travelogues. 'Mont Blanc' draws a complex analogy between an Alpine ravine and the human mind to argue for a radically materialistic and deterministic understanding of causality. The mountain, with its river flowing from its icy depths and seemingly merging with the speaker-viewer's own mind, is a powerful reminder that the 'secret strength of things', or philosophical necessity, 'governs thought' (lines 139–40).

The poem's last two lines, which question what the world would be without the imagination, have often been read as evidence of a tension between a materialist and an idealist ontology, which many critics interpreting the ending see as Shelley's tentative reassertion of the mind's transcendental primacy. Yet the poem's alien, apocalyptic images of hideously shaped glaciers wreaking havoc on the living world also point to a different interpretation. Combining James Hutton's politically radical uniformitarian theory of a self-regulating earth with the more catastrophist, but also religiously orthodox diluvialist theories popular during the Restoration, the poem suggests that the world will necessarily be revolutionized and cleansed of its 'Large codes of fraud and woe' without man's agency (lines 69–75, 105–26, 81).[33] This is the 'faith so mild' that the 'voice' of the mountain teaches: it allows us to be reconciled with nature without resorting to any supernatural myths (line 77). If the speaker believes that only 'the wise and great and good' can interpret mountains, justifying the Shelleyan poet-legislator, his is nevertheless a far more radically naturalistic and democratic version of the Alpine sublime than that found in most Romantic-period texts (lines 83–4).

It was not Shelley's philosophically challenging 'Mont Blanc' but the Second Spirit's lines on the 'monarch of the mountains' in Byron's *Manfred* (1817) that came to define the Alpine sublime in nineteenth-century popular culture (Act 1, scene 1, line 60). According to Duffy, the Alps' highest summit was commonly represented after the French Revolution 'as the image of an ideal monarchy', and we find the same regal imagery in Canto III of *Childe Harold's Pilgrimage* (1816), which casts the Alps as 'palaces of Nature, whose vast walls / Have ... throned Eternity in icy halls / Of cold sublimity' (lines 591–6). Despite the Alps' aristocratic distance, however, Byron also celebrates Swiss republicanism, eulogizing the battlefield of Morat, a favorite Whig topos, as a way to criticize the Bourbon Restoration (stanzas 64–5). Paying homage to Rousseau, he then relies on the same violent imagery of ruins drawn, as in Shelley's 'Mont Blanc', from Volney's politically radical *Les ruines* (1791), to prophesy another revolution (stanzas 77–84).

Byron's *Alpine Journal* to Augusta, which provided the poet with the principal scenes for *Manfred*, begins with a more embodied, less threatening version of the sublime: scrambling to the summit of the Dent de Jaman, then tumbling back down, he experiences an intense sense of unity with his fellow travellers, with the surrounding scenery and even with the mules, one that paradoxically 'repeopled my mind with Nature'.[34] This leads him to again endorse the myth of the Alps as a pastoral republic, as he does in *Manfred* through the figure of the Chamois Hunter. The climax of Byron's tour, however, is the summiting of the Lauberhorn, which he would later make the setting for Manfred's soliloquy upon the cliffs before the Jungfrau – an episode that, like Wordsworth's 'Simplon Pass' and Shelley's 'Mont Blanc', has become iconic of the Romantic sublime.

In the passage, the setting for which matches closely Byron's account in his Alpine journal, Manfred, renouncing all 'super-human aid' and staring down, like Milton's Satan on Mount Niphates, into the 'dizziness of distance' below, is tempted to leap yet is stopped by a 'power' that 'makes it my fatality to live' (Act 1, scene 2, lines 4, 16, 23–4). Unlike Wordsworth, Manfred regrets that the imagination separates him from nature, leading to a negative epiphany (Act 1, scene 2, lines 36–45). Manfred's soliloquy reminds us that we are divided between our desire to view the world both from above and below, that humans are at the same time autonomous, transcendent individuals and the subjects of a sovereign far more powerful than them. Like the poem as a whole, the passage thus depicts the human condition as one of tragic solitude. That such a bleak conclusion emanates from a distinctly male, classist, and heavily romanticized perspective is made clear when we compare Byron's account of the ascent with that of his companion John Cam Hobhouse. In his journal, the latter regrets that their experience was 'somewhat infringed by the apparition of two or 3 females on horseback just as we were congratulating ourselves on the superior solitariness of these scenes to Chamouny'.[35]

Repeated ad infinitum in guides, travelogues, and visitors' books, Byron's poems on the Alps also had an impact on late Romantic texts, including Felicia Hemans's 'The League of the Alps' (1823), composed like *Childe Harold* in Spenserian stanzas, and Walter Scott's *Anne of Geierstein* (1829), which opens with an epigraph from *Manfred*.[36] While both writers also draw on the Alpine myth, their interpretation of Alpine liberty is more conservative than Byron's. In the many relief models, dioramas, and panoramas of the Alps that Londoners could vicariously experience for a shilling during the 1820s and 1830s, the sublime was likewise emptied of much of its political and even religious power. These visual representations culminated in the writer and impresario Albert Smith's *The Ascent of Mont Blanc*, which ran from 1851 to 1859, drawing almost a million spectators.[37] In *The Way of All Flesh* (1903), George Pontifex experiences a 'fit of conventional ecstasy' in front of Mont Blanc, encapsulating its diminished cultural capital by the end of the century.[38] Like Smith's show, the thousands of Victorian tourists who flocked to the Alps transformed them into a spectacle for mass consumption, 'sinking' the Romantic sublime, as Ann Colley puts it, under the weight of cockneyfication, commodification, and sheer familiarity.[39]

John Ruskin, who insisted on viewing the Alps from below, blames these *déclassé* visitors, including members of the new Alpine Club, for desacralizing the Alps: 'You have made race-courses of the cathedrals of the earth.'[40] Yet while one historian has shown that the term 'sublime' was no longer used by climbers by 1900, another has argued that, as in previous centuries, they simply adapted its discourse to new circumstances, taking into account the physical experience of mountain travel.[41] Less worried than the Romantic poets with being original, or reaching the summit, tourists for their part continued, and still continue, to express their awe of Alpine scenery from below, filling albums with comments, verses, and sketches on the grandeur of God or simply of the view. As one Briton jotted down excitedly in 1852 upon discovering the Mont Blanc, 'It beats the great Exhibition!!!!!!!!!!' – thereby pointing both to the diminished status of the Alpine sublime and to its continued significance as a figure of human empowerment.[42]

NOTES

1 See, for example, Simon Bainbridge, *Mountaineering and British Romanticism*, Oxford, Oxford University Press, 2020; Peter H. Hansen, *Summits of Modern Man*, Cambridge, MA, Harvard University Press, 2013; and Charles Taylor, *Sources of the Self*, Cambridge, MA, Harvard University Press, 1989, chapters 20 and 21.

2 Thomas Gray, letter of 13 October 1739 to Mrs Gray, quoted from *Correspondence of Thomas Gray*, 3 vols., ed. Paget Toynbee and Leonard Whibley, Oxford, Oxford University Press, 1935, vol. 1, 121–3.

3 Horace Walpole, letter of 28 September 1739 to Thomas West, quoted from *Yale Edition of Horace Walpole's Correspondence*, 48 vols., gen. ed. W. S. Lewis, New Haven, CT, Yale University Press, 1937–83, vol. 13, 181.

4 Joseph Addison, 'The Pleasures of the Imagination (*Spectator* 412 and 416)', quoted in Walter Jackson Bate, ed., *Criticism: The Major Texts*, San Diego, CA, Harper Brace Jovanovich, 1970, 184, and *Remarks on Several Parts of Italy, Etc. in the Years 1701, 1702, 1703*, London, 1711, 260–1.

5 William Gilpin, *Observations in Cumberland and Westmoreland*, Poole, Woodstock Reprints, 1996 [1786], vol. 1, 83.

6 Lady Mary Wortley Montagu, *Letters of the Right Honourable Lady M...y W...y M...u*, 3 vols., London, 1767, vol. 3, 53–4.

7 See Elizabeth Bohls, *Women Travel Writers and the Language of Aesthetics, 1716–1818*, Cambridge, Cambridge University Press, 1995, 2, 15.

8 Eliza, 'A Tour to the Glaciers of Savoy', in Roger Lonsdale, ed., *Eighteenth Century Women Poets*, Oxford, Oxford University Press, 1989, 498.

9 Horace-Bénédict de Saussure, *Voyages dans les Alpes*, 4 vols., Neuchâtel, 177–96, vol. 4, 146–8.

10 Johann Wolfgang Goethe, *Goethe en Suisse et dans les Alpes*, ed. Christine Chiadò Rana, Geneva, Georg, 2003, 95–6.

11 Chatsworth House, Devonshire ms. CS5/1165–7: Letters of the Duchess of Devonshire to Countess Spencer, 13–17 August 1793.

12 [William Windham], *An Account of the glacieres or ice Alps in Savoy*, London, 1744, 5–10.

13 Louis François Ramond de Carbonnières, 'Observations on the Glacieres and the Glaciers', in Helen Maria Williams, *A Tour in Switzerland*, 2 vols., London, 1798, vol. 2, 351.

14 See Patrick Vincent, *Romanticism, Republicanism, and the Swiss Myth*, Cambridge, Cambridge University Press, 2023, chapter 1.

15 James Thomson, 'Liberty' (1734), IV, lines 322–3; quoted from *Poetical Works*, ed. J. Logie Robertson, Oxford, Oxford University Press, 1971, 366–7.

16 On the significance of the viewpoint, see Hansen, *Summits*, 128–36, and *Landscapes*, 46–50.

17 William Wordsworth, 'The Sublime and the Beautiful', in W. J. B. Owen and Jane Worthington Smyser, eds., *The Prose Works of William Wordsworth*, 3 vols., Oxford, Clarendon, 1974, vol. 2, 349–60.

18 Edmund Burke, *Reflections on the Revolution in France*, Oxford, Oxford World's Classics, 1993, 47, and Germaine de Staël, *Germany*, translated from the French, 3 vols., London, John Murray, 1813, vol. 1, 201–10.

19 See Geoffrey Hartman, *Wordsworth's Poetry 1787–1814*, New Haven, CT, Yale University Press, 1964, 33–69, and *Weiskel*, 200–2.

20 See Alan Liu, *Wordsworth: The Sense of History*, Stanford, CA, Stanford University Press, 1988, 3–31.

21 Heinrich Reichard, *Guide des voyageurs en Europe*, Paris, 1793, 407–8; translated in Henry Coxe, *The Travellers' Guide in Switzerland*, London, 1816, 65.

22 See Hansen, *Summits*, 16–17.

23 Marianne Baillie, *First Impressions of a Tour Upon the Continent in the Summer of 1818*, London, 1819, 216–17, and William Wordsworth, 'The Column Intended by Buonaparte,' in *Sonnet Series and Itinerary Poems, 1820–1845*, ed. Geoffrey Jackson, Ithaca, NY, Cornell University Press, 2004, 387–8.

24 Samuel Rogers, *The Italian Journal of Samuel Rogers*, ed. J. R. Hale, London, Faber and Faber, 1956, 159–61, and *Italy, a Poem*, London, 1830, 29–30.

25 Robert Southey, 'Southey's Journey through France, Italy, & Switzerland 1817', Keswick Museum KESMG 289, 401–3.

26 Thomas Moore, *Fables from the Holy Alliance, Rhymes on the Road, Etc.*, London, 1823, 101.

27 See, for example, Mrs. E. M. Forster, *Emily of Lucerne*, London, 1800; Anne Ormsby, *Memoirs of a Family in Swisserland*, London, 1802; and Charlotte Anne Eaton, *Continental Adventures*, London, 1826.

28 See, for example, Mary and Percy Shelley, *History of a Six Weeks' Tour*, London, 1817, 162–3, 170–1, and Lord Byron, *Byron's Letters and Journals*, ed. Leslie Marchand, 12 vols., London, John Murray, 1976–81, vol. 5, 97.

29 See *The Journals of Mary Shelley 1814–1844*, ed. Paula R. Feldman and Diana Scott-Kilvert, Baltimore, MD, Johns Hopkins University Press, 1987, 112–21.

30 Mary Shelley, *Frankenstein: 1818 Text*, ed. Marilyn Butler, Oxford, Oxford World's Classics, 1993, 75–7.

31 See Chris Baldick, 'The Politics of Monstrosity', in Fred Botting, ed., *Frankenstein: New Casebooks*, London, Macmillan, 1995, 48–57.

32 See Gavin de Beer, 'An "Atheist" in the Alps', *Keats-Shelley Memorial Bulletin*, 9, 1958, 1–15.

33 See Nigel Leask, 'Mont Blanc's Mysterious Voice: Shelley and Huttonian Earth Science', in Elinor Schaffer, ed., *The Third Culture: Literature and Science*, Berlin, De Gruyter, 1998, 182–203; Noah Heringman, *Romantic Rocks, Aesthetic Geology*, Ithaca, NY, Cornell University Press, 2004, 68–88; and Cian Duffy, *Shelley and the Revolutionary Sublime*, Cambridge, Cambridge University Press, 2005, chapter 3.

34 See *Byron's Letters and Journals*, vol. 5, 99–100.

35 John Cam Hobhouse, 'Byron in the Alps: The Journal of John Cam Hobhouse 17–29 September 1816', in John Clubbe and Ernest Giddey, eds., *Byron et la Suisse: Deux études*, Geneva, Droz, 1982, 52.

36 See, for example, Musée Alpin, Chamonix, Livre d'or de la Croix de la Flégère. 1832–55. 2015. 0. 633, entries of 24 July 1834 and 21 July 1853.

37 See Alan Macnee, *The Cockney Who Sold the Alps: Albert Smith and the Ascent of Mont Blanc*, London, Victorian Secrets, 2015.

38 Samuel Butler, *The Way of All Flesh*, ed. James Cochrane, Harmondsworth, Penguin, 1986, 45.

39 See Ann C. Colley, *Victorians in the Mountains: Sinking the Sublime*, New York, Macmillan, 2010, 3.

40 John Ruskin, 'Sesame and Lilies', quoted from *The Works of John Ruskin*, ed. Edward Tyas Cook and Alexander Wedderburn, 39 vols., Cambridge, Cambridge University Press, 1905; reprinted 2010, vol. 18, 89.

41 See Jon Mathieu and P. Gutknecht, '"Erhabene Berge": Eine korpuslinguistiche Studie zu den Periodika das Schweizer Alpenclubs 1864 bis 2014', *Gesiscchte der Alpen* 25 (2020), 215–33; and Alan McNee, 'The Haptic Sublime and the "cold stony reality" of Mountaineering', *Interdisciplinary Studies in the Long Nineteenth Century*, 19; https://doi.org/10.16995/ntn.697.

42 Musée Alpin, Chamonix, Livre d'or de la Croix de la Flégère. 1832–1855. 2015. 0. 633, entry for 30 June 1852.

8

MATTHEW SANGSTER

Urban Sublimes

Thomas Weiskel opens his study of the Romantic sublime by asserting that '[t]he essential claim of the sublime is that man can, in feeling and in speech, transcend the human' (*Weiskel*, 3). If we accept for a moment this definition, we can see immediately why cities might present a problem for Romantic artists in search of sublime experiences, even though influential theorists like Edmund Burke and Immanuel Kant cite urban architectures as instances of manmade sublimity. Cities are, by definition, human environments. Consequently, the mode John Keats characterized as the 'wordsworthian or egotistical sublime', which privileges the unique focalizing consciousness of the artist, initially struggled to find its footing amidst urban profusion.[1] In the early nineteenth century, poets often painted cities in general – and the unprecedented million-person metropolis of London in particular – as places within which it was difficult or impossible to access genuinely transcendent intimations. In 'Composed Upon Westminster Bridge' (1802), London appeared wondrous to William Wordsworth in the calm 'beauty of the morning', but the crowds and sights of the waking, bustling capital overwhelmed him in manners he figured as dulling and attenuating (line 5). In the 'Preface' to *Lyrical Ballads* (1802), he bemoaned the 'encreasing accumulation of men in cities', which he argued reduced thoughts to 'a state of almost savage torpor' (*Wordsworth*, 599). When he conjures London as a 'monstrous ant-hill on the plain / Of a too busy world' in the 1850 version of *The Prelude*, there is a form of sublimity in play, but it functions as a crushing force rather than a liberating one (Book VII, lines 149–50). Rather than being a place where a poet might reach beyond the human, London, in Wordsworth's conception, seems actively to foreclose that possibility.

In Wordsworth's writings, urban scenes almost inevitably end up as scenes of disappointment and disaffection. Post-Revolution Paris failed to live up to his great expectations:

Where silent zephyrs sported with the dust
Of the Bastille I sate in the open sun,
And from the rubbish gathered up a stone
And pocketed the relick in the guise
Of an Enthusiast; yet, in honest truth
Though not without some strong incumbences,
And glad, (could living man be otherwise?)
I looked for something that I could not find,
Affecting more emotion than I felt.   (Book IX, lines 63–71)

Fired by the prospect of a great change, Wordsworth was looking for a material correlative he could use to focalize his hopes, but the Bastille's ruins failed to provide him with the reassurance he needed. Weiskel writes that 'Wordsworth was among the first to register a disturbed awareness of urban alienation', and for Wordsworth, this awareness manifested as a feeling of lack, often expressed through what Neil Hertz helpfully characterizes as 'moment[s] of blockage' (*Weiskel*, 36; *Hertz*, 44). Later poets have found transcendent visions through being slightly out of step with the city, but for Wordsworth, breaking through urban suppression required either focusing in – as with the Blind Beggar episode Hertz discusses – or casting out to elsewhere, as when the lovely child he saw in the 'dissolute' and 'shameless' Sadler's Wells crowd appeared to him as 'a Cottage rose' (Book VII, lines 380, 387, 377; see *Hertz*, 58–60). Weiskel rightly believes that in the narratives Wordsworth spins 'the sublime enters to rescue – but not, unfortunately, to cure – an estranged mind in an alien city' (*Weiskel*, 36). In Anne Janowitz's terms, for Wordsworth, 'the urban scene works as a sort of black hole or anti-matter of the natural sublime' – if we might read a form of dislocating sublimity in his urban visions, it is a negative one defined by feeling 'menaced by the incoherence of all the things and buildings that people have made'.[2] Like Amy Lowell looking up at the 'thin and lustreless' moon she loves from her 'squalid and sinister' metropolitan environs, and like T. S. Eliot in *The Waste Land* (1922) attempting to reach beyond 'Unreal' cities, Wordsworth's poetry manifests a form of artistic consciousness that when immured in urban modernity expresses a profound need to think and feel its way out.[3]

Condemning the City

Wordsworth's anti-urban impulses were not universal among British Romantic-period versifiers, but they were relatively common. His fellow Lake Poets displayed a similar scepticism regarding the potential for genuine transcendental experiences in metropolitan environments. In *The Watchman*, Samuel Taylor Coleridge bemoaned the prospects of those 'pent up in corrupt, and corrupting towns', and when, in 'This Lime-Tree Bower My Prison' (1797), he imagined his friend Charles Lamb walking in the Quantocks, he conceived of this experience as satisfying a hunger for nature that would inevitably grow in individuals trapped in the barren surroundings of a city.[4] Coleridge later worked extensively in London, but the metropolis remained stained for him by memories of his education at Christ's Hospital and his tendency to rush ahead of himself: the 'fatigues of lecturing and Londonizing' repeatedly led him to retreat into less exhausting situations.[5]

Robert Southey also portrayed the city as enervating. In his satirical travel account *Letters from England* (1807), his Spanish narrator, Don Manuel Alvarez Espriella, describes the approach to London thus:

> The number of travellers perfectly astonished me, prepared as I had been by the gradual increase along the road; horsemen and footmen, carriages of every description and every shape, waggons and carts and covered carts, stage-coaches, long, square, and double, coaches, chariots, chaises, gigs, buggies, curricles, and phaetons; the sound of their wheels ploughing through the wet gravel was as continuous and incessant as the roar of the waves on the sea beach.[6]

The list's pilings up and the analogy with the incessant motions of the waves might suggest a kind of expansiveness cognate in some ways with the transcendental sublime, but the effect for Espriella is wearying, rather than uplifting. He writes of his entering London that he had 'never felt more deeply dejected', adding that 'the more I was surprised at the length of the streets, the lines of lamps, and of illuminated shops, and the stream of population to which there seemed to be no end, – the more I felt the solitariness of my own situation' (103–4). Such formulations represent urban experience as a form of negative counter-sublime that brings home the difficulty of generating genuine meaningfulness while feeling surrounded and immured.

Espriella's opinions reflect those of his creator and, in doing so, remind us how strange and overbearing the expanding, industrializing cities of the Romantic period could be. Writing to his wife in 1799, Southey expresses disgust at the metropolis's assault on his body and senses: 'I cannot walk a street without wanting to wash my hands – the air is so thick that my very lungs feel dirty. nothing but noise & nastiness. even the sight of my friends is fatiguing – after absence there is so much to say that I hear & talk till my head throbs with the unremitting exertion.'[7] Southey's visceral description makes it clear how hard it could be to get a perspective on London with smoke in your lungs, dirt on your skin, and a cacophony resounding in your skull. Southey often said that he despised London, writing in 1797 that 'I hate it & always hated it, with all my heart & with all my soul & with all my strength', so he cannot be taken as the most objective witness.[8] However, the idea of London as a constraining, dehumanizing environment is common in British Romantic writing. William Blake, a lover of London in many respects, nevertheless wrote of the 'mind-forg'd manacles' he could hear 'in every voice: in every ban'.[9] Blake's 'London' in *Songs of Experience* (1794) has a kind of sublimity, but it is often that of an imagined circle of hell: a stark warning for Blake's readers, but a numbing, inescapable torment for its depicted inhabitants. Novelists also tended to portray London as crushing and unsettling. In William Godwin's *Caleb Williams* (1794), the eponymous protagonist writes that London 'appears an inexhaustible reservoir of con-cealment', but finds it to be a place where he is 'harassed and ... repeatedly alarmed'.[10] Jane Austen's Elinor Dashwood finds little entertainment or ease in the city, telling Edward Ferrars that 'I expected much pleasure in it, but I have found none. The sight of you, Edward, is the only comfort it has afforded.'[11]

A Sense of Perspective

Experiencing the sublime is often contingent on finding a place of separation, as when Wordsworth ascends into the hills above Tintern Abbey, or Caspar David Friedrich's Wanderer stands above the sea of fog. When sublime sights do occur in literary descriptions of cities, they often separate the viewer from the common flow. In Walter Scott's *Rob Roy* (1817), for example, Frank Osbaldistone visits Glasgow, observing a 'principal street' that appears 'broad and important' and commenting on architecture that lends the city an 'imposing air of dignity and grandeur'.[12] However, it is not until he first encounters the 'Minster or Cathedral Church of Glasgow' that he feels sublime emotion:

> The pile is of a gloomy and massive, rather than of an elegant, style of Gothic architecture; but its peculiar character is so strongly preserved, and so well suited with the accompaniments that surround it, that the impression of the first view was awful and solemn in the extreme. I was indeed so much struck, that I resisted for a few minutes all Andrew's efforts to drag me into the interior of the building, so deeply was I engaged in surveying its outward character.   (238–9)

As Osbaldistone continues, though, it becomes apparent that this impression is caused by the way the cathedral appears to break out from the city it is ostensibly a part of:

Situated in a populous and considerable town, this ancient and massive pile has
the appearance of the most sequestered solitude. High walls divide it from the
buildings of the city on one side; on the other it is bounded by a ravine, at the
bottom of which, and invisible to the eye, murmurs a wandering rivulet,
adding, by its gentle noise, to the imposing solemnity of the scene. On the
opposite side of the ravine rises a steep bank, covered with fir-trees closely
planted, whose dusky shade extends itself over the cemetery with an appropriate and gloomy effect.   (239)

In framing Glasgow Cathedral as sublime, Scott's prose separates it from its
urban context, placing it as rearing up out of nature, which obligingly offers
sounds and shadings more conducive to transcendental contemplation than
the bustle of crowds or the striking high street architecture mentioned earlier.
In Scott's depiction, the cathedral's natural surroundings come together to
achieve a unified effect, allowing for a tight relation between the observer and
that which imparts the totalizing impression. Rather than being dirtied and
distracted, like Southey, Osbaldistone is given space to survey and process.

Escaping the rush and bustle seems essential for most Romantic-period
poets who want to conjure positive experiences of urban sublimity. In
'Scenes in London: Piccadilly' (1836), Letitia Elizabeth Landon is able to
see the city as 'Tradition's giant fane' only 'when the morning light / First
steals upon the skies'.[13] At this hour, the city:

> stands with darkness round it cast,
>   Touch'd by the first cold shine;
> Wast, vague, and mighty as the past
>   Of which it is the shrine.   (11)

The city at dawn becomes a place in which an artist might contemplate and
commune with the vastness of history. However, once people take to the
streets (in forms recalling Southey's descriptions), this potential is occluded
by the onrush of present cares:

> How wonderful the common street,
>   Its tumult and its throng,
> The hurrying of the thousand feet
>   That bear life's cares along.
>
> How strongly is the present felt,
>   With such a scene beside;
> All sounds in one vast murmur melt
>   The thunder of the tide.
>
> All hurry on – none pause to look
>   Upon another's face:

The present is an open book
None read, yet all must trace. (12)

While Landon's poetry employs rather grander sweeps than Wordsworth's generally does, she takes a broadly similar approach to the material impositions of the city, seeing these as encouraging people to skim across the surface of things. Like Wordsworth, she locates the potential for genuine communion and community outside the metropolis. Her Savoyard in Grosvenor Square – 'a tomb which wealth and rank / Have built themselves around' – is cheered by an unexpected orange tree because this recalls 'his distant native vale'.[14] In another poem, she implores her executors to inter her body not in a city graveyard but in 'the far green fields'.[15] 'If there be one object more material, more revolting, more gloomy than another,' she adds in an opening commentary, 'it is a crowded churchyard in a city... The pressed-down stones lie heavy upon the very heart' (36). Rather than allowing the 'memory of the loved and the lost' to act as 'the earthly shadow of their immortality', the city churchyard precludes the possibility of a cathartic encounter with lineages and mortality (36). 'The grave is bought – is closed – forgot!' Landon asserts, 'And then life hurries on' (37).

The preceding examples demonstrate that there was a powerful anti-urban strand in Romantic-period literature. One of this strand's key contentions was that cities degraded human potential, and one of the main means of figuring this degradation was by showing urban environments as blocking to a greater or lesser extent authors' access to what they depicted as higher thoughts. There is, however, a complication in accepting such writing as straightforwardly lacking in urban sublimity, a complication implied in its insistence on the importance of subjective, focalizing consciousnesses. Removed from Wordsworth's London by 200 years, we might now feel we have the kind of perspective he was unable to access. We might, for example, see his account of Bartholomew Fair as a transcendent literary experience even though he seems to deny that possibility in the account itself. This is one of the tricky things about discussing the sublime – it can be rhetorically invoked or rejected, but whether this invocation or rejection works for any given audience can be difficult to determine. Regardless, it seems fair to claim that most early nineteenth-century British poetry deliberately veers away from modern cities when seeking restorative experiences of sublimity.

Metropolitan Glory

However, Romantic lyric poetry is not the totality of the period's cultural productivity. Other discourses deliberately located sublimity in urban scenes – albeit often somewhat ambivalently – as part of what James Chandler and Kevin Gilmartin characterize as an emerging 'metropolitan aesthetic' self-consciously concerned with modernity.[16] Weiskel writes that 'In Victorian architecture ... the sublime was a constitutive idea in the construction of local environments – jails, railway stations, street edifices, public works – whose aggregate was the swarming imperial city' (*Weiskel*, 6). Framing great public buildings as sublime was not new in Victoria's reign; a similar impulse shapes Thomas Malton's *A Picturesque Tour through the Cities of London and Westminster* (1792–1801), which contains 100 impressive, large-scale aquatints of London landmarks. Malton writes that his plates of the city will 'give a true idea of its RESOURCES, WEALTH, and MAGNIFICENCE'.[17] This language recalls eighteenth-century poems like John Dyer's *The Fleece* (1757), which depicts the 'ruddy roofs, and chimney-tops ... Of busy Leeds, up-wafting to the clouds / The incense of thanksgiving'.[18] Illustrations and architectural plans often sought to sell the city based on either its impressing directly or its serving as a synecdoche for mercantile, industrial, or state power. Sublime scales also operated in popular entertainments like Robert Barker's spectacular panorama of London from the roof of the Albion Mills, a vast painting of '1479 square feet' displayed in a rotunda in Leicester Square during the 1790s.[19] However, despite the seeming sublime potential of such images, their reception often had more in common with Enlightenment attitudes than nascent Romantic ideologies. Malton's aquatints were seen as 'valuable picturesque representations', characterized as 'elegant and useful' rather than sublime, despite their drama and scale.[20] Markman Ellis writes that the reception of Barker's panoramas evidenced a 'contest between the discourse of connoisseurship and that of delusive wonder', with the former framed as a more rational response.[21] Burke argued that the clarity of visual art was less likely to arouse strong emotions than more 'obscure and imperfect' verbal descriptions (see *Enquiry* II iv). In line with this assumption, visual representations of the urban were often characterized as means of rationally mastering the modern city, rather than sources of ambiguous grandeur.

Statistical accounts displayed similar patterns, flirting with the possibility of overwhelming urban scale before promising means of mastery. In his *Treatise on the Police of the Metropolis* (1796), Patrick Colquhoun writes that 'London is not only the grand magazine of the British Empire, but also the general receptacle for the idle and depraved ... where the temptations and resources for criminal pleasures – gambling – fraud and depredation, as well as for pursuits of honest industry, almost exceed imagination.'[22] Colquhoun, however, is constructing an argument that the city is ultimately governable by state authorities informed by accurate numbers. In his treatise, as in city guidebooks, London's complexity is invoked as a potential sublime threat before the author proves that selectivity and abstraction can render the metropolis rewardingly legible. A transcendent understanding is ultimately unnecessary – a practical or scientific one will suffice.

Despite his permissive attitude to activities Colquhoun would see as criminal pleasures, Pierce Egan's collaborative novel/tour guide/satire *Life in London* (1820–1) takes a similar stance on the impressive variety of the capital, arguing that 'almost at every step, TALENT will be found jostling against TALENT, – and greatness continually meeting with greatness'.[23] Gregory Dart sees *Life in London* as being 'completely immersed in the Cockney culture of the period', characterized by promiscuous generic and social mixing.[24] While a tendency Egan calls sublime exists within the city, it rubs shoulders with a vast array of other registers. Apostrophizing the Cruikshank brothers, his collaborators and illustrators, Egan exhorts them to:

> *grapple* with an *Hogarthian* energy, in displaying *tout à la mode* the sublime and *finished* part of the creation, whether *screwed* up to a *semi-tone* of ART, or in nobly delineating, what must always be a welcome visitor at every residence, and likewise an admired portrait over all the chimney-pieces in the kingdom, a PERFECT GENTLEMAN. (12)

Egan thus frames the sublime as a form of practiced refinement, implying that affecting access can be a useful mode of aesthetic social posturing. One of his principal characters, Corinthian Tom, encourages his cousin Jerry to 'call to your assistance the shades of HERVEY, ADDISON, and MILTON, to ornament your style of conversation with a few of their irresistible touches of the *flowery*, ELEGANT, and SUBLIME' in order to impress women (295). 'To become a hero in this *looking-glass* sort of life, my dear JERRY,' he advises, 'you ought to be as much *made-up* as the *measured* statue of the *Venus de Medicis*' (296). Romantic writers often condemned the performative aspects of city living; Egan helpfully reminds us that evoking the sublime was itself a performative position denoting perception and refinement.

While poetry tended to reserve sublime experiences for individuals, more democratic forms argued that urban environments allowed for experiences of collective power. In his essay 'On Londoners and Country People' (1823), William Hazlitt saw city living as a liberating force likely to expand citizens' intellectual and moral horizons:

> We comprehend that vast denomination, *the People*, of which we see a tenth part daily moving before us; and by having our imaginations emancipated from petty interests and personal dependence, we learn to venerate ourselves as men, and to respect the rights of human nature. Therefore it is that the citizens

and freemen of London and Westminster are patriots by prescription, philosophers and politicians by the right of their birth-place.[25]

Kevin Gilmartin reads Hazlitt as working towards an urban 'popular Leviathan', 'a collective and spectacularly magnified embodiment of "the stream of human life pouring along the streets"'.[26] For Hazlitt, London represented a scene of advancement rather than of degradation, its relatively emancipated populace serving as the spearhead for much-needed reforms. The city thus provided the most obvious place to experience the sublimity of the majesty of the people.[27]

Hidden Corners and Ruination

Other writers found metropolitan sublimity by exploring hidden nooks and curious counter-currents, rather than aligning with the crowd. This mode of engagement became more strongly codified in the later driftings of the flâneur, who would see the city as a site of near-infinite potential encounters. Charles Baudelaire's rhapsodic addresses to Paris are a good mature example:

> Fourmillante cité, cité pleine de rêves,
> Où le spectre en plein jour raccroche le passant!
> Les mystères partout coulent comme des sèves
> Dans les canaux étroits du colosse puissant.[28]

However, the city as a slumbering colossus full of mysteries has a long pedigree, and the itinerant, alienated position Baudelaire occupies was also evoked by earlier Romantic essayists. Thomas De Quincey, whose reputation-making *Confessions* (1821) Baudelaire translated, provides a more negative version of the picture. His own experiences of floating through the city were characterized by deprivation and want, and he often found that the twists of London would turn against him. Of his fruitless attempts to locate Ann of Oxford Street, who was kind to him, De Quincey writes, 'doubtless we must have been sometimes in search of each other, at the very same moment, through the mighty labyrinths of London; perhaps, even within a few feet of each other – a barrier no wider than a London street, often amounting in the end to a separation for eternity!'[29] This is the metropolis as gothic maze – vast and haunted, terrible in its scale, capriciousness and power.

I mentioned earlier that Coleridge addressed Charles Lamb as if the city in which he dwelt would inevitably drain him. However, Lamb himself took a very different view. The essays he wrote in the early 1820s are often playful and ironic, but they engage seriously with London as a space of regenerative wonder. Consider, for example, the account Lamb gives of the South Sea House in the first essay he wrote for the *London Magazine* under the pseudonym Elia:

> This was once a house of trade, – a centre of busy interests. The throng of merchants was here – the quick pulse of gain – and here some forms of business are still kept up, though the soul be long since fled. Here are still to be seen stately porticos; imposing staircases; offices roomy as the state apartments in palaces – deserted, or thinly peopled with a few straggling clerks; the still more sacred interiors of court and committee rooms, with venerable faces of beadles, door-keepers – directors seated in form on solemn days (to proclaim a dead dividend,) at long worm-eaten tables, that have been mahogany, with tarnished gilt-leather coverings, supporting massy silver inkstands long since dry; – the oaken wainscots hung with pictures of deceased governors and sub-governors, of queen Anne, and the two first monarchs of the Brunswick dynasty; – huge charts, which subsequent discoveries have antiquated; – dusty maps of Mexico, dim as dreams, – and soundings of the Bay of Panama! – The long passages hung with buckets, appended, in idle row, to walls, whose substance might defy any, short of the last, conflagration; – with vast ranges of cellarage under all, where dollars and pieces of eight once lay, an "unsunned heap," for Mammon to have solaced his solitary heart withal, – long since dissipated, or scattered into air at the blast of the breaking of that famous BUBBLE.[30]

Lamb commonly takes delight in aged and peculiar things, and while there is a certain amount of undercutting going on in this passage, the South Sea House's vast architecture and the remnants of its luxuries and safeguards nevertheless serve as a portal to a time that has almost vanished. While the rush of the new can be a sublime experience, Lamb celebrates the inspiring persistence of the old, which provides refuge, inspiration, and a mode of connection.

While exploring the South Sea House, Lamb describes the 'heavy odd-shaped ivory-handled penknives' he finds as being 'as good as any thing from Herculaneum' (1–2). The sublime potential of urban ruination was something on which most Romantic-period creatives agreed. John Martin painted vast, glowering canvasses in which Pompeii and Herculaneum drowned beneath lava and ash, and the towers of Tyre toppled into raging seas. In these images, nature rises furiously to destroy the works of man. Less showy falls were also prophesied. In *Eighteen Hundred and Eleven* (1812), Anna Laetitia Barbauld depicts future tourists visiting the ruins of London, ascending 'crumbling turrets' to view the Thames flowing again through 'reeds and sedge'.[31] Barbauld's visitors find the remnants benevolently haunted by great writers, orators, generals, and natural philosophers. High points of a social and cultural history remain entangled with London's ruins, although Baurbauld asserts that local knowledge is necessary to decode what 'Time has cast behind' (line 188). The strangers also find within London more ruins than its own:

> On spoils from every clime their eyes shall gaze,
> Ægyptian granites and the Etruscan vase;
> And when midst fallen London, they survey
> The stone where Alexander's ashes lay,
> Shall own with humbled pride the lesson just
> By Time's slow finger written in the dust.   (lines 205–14)

In encountering the sublime fragments of ancient cultures in the remains of the British Museum, Barbauld's pilgrims and readers are invited to dwell on the seemingly inevitable fall of empires. The flotsam of time occasions stark meditations on what is absent. The living city is often figured as containing too much to teach consistent lessons. By contrast, the ruined fragments of past metropolises facilitate deep reflections on history, memory, and death.

Writing to Thomas Love Peacock in 1819, Percy Bysshe Shelley described Rome as 'a city of palaces & temples more glorious than those which any other city contains, & of ruins more glorious than they', creating a similar hierarchy to Barbauld, in which urban environments acquire transcendental potential as they age and decay.[32] In *The Last Man* (1826), a novel that both remembers and reworks her husband, Mary Shelley stages the same city as a place of refuge and reflection. The titular character, Lionel Verney, shorn of other purposes, travels to Rome after losing his last human companions to the plague ravaging the world:

> I entered Eternal Rome by the Porta del Popolo, and saluted with awe its time-honoured space. The wide square, the churches near, the long extent of the Corso, the near eminence of Trinita de' Monti appeared like fairy work, they were so silent, so peaceful, and so very fair. It was evening; and the population of animals which still existed in this mighty city, had gone to rest; there was no sound, save the murmur of its many fountains, whose soft monotony was harmony to my soul. The knowledge that I was in Rome, soothed me; that wondrous city, hardly more illustrious for its heroes and sages, than for the power it exercised over the imaginations of men.[33]

Perhaps the sprawl of Rome soothes Verney precisely because he has its vastness to himself. On waking, he celebrates his ability to 'familiarly converse with the wonder of the world, sovereign mistress of the imagination, majestic and eternal survivor of millions of generations of extinct men' (461). The existence of other people is often a blocking factor for Romantic sublime experiences, which commonly aspire to connect the inspired individual with something greater, rather than with a plethora of putative equals. While Verney mourns the end of the humanity, he will never again need to grapple his way out of the crowd to gain perspective.

NOTES

1 John Keats to Richard Woodhouse, 27 October 1818, in *The Letters of John Keats*, ed. Hyder Edward Rollins, 2 vols., Cambridge, MA, Harvard University Press, 1958, vol. 1, 387.

2 Anne Janowitz, 'The Artifactual Sublime: Making London Poetry', in James Chandler and Kevin Gilmartin, eds., *Romantic Metropolis: The Urban Scene of British Culture, 1780–1840*, Cambridge, Cambridge University Press, 2005, 246–60 (250, 251).

3 Amy Lowell, 'A London Thoroughfare. 2 A.M.', in *Sword Blades and Poppy Seed*, New York, Macmillan, 1914, 43–4.

4 Samuel Taylor Coleridge, *The Watchman*, 11 April 1796, in *The Collected Works of Samuel Taylor Coleridge: The Watchman*, ed. Lewis Patton, London, Routledge, 1970, 199–234 (223).

5 Charles Lamb to George Dyer, 5 July 1808; Letter 227 in *The Letters of Charles and Mary Lamb*, 3 vols., ed. Edwin W. Marrs, Ithaca, NY, Cornell University Press, 1975–81, vol. 2, 284–5 (284).

6 Robert Southey, *Letters from England by Don Manuel Alvarez Espriella*, ed. Carol Bolton, New York, Routledge, 2016, 103.

7 Robert Southey to Edith Southey, 1–3 May 1799; Letter 403 in *The Collected Letters of Robert Southey*, ed. Lynda Pratt, Tim Fulford, and Ian Packer, Romantic Circles Electronic Editions, 2009–, (https://romantic-circles.org/editions/southey_letters).

8 Robert Southey to Thomas Southey, 16 March 1797; Letter 206 in *Collected Letters*. I discuss Southey's negative reactions to London at greater length in Matthew Sangster, 'Southey versus London: Proto-Romantic Disaffection and Dehumanisation in the British Metropolis', *Romanticism on the Net*, 68–9, 2017, https://doi.org/10.7202/1070626ar.

9 William Blake, 'London', in *Songs of Innocence and Experience*, London, 1794, lines 8, 7. Accessed via *The William Blake Archive*, www.blakearchive.org/.

10 William Godwin, *Caleb Williams*, ed. Pamela Clemit, Oxford, Oxford University Press, 2009, 246, 299.

11 Jane Austen, *Sense and Sensibility*, ed. Ros Ballaster, London, Penguin, 2004, 228.

12 Walter Scott, *Rob Roy*, ed. Ian Duncan, Oxford, Oxford University Press, 2008, 237.

13 Letitia Elizabeth Landon, 'Scenes in London: Piccadilly', in *Fisher's Drawing Room Scrap-Book*, London, 1836, 11–12 (11).

14 Landon, 'Scenes in London: The Savoyard in Grosvenor Square', in *Fisher's*, 28–9 (28).

15 Landon, 'Scenes in London: The City Church-yard', in *Fisher's*, 36–7 (36).

16 James Chandler and Kevin Gilmartin, 'Introduction: Engaging the Eidometropolis', in James Chandler and Kevin Gilmartin, eds., *Romantic*

Metropolis: The Urban Scene of British Culture, 1780–1840, Cambridge, Cambridge University Press, 2005, 1–41 (5).

17 Thomas Malton, *A Picturesque Tour through the Cities of London and Westminster*, London, 1792–1801, iv.

18 John Dyer, *The Fleece*, London, 1757, Book 3, 109–10.

19 Markman Ellis, '"Spectacles within doors": Panoramas of London in the 1790s', *Romanticism*, 14, 2, 2008, 133–48 (137).

20 'Malton's Picturesque Tour through London', *Monthly Review*, 41, July 1803, 295–305 (295, 305).

21 Ellis, 'Spectacles', 143.

22 [Patrick Colquhoun], *A Treatise on the Police of the Metropolis*, 3rd edition, London, 1796, xi–xii.

23 Pierce Egan et al., *Life in London*, London, 1821, 20.

24 Gregory Dart, *Metropolitan Art and Literature 1810–1840: Cockney Adventures*, Cambridge, Cambridge University Press, 2012, 108.

25 William Hazlitt, 'On Londoners and Country People', in *The Complete Works of William Hazlitt*, 21 vols., ed. P. P. Howe, London, 1930–4, vol. 12, 66–77 (77).

26 Kevin Gilmartin, 'Hazlitt's Visionary London', in Heather Glen and Paul Hamilton, eds., *Repossessing the Romantic Past*, Cambridge, Cambridge University Press, 2006, 40–62 (51).

27 For a detailed exploration of this discourse after the French Revolution, see Georgina Green, *The Majesty of the People*, Oxford, Oxford University Press, 2014.

28 Charles Baudelaire, 'Les sept viellards', in *Selected Poems*, ed. Carol Clark, London, Penguin, 2004, 89. 'Swarming city, city full of dreams / Where ghosts in broad daylight catch the walker's sleeve! / Mysteries everywhere run like sap / Through the narrow channels of the powerful colossus' (Clark's translation; punctuation adapted).

29 Thomas De Quincey, *Confessions of an English Opium-Eater and Other Writings*, ed. Robert Morrison, Oxford, Oxford University Press, 2013, 34–5.

30 Elia [Charles Lamb], 'The South-Sea House', in *Essays of Elia*, London, 1823, 1–14 (1–2).

31 Anna Laetitia Barbauld, *Eighteen Hundred and Eleven*, London, 1812, lines 171, 176.

32 Percy Bysshe Shelley to Thomas Love Peacock, 23 March 1819, in *Letters of Percy Bysshe Shelley*, 2 vols., ed. Frederick L. Jones, Oxford, Clarendon Press, 1964, vol. 2, 87. Cited in Jonathan Sachs, *Romantic Antiquity*, Oxford, Oxford University Press, 2010, 146, which contains a full and interesting exploration of Shelley's engagements with Rome.

33 Mary Shelley, *The Last Man*, ed. Morton Paley, Oxford, Oxford University Press, 2008, 460–1.

9

SIMON BAINBRIDGE

Highlands, Lakes, Wales

'Mountains and their accompaniments are amongst the finest specimens of the sublime.'[1] So wrote the landscape gardener and adventurous fell-walker Thomas Wilkinson in his *Tours to the British Mountains* (1824), an early example of what has since become a popular form, the mountaineering memoir. As a lifelong 'admirer of the sublime in Nature', Wilkinson's search for lofty landscapes and elevated emotions inspired him to make numerous ascents of both popular and little-climbed peaks around Britain. In this, Wilkinson was not alone; during the Romantic period, there was a remarkable growth in the popularity of mountain climbing, particularly as undertaken by those touring what were regarded as the country's three most sublime regions: the Highlands of Scotland, the Lake District in the north-west of England, and Snowdonia in the north of Wales. Romantic-period travel literature, whether in the form of guidebook, letter, or poem, regularly presented the mountain top as the ultimate sublime location. Having made a pioneering climb in 1818 to England's highest summit, Scafell Pike, Dorothy Wordsworth wrote to a friend that 'never before did I behold so sublime a mountain prospect'.[2] In his epic autobiographical poem *The Prelude* (1805), Dorothy's brother William described the environment on Wales's highest peak, Snowdon, as possessing 'circumstances most awful and sublime' (Book XIII, line 76). Reinforcing such personal testimonies, guidebooks presented mountain climbing as a guaranteed way of accessing the sublime. *The Scottish Tourist and Itinerary* (1830) instructed its readers as follows in reference to Britain's loftiest mountain: 'The stranger, at Fort William, if ambitious of enjoying the most sublime prospect to be met with in Great Britain, will ascend to the summit of Ben Nevis.'[3]

Mountain summits, and the prospects they offered, not only were seen as among the most powerful forms of the natural sublime in the period; they also provided the location where the climber could experience 'the most sublime sensations'.[4] This was a phrase used by the lawyer, journalist, and travel-writer John Stoddart in describing an ascent of Ben Lomond he made during his Scottish Tour of 1799 and 1800. Stoddart's narrative offers a textbook account of how, through the act of climbing, sublimity of landscape could become sublimity of feeling and, ultimately, sublimity of self. Exploring Ben Lomond's summit, Stoddart discovers that the mountain's north side 'excites a degree of surprise arising almost to terror' (vol. 1, 236). His proximity to the mountain's edge and to the sensation of 'terror', the key emotion of the Burkean sublime, prompts him to consider the necessary conditions and workings of the sublime: 'In such a situation, the most sublime sensations cannot be felt, unless you are alone. A single insulated being, carrying his view over these vast, inanimate masses, seems to feel himself attached to them, as it were, by a new kind of bond; his spirit dilates with magnitude, and rejoices in the beauty of the terrestrial objects' (vol. 1, 236). Here, the sublime is essentially a solitary experience, produced by the viewer's changed relationship with the mountain landscape. For Stoddart, the sublime aggrandizes the viewing subject, whose spirit grows to the mountainous proportions of the 'terrestrial objects' it looks upon and attaches itself to. Stoddart develops these reflections on the 'sublime sensations' experienced on a summit through reminiscence of a previous climb of 'a mountain in Cumberland':

> It was a bright, lovely day, and I stood contemplating with admiration a beautiful vale, with its glittering lake, rich woods, and numerous buildings. Gradually, a thick mist rolled, like a curtain, before it, and took away every object from my view. I was left alone, on the mountain top, far above the clouds of the vale, the sun shining full upon my head; it seemed as if I had been suddenly transported into a new state of existence, cut off from every meaner association, and invisibly united with the surrounding purity and brightness. (vol. 1, 237)

One of many of the period's descriptions of a cloud inversion, in which the climber stands sunlit above the clouds, Stoddart's account offers a classic statement of the mountain-top sublime and its power to 'transport' the viewer. Having ascended from the world below, he has elevated himself above 'meaner associations' into a 'new state of existence'. Physically, psychologically and even morally uplifted, the climber has become, literally, sublime – 'Set or raised aloft; high up', to quote the *Oxford English Dictionary*.[5]

From the Alps to the British Mountains

The link between mountains and the sublime had been a major element of aesthetic theory since the turn of the eighteenth century, particularly in relation to the Alps. It was while crossing a precipitous Alpine pass in 1688 that John Dennis described feeling 'a delightful horror' and 'a terrible Joy', seeming oxymorons that anticipate Burke's influential account of the sublime as the pleasurable experience of terror in his *Enquiry*.[6] Similarly, in his 'Essay on the Pleasures of the Imagination' of 1712, Joseph Addison recalled how 'a pleasing Astonishment' was produced by mountainous landscapes.[7] Addison's 'astonishment' would become the crucial sublime emotion for Burke, who defines it, in *Enquiry* II i, as the 'state of the soul, in which all its motions are suspended, with some degree of horror', adding that 'the mind is so entirely filled with its object, that it cannot entertain any other, nor by consequence reason on that object which employs it'. Burke described this state of astonishment as 'caused by the great and sublime in *nature*, when those causes operate most powerfully' and classed it as 'the effect of the sublime in its highest degree' (*Enquiry* II i). While Dennis, Addison and Burke primarily saw the sublime as produced by looking *at* mountains, the Scottish philosopher and poet James Beattie emphasized how sublimity could be experienced by looking *from* peaks. In his *Dissertations Moral and Critical* (1783), Beattie articulated the sublimity of looking down from the summit:

> Great depth, being the correlative of great height ... and because it astonishes and pleases the imagination, is also to be considered as sublime. For, if we be ourselves secure, every one must have observed, that it is agreeable to look down from a mountain, upon a plain ... it is pleasant to look down from an elevated situation, because here too there is greatness and delightful astonishment.[8]

While Beattie shifts the sublime viewpoint to the mountain top, it is noticeable that he, like Burke, saw a sense of personal security as necessary for the sublime experience to be agreeable, pleasant, and delightful.

It was the development of domestic tourism within the British Isles that made it possible to experience the sublimity of summits, with parallels regularly being made between the native peaks and the Alps. Indeed, the relative accessibility of British summits, compared with those of the Alps, was seen as one of the attractions of remaining on home soil (or rock), even before the Revolutionary and Napoleonic Wars of 1793–1815 prevented most travel to mainland Europe. As Thomas West wrote in 1778 in *A Guide to the Lakes*, probably the period's most influential Lake District guidebook: 'The mountains here are all accessible to the summit, and furnish prospects no less surprising, with more variety than the ALPS themselves. The tops of the highest ALPS are inaccessible, being covered with everlasting snow.....'[9] West even incorporated the summit position into the burgeoning picturesque tour when he made 'the top of Castle-rock or crag, in Borrowdale' the fourth of his famous stations, describing it as offering 'a most astonishing view of the lake and vale of Keswick, spread out to the north in the most picturesque manner' (98).

West's was one of a number of publications of the 1770s that started to describe the sublime pleasures of ascents to British summits. In 1773, the antiquary and topographer William Hutchinson was a member of a party that made a 'laborious ascent' of the Lake District peak Skiddaw, finding that 'The prospect which we gained from this eminence very well rewarded our fatigue.'[10] As Hutchinson's economic language of effort and reward suggests, his motivation for ascent was visual; he was seeking an elevated 'prospect', which he duly described in detail. Yet Hutchinson's account also reveals that the sources of the sublime were not always as expected on the mountain top. Initially this was the result of a gathering storm, which obscured the initial prospect but produced an alternative form of sublimity as the summit party 'looked down upon an angry and impetuous sea' of clouds and rejoiced 'in this grand spectacle of nature' (159). These visual sublime sights were dramatically upstaged by the storm itself, as Hutchinson describes:

> to our astonishment and confusion, a violent burst of thunder engendered in the vapour below stunned our sense, being repeated from every rock, and down every dell, in the most horrid uproar; at the same time, from the agitation of the air, the mountain seemed to tremble; – at the time of the explosion, the clouds were instantaneously illuminated, and from innumerable chasms sent forth streams of lightning. (159–60)

Hutchinson emphasizes the storm's aural and somatic impacts at least as much as its visual ones. The whole experience borders on going beyond the sublime into the purely terrifying; as Hutchinson writes: 'danger made us solemn indeed, we had no where to fly for safety' (159).

Hutchinson presents his Skiddaw climb as comparable to an Alpine adventure; he writes of the storm that 'A like event has frequently happened to travellers in the heights of the Alps, from whence the thunder storms are seen passing over the countries beneath them' (161). Even more remarkably, the antiquarian presents his physical experience on this Lake District summit as if he were at the sort of elevated Alpine altitude where breathlessness is produced by the reduced air pressure resulting in a decreased level of oxygen: 'The air was remarkably sharp and thin, compared with that from which we passed to the valley; and respiration seemed to be performed with a kind of asthmatic oppression' (42). Hutchinson is so immersed in Alpine literature, with its accounts of altitude's challenges, that he experiences Skiddaw's summit as if he was in that more elevated sublime environment.

This parallel between Britain's mountains and the Alps was also a strong feature of the literature of the Snowdonian sublime in the 1770s. A key early publication here was *Letters from Snowdon: Descriptive of a Tour through the Northern Countries of Wales* of 1770, which has usually been ascribed to Joseph Cradock, though his authorship of this influential volume has been questioned recently. Like West's championing of the Lake District's fells, this volume presented 'the Welsh Alps' as worthy rivals to their European counterparts, a claim that Cradock did himself make in *An Account of Some of the Most Romantic Parts of Wales* of 1777 where he expressed an excited hope that recent road improvements would 'induce the Curious to visit the Wonders of the British Alps, in preference to the Mountains of Switzerland, or the Glaciers of Savoy'.[11] Both *Letters from Snowdon* and Cradock's *Account* offered detailed narratives of Snowdon ascents, with the author of *Letters* giving early expression to the idea that elevating the body through climbing could also elevate the mind: 'As our situation was exalted above the globe, so were our ideas. And the nearer we were to the etherial regions, the more our souls seemed to partake of their purity. Our minds like the serene face of the sky, undisturbed with the storms of the passions became equal and composed.'[12] These sentiments exemplify another way in which Alpine ideas were shaping the experience of British mountains, heavily influenced as they are by a highly influential passage from Jean-Jacques Rousseau's *Julie, ou La nouvelle Héloïse* in which the protagonist, Saint-Preux, remarks: 'It seems that by rising above the habitations of men one leaves all base and earthly sentiments behind, and in proportion as one approaches ethereal spaces, the soul contracts something of their inalterable purity.'[13] Snowdon, as much as Switzerland, offered the possibility of an escape from ground-level cares to the pure atmosphere of the skies.

The Three Peaks: Snowdon, Skiddaw, Ben Lomond

Snowdon's and Skiddaw's status as the pre-eminent sublime locations in Wales and the Lake District were confirmed by two major publications of the following decades, Thomas Pennant's *The Journey to Snowdon* (1781) and Ann Radcliffe's *Observations during a Tour to the Lakes* (1795). In 1781, the Welsh antiquarian Pennant published the second volume of his *A Tour In Wales*, entitled *The Journey to Snowdon*, in which he conflated Snowdon ascents he had made in 1752 and 1776. Pennant's detailed accounts provided practical information for those wishing to ascend Wales's highest mountain, and though he rarely used the word 'sublime' itself, his narrative evoked the excitements afforded by the Snowdonian landscape:

OBSERVE, on the right, a stupendous *rock fendue*, or split rock, called *Twll-Du*, and *The Devil's Kitchen*. It is a horrible gap, in the center of a great black precipice, extending in length about a hundred and fifty yards; in depth, about a hundred; and only six wide; perpendicularly open to the surface of the mountain. On surmounting all my difficulties, and taking a little breath, I ventured to look down this dreadful aperture, and found its horrors far from being lessened, in my exalted situation; for to it were added the waters of *Lyn y Cwm*, impetuously rushing through its bottom.[14]

Pennant's combination of practical instruction and exciting description, seen in this passage, encouraged many of his readers to attempt Snowdon themselves and helped establish standard routes and itineraries for those wishing to climb the mountain. For example, in his 1752 ascent, Pennant had sought to heighten the sublimity of the prospect view by arriving on the summit in time for the sunrise: 'I took pains to see this prospect to advantage; sat up at a farm on the west till about twelve and walked up the whole way' (163). Pennant popularized this nocturnal itinerary, with one writer noting in 1821 that 'Many go up to see the sun-rise.'[15] William Wordsworth was consciously following Pennant's timetable when he climbed Snowdon in 1791 with Robert Jones. Having already met Pennant earlier in their tour, the two friends set out with a guide at 'couching-time ... to see the sun / Rise from the top'.[16] Near the summit, Wordsworth experienced a spectacular cloud inversion, which became the focus for the revelatory conclusion of *The Prelude*. Notably, though, while Wordsworth celebrates the scene as a 'universal spectacle ... shaped for admiration and delight', he ultimately presents it as metaphor: 'The perfect image of a mighty Mind' (Book XIII, lines 60–9). For Wordsworth, it is testimony to the Mind's own sublimity that it predominates over Nature's most sublime spectacle.

In the Lake District, Ann Radcliffe wrote what became the definitive account of a Skiddaw ascent in her *Observations during a Tour to the Lakes*. Her dramatic description was included in several guidebooks, including West's *Guide*, and was frequently quoted extensively on the grounds that it could not be surpassed; four decades after the initial publication of *Observations*, the author of *Leigh's Guide to the Lakes* wrote of Skiddaw's summit that 'it cannot be better described than in the language of Mrs Radcliffe'.[17] Radcliffe had already achieved renown as a Gothic novelist of Alpine landscapes (even without having seen the Alps themselves) and, following an aborted trip to Switzerland, she turned to the Lake District as a source for sublime thrills. Her ascent account emphasized the terrors of the experience:

About a mile from the summit, the way was, indeed, dreadfully sublime, laying for nearly half a mile, along the ledge of a precipice, that passed, with a swift descent, for nearly a mile, into a glen within the heart of Skiddaw...our situation was too critical, or too unusual, to permit the just impressions of such sublimity. The hill rose so closely above the precipice as scarcely to allow a ledge wide enough for a single horse. We followed the guide in silence, and, till we regained the more open wild, had no leisure for exclamation.[18]

Here, Radcliffe goes beyond the standard trope of the sublime – that it defeats all attempts at proper description; rather, the perceived terrors of her precipitous ascent are such that they overwhelm comprehension itself, making it impossible to gain a 'just impression' of the sublime landscape.

A notable feature of Radcliffe's Skiddaw ascent, as indicated in the quotation above, was that it was made on horseback. Indeed, the ability to ride to the summit of Lake District's sixth highest mountain was one of the major factors that made it the region's most regularly ascended peak in the period. As Jonathan Otley commented in his *A Concise Description of the English Lakes* (1823), Skiddaw offered the perfect combination of (relative) convenience and aesthetic power: 'Skiddaw is, on several accounts, generally selected [by those wishing for a mountain-top view]. It is nearest to the station at Keswick, most easy of access, (as ladies can ride on horseback to the summit,) and standing some measure detached, the view, especially in the north and west, is less intercepted by other mountains.'[19]

As Otley's comments indicate, during the romantic period, horseback was becoming increasingly seen as the appropriate mode of ascent for women. Edward Baines gives a detailed account of one such ascent in his *A Companion to the Lakes* (1829), describing how his two female friends rode up the mountain while he and another male member of the party walked alongside them. The horses, ponies, or mules used for such expeditions were usually supplied by local inns, an indication of the increasing commodification of ascent during the period. Inns acted as organizational hubs for many mountain expeditions, bringing together like-minded tourists and providing them with guides and provisions to support their climbs.

In Scotland, Ben Lomond became the key location for ascent on the Highland Tour. Located next to picturesque Loch Lomond, this peak was the prime target for those with a 'taste for grandeur or the dread sublime', according to a widely quoted rhyme scratched on the window of a local inn.[20] As at Snowdon and Skiddaw, an infrastructure of accommodation, guides, and ponies developed around Ben Lomond that made it possible for large groups to reach the summit. As early as 1787, Thomas Wilkinson encountered one such group on the mountain, defining it as 'a genteel company' and adding that it consisted of 'twelve persons, (six of either sex,) two guides, a black servant, and a pony with provisions' (*Tours*, 16).

Though Ben Nevis was already known to be the highest point in Britain, its size and relative inaccessibility meant that it never gained Ben Lomond's popularity, a context that makes John Keats's 1818 climb of the loftier peak all the more impressive. Keats's determination to climb a major British mountain as part of the walking tour he believed would be a necessary 'sort of Prologue' to his poetic career reveals how essential sublime experience had become to ideas of literary creativity and authority.[21]

While the search for the sublime contributed to the rapid growth in popularity of mountain climbing in the Romantic period, increasing numbers of climbers on the peaks began to imperil the sublimity of the summit experience itself. As John Stoddart commented in his account of climbing Ben Lomond quoted above, 'the most sublime sensations cannot be felt, unless you are alone'.[22] By the end of the period, such solitariness was becoming harder to find on the more popular mountains; peaks were becoming surprisingly busy places, according to some accounts, and the make-up and motivations of summit parties reflected wider societal changes. In the year after Queen Victoria's accession to the throne, the Scottish naturalist William MacGillivray complained as follows:

> I cannot but look upon it as a gross profanation to enact in the midst of the sublimities of creation a convivial scene, such as is usually got up by parties from our large towns, who seem to have no higher aim in climbing to the top of Benlomond or Benlevi than to feast there upon cold chicken and 'mountain dew,' and toss as many stones as they can find over the precipices.[23]

Here, MacGillivray presents the town-based tourists, driven by their appetites and sense of fun, not only as oblivious to 'the sublimities of creation' but as profaning them through their behaviour. His account indicates how divergent mountain experience was becoming in the period, even for those who stood on the same summit. For MacGillivray, there was a sacredness about the mountain-top sublime, an idea expressed even more directly by other climbers who shared his sense of ascent's 'higher aim'. Thomas Wilkinson, with whom I began this essay, was a Quaker who similarly linked the sublime and the sacred, claiming that 'Mountains may be said to be among the most conspicuous and imperishable monuments of the Creator's power that we behold'.[24] For all the aesthetic appeal and physical excitements peaks afforded, Wilkinson ultimately valued them in religious terms: 'Mountains, rocks, woods, and waters, are innocent objects in themselves, and are the productions of a Divine hand: thy impress us with awe, as works of Almighty Power.'[25] As the 'finest specimens of the sublime', mountains provided Wilkinson with a reminder of Almighty Power; for him, climbing offered a form of worship.

Beyond the Three Peaks to 'sublime and dreadful regions'

As the popularity of mountain ascent grew, adventurous climbers such as Wilkinson sought the sublime in locations other than the increasingly crowded summits of Snowdon, Skiddaw, and Ben Lomond. These less frequented and more challenging locations often posed a greater physical danger to the climber, further enhancing the sense of sublime. With a knowing nod to Burke, Wilkinson commented of a perilous descent down the Old Man of Coniston in the Lakes that 'it was not amiss to have a little sprinkling of terror in the expedition'.[26] Such experiences of terror could produce feelings of exhilaration, especially once the immediate dangers had been overcome. Of another hazardous descent, this time down 'the reputed Cobbler', Beinn Artair in Scotland, Wilkinson wrote that 'I had now spirits, and experienced feelings that I do not remember to have known before.'[27] Wilkinson's account of his risky adventure, undertaken on his 'hands and knees ... with much difficulty and some danger', suggests possible physiological and psychological explanations for these unprecedented 'spirits' and 'feelings'.[28] This sense of how the physical and mental stresses of navigating challenging mountain terrain could produce a transformed state of mind is most famously captured in the period in Samuel Taylor Coleridge's 'Sca' Fell Letter' in which the poet brilliantly describes how a series of life-threatening drops down the perilous rock-face of Broad Stand led to 'a state of almost prophetic Trance & Delight' once he had reached a place of relative safety.[29]

Coleridge made his Broad Stand descent as part of his nine-day 'Circumcursion' of the Lakes, a walking tour of what was then a very remote part of the region and included the first recorded of ascent of Scafell.[30] Other pioneering climbers ventured beyond the popular tourist mountains to explore terrain known only to local residents. The ex-soldier and travel writer Joseph Budworth climbed the Grasmere fell Helm Crag in 1792, claiming it as the first ascent by a 'stranger' in his *A Fortnight's Ramble to the Lakes*.[31] He returned to the Lakes five years later, exploring the more rugged Langdale valley where he made another first ascent for a 'stranger', this time of Pike O'Stickle, a climb that required him and his guide to 'haul ourselves by rocks to bring us to the crown'.[32] Langdale was also the scene for some daring, exploratory rock climbing undertaken by the Smith sisters of Coniston, accompanied by Thomas Wilkinson, who described the start of the adventure as follows:

> To these sublime and dreadful regions I ascended with my intrepid maids, and was the first to express any fear. Catherine, who feels a kindness for the whole creation, offered me her hand; while Elizabeth, with a courage I had never met with before, proposed to explore what remained, and, winding round the corner of a rock, presently ascended out of sight.[33]

Wilkinson and his 'intrepid maids' undertook this climb five years before Elizabeth Smith's death from illness in 1806. It is an indication of how rapidly mountain climbing was developing in the period that within the next two decades, the 'sublime and dreadful' Langdale region explored by Budworth, Wilkinson, and the Smith sisters was becoming a part of more standard tourist trips. In *The Tourist's New Guide* of 1819, the Ambleside painter and guide William Green describes leading a party of sixteen people on an ascent from the Langdale Valley as far as the mountain lake of Stickle Tarn and invites his readers to follow in their footsteps.[34]

In Wales and Scotland, as in the Lake District, a number of individuals who had initially ventured into the mountains for specific reasons, such as the collection of botanical samples or the creation of maps, found the sublime landscapes and the feelings they stimulated to be a reward in themselves. The Cambridge undergraduate and clergyman-to-be, William Bingley, travelled to Snowdon in 1798 to collect rare plants but after a perilous climb of the crag Clogwyn Du'r Arddu began to explore other mountains for the sheer thrill of the experience, as in his climb of Tryfan, where he 'stood on a mere point' and 'contemplated all the scene around . . . which was rude as mountain horror could render it'.[35] In Scotland, John MacCulloch's work as a geologist for the Trigonometrical Survey from 1811 to 1820 took him to many remote Highland regions and he seized any opportunity to reach summits, as in a climb of the Cobbler, where he found himself astride the peak's rocky saddle, 'with one foot in Loch Lomond and the other in Glencro'.[36]

Bingley's and MacCulloch's perilous summit experiences, enacted at the very limits of the landscape, indicates how adventurous mountain climbing had become for some of the most daring climbers of the Romantic period. Yet, in large part, the motivations that took these climbers to the extremes were shared with those domestic tourists who participated in organized group excursions up Ben Lomond, Snowdon, and Skiddaw. Through ascent, all were seeking to be physically and psychologically elevated; by climbing Britain's mountains, all were seeking the complex combination of visual, physical, and psychological experiences that they understood in terms of the idea of the sublime.

NOTES

1 Thomas Wilkinson, *Tours to the British Mountains*, London, 1824, v.
2 *The Letters of William and Dorothy Wordsworth: Volume III: The Middle Years: Part 2: 1812–1820*, ed. Ernest de Selincourt, 2nd edition, revised by Mary Moorman and Alan G. Hill, Oxford, Clarendon Press, 1970, 495.

3 *The Scottish Tourist and Itinerary*, 3rd edition, Edinburgh, 1830, 259.

4 John Stoddart, *Remarks on Local Scenery and Manners in Scotland during the Years 1799 and 1800*, 2 vols., London, 1801, vol. 1, 236.

5 "sublime, adj. and n." OED Online, Oxford University Press, December 2021, www.oed.com/view/Entry/192766. Accessed 9 December 2021.

6 John Dennis quoted in Clarence DeWitt Thorpe, 'Two Augustans Crossing the Alps: Dennis and Addison on Mountain Scenery', *Studies in Philology*, 32, 3, 1935, 465.

7 Joseph Addison, 'The Pleasures of the Imagination', *The Spectator*, 412 (23 June 1712), in *The Spectator*, ed. Donald F. Bond, Oxford, Clarendon Press, 1965, 540.

8 James Beattie, *Dissertations Moral and Critical*, London, 1783, 606.

9 Thomas West, *A Guide to the Lakes*, London, 1778, 6.

10 William Hutchinson, *An Excursion to the Lakes, in Westmorland and Cumberland, in August 1773*, London, 1774, 156.

11 Anon., *Letters from Snowdon*, London, 1770, 55; Joseph Cradock, *An Account of Some of the Most Romantic Parts of North Wales*, London, 1777, 49–50.

12 *Letters from Snowdon*, 58.

13 Jean-Jacques Rousseau, *Julie, or the New Heloise*, trans. and ed. Philip Stewart and Jean Vaché, vol. 7 of *The Collected Writings of Rousseau*, Roger D. Masters and Christopher Kelly, 14 vols., Hanover, University Press of New England, 1997, 64.

14 Thomas Pennant, *The Journey to Snowdon*, London, 1781, 154–5.

15 Robert Hassell Newell, *Letters on the Scenery of Wales*, London, 1821, 158.

16 Wordsworth, *Prelude* (1805), Bool XIII, lines 3–5; Kenneth R. Johnston, *The Hidden Wordsworth: Poet, Lover, Rebel, Spy*, London, Pimlico, 1998, 198.

17 *Leigh's Guide to the Lakes*, 3rd edition, London, 1835, 75.

18 Ann Radcliffe, *A Journey Made in the Summer of 1794 ... To which are added, Observations during a Tour to the Lakes*, London, 1795, 456–7.

19 Jonathan Otley, *A Concise Description of the English Lakes*, Keswick, 1823, 36–7.

20 T. Richardson, *Guide to Loch Lomond*, Glasgow, 1798, 67.

21 John Keats, *The Letters of John Keats, 1814–1821*, ed. Hyder Edward Rollins, 2 vols., Cambridge, Cambridge University Press, 1958), vol. 1, 264.

22 Stoddart, *Remarks*, 56.

23 William MacGillivray, *A History of British Birds*, 5 vols., London, 1837, vol. 1, 204.

24 Wilkinson, *Tours*, vi.

25 Ibid., vi.

26 Ibid., 106.

27 Ibid., 43.

28 Ibid., 43.

29 Samuel Taylor Coleridge, *Collected Letters of Samuel Taylor Coleridge*, ed. Earl Leslie Griggs, 6 vols., Oxford, Clarendon Press, 1956–71), vol. 2, 842.

30 Ibid., 848.

31 Joseph Budworth, *A Fortnight's Ramble to the Lakes*, 3rd edition, London, 1810, 264.

32 Ibid., 266–7.

33 Wilkinson, *Tours*, 99.
34 William Green, *The Tourist's New Guide*, 2 vols., Kendal, 1819, vol. 1, 256.
35 William Bingley, *North Wales*, 2 vols., London, 1804, vol. 1, 271–2.
36 John MacCulloch, *The Highlands and Western Isles of Scotland*, 4 vols., London, 1824, vol. 1, 255.

10

RICHARD C. SHA

Science and the Sublime

In 1752, Benjamin Franklin decided to fly, in a thunderstorm, a simple kite made from a silk handkerchief and hemp string, to which he tied a house key to attract electrical charges. Franklin guessed that lightning was the same as earthly electricity. By tackling the sublime – potently symbolized by electricity from the heavens – Franklin helped inaugurate the second scientific revolution, freighting science with Promethean risk. But not every sublime risk taken by Romantic-period scientists, either actual or imagined, would achieve such resounding success.

Franklin had no way to grasp lightning without bringing it down to earth. By arguing that this heavenly electrical explosion was an equalizing of positive and negative charges, Franklin tamed sublime electricity by making it calculable and measurable. But to do so, he employed the concepts of charge and discharge. Charge did not become a fundamental entity until James Maxwell formulated his equations in the 1850–70s, when metaphor met precision. The sublime names the limit of human experience and thus represents a threat to science. The essence of sublime experience has been described as the "subject's inability to grasp, embody, or personify the power or authority offered to it," a threat compounded by the fact that one is generally overwhelmed by the experience.[1] The experiencing subject is rendered a passive object, a process often visible when Romantic-period scientists register the overwhelming affective power of the landscapes or phenomena with which they are confronted. Paul Fry suggests that the sublime "is what we cannot resist," and thus the sublime is often represented in Romantic-period cultural texts as feminizing, by transforming what otherwise would be active disciplined scientific observation into an experience that is suffered, something akin to a passion.[2] For the same reason, the sublime is often represented as Orientalizing. Frequently associated in the Romantic period with Eastern authors and exotic climates, the sublime allegedly appeals to those supposedly predisposed to overheated imaginations. In his *Natural History of Barbados* (1750), for example, the Welsh naturalist Griffith Hughes contrasts the Eastern sublime with Western method. Hughes writes of "the more sublime compositions of almost all Eastern authors," with "their lively imaginations transporting them, with incredible Warmth and Activity, from one Thing to another, and thereby causing them to overlook the rules of Method and connection" – unlike the supposedly cooler fancies of Northern authors like himself.[3]

Neil Hertz calls this state of being overwhelmed "blockage" – and contrary to Hughes, no one has immunity to it (see *Hertz*). Hence, in *Frankenstein* (1818), the Creature's initially overwhelmed senses upon birth mirror Victor's inability to articulate anything scientifically meaningful about his discovery, symbolized by the fact that he never mourns his missing laboratory notes. Hertz highlights a transcendent identification with whatever is causing this blockage as a typical work-around, and Victor accordingly identifies himself with the principle of life (*Hertz*, 54–5). Such identification is necessary because the thinking self needs confirmation of its integrity, an integrity all the more tenuous given the sublime's already-noted tendency to (in Romantic-period discourse) Orientalize and feminize. The self and its integrity – Immanuel Kant's name for these is reason – are never experienced with the epistemological certainty of the a priori. Sircello warns that such inability cannot rest there: "the experience of radically limited access to reality," he writes, "must be transformed into a thesis about the experience of an object, or perhaps realm."[4] The very naming of the limit entails the need to overcome it, which science tries to do through method. But not all speculation, as Fry insists and Victor Frankenstein shows, can be tamed by method. Because the sublime intimates the very possibility of the defeat of empirically grounded understanding itself, its stakes could not be higher for science. When Victor accepts life as a principle, he has made it metaphysical and thus beyond experiment.

Science, Mystery, and the Sublime

Sublime mystery needs to be transformed by science into precision, often understood in terms of measurement. Without precision, neither refutation nor experimentation is possible, but with his speculations on the forces of matter (later transferred onto an ether), even Newton recognized not all mystery can be measured.[5] Humphry Davy lamented the fact that chemistry had yet to find "precise ... theory" and his attempts to equate chemical and electrical force were in service of this missing precision.[6] Georges Cuvier looked at the gaps in the fossil record and developed the theory of catastrophism: the idea that sublime natural events had shaped the history of the earth. Catastrophism made possible the terrifying prospect of human extinction, which Percy Bysshe Shelley engages in "Mont Blanc" (1816) and *Prometheus Unbound* (1820).

Not just any precision will do. Required is a precision that lessens mystery. Because Kant had only just begun to separate theology and science, transcendent identification is an initial possible response to blockage.[7] Following Franklin's celebrated experiment with the kite, Immanuel Kant dubbed him "the Prometheus of recent times" ("dem *Prometheus* der neuern Zeitern"), while the subtitle of Mary Shelley's *Frankenstein* similarly bills Victor as "the modern Prometheus."[8] However, the sublime must provoke scientists to do something besides worship or else they remain powerless and ignorant in the face of mystery, and worse off because bereft of powers of scientific observation. Hence, Mary Shelley's subtitle demands that readers compare Frankenstein with Franklin – and find Frankenstein wanting.

Due to its mysterious nature, the sublime threatens to overturn the scientific principle of Occam's razor: the idea that the simplest explanation suffices. How could simplicity snuff out all that infinite mystery, especially since simplicity and mystery seem to work at different scales? Burke's *Enquiry* (1757) attempts to reduce the affective properties of the sublime to just one – terror – and thereby opens the door to precision by drastically reducing the data sets associated with the sublime. Burke then further reduces terror to the efficient cause of the agitation of the nervous system. The sublime flood of data is thereby transformed into information whose patterns require a theory. Burke's example allows us to see how the correlation between mystery and precision necessary to tame the sublime thrives upon the slide from one empirical arena (the felt experience) to another (the workings of the nerves), as if physiology makes consciousness transparent.

However, the sublime's aesthetic prestige also promises to transmute an otherwise mechanical scientific practice into knowledge, provided of course that the sublime's overwhelming affect can be overcome and that its mystery can be somehow punctured. Kant insisted that the sublime was located not nature but rather in the mind because only the mind could produce concepts like infinity that would allow a "purposive relation of the cognitive faculties," which Kant argues produces knowledge of the conditions of human experience, perhaps the only secure knowledge humans can have (*COPJ* §31 161).

Affinity, Curiosity, Skepticism

Because the sublime begins as an experience not quite understood, it calls upon theory to make sense of it as an experience by providing patterns to exploit – hence, in some respects at least, the genesis of the extensive speculation about the sublime within eighteenth-century philosophical aesthetics, a genre that, as De Bolla argues, at once examines and produces sublime affect (see *Discourse*). The sublime thus models scientific work, by demanding that local observation become generalizable into knowledge, theory, and rules through patterns, which, in turn, must be subject to more verification. By provoking what are essentially figures of speech like "affinity" or "rapports" or "vitality" that smooth over the gap between local observation and systematic knowledge, the sublime shows why and how science leans upon the artifice of art. When pondering terminology in his *New System of Chemical Philosophy* (1808), for instance, John Dalton experiments with "attraction of cohesion," then "attraction of aggregation," and finally "more simply, affinity."[9] Dalton concludes that "whatever names it may go by, they still signify one and the same power" (113). Tropes facilitate the transformation of particular observations into general ideas or theories, while their fictiveness provokes the need for constant testing and further refinement of models. Evelyn Fox Keller argues of the use of tropes in scientific writing that "making sense of what is yet not known is a ... groping in the dark; and for this the imprecision and flexibility of figurative language is indispensable."[10] The trope's ability to shuttle back and forth between empirical particulars and abstract generalizations grants the scientist the illusion of understanding these competing domains even as the trope enables the provisional specification of empirical detail and, because of that same provisionality, the evasion of charges of materialist atheism.

The ability of the sublime to foster skepticism as a bulwark against mystery further intensifies the sublime's scientific influence. As mystery provokes skepticism, which teeters between the sublime and the ridiculous, skepticism allows scientific investigation to remain an open-ended process while shifting precision into a process instead of a product. For Hilary Putnam, the antidote to skepticism seems like more skepticism insofar as both "scientific positivism and metaphysical realism concede the correctness of almost everything the skeptic says" in hopes of holding onto a "minimalist sort of scientific knowledge" and onto a common perceptual dissatisfaction with the human as opposed to a God's-eye view.[11] At once, then, a prod to science and a sense of the real limitations of human knowledge, the sublime provides space and boundaries for a recursive loop that can be filled by operationalization itself, but one requiring speculative taming to prove its worth. Thus, the sublime scientific road often leads to the quotidian, to what Thomas Kuhn refers to as the dominant work of science or "mop-up work."[12]

Aided by Lorraine Daston's and Katherine Park's thesis that curiosity shifts in the Early Modern period from being associated with lust to becoming avaricious, we can see how a revised curiosity can leverage desire as opposed to being controlled by it.[13] Unlike lustful curiosity, avaricious curiosity can be made noble, or sublime, because it is always on the move and preoccupied with precision in the form of particulars.[14] With teleology suspended, and with greedy curiosity agitating inquiry, operationalization can become its own end, and scientific observation can be reified or made sublime. On the one hand, the sublime's resistance to closure further threatens to impose either an endless chain of experiments, potentially devolving into what Samuel Taylor Coleridge called a "crass idly-busy empiricism," or an endless series of hypotheses, which Coleridge dubbed "suffictions": the fruitless piling up of one hypothesis upon another.[15] On the other hand, empiricism and hypothesis do not have to remain separate dead ends: dialectic can transform what were cul-de-sacs into the operationalizing traffic between them.

Sublime threat thus becomes especially charged within science, which we witness when the sublime marks the difference between practitioner of science and the quack. Daniel Turner, himself on the fringes of science, insists in *The Art of Surgery* (1736) that quacks "know nothing of the sublime subject they work upon."[16] Because surgeons were, until 1745, incorporated with barbers, with bloodletting and purgation two of the most common procedures, Turner harnesses the sublime to elevate surgery beyond butchery, but elevation hints at quackery. Even the eminent surgeon John Hunter was known as "the knife man." Sublime power was all the more necessary given that under a patronage model, the patient exacts control over the practitioner, and the practitioner is forced to traffic in gentility over medical and scientific knowledge. Stephen Jacyna argues that by 1800 the increased importance of the hospital setting reduced the genteel patient patron into a body, wholly subject to medical knowledge.[17] Turner disseminates sublime knowledge through his 110 case studies, which together aspire to methodize surgery into an art. And yet the danger of such methodizing is that surgery will return to a series of rote procedures no more intricate than hair cutting or bloodletting. Some mystery in the form of speculation, it would seem, can ennoble science.

During the Romantic period, Franz Anton Mesmer, the inventor of the theory and therapeutic practice of Mesmerism, provided the most challenging case for discerning the difference between the scientist and the quack. Radicals embraced Mesmer because he allowed them to mock the French medical establishment.[18] Louis XVI of France empaneled a commission in 1784 to examine Mesmer's animal magnetism: a universal, magnetic fluid that supposedly informed all organized life. Benjamin Franklin, one of four commissioners (chemist Antoine Lavoisier was another), argued in a secret report that the people were divided between an "announced ... discovery useful and sublime [and] ... a dangerous and ridiculous illusion."[19] But how was one to prove this "sublime" fluid of animal magnetism was an illusion, especially when it escaped the senses of the examiners? Mesmer, who argued that the universal cause of disease in the body is poor circulation of its hypothetical magnetic fluids, studiously avoided the occult and first modeled his fluid on Newtonian attraction and on his universal ether and then on magnetism. In drawing upon topical eighteenth-century theories of emotional and physiological "sympathy" between individuals, ideas that bound together inner sense and pantheistic vitalist electrical forces, Mesmer was in keeping with current scientific speculation.

In the commissioners' unpublished response, written originally in French, they insist, by contrast, that sometimes nature cures without a remedy, implying that Mesmer's putative cures are merely the work of nature. They challenge Mesmer's sublime idea of an animal magnetic fluid as a universal explanation for human disease by pointing to an infinite number of causes ("une infinité de causes") working on the body: "a psychological and physical being." They argue that "his inclinations, his pains, his movements all depend as much on his thinking as on the irritability of his organs." The commissioners explain that these forces amount to a labyrinth of difficulties ("un dédale de difficultés"). Mesmer uses Occam's razor to try to reduce this totality of possible causes to a single, postulated cause: animal magnetism. But by yoking Mesmer with Daedalus, the creator of the labyrinth on Crete, the commissioners rupture any proffered precision, and return us to the charlatan's seeming triumph over mystery. To counter Mesmer, the commissioners explicitly modeled themselves on the synthetic methods of contemporary chemistry and the chemical sublime: first decomposing the substances, discovering their principles, assuring themselves of the exactitude of their analysis, and then recomposing the substance. They conclude: "while proceeding in our investigation, we witnessed the disappearance, one after another, of the properties attributed to this supposed fluid, and that the whole theoretical construction, built upon an imaginary basis, crumbled before our eyes." The commissioners even blindfolded patients so that when they claimed to be cured even though nothing had been done to them, the commissioners could proclaim any alleged cure to be the work of the imagination.

Chemistry and Biology

In Romantic-period chemistry, the verb "sublime" is invoked to describe the transitions of matter from one state to another. Ruston argues that chemistry and poetry had symbiotic power in the period because both were considered transformative.[20] Yet without a demonstrable theory about the elements of matter, and without some sense of how chemical bonds work, how are those transformations to be understood? Nor was it clear whether the chemist had much control over these sublime transitions. Hence chemistry, as we have seen, turns to the language of affinity to provide explanations and harnesses the power of affinity tables both to predict which combinations are more likely and to hypothesize new substances. Humphry Davy considered chemistry sublime insofar as it unified all of nature's forces under electricity.[21] Chemists were not to be passive in the face of nature's transformations; rather, they had to actively manipulate them, or subject them to reduction.[22] Davy paraded his manipulations of the Royal Institution's massive galvanic batteries that pulled compounds apart into their elements and confirmed electricity's powers to unify chemistry. At the same time, the French chemist Antoine-François de Fourcroy refers to Georg Ernst Stahl's theory of salts as being comprised of earth and water as his "sublime theory," meaning by this that it reaches beyond what facts will support.[23] Salts were vexing to the concept of affinity because they were composed of alkalis and bases but had the properties of neither. Enter the sublime corpuscular theory to posit the one having the shape of daggers, the other to have the shape of a sheath, and the transformation could once again be explained.[24] Even when levied as a criticism, then, the sublime was still scientifically useful when it prompted theories that made what otherwise seems total mystery intelligible. Science tames sublime threat when it is the start of scientific work, not its end.

In Romantic-period biology, operationalizing life into something that could be studied tempers sublime blockage. That life has many levels of organization, each of which provides new ways of considering the formation of living beings, only adds to the challenges. The French anatomist and pathologist Xavier Bichat thought that Newton's "truly sublime idea" of attraction unified all physical phenomena, and he sought to determine what unified biology.[25] Although maligned, Bichat's circular definition of life, outlined in his *Physiological Researches upon Life and Death* (1800) as the sum of processes that resist death, makes life not a cause, which resists ocular proof, but rather a result. As the sum total of physiological (vital) processes, Bichat allows one to compile physiological data into a meaningful aggregate: "life" names as an ensemble what really is the fruit of methodical assembly. Literally assembled from dead parts, Frankenstein's Creature allegorizes Bichat's grounding definition of biology. Bichat's empirical sleight-of-hand transforms life from a sublime cause or principle into something demonstrable (an effect), and thereby attempts to rival Newton's sublime theory of attraction. Mary Shelley's *Frankenstein* similarly wonders, against the backdrop of the ongoing contemporary debate about the nature of life, whether life should be considered as something added to dead parts and about whether it is a cause or an effect.

The German physician Johann Friedrich Blumenbach's *An Essay on Generation* (1789) provides another apt illustration of how biologists struggled to make advances against the sublime mystery of life, with Blumenbach choosing to reduce life to a formative nisus (perfective urge) irreducible to chemical and mechanical forces. The scientific study of generation was thwarted by many obstacles, the first of which was, as Daston and Park point out, the need to sever the connection between lust and curiosity.[26] After tarring the Middle Ages with the brush of "monastic barbarism," Blumenbach notes that the "holy fathers of those times ... awakened by a spark of curiosity ... composed sensuous and obscene works."[27] The second obstacle was that it was all too easy to provide evidence for the two reigning but contradictory theories surrounding generation: evolution and epigenesis. By "evolution," Blumenbach means preformation: the idea that the first parent embodies all the germs of every succeeding generation. Epigenesis, by contrast, insists that the prepared but unorganized rudiments arrive at the requisite location at the right time and then begin to organize themselves. At what scale do we look for the rudiments of life, and what to look for? Note how the objectification – achieved through labeling something as the component of life – short-circuits speculation, dismantling the blockage caused by the sublime.

Natural History, Neurology, and Astronomy

In Romantic-period natural history, the threat to science posed by sublime excess was magnified by the exponential rise in the discovery of new species, due to exploration and colonization. Jean-Jacques Rousseau, for example, remarked that "extensive voyages incessantly enriched Botany with new treasures."[28] With the help of his cosmopolitan scientific network, Joseph Banks, president of the Royal Society, increased the numbers of plant species at Kew Gardens from 3,400 to 11,000. Economist Adam Smith warned that wonder would not rest until it had connected the singular natural specimen to others of its kind.[29] The German explorer and scientist Alexander von Humboldt described the challenge as follows: "it remains to be considered whether, by the operation of thought, we may hope to reduce the immense diversity of phenomena comprised by the Cosmos to the unity of principle."[30] Over this sublime ("immense") diversity, Humboldt wielded what we would now call ecological thinking, developing the idea of species grouped into climate zones stretching across the world. In his *Views of Nature* (1807), Humboldt often uses the aesthetics of the sublime to represent natural phenomena, as in his account of grassland plains: "like a limitless expanse of waters," he writes, "the Steppe fills the mind with a sense of the infinite, and the soul, freed from the sensuous impressions of space, expands with spiritual emotions of a higher order."[31] In many eighteenth-century and Romantic-period accounts of the sublime, this "infinite" vacancy could be filled in with contemplation of the supposed Creator. Because no scientist could afford to appear to deny God, the sublime within science could merge with the theological, enabling mystery to enhance empirical evidence of omnipresent harmony.

In *The Neural Sublime*, Alan Richardson explores how Romantic-period literature and brain science invokes the sublime to show the power and complexity of the brain at the moment of cognitive collapse (*Richardson*, 28–30). Tensed against a Kantian sublime that reveals the supersensible, Richardson's neural sublime peels away reason and language to illuminate the workings of the ordinary mind. Rather than a puncturing of mystery, however, this move tends to the substitution of one form of mystery for another, as the ordinary and extraordinary change places, and as dumb matter achieves some intelligibility. Once consciousness has been replaced by the brain as the object of enquiry, cognitive collapse can be deferred onto an intelligible theory of how the brain and the nervous system function. We witness such deferral especially in Emanuel Swedenborg's *Three Transactions on the Cerebrum* (1744). If Swedenborg's almost 1,500-page manuscript lavishly maps out the labyrinthine brain connections, along with quoting from almost every authority, what is most striking is how little this atlas actually explains. Swedenborg's declared method underscores the connectedness of every fact: "there is a connection between all things in the world, since they spring from a single universal source."[32] He continues, "thus whatever comes now to be treated of concerning the brain, that same must be confirmed by everything that depends upon the brain" (vol. 1, xxxiii). Having connected the brain with everything else, Swedenborg once again reveals the strength and the weakness of operationalization: a mania for finding what he argues are ontological connections reveals the connectedness of facts for which only a God's-eye view could provide true illumination. Missing from the method is any actual connective essence. To wit, Swedenborg calls for a "universal mathesis or a philosophy of universals . . . a science of sciences [which can] designate by signs those things in prior nature, and the nature of causes, which analogically refer themselves to visible phenomena and effects" (vol. 1, 86). Here, Swedenborg returns to the Cartesian promotion of mathematics as a universal language, an idea picked up again in the sublime "dream of poetry and science" passage from Book V of William Wordsworth's *Prelude* (1805). This quest for the Romantic neural sublime endures today: neuroscientists are still in pursuit of the connectome: a comprehensive map of every nervous connection in the human brain.

Conclusion

Let me conclude by returning to the heavens. In his essay "The Principles Which Lead and Direct Philosophical Enquiries; Illustrated by the History of Astronomy" (1795), Adam Smith insisted that sublime wonder be transformed into connections that show the harmony and coherence of the "beautiful machinery" of the universe.[33] Not only did Smith praise astronomy for its attempts to connect the human "imagination [with] the phenomena of the heavens," but he also applauded "the discovery of an immense chain of the most important and sublime truths" (93). Once again isolated empirical facts must be operationalized into connections. The astronomer John Herschel, whose famous father William discovered Uranus in 1781, celebrates the fact that "all is harmony in nature ... as rules advance in generality; apparent exceptions become regular; and equivoque, in her sublime legislation, is as unheard of as maladministration."[34] In this fantasy of the sublime, chaos, entropy, and ambiguity are denied. The astronomer Mary Somerville, the first person referred to in print as a "scientist," noted in her *On the Connection of the Physical Sciences* (1834) that the "heavens afford the most sublime subject of study which can be derived from science."[35] She continues: "equally conspicuous is the goodness of the great First Cause, in having endowed man with faculties, by which he can not only appreciate the magnificence of His works, but trace, with precision, the operation of His laws" (2). Although the sublime in part sustains worship, Somerville's end goal is Newtonian measured "precision," and she shows how geometry and its imagined vectors "join[] the centers of the sun and the planets" along with how calculus reveals the essential continuity between the motions of the heavens and the earth (8). Moreover, cosmic disturbances and perturbations are met with compensations, as when Somerville concedes that the orbits of the planets are elliptical and lose their symmetry. However, when data is compiled over the course of centuries, the inequalities in the motions of Jupiter and Saturn, for instance, can be shown to be periodic, with an interval of "no less than 918 years" (15). Yet as the observing self dissolves into the transparency of method, the very excess that the sublime provides – its overwhelming affective power – becomes the only trace of the scientific self's lapsed integrity.

NOTES

For helpful comments on earlier drafts of this essay, I thank Cian Duffy, Nathan Harshman, Anita Sherman, April Shelford, Frank James, and Trevor Levere.

1 James Noggle, *The Skeptical Sublime*, Oxford, Oxford University Press, 2001, 10.

2 Paul Fry, *The Reach of Criticism*, New Haven, CT, Yale University Press, 1983, 57.

3 Griffith Hughes, *The Natural History of Barbados*, London, 1750, 33.

4 Guy Sircello, "How Is a Theory of the Sublime Possible?," *Journal of Aesthetics and Art Criticism*, 51, 4, 1993, 541–50 (545).

5 See Amos Funkenstein, *Theology and the Scientific Imagination*, Princeton, NJ, Princeton University Press, 1986, 16.

6 Humphry Davy, *Collected Works*, ed. John Davy, 9 vols., Bristol, Thoemmes, 2001, vol. 2, 230.

7 Funkenstein credits Leibniz for distinguishing between logical and physical necessity, a move that allowed one to be a good scientist and an obedient theologian (120–4). David Knight notes that until 1800, almost everyone considered scientific study a part of religion (*Science and Spirituality*, London, Routledge, 2004, 1).

8 For Kant on Franklin, see James Delbourgo, *Electricity and Enlightenment in Early America*, Cambridge, MA, Harvard University Press, 2006, 3, 285n.2.

9 John Dalton, *A New System of Chemical Philosophy*, New York, Philosophical Library, 1964, 112.

10 Evelyn Fox Keller, *Making Sense of Life*, Cambridge MA, Harvard University Press, 2002, 110.

11 Hilary Putnam, "Preface: Introducing Cavell," in Ted Cohen, Paul Guyer, and Hilary Putnam, eds., *Pursuits of Reason*, Lubbock, Texas Tech University Press, 1993, vii–viii.

12 Thomas Kuhn, *The Structure of Scientific Revolutions*, Chicago, University of Chicago Press, 2012, 24.

13 Lorraine Daston and Katherine Park, *Wonders and the Order of Nature, 1150–1750*, New York, Zone Books, 1988, 303–10.

14 Ibid., 316–21.

15 See Trevor Levere, *Poetry Realized in Nature*, Cambridge, Cambridge University Press, 1981, 87; and Samuel Taylor Coleridge, *Biographia literaria*, ed. James Engell and W. Jackson Bate, 2 vols., Princeton, NJ, Princeton University Press, vol. 1, 101.

16 Daniel Turner, *The Art of Surgery*, London, 1736, 131. Turner's first book, *Apologia chyrurgica* (1695), explains how to detect the overpromises of a quack.

17 Stephen Jacyna, "Medicine in Transformation, 1800–49," in W. F. Bynum, Anne Hardy, Stephen Jacyna, Christopher Lawrence, and E. M. Tansey, eds., *The Western Medical Tradition 1800–2000*, Cambridge, Cambridge University Press, 2006, 11–97 (54–5).

18 See Robert Darnton, *Mesmerism and the End of the Enlightenment in France*, Cambridge MA, Harvard University Press, 1968, 164–5.

19 Benjamin Franklin et al., "Exposé des expériences" (September 4, 1784); quoted from the Benjamin Franklin Papers, Packard Humanities Institute/Yale University: https://franklinpapers.org/yale?vol=42&page=187&rqs=573 (my translation).

20 Sharon Ruston, *Creating Romanticism*, London, Palgrave, 2013, 133–5. For Lamarck, transformation was a gradual process, refuting Cuvier's catastrophism.

21 See Jan Golinksi, "The Literature of the New Sciences," in James Chandler, ed., *The Cambridge History of English Romantic Literature*, Cambridge, Cambridge University Press, 2009, 527–52 (534).

22 Ruston, *Creating Romanticism*, 173.

23 Antoine-François de Fourcroy, *Elements of Chemistry and Natural History*, trans. William Nicholson, London, 1800, 350.

24 See Trevor Levere, *Transforming Matter*, Baltimore, MD, Johns Hopkins University Press, 2001, 44.

25 Xavier Bichat, *General Anatomy Applied to Physiology and Medicine*, trans. George Hayward, 3 vols., Boston, 1822, vol. 1, 11.

26 Daston and Park, *Wonders*, 305.

27 Johann Friedrich Blumenbach, *An Essay on Generation*, trans. A. Crichton, London, 1792, 3.

28 Jean-Jacques Rousseau, *The Reveries of the Solitary Walker, Botanical Writings, and Letter to Franquières*, ed. Christopher Kelly, trans. Alexandra Cook, Hanover, NH, University Press of New England, 1990, 95. For more on botany in the Romantic period, see Theresa Kelley, *Clandestine Marriage: Botany and Romantic Culture*, Baltimore, MD, Johns Hopkins University Press, 2012.

29 Adam Smith, "History of Astronomy" (1795), in *Essays on Philosophical Subjects*, ed. W. P. D. Wightman and J. C. Bryce, Carmel, IN, Liberty Fund, 1980, 40.

30 Alexander von Humboldt, *Cosmos*, trans. E. C. Otté, Baltimore, MD, Johns Hopkins University Press, 1997, 73.

31 Alexander von Humboldt, *Views of Nature*, trans. E. C. Otté and Henry Bohn, London, 1850, 2.

32 Emanuel Swedenborg, *Three Transactions on the Cerebrum*, 2 vols., Philadelphia, Swedenborg Scientific Association,1938, vol. 1, xxxiii.

33 Adam Smith, "The Principles Which Lead and Direct Philosophical Enquiries; Illustrated by the History of Astronomy," in *Essays on Philosophical Subjects*, ed. Dugald Stewart, Edinburgh, 1795, 1–93 (54).

34 John Herschel, *A Preliminary Discourse on the Study of Natural Philosophy*, London, 1831, 33.

35 Mary Somerville, *On the Connection of the Physical Sciences* [1834], London, 1846, 1. William Whewell, the first person to use "scientist" in print, does so in his review of Somerville's *On the Connection* (*Quarterly Review* 54, 1834, 64–68 [65–6]).

11

MIRANDA STANYON

Musical Sublimes

In November 1828, a new musical farce was presented at Covent Garden: the composer George Alexander Lee and playwright Thomas Morton Senior's *The Sublime and Beautiful*.[1] Long forgotten, the music was popular enough to be printed for domestic consumption, and the farce served as a relatively successful vehicle for its lead, the contralto Lucy Vestris. Vestris created a number of Rossini roles on the English stage, but is perhaps still better known as a star and later manager of burlesques, who played the title pants-role in *Giovanni in London* (1817), a parody of the sublime antihero known to us from Mozart's *Don Giovanni* (1787) and, later, Byron's *Don Juan* (1819–24).[2] As Lee and Morton's farce suggests, by the end of the Romantic period, musical culture had fully absorbed – and could indeed present as comical or trite – the opposition of beauty and sublimity. A variation on the captivity dramas that delighted European audiences during the Enlightenment and Romantic periods, *The Sublime and Beautiful* pitted an English beauty, Elizabeth, against a sublime despot, the Sultan of Constantinople, who has enslaved Elizabeth's sister-in-law in his harem. Elizabeth cannily deploys her beauteous person, smart mouth, physical weakness, and apparently artless love of English conviviality, informality and liberty in order to insult with impunity (and partially reform) the Sultan's court, and to woo the tyrant for herself, eventually securing the release of all his captive women and her own coronation as 'new and favoured Queen' (70). While both aesthetics are approached with tongue in cheek, the joke is clearly on the sublime. If in 1757, according to Edmund Burke's *Enquiry*, the 'ideas of pain, and danger' were sources of sublimity because they produced 'the strongest emotion which the mind is capable of feeling', then by 1828 those same ideas could be sources also of laughter (*Enquiry* I vii).

Lee and Morton's farce provides a catalogue of the tropes of the beautiful and sublime after Burke, contrasting the female and male, domestic and other, sociable and anti-social, persuasive love and forceful fear, weakness and power, modern and archaic, common sense and irrationality, and, here, a society that is reasonable, modern and civilized with one that is unreasonable, absolutist and barbarous.[3] While the musical 'tropes' are not pronounced in the way that the narrative tropes are, Lee suggests the contrasting aesthetics in numerous ways.[4] For instance, an overture that moves between a lively, playful C major melody marked *Allegro con spirito*, and foreboding, brooding semi-demi-quaver figures in C minor creates (predictable) surprises through abruptly alternating dynamics. In the solos, Lee presents a 'Celebrated Bravura' aria that highlights the Sultan's tumid passion and the virtuosity of the tenor playing him, in contrast to a lighter, gracious air introduced by Vestris for Elizabeth, whose feelings remain moderate throughout. And he composes choruses that range from evocations of awed subjection to the Sultan – conjuring up stilted and grand ceremonial music through their repeated, homophonic, syllabic chants (in the Grand Chorus 'The Clank of the Sabre the Tramp of the Guard', or the Act 1 finale 'Make Your Salam to the Grand Signor') – to a winsome glee for a picturesque scene at a Turkish bazaar, or a pretty madrigalesque Act 2 finale celebrating Elizabeth's triumph over the sublime despot.

These musical characteristics are by no means specific to evocations of the sublime and beautiful and cannot be said to *represent* or *refer to* them in the same way as the verbal text. This is hardly surprising, since the power of music to move listeners strongly without telling them anything clearly had both attracted and repelled theorists of the sublime from pseudo-Longinus to Burke and Kant, and has continued to vex scholars of the musical sublime in more recent years. In many cases, a lack of (semantic) specificity made music an epitome of the Romantic sublime; for some, it excluded music from sublimity; and for others, it made music an ambiguous limit case *within* an aesthetic of thresholds and boundary-crossings. This chapter outlines tensions and varieties in Romantic musical sublimes, setting out from the premise not that music could only truly become sublime in this period (as is sometimes assumed), but that music epitomized some of the attractions and perplexities of the sublime for the Romantic period.

But before leaving *The Sublime and Beautiful*, we can note that Vestris's career also raises the ticklish question of periodization. Stretching as it did from the mature music of Rossini, conventionally aligned with the beginnings of Romantic opera, to the peak of Victorian burlesque, Vestris's professional life points to the asynchrony of Romanticism across media as well as between regions. Romantic music is traditionally classified as beginning later than Romanticism in other cultural spheres (perhaps especially in Britain), and often covers much of the nineteenth century, running from the later works of Ludwig van Beethoven to the oeuvres of Franz Liszt, Richard

Wagner, Pyotr Ilyich Tchaikovsky, Antonín Dvořák, Gustav Mahler and so-called late Romantics such as Camille Saint-Saëns.[5] One way of imagining the history of 'Romantic' music over this extended, even distended, period has been as a story of the victory of the sublime over the beautiful during the nineteenth century, in tandem with the rise in status of instrumental music.

Instruments of the Infinite

Perhaps the pithiest praise for instrumental music in this period came from the critic, musician and literary fantasist E. T. A. Hoffmann, who in an 1810 essay on Beethoven called instrumental music 'the most romantic of the arts ... for only the infinite is its object' ('Sie ist die romantischste aller Künste ... denn nur das Unendliche ist ihr Vorwurf').[6] Hoffmann's now influential formulation implicitly aligns Romanticism *tout court* with the post-Kantian sublime, as the aesthetic of the infinite. Tellingly, Hoffmann uses a term, *Vorwurf*, which can suggest both the *object* of aesthetic contemplation – foregrounding the subjective or phenomenological understanding of the sublime so important to Kant, and more broadly to aesthetics as a discipline grounded in sensations, tastes and reflections – and by contrast the *model*, pattern or material for artistic creation. Instrumental music *need not* follow any model or imitate any determinate object (*Vorwurf*) in the world, Hoffmann claims, turning on its head the neoclassical regret that music *cannot* properly imitate nature.[7] Finally, and curiously, *Vorwurf* also commonly means 'reproach' or 'reproof', as if the infinite were somehow a reproach to music.

The idea of infinite reproach arguably colours Hoffmann's celebration of music with that sense of incompletion and striving, of thresholds reached but not quite transcended – of unending quantity or power that we can 'think' or negatively enjoy but not possess (argues Kant) – which becomes so central to the Romantic sublime, as it is to Hoffmann's more general understanding of the infinite longing unleashed by music (see *COPJ* §26 254–6). This would make sense insofar as music is regarded as a sensuous art that must ultimately fall short of either representing or contemplating the infinite, and if one grants that we are empirical subjects, limited by our finite senses and able to perceive only what Burke called an 'artificial infinite': an 'indefinite' series, such as the series of vibrations within a prolonged sound, or a series of bell-sounds or cannon-shots; sonic vibrations, Burke suggested, could rise to the pitch of the sublime either through their seemingly infinite extent or through an extreme psychological 'tension' attendant on our inability to predict their recurrence (*Enquiry* IV ix). This sense that the sublime confirms humans' proper limits alongside their grandeur was less prominent in the classical and neoclassical discourses of the sublime, but was increasingly important to theorists from Burke onwards. It resonates, for example, with Schlegel's provocative reflection that the infinite itself is 'a *fiction* ... an *error*, or *illusion*, or *misunderstanding* ... But an absolutely necessary fiction.'[8] While for Burke and Kant music per se stood outside the sublime, nonetheless, in their wake, Romantic-period Europeans frequently saw music as the art best suited to representing that necessary fiction, the infinite.

The apparent emancipation of music from the determinacy and finitude of language, epitomized by Hoffmann's treatment of Beethoven, has seemed to chime not only with the rage for the sublime in Romanticism but also with the ascendancy of genius composers who, no longer tied to institutions or noble patrons, transgressed the expectations of audiences and the rules of harmony and counterpoint to become tortured and titanic heroes, themselves sublime even in their extreme gestures of 'prostration' (what postmodern theories of the sublime might call 'abjection') before great composers of the past.[9] Handel was acclaimed as a sublime composer of oratorio and opera from at least the 1720s, a creator of overwhelming sounds to render the awe-inspiring text of scripture, and a counterpart to the sublime poets Dryden and Milton. Wagner's operas were routinely received through the aesthetic of the sublime, which, as a prose writer, he himself helped to theorize. But it was Beethoven who became the sublime musician par excellence within imaginings of the Romantic sublime as an art of instrumental and especially symphonic music: experientially intense, thematically involved and complex, formally audacious, generally non-referential, texturally big, undeniably 'serious'.

Ironically – and fittingly – the centrepiece of this reception history is a symphony that transgressed the limits of 'pure' or 'absolute' instrumental music and absorbed texted vocal music into the arsenal of the orchestra: Beethoven's Ninth (1824) with its setting of Schiller's 'Ode to Joy' (An die Freude) (1785). The 'orthodoxy' that the Ninth is 'the most sublime musical composition known' has its origins in contemporary responses to Beethoven.[10] It has hardly been challenged either by the fact that sublimity has no very definite meaning in contemporary culture or that musicologists have spent decades worrying over the Symphony's moral standing in the wake of its celebration by both Nazi and Soviet regimes. It is not the status of the Ninth as sublime that is put on trial here, but the status of the sublime itself. Beethoven's symphony has been excoriated as an extended analogue for and sometimes tool of nationalist and sexualized violence, culminating in the hard-won thematic unity and closure of 'the "triumphal" end of the symphony'.[11] If, for Hoffman, instrumental music was above reproach from mere mortals, then for half a century it has been a key site for reproaches to the high ideals and ideologies of the West, and the 'dangerous aesthetic' of the sublime that bodied them forth.[12]

Infinite Variety

The (German) Romantic symphony, then, has had a continuous though rocky relationship with the sublime. Scholarship has had to wait longer and push harder for recognition of the variety of the musical sublime. This variety pertains partly to repertoire and genre: in vocal music by composers as diverse as Palestrina, an 'old master' of sacred polyphony, and Cherubini, the 'terrorist' Italian opera composer who staged cataclysmic operas in Revolutionary Paris; in smaller-scale instrumental and intimate song genres; and in so-called folk music (a category that emerges in the eighteenth century and becomes highly loaded in Romantic-period nationalist and ethnocentric discourses).[13] But the variety also marks the conceptualizations of the musical sublime across the period. Thus, for example, in the domain of compositional techniques, Christian Friedrich Michaelis, a sedulous early adaptor of Kantian aesthetics to music, explained that music could trigger the sublime either through complexly ordered polyphonic textures with multiple interweaving voices or through 'wild music' that resembled a 'downward-rushing, foaming waterfall' or 'flooding seas': such sounds 'tear the imagination along with such violence [*Gewalt*] that it cannot grasp any totality, but instead, driven to and fro ... floats in the infinite, and raises reason to the thought of eternity'.[14] Or again, the compositions of C. P. E. Bach were received as sublime partly because his innovative solo keyboard music rested on audacious and shocking harmonic progressions – leaps between contrasting chords that broke traditional rules, and yet escaped any charge of mere ineptitude by their adherence to a suppressed logic of omitted, hidden transitions. Friedrich Gottlieb Klopstock, no straightforward fan of instrumental music, called Bach 'great / in music led by words / greater / in bold, wordless' music.[15] Yet Bach also strove for sublimity through the evocation of colossal grandeur in compositions such as *Heilig* (Holy) (1776), an ambitious sacred work for double choir and orchestra. While hardly simple, *Heilig* is harmonically much less adventurous, and with its mystical paratexts it can be heard as keying into unchanging celestial consonances that overwhelm the listener through sheer accumulation of harmonies – not unlike the 'masses of harmony' that Charles Burney praised in Handel's music – rather than startling, tortuous leaps or crunchy dissonances.[16] *Heilig* significantly harkened back not only to the high style of *Messiah* but also to sacred music featuring double choirs by C. P. E. Bach's father – works that would be revived for nineteenth-century listeners by Felix Mendelssohn, and transformed from Lutheran church music into monuments of the sublime for modern secular concert audiences.

Further illuminating the contrast between sublime complexity and sublime simplicity, we can observe that sublimity was claimed both by proponents of musical virtuosity and scientific mastery and by opponents of virtuosity who championed natural and heartfelt performances, whether by professional opera singers or 'untaught' improvisors and repertoire-holders, such as the representatives of the Gaelic bardic traditions that British Romantics simultaneously cherished and relegated to the past of the modern empire. In an age of celebrity, an important dimension of this contrast lay in the personae and vocal profiles of individual performers, such as the 'sublime voice' of Giuditta Pasta, whose vocal vulnerabilities and apparently uneven production called up rapturous defences from her admirers; the 'sublimely pathetic' Giuseppina Grassini, who captivated some listeners while others scorned her limited, allegedly damaged voice; or the dramatically powerful but physically frail Julie-Angélique Scio, whose performances as the infanticide Medea were hailed as sublime in post-Terror Paris.[17] The reception of these three opera stars points to the complication of reading the Romantic sublime as masculine and the limits of approaching it purely through the history of genius composers and enduring 'works'. More broadly, their mixture of power and perceived simplicity and/or weakness suggests how an old rhetorical contrast between the *stylis sublimis* (high style) and *sermo humilis* (low/humble words) – both associated with astonishing effects – continued to inform Romantic tastes and debates in the domain of performance practice and musical celebrity.[18]

This contrast between sublime music as virtuosic or heartfelt also resonated with the Longinian observation that emotion was a chief source of the sublime – and yet that the sublime could exist without targeting the movements of the soul associated with *pathos*. Accordingly, much like writers on the poetic sublime before him, Michaelis asserted the existence of a musical sublime that depicted feelings being 'stirred, shattered, moved hither and thither', and a musical sublime quite separate from the 'expression of feeling'.[19] This was no doubt an important ingredient in allowing music to achieve the prominence it did within Romantic hierarchies of the arts. Whereas in pre-Romantic criticism, music could be praised as a universal language of passion, powerfully moving and manipulating the heart (in this regard serving as a mirror to verbal rhetoric), from the later eighteenth century we witness more frequent doubts about the relevance of passion (and 'emotion', the category that would overtake it) to aesthetic enjoyment and value.[20] Music comes to be associated with aesthetic *disinterest*, as well as with extremes of excitation that are interpreted less through the vocabulary of particular, alternating passions, and more through the discourse of shocks or stimulations to the nervous system – a system increasingly understood, following the work of Hartley and Burke, as operating, like music, via vibration.[21] By offering ways beyond artistic paradigms focusing on the passions – their movement and imitation – music could chime with theorizations of aesthetic disinterest and 'austere' varieties of the sublime, as well as with intersecting materialist discourses that investigated the nerves and speculated that consciousness and subjectivity were the mere products of a play of empirical sensations.[22] Thus, while the Romantic sublime continued to be associated with passions of fear or terror as triggers, the belief that aesthetic responses ultimately transcended self-centred or interested passions could nonetheless profit from music's representations in the European tradition: a construction as an abstract play of forms; as an art whose medium, the evanescent vibrations of the air, apparently transcended sight and touch, approaching the irreal, non-sensual enjoyments of the imagination that escaped mortality and lay 'All breathing human passions far above', as Keats put it in 'Ode on a Grecian Urn' (1818; line 28); as an art of harmony and therefore composure, connected with super-passionate Epicurean states of tranquillity; or with the Boethian ideal of aligning the well-ordered human soul (*musica humana*) with cosmic harmony (*musica mundana*) via the heard harmonies of music (*musica instrumentalis*).

We are perhaps so accustomed to associating the sublime with rupture, disorder and, conceptually, with discord that musical sublimes of composure and resolution have become more difficult to discern in Romantic culture. This issue goes beyond the expanded toleration of dissonance in this period (evident with Beethoven, and extended by Wagner so that, in his famous 'Tristan' motif, a dissonant chord can even function as a resolution), and beyond the formal question of whether, after strife, harmonious resolutions finally appear (such resolutions again are abundant with Beethoven, as in the emphatic, repetitious cadences closing the Ninth). As Elaine Sisman has recently argued with reference to Haydn's *The Seasons* (Die Jahreszeiten) (1801), the end of the sublime is much more elusive than its beginning: When quotidian contentment sets in after the ruckus of a sublime storm, an astonishing blaze of light, or a life-endangering ordeal, is this ending always a beautiful let-down that *follows* the sublime – a betrayal, even, of the turmoil, indeterminacy and irresolution characteristic of the (musical) sublime – or can the end of the sublime in harmony represent its culmination or fulfilment, an 'end' in the sense of a goal?[23] After all, a characteristic eighteenth-century parsing of the experience of the sublime would separate it into stages of astonishment (stand-still and diminution), rapture (being carried away), and an inflation (pride and self-aggrandizement) that can be read as the phenomenon's climax or its aftermath. And to return to a more general point about analytic elusiveness, in the Romantic period the discourse of the musical sublime was well-recognized, capacious and diffuse enough to colour neighbouring aesthetics and to 'trail its binary Others, among them the beautiful, the ridiculous, the sentimental, the grotesque, the comic'.[24]

From this perspective, we can read as inflected by the sublime scenes of music-making that at first sight obey a different logic, such as those in Ann Radcliffe's *Mysteries of Udolpho* (1794). Radcliffe's imperilled heroine finds a moment of repose when a strange, inexplicable music sounds from the woods below the castle where she is trapped. Like the appearance of the planet Venus in the night sky above (an image from the playbook of the cosmic sublime), the appearance of music below is comforting and easily glossed as beautiful or melancholy. Yet it also raises 'superstitious' 'fear and surprise' that 'yielded' to transporting 'enchantment' and finally reflective 'solemn awe'.[25] The music intimates a higher and (for the time being) hidden order governing the machinery of the novel, one that will eventually lead to the heroine's release and affirm her superiority to the surrounding world of masculine violence, superstitious obscurity, self-interest and destructive passions. The trope of hidden but astonishing harmony is an old one, deriving from Cicero's imagining of a statesman who is lifted into the heavens and granted a vision of cosmic harmony that models the normative harmony of the *polis*, and rehearsed with variations in scenes of complex cosmic music in Milton's *Paradise Lost* (1667), Dryden's *Song for St Cecilia's Day* (1687), or Percy Bysshe Shelley's *Queen Mab* (1813). Set in this context, Radcliffe's musical scene parallels more overt stagings of the sublime in her later novels, like the canonical moment in *The Italian* (1797) in which a captive heroine surveys the 'freely-sublime scene' beyond her convent walls with 'dreadful pleasure', forgetting her physical powerlessness and insignificance in her sense that 'man, the giant who now held her in captivity' cannot in fact 'enchain her soul, or compel her to fear him'. For Radcliffe, who formulated a theory of the sublime in dialogue with Burke, the sublime lay not in encounters with obscurity and fear per se, but in glimpses such as these 'beyond the awful veil which obscures the features of the Deity', glimpses that – like the Ciceronian scene where a mere mortal perceives celestial harmony – suggest a super-sensuous justness and harmony rarely apparent in the thick of human action.[26] While Kant rules out any sensuous clues to morality and freedom in the sublime – its empirical stimuli only reveal our *failures* of cognitive and physical power – his sublime offers indirect proofs of the possibility of these same capacities, morality and freedom (see *COPJ* §§25-8 248-64).

We can push further at the sublime's interaction with its apparent 'binary Others' (to return to Sisman's observation). We might discern one canonical pattern for the Romantic sublime that moves from strife to harmonious resolution – the model of the Ninth, for many critics – and another that locates the Romantic sublime in states of 'irresolvability', 'indeterminacy' and failure that remain resistant to transcendence and closure – a counter-model that becomes a resource for postmodern thought.[27] But we can also discern a third pattern that challenged the later eighteenth-century dichotomy of the beautiful and sublime, and its alignment with harmony/discord, feminine/masculine, masterable/overpowering, clarity/obscurity, determinacy/indeterminacy. A striking formulation of this challenge came from Johann Gottfried Herder, a thinker often associated with Enlightenment or Counter-Enlightenment, but whose work eludes easy labels and runs well into the Romantic period. Writing explicitly against Burke and Kant, Herder in *Kalligone* (1800) presented the sublime as the apotheosis of the beautiful, and argued that celebrations of privation, pain and obscurity missed the true sublime and the proper anthropology, theology and cosmology – the proper approach to an infinite but, for him, measure-ful cosmos – opened up by this aesthetic. Herder has frequent recourse to music, classically the art of ratio and 'measuring well' (Augustine's *bene modulandi*): musical examples, metaphors and genres appear alongside models of aurality and vibration that suggest for him the omnipresence of mediation and interconnection within an infinitely resonating cosmos.

Conclusion

The three models of the sublime sketched above involve different approaches to musical harmony. The broader implications of harmony as a cultural category suggest why music was such a potent domain for debating and practicing the sublime when Romantics were working through the implications of an infinite cosmos for what we can crudely call 'traditional' understandings of order and hierarchy, of access to certain truth and meaning, so that for some even the infinite itself appeared as a necessary fiction – an ultimate quantity and reality inferred and relied upon but never experienced in itself. As the range of sublimes addressed here suggests, this context could spawn varied and contradictory musical sublimes. But we should recognize in closing that Romantic thought could equally *exclude* the possibility of a musical sublime. Thus Samuel Taylor Coleridge could complain, annotating his copy of Herder's *Kalligone*: 'We call an object sublime, in relation to which the exercise of Comparison is suspended; while, that object is most beautiful, which in the highest perfection sustains[,] while it satisfies[,] the Comparing Power.'[28]

Coleridge would have accepted Herder's understanding of music as an art of measure and ratio – mechanisms of comparison – but for this very reason he would deny the existence of a musical sublime. Indeed, his experience listening to a nocturnal storm with 'thunders and howlings of the breaking ice' during his studies in Germany 'left a conviction ... that there are sounds more sublime than any sight *can* be, more absolutely suspending the power of comparison, and more utterly absorbing the mind[']s self-consciousness in its total attention to the object working upon it'.[29] Unlike for Hoffmann, for Coleridge this 'object' can be aural – a noise – but not a musical *Vorwurf*. When, in 'Dejection: An Ode' (1802), Coleridge wishes for 'Those sounds which oft have raised me, whilst they awed, / And sent my soul abroad' to 'startle this dull pain, and make it move and live!', he is invoking the aesthetic of the sublime and the nerve-theories that had fascinated Burke and shaped his understanding of the sublime as a psychologically tonic exercising of our vibrating nerves (lines 17–20). The sounds Coleridge longs for are the wind's 'blast', 'rushing' and 'deepest silence': the wind is an 'Actor, perfect in all tragic sounds' but only an ironic, 'Mad Lutanist', an anti-musician with 'worse than wintry song' (lines 15, 21–2, 108, 104). There does exist a 'strong music in the soul': the internal harmony of 'Joy' that transforms the subject and its world (lines 60, 64). This was the subject of Schiller's ode, too, of course – yet rather than inspiring a sublime symphony, in 'Dejection' joy is an absence that calls for the shock therapy of the sonic, anti-musical sublime.

Still, perhaps music has the last laugh. It is not so easy, even within Coleridge's poem, to separate the eloquent voice of the wind as a 'perfect' 'Actor' from the inarticulate 'Mad Lutanist'; nature from spirit; music from non-musical sounds, mere sonic matter, and even silence. Long before postmodern composers harnessed and echoed the sublime in creating noise art, silent compositions, durational works of astonishing dullness, and repetitious serialist scores that mimic infinity, Romantic-period composers as different as Beethoven, Wagner and Meyerbeer were engaging in their operas with a-musical sounds ranging from silence to industrial machinery, cannon-fire to deafening bells, and absorbing the apparently extra-aural effects of light, space, movement and visual spectacle into their musical sublimes.[30]

One of the abiding fascinations of Romantic thought that found expression in the vogue for the sublime was testing the boundaries between presence and absence, between ordered and formless phenomena, between joyful and painful sensations, and between the arts and senses. With its long and contradictory history as an art of cosmic harmony and of passionate sensuality, music was a prime site for marking and transgressing such boundaries. Although music rose to an exalted place in Romantic aesthetics, the Romantic period did not inaugurate the musical sublime. As is often observed, the sublime's history is one of countless and perhaps interminable revivals, and the musical sublime is no exception. Just as a narrow definition of music falls short of Romantic engagements with the sublime, so too an excessively developmental music history would limit understanding of this capacious aesthetic and the live relationships we continue to have with Romantic-period music. Marx famously quipped that history repeats itself: first as tragedy, then as farce. The premiere just a few years apart of Morton and Lee's *The Sublime and Beautiful* and Beethoven's Ninth Symphony reminds us that, in the musical sublimes of Romanticism, history plays out simultaneously as 'triumph', as tragedy and as farce.

NOTES

1 See 'Sublime and Beautiful', in *Lord Chamberlain's Plays, 1824–1858*, xxix, November–December 1828, 34–70 (British Library Add MS 42893); *The Overture and Whole of the Music in the Musical Farce of 'The Sublime and Beautiful'*, London, 1828.
2 W. T. Moncrieff's *Giovanni in London* premiered in the same year as Thomas Dibdin's *Don Giovanni – or A Spectre on Horseback, a Comic, Heroic, Operatic, Tragic, Pantomimic, Burletta-Spectacular-Extravaganza*, whose introduction wisely remarked that 'there is but one step from the sublime to the ridiculous'. George Daniel, 'Remarks', in Dibdin, *Don Giovanni*, London, 1817, 3.
3 On the eighteenth-century alignment of modernity with femininity, see Matthew Head, *Sovereign Feminine: Music and Gender in Eighteenth-Century Germany*, Berkeley, University of California Press, 2013.
4 On whether the sublime can be located in musical tropes, see Wye Allanbrook, 'Is the Sublime a Musical Topos?', *Eighteenth-Century Music* 7, 2, 2010, 263–79.
5 On music and Romanticism, see Benedict Taylor, *The Cambridge Companion to Music and Romanticism*, Cambridge, Cambridge University Press, 2012, 3–16.
6 E. T. A. Hoffmann, 'Beethovens Instrumental-Musik', in *Sämtliche Werke in Sechs Bänden*, ed. Hartmut Steinecke, Gerhard Allroggen and Wulf Segebrecht, Frankfurt, Deutscher Klassiker Verlag, 1993, vol. 2.1, 52. Unless otherwise noted, translations are my own.
7 Hoffmann represents here a broader trend: see Carl Dahlhaus, *Die Idee der absoluten Musik*, Kassel, Bärenreiter, 1978, 12 and passim.
8 Friedrich Schlegel, 'Transzendentalphilosophie' (1801), in *Kritische Friedrich-Schlegel-Ausgabe*, vol. 12, ed. Jean-Jacques Anstett, Paderborn, Ferdinand Schöningh, 1964, 1–106 (9).
9 See Nicholas Mathew, 'Beethoven's Political Music, the Handelian Sublime, and the Aesthetics of Prostration', *19th-Century Music* 33, 2, 2009, 110–50.
10 Donald Tovey, 'Symphony in D Minor, No. 9, Op. 125', in *Symphonies and Other Orchestral Works*, Oxford, Oxford University Press, 1981, 89.

11 Susan McClary, *Feminine Endings: Music, Gender, and Sexuality*, 2nd ed., Minneapolis, University of Minnesota Press, 2002, 129. See Richard Taruskin, 'Resisting the Ninth', Review of Beethoven Symphony No. 9 in D Minor, Op. 125, dir. Roger Norrington, *19th-Century Music* 12, 3, 1989, 241–56; David Dennis, *Beethoven in German Politics, 1870–1989*, New Haven, CT, Yale University Press, 1996; Reinhold Brinkmann, 'The Distorted Sublime: Music and National Socialist Ideology – A Sketch', in *Music and Nazism: Art under Tyranny, 1933–1945*, ed. Michael Kater and Albrecht Reithmüller, Laaber, Laaber, 2003, 43–63.

12 Judy Lochhead, 'The Sublime, the Ineffable and Other Dangerous Aesthetic Concepts', *Women and Music* 12, 2008, 63–74.

13 For Cherubini as 'terrorist-musician', see Sarah Hibberd, 'Cherubini's Médée and Sublime Vengeance', in Sarah Hibberd and Miranda Stanyon, eds., *Music and the Sonorous Sublime in European Culture, 1680–1880*, Cambridge, Cambridge University Press, 2020, 121–41 (123).

14 C. F. Michaelis, 'Ueber das Erhabene in der Musik', *Deutsche Monatsschrift* 1, 1801, 42–52 (44).

15 Epitaph for Bach in Friedrich Gottlieb Klopstock, *Werke und Briefe: Historisch-kritische Ausgabe*, *Werke*, 12 vols., ed. Klaus Hurlebusch, Berlin, de Gruyter, 2003, vol. 7, pt. 2, 771. This account of Bach draws especially on Annette Richards, 'An Enduring Monument: C. P. E. Bach and the Musical Sublime', in Annette Richards, ed., *C. P. E. Bach Studies*, Cambridge, Cambridge University Press, 2006, 149–73.

16 Charles Burney, *Account of the Musical Performances in Westminster Abbey*, London, 1785, 106.

17 On Pasta, see Stendhal, *Vie de Rossini suivie des Notes d'un dilettante*, ed. Henry Prunières, in *Œuvres complètes*, vol. 33, Geneva, Slatkine Reprints, 1986, 152; on Grassini, see Michael Kelly, *Reminiscences*, 2nd ed., London, 1826, vol. 2, 214; on Scio, see Hibberd, 'Cherubini's Médée'.

18 See Dietmar Till, *Das doppelte Erhabene: Eine Argumentationsfigur von der Antike bis zum Beginn des 19. Jahrhunderts*, Tübingen, Niemeyer, 2006, and Keith Chapin, 'C. P. E. Bach and the Neoclassical Sublime: Revisions of a Concept', in Hibberd and Stanyon, eds., *Music and the Sonorous Sublime*, 93–120.

19 C. F. Michaelis, 'Einige Bemerkungen über das Erhabene der Musik', *Berlinische musikalische Zeitung*, 46, 1, 1805, 179–81 (80).

20 See Miranda Stanyon, *Resounding the Sublime: Music in English and German Literature and Aesthetic Theory, 1670–1850*, Philadelphia, University of Pennsylvania Press, 2021, chapter 2; Thomas Dixon, *From Passions to Emotions: The Creation of a Secular Psychological Category*, Cambridge, Cambridge University Press, 2003.

21 On music and nerves, see James Kennaway, *Bad Vibrations: The History of the Idea of Music as a Cause of Disease*, Farnham, Ashgate, 2012.

22 On austerity, see Anne Janowitz, 'The Artifactual Sublime: Making London Poetry', in James Chandler and Kevin Gilmartin, eds., *Romantic Metropolis: The Urban Scene of British Culture, 1780–1840*, Cambridge, Cambridge University Press, 2005, 246–61 (248–50).

23 For a reading of the musical mode of the sublime as essentially indeterminate and irresolvable, see Kiene Brillenburg Wurth, *Musically Sublime: Indeterminacy, Infinity, Irresolvability*, New York, Fordham University Press, 2009.

24 Elaine Sisman, 'When Does the Sublime Stop? Cavatinas and Quotations in Haydn's *Seasons*', in Hibberd and Stanyon, eds., *Music and the Sonorous Sublime*, 142–76 (143).

25 Radcliffe, *Mysteries of Udolpho*, Oxford, Oxford University Press, 1998, vol. 2, chapter 11, 330–31.

26 Radcliffe, *The Italian*, Oxford, Oxford University Press, 1998, vol. 1, chapter 8, 90–1. Compare Peter Otto, 'The Sublime', in *The Encyclopedia of the Romantic Era, 1760–1850*, ed. Chris Murray, London, Fitzroy Dearborn, 2004, 1102–4.

27 See Kiene Brillenburg Wurth, *Musically Sublime: Indeterminacy, Infinity, Irresolvability*, New York, Fordham University Press, 2009.

28 Samuel Taylor Coleridge, *Marginalia*, in *The Collected Works*, vol. 2, ed. George Whalley, London, Routledge, 1984, 1069.

29 Samuel Taylor Coleridge, *The Friend*, 19, 1809, discussed in Tim Fulford, 'The Politics of the Sublime: Coleridge and Wordsworth in Germany', *Modern Language Review* 91, 4, 1996, 817–32 (819).

30 See David Trippett, 'Wagner's Sublime Effects: Bells, Cannon and the Perception of Heavy Sound', in Hibberd and Stanyon, eds., *Music and the Sonorous Sublime*, 245–72; Emily Dolan and John Tresch, 'A Sublime Invasion: Meyerbeer, Balzac, and the Opera Machine', *Opera Quarterly* 27, 1, 2011, 4–31.

12

ROBERT W. RIX

The Arctic Sublime

The connection between the Arctic and the sublime was not an invention of the Romantic period, but it is safe to say that the Arctic came into its own as a source of the sublime during the Romantic period. If the vocabulary used by both literary writers and explorers was anticipated by Burke, *Enquiry* nevertheless predated the intensified interest in the Arctic during the Romantic period and makes no direct references to the polar regions. However, as Loomis has suggested, Burke probably would have included references to icy landscapes had he written a century later.[1] One of the best-known illustrations of how the Arctic sublime is used in literary works is Mary Shelley's *Frankenstein* (1818), a novel that both opens and closes on board a ship bound for the North Pole. The character of the polar explorer Robert Walton embodies the hubris of the contemporary attempt to discover the secrets of the North. Shelley nods towards Burke's discussion of vastness and infinitude when she has Walton behold the 'vast and irregular plains of ice', which are 'stretched out in every direction' with seemingly 'no end'.[2] For Shelley, the isolated territory towards the North Pole symbolizes God's creation at its most magnificent and yet destructive, qualities that correlate with Frankenstein's Creature. For this reason, the Creature is appropriately carried away on an ice raft in the conclusion of the novel, engulfed by the desolate Arctic landscape that he spiritually resembles.

In another famous Romantic-period work, Antarctica is cast as a 'dark continent' of spiritual terror. Samuel Taylor Coleridge's 'The Rime of the Ancient Mariner' (1798) is the tale of the ill-fated sailor who experiences the terrors of 'Storm and Wind' and ice as it 'crack'd and growl'd, and roar'd and howl'd' to eventually 'split' with a 'Thunder-fit'; he also describes the sublime fright of being engulfed in the obscurity of 'mist and snow' on the endless frozen sea: 'The ice was all between. / The ice was here, the ice was there' (lines 44–60).

The Arctic is home to various indigenous nations, whose concept of nature differs from interpretive frameworks imposed upon it by Western visitors. In

Figure 12.1 Caspar David Friedrich, *Das Eismeer* (The Sea of Ice) (1823–4). Hamburger Kunsthalle, Hamburg.

fact, the Arctic sublime was often cultivated as a discourse by those who never visited these northern reaches. In this respect, one cannot fail to mention the German Romantic painter Caspar David Friedrich, who created probably the most famous painting of the Arctic sublime: *Das Eismeer* (The Sea of Ice) (1823–4), a striking vista of a pyramidal mass of sharp, broken ice floes, under whose frozen ridges a ship has been crushed (see Figure 12.1). Friedrich was fascinated by the ice formations he observed on the Elbe and sketched its heaped-up shards, transposing them to an imaginary Arctic landscape. Friedrich's painting concurs with Burke's list, in *Enquiry* III xiv, of features that will elicit a sublime response in the viewer: the representation of 'rugged and broken surface' and 'any sudden projection, any sharp angle'. Friedrich's scene of a frozen and unforgiving nature, which has overwhelmed the manmade vessel, also fits Burke's definition of the sublime in another and more fundamental way. It epitomizes Burke's principal theory that pain, powerlessness, and threat of annihilation can be transmogrified into thrill and enjoyment when perceived at a safe distance.

As Duffy points out, the Romantic-period public became acquainted with sublime icescapes not only through artistic representations but also through the many travel accounts published at the time (*Landscapes*, 102–34). With

Friedrich's canvas in mind, one might identify in particular the Arctic ship-wreck as a trope that received much attention in the Romantic period. Accounts of visceral and violent encounters with the dangers of the Arctic were popular. The second volume of *Naufragia, or, Historical Memoirs of Shipwrecks and of the Providential Deliverance of Vessels* (1806), for example, anthologized real-life stories of extreme hardship and narrow escapes against the backdrop of what the editor describes as the 'sublime Scenery of the North Pole' with its 'vast and watery Deserts'.[3]

Exploring the Arctic Sublime

In the Romantic period, the most intense effort to the map the Arctic both geographically and artistically was through the expeditions in the early nine-teenth century that sought to locate a navigable trade route to Eastern markets through the so-called Northwest Passage. This was the mythical waterway in the Arctic Ocean, which Captain Robert Walton refers to as 'a passage near the pole' in *Frankenstein* (vol. 1, 4). In Britain, ships and men became available after the end of the Napoleonic Wars. Thus, John Barrow, the influential Second Secretary of the Admiralty, announced two expeditions to the Arctic in 1818. With a view to documenting the explorations, the Admiralty hired artists to teach navy recruits to draw. The drawings made on location were subsequently touched up for engravings to be marvelled at by the many newspaper and journal readers who avidly followed accounts of Arctic explorations. This marked the beginning of a commercially successful genre. Illustrations of ships dwarfed by monumental icebergs, or men looking out over endless icy vistas, were part of the attraction when one picked up a copy of John Franklin's bestselling *Narrative of a Journey to the Shores of the Polar Sea* (first published 1823). Franklin's report not only contributed to the aesthetic construction of the Arctic as a landscape of the sublime, but also helped to define it as a highly saleable commodity on the book market. The selling point of the illustrated travel account was its promise to provide a unique view of unfamiliar horizons, yet textual and visual representations of the Arctic borrowed from already familiar ideas about the sublime.

The images of mountains and icy vistas were in many respects a continu-ation of a well-established sub-zero aesthetics promoted in relation to Alpine glaciers, visible in the work of painters like Philip James de Loutherbourg and J. M. W. Turner and in the writings of Marc-Théodore Bourrit and Horace Bénédict de Saussure. Yet there is no doubt that exploration of the Arctic raised the bar in terms of the danger and magnitude associated with the sublime. Focusing on the divine magnificence of God's creation around the world (a key trope of the discourse on the sublime in various contexts),

Reverend Pleydell Wilton reflects on this Arctic sublimity in his poem 'The Polar Ice' (1818), where the sublimity of the European Alps is surpassed by the Arctic's 'roar of clashing ice bergs – and the sound / Of moving masses', which are 'fell sounds' in 'scenes of death', to which no human can lay ear and not tremble.[4] In *Enquiry* II xvii, Burke had emphasized how 'excessive loudness' creates in the mind 'great and aweful sensation' and it is therefore no surprise that terrible sounds became a regular feature in imaginations of the frigid zones.

It is no coincidence that Wilton published his poem in 1818, in connection with the revival of British Arctic exploration that year. Barrow, the Second Secretary to the Admiralty, sent out two expeditions to navigate either side of Greenland for the discovery of the Northwest Passage and to approach the North Pole. As with early explorations of the Alps, Arctic exploration, too, mixed adventure with significant scientific enquiry. The confrontation with the Arctic sublime was intrinsically bound up with a sense of national pride in conquering the polar seas and in making scientific and commercial discoveries. This is visible in the crescendo of Wilton's poem: 'Ride on, ye barks! – and bear ye wide unfurl'd / The British colours to a Polar sky / And proudly tell it to a Northern world / How Britons learn to conquer or to die!' (85). Burke had made the sublime a metaphor for masculine potency, and descriptions of sublime Northern landscapes are often used to emphasize the national heroism of British explorers.

Eleanor Anne Porden's 1818 poem 'The Arctic Expeditions' also reflects this dynamic. Porden, who had met Franklin (her future husband) before he left for the Arctic under David Buchan's command, describes at length the sublime nature the British would encounter on their voyage:

> Awful it is to gaze on shoreless seas
> But more to view those restless billows freeze
> One solid plain, or when like mountains piled,
> Whole leagues in length, of forms sublimely wild.[5]

It is against this hostile nature that the Royal Navy's heroism would stand out: 'Yet Britons! Conquerors on the subject deep / . . . Fired by your fathers' deathless deeds defy / The frozen ocean and the flaming sky' (lines 130–3). Porden, who would go on to write poetry with imperial themes, published 'The Arctic Expeditions' with John Murray, who was responsible for publications connected with the British Admiralty. Hence, it is difficult not to see the poem as a promotional piece that utilizes sublime imagery to aggrandize British Arctic expeditions. As ice literally blocked Britain's destined path to prosperity, by preventing passage to Eastern markets, it was cast as a formidable adversary to be defeated.

The heroism of Arctic explorers was celebrated in books, engravings, and souvenir prints throughout the nineteenth century.[6] Arctic expeditions gave impetus to what Francis Spufford identifies as a British 'national tradition of endurance', while, in the American media, as Michael F. Robinson points out, the Arctic became 'the coldest crucible', in which men could emerge as heroes.[7]

The Wonders of Ice

In Romantic-period accounts of Arctic journeys, we often find the notion that those who brave a journey to the North would find themselves in the presence of one of the last places of God's divine creation not yet spoiled by human civilization. In *The Greenland Minstrel* (1839), a poem based on personal observations from a voyage to Greenland, the Reverend Frederick Rogers Blackley foregrounds the religious awe felt when surrounded by Arctic landscapes. In one place, he proclaims: 'GREAT are the terrors which surround the pole, / Dread the alarms that rack the native's soul', and when he is confronted with a 'scene sublime, / So grand and boundless in the wild extent', he is led to reverence of the 'striking grandeurs nature's God had made'.[8] The combination of danger and divine presence is replicated in the illustrations of ships dwarfed by magnificent icebergs, symbolizing man's insignificance.

Blackley describes a visit to a Danish Christian mission station in western Greenland, and missionary texts were important sources for readers in Europe to learn about the Arctic. Probably the most popular example of this is the German historian David Cranz' *Historie von Grönland* (History of Greenland) (1765, English trans. 1767 and 1820), in which he sets out to detail the land and people of a fairly recently colonized space (a Dano-Norwegian settlement was first established in Greenland in 1721). Occasionally, Cranz abandons his dry, matter-of-fact style to embellish the landscape descriptions with a vocabulary borrowed from the tradition of eighteenth-century European landscape aesthetics. For example, he describes how a bay on the west coast presents a 'sublime spectacle of a stupendous bridge of ice', under the arches of which boats were in danger of 'destruction by the masses impending from above'.[9]

A similar example is 'the terribly magnificent mass of icebergs' in Disko Bay, which Hans Egede Saabye describes in a popular book published in 1816. Saabye was a Danish missionary in Greenland, for whom this spectacle leads to a crisis of comprehension as well as representation: 'If a person who has never seen this bay were to exert his imagination to the utmost, he would not be able to form a just idea of it.'[10] However, the sublime power of the icebergs is tempered by Saabye projecting onto them his own visions of human-made buildings or cities: 'I saw, among other magnificent buildings, the great gate of the Palace of Christianburg [royal buildings in Copenhagen] with its pillars and side doors; and my eye dwelt on the mezzanine story, which [it] was astonishingly resembling' (101). Imaginatively morphing the otherworldly ice formations into something that may still be sublime but now familiar and relatable is a common trope in Arctic exploration litera-ture. The effect of this exertion of the imagination is that Saabye can now describe the sublime view as 'a very agreeable illusion, as long as we do not know how dangerous it is to approach them; but even when we know this danger, we take pleasure in looking at them' (101).

Arctic Illusions

The discourse of illusions was regularly connected with an idea of the Arctic sublime in Romantic-period writing, especially with respect to how optical mirages imposed themselves upon the traveller in northern climes. One of the most widely read descriptions of such phenomena was provided by the English whaler and explorer William Scoresby Jr. In his *Account of the Arctic Region* (1820), we find a long section on 'Atmospheric Phenomena Dependent on Reflection and Refraction', which is an account of how microscopic ice crystals refract or bend light rays in the Arctic climate. The sublime is invoked, for instance, when Scoresby observes how 'the moun-tains along the whole coast assumed the most fantastic forms; the appear-ance of castles with lofty spires, towers and battlements', and after a few minutes, 'converted into a vast arch or romantic bridge' taken out of 'fairy descriptions'.[11] These experiences challenged European knowledge-claims and therefore pulled these optical effects into the orbit of the sublime.

Scoresby's sightings were extensively summarized by the natural philoso-pher and pioneer of optical science David Brewster in his *Letters on Natural Magic* (1832), which reached several editions and reprints during the nine-teenth century. Brewster aims to replace an old order of superstitious beliefs with rational elucidation, and in this context he discusses observations that may seem like supernatural spectacles but can be explained scientifically as optical phenomena. With respect to the Arctic, often designated as an unworldly space, Brewster accounts for its strange and awe-inspiring mirages by references to atmospheric physics. It is not to deflate these experiences; rather, Brewster embraces the frisson that the subject feels when confronted with 'the grand and sublime in the universe'.[12] This is because he thinks the affective appeal of the phantasmagoria will help promote an interest in an empirical investigation of the mirages as natural phenomena, perhaps echoing Adam's Smith's idea in his essay on 'The History of Astronomy' (1797) that scientific enquiry began with the desire of early human societies to understand sublime natural phenomena. The fascination with sightings that appear to be magical will 'inspire the reader with a portion of enthusiasm of love and gratitude which can prepare the mind for its final triumph', which is an inquisitive mindset that aids the progress of '[m]odern science'.[13] In other words, the public's attraction to sublime experiences can be utilized to promote the introduction of an age of science.

The affective experience created by atmospheric illusions is also made a theme in the Irish explorer Bernard O'Reilly's *Greenland, the Adjacent Seas, and the North-West Passage to the Pacific Ocean* (1818), a richly illustrated book published to capitalize on the public interest in Arctic discovery. O'Reilly gives an account of the 'luminous phenomenon' he experienced near Greenland's Sugar Loaf Bay. On this occasion, the sunlight illuminated an icy mist onto which he saw his own shadow backscattered and strangely magnified.[14] He includes a full-page illustration of this uncanny vision. This sighting is a version of what was otherwise known as a Brocken Spectre, an eerie and sublime phenomenon known to wanderers in European mountain landscapes. Scholars of Romanticism will be familiar with this optical illusion from references to it in several well-known texts: the supernatural figure in the Scottish landscape of James Hogg's *Private Memoirs and Confessions of a Justified Sinner* (1824), the illusion rustics worship as a spirit in Coleridge's poem 'Constancy to an Ideal Object' (1828), and the mysterious apparition in Thomas De Quincey's *Suspiria de Profundis* (1845). In viewing the diffracted projection of his own body on the mist, O'Reilly literally views himself as both object and subject of the sublime experience. However, he shirks the ontological implications of this experience and insists on leaving it to the 'philosophic reader' to 'form a better conclusion than I can presume to do' about the utility of this strange vision (162). That an encounter with the sublime can lead to a recognition of one's own position as a perceiving subject is clear in Kant's writing, and Burke (drawing on pseudo-Longinus) argues in *Enquiry* I xvii that the sublime experience can foster self-consciousness as 'the mind always claim[s] to itself some part of the dignity and importance of the things which it contemplates'.

Another version of a confrontation with a magnified figure is found in Edgar Allan Poe's only complete novel, *The Narrative of Arthur Gordon Pym of Nantucket* (first published 1838), which concludes with a journey towards the South Pole. In a small boat, a group of survivors is carried headlong towards a 'white curtain', which Pym sees as a spirit-like figure rising up in front of them. This figure was 'very far larger in its proportions than any dweller among men' and with 'the perfect whiteness of the snow'.[15] With this scene, the novel comes to an abrupt end, as the boat is swallowed up in a cataract. Just as eighteenth-century investigations of the sublime in philosophical aesthetics often theorized the faculties to be incapacitated by the confrontation with the sublime, so the ability to continue the narration seems overwhelmed at this point. Like his contemporaries, Poe would have read the numerous accounts of strange atmospheric illusions experienced in polar climates, and the snow figure in his novel is perhaps meant to echo the accounts of such fata morganas.

Failed Colonization

Having written both fiction and non-fiction about the climatic phenomena experienced in his native Scottish hills, the author James Hogg provided the age with a fictional travel narrative that most resolutely exploited the public's fascination with the Arctic sublime: *The Surpassing Adventures of Allan Gordon* (1837), a novella he dedicated to the pioneer of optical science, David Brewster.[16] The story concerns the seventeen-year-old Scot Allan Gordon, who finds himself to be the only survivor of a shipwreck in the Greenland Sea. Drifting on an ice floe, Gordon's senses are often disorientated; there are strange sightings and ghostly sounds. However, the sublime is most clearly manifest in Gordon's observation of new ice forming. He is rudely awakened by an ear-splitting sound, of 'undefinable terror', which soon modulates into 'loud crashes, like discharges of artillery'. There follows a scene in which Gordon tells us he 'shall never see any thing again to compare':

> The ice heaved up the field into broad crystal flakes, which gradually rising to a perpendicular position to the height of an hundred feet and more.... Again and again was the great frozen space broken up with crashes not to be equalled by any thing in nature, and therefore incomparable, unless we could conceive the rending of a sphere to pieces. (277–8)

The focus on terrible sounds is Burkean, while the spectacle of ice shards rising up is reminiscent of Friedrich's *Das Eismeer*. The passage is nonetheless probably directly inspired by a scene Brewster reported in his entry 'Ice' for the *Edinburgh Encyclopædia* (1830). Here it is related how Moravian missionaries in Labrador had seen the 'immense fields of ice rising out of the ocean, clashing against each other, and then plunging into the deep with a violence which no language can describe, and a noise like the discharge of a thousand cannon was a sight which must have struck the most unreflecting mind with solemn awe'.[17] Hogg's possible use of such testimonies for literary effects shows us how fiction writers would seize on the ample supply of sublime scenes from this part of the world, which only a few of them would ever visit.

The Arctic with its deadly land- and seascapes was an obvious stage for sublime images in the form of strange phantasms, apparitions, and Gothic terror.[18] Hogg also lets a horrific scene play out in the second part of *The Surpassing Adventures of Allan Gordon*. Gordon comes upon a struggling colony of Norse Greenlanders (who had lived in Greenland from 785 to the early fifteenth century). At the time Hogg wrote, it was still discussed whether descendants survived and what terrors they may have experienced as an isolated colony cut off from the world. Hogg imagines in graphic detail that the colonists are attacked and devoured by hungry polar bears. The animals show 'apparent joy and triumph' when they 'embraced [the women] to death and sucked their blood', celebrating their frenzied feasting with 'growls of voluptuous joy' (313–14). The polar bears, like Burke's list of large carnivores in *Enquiry* II ii and iv, embody the sublime, as does the field of slaughter.[19] But, more concretely, the ravenous polar bears epitomize the merciless ravages of an Arctic nature fundamentally hostile to human intrusion. As Sarah Moss notes in a short commentary on *The Surpassing Adventures of Allan Gordon*, 'Hogg's Norse Greenlanders die, essentially, of polarisation, fearing and at last consumed by the frozen shapes that kill.'[20]

Hogg's scenario foreshadows the English painter Edwin Landseer's shocking painting, *Man Proposes, God Disposes* (1864), now in the collection of Royal Holloway. This is an imaginative depiction of the fate of the unfortunate Franklin expedition. Two bears are crunching on human remains and tearing at a red British ensign. Landseer's visualization of how the Canadian Arctic had literally devoured his countrymen was a patriotic diversion to the unwelcome suggestion that the expedition had turned to cannibalism, which had been raised (controversially) after the Scottish explorer John Rae, who had gone in search of the expedition, found cut marks on the human bones that he recovered.

To return to the demise of the Norse colony, a popular explanation in the Romantic period was that Greenland's climate had cooled, destroying the settlers' livelihood. This speculative history was taken up by James Montgomery in his unfinished epic poem *Greenland* (1819). Although practically forgotten today, *Greenland* sold 37,500 copies, making it one of the bestsellers of the age.[21] Montgomery creates a series of sublime scenes when imagining the cold that brought the first European occupation of Greenland to an end. Instead of bear fangs, Montgomery has shards of ice pierce the Norse colonists. A towering Greenland glacier, described as a 'splendid peak the Power (which to the spheres / Had piled its turrets through a thousand years)', becomes so heavy that it tumbles down to fall upon a Norse village, shattering in 'ten thousand, thousand spangles' so that its mass of ice 'piles a hill where spread a vale before'.[22] The sublime image conveyed in these lines speaks to a sense of human disempowerment in the face of natural forces, not unlike the people succumbing to the falling lava in Jacob More's famous painting *Mount Vesuvius in Eruption: The Last Days of Pompeii* (1780).

Conclusion: The Arctic at Home

In addition to its commoditization in books and paintings, the Arctic sublime also came to be sold through the medium of the panorama exhibition, which was marketed by showmen as part of a thriving experience economy.[23] The panorama was first introduced in Britain as a 360-degree view painted on a large canvas strip hung on the inside of a specially built circular building. Viewers paid an entrance fee to stand at the centre of the circle, thus wholly surrounded by the painting, which would give the viewer the impression of actually being in a landscape. In 1819–20, Henry Barker, painter and exhibitor, gave the public the first large-scale treatment of the Arctic in London's Leicester Square, entitled *View of the North Coast of Spitzbergen*, a painting based on drawings by Lieutenant Frederick William Beechey, second in command on the Admiralty's 1818 expedition to find a sailing route across the Pole. The panorama would recreate the sublime experience for a receptive audience who could vicariously take part in the Arctic journey. In 1821–2, the first moving panorama – a canvas unwound across a stage in anticipation of later motion pictures – was created by Messrs. Marshall, who toured Britain and then the continent with *New Peripstrephic Panorama of the Sublime Scenery of the Frozen Regions, with Eight Views of Captain Parry, Ross, Franklin, and Buchart's Voyages of Discovery in the Polar Regions*. The advertisement prepared audiences for an immersive effect and promised that 'the Frozen Regions are always rendered in a comfortable temperature by Stoves'.[24] No fewer than sixteen panoramas or dioramas were exhibited between 1819 and 1858.[25]

The fact that explorers licensed their drawings to such exhibitions, as well as to artists who prepared them for illustrations in books, helped to bring the far-flung Arctic space into national view. Sublime images were intended to both titillate and inform the public about national achievements in the Arctic. In effect, spaces at the end of the world became as much artistic and intellectual concepts as actual physical locations. During the Romantic period, the use of the Arctic sublime in texts and imagery became both familiar and conventionalized. By making representational claims over the Arctic, it was possible to assuage national anxieties about failure to control this space. But while the public could – virtually – occupy the Arctic and enjoy the representations of its sublime landscapes in books and at exhibitions, the actual Arctic remained ungovernable and its conquest elusive. At the close of the Romantic period, the fatal failure of the Franklin expedition, which had left England to search for the Northwest Passage in 1845, provided a stark reminder of the Arctic as hostile to human interference. The loss of the expedition became a national trauma, which was compounded by the fact that Franklin had long been celebrated as a national hero, an image he had cultivated through his published accounts of boldly navigating the Arctic.

NOTES

1 See Chauncey C. Loomis, 'The Arctic Sublime', in U. C. Knoepflmacher and G. B. Tennyson, eds., *Nature and the Victorian Imagination*, Berkeley, University of California Press, 1977, 95–112 (102–3).

2 Mary Shelley, *Frankenstein*, 3 vols., London, 1818, vol. 1, 21.

3 James Stanier Clarke (ed.), *Naufragia, or, Historical Memoirs of Shipwrecks and of the the Providential Deliverance of Vessels*, London, 1805, vol. 2, xv–xvi.

4 Pleydell Wilton, 'The Polar Ice', in *Geology, and Other Poems*, London, 1818, 84.

5 Eleanor Anne Porden, *The Arctic Expeditions*, London, 1818, lines 102–5.

6 See Huw Lewis-Jones, *Imagining the Arctic*, London, I. B. Tauris, 2017; and Russell A. Potter, *Arctic Spectacles*, Seattle, University of Washington Press, 2007.

7 Francis Spufford, *I May Be Some Time*, New York, St. Martin's Press, 1997, 54.

8 Frederick Rogers Blackley, *The Greenland Minstrel*, London, 1839, Canto IV, 43, 50–1.

9 David Crantz, *The History of Greenland*, London, 1820, vol. 1, 5. Cranz was spelt 'Crantz' in English-language publications.

10 Hans Egede Saabye, *Journal in Greenland*, London, 1818, 100.

11 William Scoresby Jr., *An Account of the Arctic Regions*, 2 vols., Edinburgh, 1820, vol. 1, 386.

12 David Brewster, *Letters on Natural Magic*, London, 1832, 7.

13 Ibid., 7.

14 Bernard O'Reilly, *Greenland, the Adjacent Seas, and the North-West Passage to the Pacific Ocean*, London, 1818, 203–4.

15 Edgar Allan Poe, *Narrative of Arthur Gordon Pym*, in *The Works of the Late Edgar Allan Poe*, New York, Redfield, 1856, vol. 4, 185.

16 James Hogg, *Surpassing Adventures of Allan Gordon*, in *Tales and Sketches by the Ettrick Shepherd*, Glasgow, 1837, dedication on 241.

17 [David Brewster], 'Ice', in *The Edinburgh Encyclopædia*, Edinburgh, 1830, vol. 11, 638.

18 See, for example, Shane McCorristine, *The Spectral Arctic: A History of Dreams and Ghosts in Polar Exploration*, London, UCL Press, 2018; and Katherine

Bowers, 'Haunted Ice, Fearful Sounds, and the Arctic Sublime: Exploring Nineteenth-Century Polar Gothic Space', *Gothic Studies* 19, 2, 2017, 71–84.

19 Compare *Longinus* (90) on the sublimity of the description of a massacre by the Athenian historian Thucydides.

20 See Sarah Moss, 'Romanticism on Ice: Coleridge, Hogg and the Eighteenth-Century Missions to Greenland', *Romanticism on the Net* 45 (2007): https://id.erudit.org/iderudit/015816ar. Accessed 15 December 2021.

21 William St Clair, *The Reading Nation in the Romantic Period*, Cambridge, Cambridge University Press, 2007, 218, see also 619.

22 James Montgomery, *Greenland, and Other Poems*, London, 1819, 96.

23 See Richard Altick, *The Shows of London*, Cambridge, MA, Harvard University Press, 1978, esp. 177 and 321 on the Arctic.

24 Quoted in Karal Ann Marlin, *Ice: Great Moments in the History of Hard, Cold Water*, St. Paul, MN, Borealis Books, 2008, 146.

25 Russel Potter and Douglas Warmsley, 'The Sublime yet Awful Grandeur: The Arctic Panoramas of Elisha Kent Kane', *Polar Record* 35, 194 (1999), 194.

13

NORBERT LENNARTZ

The Body and the Sublime

It is one of the Romantics' persistent paradoxes that despite their constant pursuit of awe-inspiring sublimity in nature and despite their wish to connect their corpora of poetry to the *genus sublime* of Milton's *Paradise Lost* (1667), they tended to look disparagingly at the human body, saw it belittled by nature and more often than not reduced to its ailing, fretting and cumbersome husk. It was in particular John Keats who, as a dresser in Guy's hospital, was not only confronted daily with the fragility of the human body, but who was, in his advanced state of consumption, made painfully aware of his own body's abject dissolution. When in his 'Ode to a Nightingale' (1819) he refers to youth as "grow[ing] pale, and spectre-thin," he seems to be giving an appalling description of his own and other young people's decaying bodies, frighteningly on the cusp between life and death and soon to be devastated by cruel hemorrhages (line 26). In this respect, it is not surprising that Keats's concept of the body is infinitely remote from the sublime and that his ideal is the disembodied body, precariously on the verge of insubstantiality, bereft of its onerous mortal fleshiness and on the point of fading away into the realm of what Yeats later calls the "artifice of eternity."[1]

Keats's Platonic reveries of either evaporated or petrified bodies (as shown in the "leaf-fringed legend" of the Grecian urn) are thus the radical opposite of the spasmodic forays into the priapistic sublime that eighteenth-century readers found both in John Cleland's diaristic novel *Memoirs of a Woman of Pleasure* (1748), nowadays simply abbreviated as *Fanny Hill*, and in Johann Wolfgang von Goethe's *Roman Elegies* (1795).[2] Long condemned as impenetrable dungeons of the incarcerated souls, bodies not only came to be discovered in all their ooziness in the decades of tear-drenched sentimentality; they were also (briefly and furtively) appreciated in their intimidating and awe-inspiring sexuality. In a salacious rewriting of Samuel Richardson's prim *Pamela* (1740), John Cleland daringly introduces the sublime into the boudoir and shows sexual intercourse as a pleasure/pain congress between the outsized penises of *hommes machines* and the lacerated genitals of their battered victims. Endowed with a monstrous "man-machine," the country bumpkin – tellingly nicknamed "Good-natur'd Dick" – epitomizes the Rousseauistic noble savage who, unlike Mr. B, encounters no obstacles to the pornographic sublime of his well-performing body and readily injects his fertilizing juices into female bodies that, at that point, are still unhampered by barricades of cloth, Puritan religion and Platonic philosophy.[3]

As a naughty provocation to burgeoning Evangelical body shaming, Cleland's novel trivializes and deflects Pamela's distress into the frivolous atmosphere of the Rococo *fêtes galantes* and foreshadows both Thomas Rowlandson's outrageously facetious caricatures and Goethe's scandalous eulogies of Priapus, which, in the tradition of the ancient Priapeia, were attached as a frame to his hedonistic *Roman Elegies*. Priapus, as a lustful guardian of the *jardin d'amour* who punishes any trespassers with the "the red post / that shoots from his loins," is shockingly incompatible with overly sentimental Werther, whom in 1774 Goethe had shown as a suicidal, hyperbolic and sexually frustrated young man.[4] While some inveterate critics of Goethe's works were dismayed at Werther's contagious loss of masculinity, others later objected to the other extreme, the ostentatious display of virility, finally inducing Goethe to put the Priapus poems, the two most transgressive poems of the *Roman Elegies*, into what he called the "Walpurgissack," the bin of his self-censored and riotous imagination (to be opened only after his death in 1832). Yet it was not only Goethe's Priapus poems that were to lie dormant there for decades; next to Shakespeare's smutty lines that were not considered decent enough to be included in Bowdler's *Family Shakespeare* (1818), the Romantics chose to relegate numerous other examples of the pornographic sublime to a negative canon of bodily monstrosity, letting it sit there like the oppressive incubus on the swooning lady's breast in Henry Fuseli's *The Nightmare* (1782).

The Body as the Mind's Abject Antipode

Putting the corporeal squeamishly on a par with a leg of mutton in a gin shop, as Percy Bysshe Shelley flippantly did in a letter to John Gisborne, most of the Romantics saw the human body disadvantageously locked in a Manichaean dichotomy, dwarfed while the mind was growing and expanding to sublime dimensions.[5] Even though Schiller's Karl Moor in the Sturm-und-Drang play *The Robbers* (1781) is dismayed to find the mind-obsessed eighteenth century turned into a "century of limp eunuchs," the Romantics imperturbably continued to devote their poetry to the growth of the poet's mind and – in the manner of Carlyle's dithyrambic Professor

Teufelsdröckh in *Sartor Resartus* (1836) – to the image of the body as the insufficient and ill-fitting garment of the spirit.[6] The apotheosis of the mind, which grows unlike "a vegetable ..., by mysterious contact of Spirit," is the central idea towards which Wordsworth's *The Prelude* had been gravitating since 1799.[7] On the summit of Mount Snowdon, standing there on the promontory like Caspar David Friedrich's wanderer over the "silent sea of hoary mist," the speaker learns to interpret this sublime scenery, this awe-inspiring "billowy ocean" as an "emblem of a mind / That feeds upon infinity."[8] At the end of a long and zigzagging trajectory, Wordsworth arrives at the image of an all-encompassing mind that by "brood[ing] / Over the dark abyss" evokes the Spirit of God as it was hovering over the primeval chaos and molding it into pre-lapsarian creation (Book XIV, lines 71–2).[9] The more the apotheosized mind of the poet is eventually in the God-like position to turn a wasteland into a cosmos, making ample use of the "plastic power" of the redemptive imagination, the more conspicuous is Wordsworth's reticence about bodies in his mind-centered poetry.

When bodies do appear in the *Prelude*'s secular pilgrimage, in particular in the carnivalesque London section, they are alarmingly devoid of theo-morphic qualities and thus far below any categories of the sublime. In this context, it is noteworthy that London, the ontological antipode of Wordsworth's elevation on Mount Snowdon, is visualized as a "monstrous ant-hill," as a teeming place where monstrosity finds its expression in the diminution of insects, in the grotesque transformation of human beings into myriads of Kafkaesque crawling animals (Book VII, line 149). The grotesque heart of this ant-hill towards which the speaker is perversely attracted is Bartholomew Fair, a place notorious for its riotousness since at least Ben Jonson's play of the same name. Helplessly imploring his Muse's assistance, the poet in *The Prelude*, on his uneven way to the deification of his mind, is forced to undergo a descent into the nadir of metropolitan hell, where not only "anarchy and din / Barbarian and infernal" assail his senses, but where an asyndetic array of phantasma, "[m]onstrous in colour, motion, shape, sight, sound!," assaults him with the horror of a perverted sublimity of brazen corporeality (Book VII, lines 686–8). In order to add emphasis to this evocation of the corporeal pandemonium, Wordsworth arranges this part of the poem as a vertiginous list suggestive of what Umberto Eco later diagnoses as the mind-baffling confusion of things in baroque works.

Before this backdrop of a dizzying sequence of animals, buffoons and prodigies, there is an unsettling number of bodies that Wordsworth describes as being in a precarious state of liminality: "Albinos, painted Indians, Dwarfs, / ... / The Stone-eater, the man that swallows fire, / Giants, Ventriloquists, the Invisible Girl / The Bust that speaks and moves its goggling eyes" (Book VII, lines 707–11). Apart from people who transgress the demarcation line between humanity and the world of things by either eating stones or swallowing fire, and apart from the "Invisible Girl" who seems to meet Keatsian expectations of rendering her body immaterial, Wordsworth is struck by the ubiquity of bodily disproportion and, with a brief nod to the "Genius of Burke" before, seems to insinuate that the city breeds a new, monstrous sublimity of the body (Book VII, line 512). While the countryside is depicted as being idyllically involved in a cosmic dance that affects daffodils, waves and human hearts, London is the place where bodies either dwindle to entomic nonentities or are showcased as those of dwarfs and giants who appear to have stepped out of the gaudy plots of Gothic novels. As if parodying the elitist idea of the poet's disembodied philosophical mind, the pleasure-seekers at the fair are jumbled up into a huge tangle of convulsive bodies, into a Babelian "Parliament of Monsters," which like a "vast mill" churns them around and eventually vomits them up on all sides of the tents and booths (Book VII, lines 718–19). While the sublime philosophical mind feeds on the rarefied atmosphere of infinity, the carnivalesque body of the monstrous city vomits and discharges an endless flow of pulpy flesh that has forfeited its likeness of God.

This "vast mill" of convulsive bodily refuse is a nightmarish reverberation of the eighteenth-century concept of the *homme machine*, its "Clock-work" now transformed into a nullifying super-machine (Book VII, line 712). Yet what, in this context, is even more revealing and a sign of a momentous paradigm shift is the fact that Wordsworth sees in all these "freaks of nature" the utter bankruptcy of "all Promethean thoughts / Of man" (Book VII, lines 715–16). The abrupt turn of Promethean sublimity into abjection and detestable monstrosity also impels Lord Byron's poetry when, into his *succès de scandale Don Juan*, he inserts a relentless description of Prometheus's (self-)destruction and leads (not only) Wordsworth to think that the poem has the power to inflict irrevocable harm on the character and literature of the British people. Starting from the premise that there are no longer any heroes, Byron's post-Napoleonic poem not only shows the ruthless extent to which flights of Icarian grandeur are eclipsed by the demands of crude bodily materialism, but, in the notorious shipwreck scene in Canto II (1819), he also underlines that Prometheus, the transient Geneva epitome of Byronic heroism, has ceded his reign to modern man as the carnivorous vulture. In what sounds like a law inevitably imposed on the debased ship's crew ("'Twas nature gnawed them to this resolution"), Byron's narrator almost nonchalantly marks the transition from man as a mythological hero to a repulsive carrion eater that, at the end of a seven-day anti-Genesis, is at the beck and call of his bestial instincts: "the savage hunger which demanded, like the Promethean vulture, this pollution."[10]

Within a few years, Byron had moved away from his conception of the Faustian hero as a compound of "fiery dust" in which man's Promethean ambition, his transgressive spark of reason, is in a precarious equilibrium with the body's flesh. Apart from Wordsworth, most of the Romantics saw life as a miserable Laocoon-like struggle under the yoke of corporeality, but they invariably stuck to the belief that the beacon of man's Enlightenment mind was finally triumphant over the body's dross, and that in utopian visions of the "richest Alchymy," life's ordeal eventually culminated in what Keats and Shelley unanimously hailed as the advent of "unbodied joy."[11]

When Byron has Pedrillo's body dismembered and divided among the human vultures and, in a last act of utter repudiation of Promethean Enlightenment, the tutor's brains (on a par with his entrails) are flung overboard to regale two sharks, the Romantics' loss of faith in the paradox of man's partial divinity or his antithetical makeup is irreversible. Consigning the cannibals, the maritime version of Wordsworth's "Parliament of Monsters," to a convulsive death accompanied by abject "hyena laughter," Byron disavows all sublime trajectories and would certainly have responded with bewilderment at the operatic death that Goethe, the "illustrious" dedicatee of his tragedies *Sardanapalus* (1821) and *Werner* (1822), envisions for the Byronic Euphorion in the surreal second part of *Faust* (1832).[12]

Three Workshops of the Filthy Sublime

With the Romantic body becoming ever more invisible, its Promethean *grandezza* being increasingly eclipsed by bodily abjection, it is, however, intriguing to see what happens when, in Schiller's terminology, the "bold gigantic mind," the outsized philosophical mind, no longer feeds on infinity, but runs riot and suddenly, like a sick Pallas Athene, is delivered of monstrous shapes that go far beyond Wordsworth's *grand guignol* of oozy carnivalism in London.[13] In *The Neural Sublime*, Richardson shows the extent to which "the brain provides the locus of our experience of the sublime," and, referring to Percy Bysshe Shelley's truncated last work *The Triumph of Life* (1822), he pinpoints the moment in the poet's work when "the mind blanks out and seems to undergo a physical collapse or meltdown" (*Richardson*, 31). This "cognitive dissolution" that Shelley depicts as the process of the brain crumbling into sand is, however, different from the Walpurgis-night sequences of chimeras, giants, imps or other forms of riotous disorder that suddenly leap up from a brain which, according to Francisco de Goya's famous engraving, has lulled reason to sleep. Taking into account the fact that the effacing of the body has a long tradition in the discourse of the sublime, going back to Kant, it is striking to see that the most prominent examples of the monstrous sublimity seem to be the perverse offshoots of what the allegedly omnipotent mind fails to suppress. A careful look at the subtexts and the semantic camouflages with which the overtaxed philosophical minds grapple with the lurking figurations of untrammeled chaos reveal pandemoniums that rival Bosch's teeming imagination. While Coleridge clumsily sought refuge in the self-censorship of the undefined person from Porlock when the ejaculations around the awesome pleasure dome in his poem "Kubla Khan" (1797) were getting out of control, other poets and novelists prove to be less restrictive and allow their readers spine-chilling glimpses into the forbidden recesses where their tragic stories germinate.

One of these progenitors of the unleashed monstrous sublime is Victor Frankenstein, who follows in the footsteps of the historic Johann Faust and, at the age of seventeen, becomes a student at the University of Ingolstadt in Bavaria. Frankenstein's craving for knowledge is given an unparalleled erotic slant when fate drives him into the presence of Professor Waldman, whose lectures not only touch the various "keys" and fibers of his body, but also seem to fill him and to make him pregnant with "one conception."[14] More than any other Romantic text, Mary Shelley's *Frankenstein* (1818) translates the old concept of the *conceptio per aurem* from the biblical context of Mary's Annunciation into the (homo)erotic desires of a young scholar who feels his "internal being," his intellectual womb, "in a state of insurrection and turmoil" (48). What the insemination of the professor's transgressive mind creates is a paradoxical aberration: an "abortion" of gigantic proportions and a newborn creature that is made up of dead fragments collected, in truly Gothic fashion, from charnel-houses and dissecting rooms.[15] After a prolonged period of "incredible labour and fatigue" and turning his delivery room into a messy "workshop of filthy creation," Frankenstein gives birth to the monstrous parody of a homunculus, an abhorrent giant that ridicules not only Paracelsus's outlandish ideas in *De generatione rerum naturalium* (The Generation of Natural Things) (c. 1530), but also Goethe's later creature engendered by Wagner and Mephisto.[16]

After infusing the "spark of being" and galvanizing the monster into life, the modern, but deficient Prometheus is so much taken aback at the incomprehensibly monstrous sublimity of the creature that he precipitately rushes out of the room and henceforth acts as a *deus absconditus*, recoiling from his animated mummy in disgust. What is disturbing about the monster is not only its repulsive ugliness – arguably the result of an unnatural and homoerotic conception – but its contradictoriness and blatant disharmony, which challenges Burke's inherent paradoxicality in the concept of the sublime: as the Creature's embedded narrative shows, it is, right from the moment of its artificial birth, voluble and takes its cue from Milton's Satan in *Paradise Lost*. While challenging its creator to an acerbic debate of wits, the deformed wretch is also an avid reader of Goethe's *Sorrows of Young Werther* (1774), only to become, after imbibing the racial prejudices of its age – hearing about the "slothful Asiatics" and the "ingratitude of the Turk" – a raging avenger outdoing Othello and all personifications of wrath in literature. That the offshoot of Frankenstein's mind is a strange cross-breed between Werther, whose tear-drenched "despondency and gloom" Goethe himself had decried as being sick, and Milton's Satan, underlines the modern Prometheus's inability to body forth a palatable human being and to pay due homage to the body as a Vitruvian work of art (119, 126, 128). Reluctant to create a female companion for the Creature, to repeat the abortive atrocity or at least to engineer a dull *femme machine* in the way E. T. A. Hoffmann's Professor Spalanzani had achieved in the 1816 story "The Sandman," Frankenstein admits the failure of the Promethean mind to move beyond "the filthy mass," the heap of unmalleable cadaverous flesh that his heart cannot help sickening at and that instills nothing but sheer "horror and hatred" (147).

In what looks like a sudden parodic reversal of roles, the Promethean creator, the master mind, becomes the Creature's slave, and cast into the role of an exiled wanderer, Frankenstein is thrust into "eternal hell" for having allowed his ear to be penetrated by the Iago-like, malicious professor. It is an ironic twist that the Creature's mad revenge is enacted before the backdrop of the Alpine scenery of the Mont Blanc, the symbol of Romantic sublimity at least since Percy Bysshe Shelley's 1816 poem of the same name. The fact that the mountains echo with the Creature's fiendish laughter and its layers of snow are disfigured by the unwieldy bulk of the wretch's body makes it unmistakably clear that the "everlasting universe of things" which "[i]n day" supposedly "[f]lows through the mind" also encompasses monstrous nocturnal counter-worlds: in the dark, "still cave of the witch Poesy," there are negative figurations of a monstrous carnivalism surreptitiously con- cocted in the cauldron of the poet's mind (lines 1–2, 45). By the end of the story, in which good and evil are inextricably mixed, the Creature – even though pitying its progenitor – has adopted the role of the Byronic Prometheus waiting to "ascend [its] funeral pile triumphantly, and [to] exult in the agony of the torturing flames," an *auto da fé* for the perverse offspring engendered in the minds of two transgressively Faustian scholars, perverting the time-honored Platonic love between the passive *erastes* and the energetic *eromenos* (223).

In the context of the Romantic mind spawning bodies of perverse sexuality, Matthew Gregory Lewis's *The Monk* (1796) predated and inspired Mary Shelley's *Frankenstein*. Lewis's role as a Mephistophelean purveyor of Goethe's *Faust* I to the Shelleys and Byron in the Villa Diodati has been variously commented on, but to what extent his debut novel can also be understood as a story of a diseased and perverted mind that, in the blurry liminality of nightmarish reveries, creates a proliferation of tempting, but also monstrously sublime figures still merits closer investigation. The first figure that seems to spring from Ambrosio's mind is a creature in which at least three phantoms are dizzyingly (and falsely) conflated: in the abbey garden, the novice Rosario insidiously morphs into Matilda, who bewitches the monk with the ostentatious display of her left breast: "His eye dwelt with insatiable avidity upon the beauteous Orb."[17] The intricate choreography of the breast-flaunting Matilda/Rosario as it coalesces with the image of a *Madonna lactans* is part of a luscious hagio-porn that is unfolding in Ambrosio's riotous mind. After the oral-genital experience in which Matilda sucks the poison out of the monk's wound, he is imperceptibly taken on a trajectory that – as so often in Romantic literature – ends in the body's utter abjection before the imperative of the mind. At first, in what seems to be a passing tribute to Milton's Satan, the devil appears in the guise of a beautiful young man, a second Rosario, "seemingly scarce eighteen, the perfection of whose form and face was unrivalled" (237). Meeting the devil's appearance with "terror," a typical emotional response to the sublime, Ambrosio is dazzled not only to find Lucifer lavishly adorned with gems, but also to view the lord of hell in a state of perfect nakedness, with feminized silken locks "confined by a band of many-coloured fires" (237). Ambrosio is not aware of the extent to which the feminization of the devil is only one glittering illusion in a whole pageantry of deceit, nor is he able to see that the thrilling erotic imbroglio in which he finds himself with Rosario-Matilda, the Madonna and Satan is only the entry into a vortex of unfathomably sublime depths of corporeal monstrosity.

Having gone through the grotesque motions of being a voluptuous parody of Shakespeare's Romeo and found his obsession with sex frustrated in the sepulcher, Ambrosio is suddenly faced with the devil who has, by this time, discarded the splendor of seraphic beauty in favor of an inexpressible ugliness: "A swarthy darkness spread itself over his gigantic form: His hands and feet were armed with long Talons" (369). His limbs of gigantic disproportion show his affiliation with all the monsters that had been inadvertently slipping from the Romantics' Promethean minds. What in Goethe's *Faust* remains conspicuously vague and in Mary Shelley's novel is depicted as an intellectual penetration is, in Lewis's novel, eminently corporeal and has clear sexual reverberations. The sexual frame of the duplicitous Faustian bargain (with the iron pen thrust into the arm with the genitalized wound) is then widened into a soaring Icarian flight over mountain ridges whose phallic rocky spikes are not so much the emblem of a redemptive mind as the site of sexualized metaphysical justice (perversely administered by the devil!). Thus, in an anachronistic translation of Dante's idea of the *contrapasso* into the Enlightenment world, the monk's body is buffeted from one precipice to another and, in what looks like a spectacle of bodily abjection, is eventually subjected to a mass penetration by myriads of insects: "they fastened upon his sores, darted their stings into his body, ... and inflicted on him tortures the most exquisite and insupportable" (376). In the wake of the Marquis de Sade's idea of life as an enormous Piranesian torture chamber (designed by a perfidious mind), Ambrosio's body undergoes an ordeal of excruciating pain that, due to its macro-geological dimensions, seems to have been devised by a philosophical super-mind that exceeds in Ambrosio's fiendishness. When on the apocalyptic seventh day diluvian rains eventually wash the monk's corpse into a river, Ambrosio's body has not only become pulpy refuse, but also a glaring example of the way the abject corpus is crushed and nullified when it comes into close contact with the henchmen of the mind's monstrous sublime.

While Lewis's and Shelley's novels seem to visualize what Pope facetiously describes as the process when "bards, like Proteus long in vain tied down, escape in monsters, and amaze the town," unleashing a sudden pandemonium from their brains, Byron premises his late poetry on a different, but not less unsettling idea.[18] Pondering man's origin and eschatology in the frivolous lines of his *Don Juan*, Byron's narrator posits the image of a colossal female abdomen that ejects mankind into the bustle of life only to reclaim and to suck it into its all-devouring genitals again. In Canto IX (1823), using an intertextual detour via Horace, Byron apostrophizes the female genitals as the "gate of life and death ... / Whence is our exit and our entrance" (lines 434–5). The alpha and omega of man's transient life is thus not Christ, as promised in John's book of Revelation (1:8), but a female body inflated to grotesque Brobdingnagian dimensions that dwarfs the male protagonists and reduces them to helpless (ant-like?) nonentities. In Byron's poem, the unnerving dichotomy between the outsized (masculine) mind and its (often feminized, or sentimentalized) progeny of monstrous and abhorrent bodies has been replaced by the surreal image of life as a perilous cruise on a female body.[19] If there is still a vestige of the former antithesis, it is now that between a disproportionate body and a shriveled and insignificant mind, leaving man in the relentless jaws of a horrific *vagina dentata*. When Byron identifies the gigantic vagina with a "perennial fountain" – an image going back to Venus's "pleasant fountains" in Shakespeare's *Venus and Adonis* – and even goes so far as to trope it as the "sea of life's dry land," he invites his readers to finally reread the shipwreck scene in Canto II (1819) as the crucial and shocking moment when philosophical, dry and cerebral ideas (in this case, of trinity) are suddenly sucked into the vortex of the female body: "the sea yawned around her like a hell, / And down she sucked with her the whirling wave" (Canto IX, lines 437, 448; Canto II, lines 413–14). Although the use of pronouns here is confusing – conflating the ship and the sea – there are good reasons to understand the sea in terms of an all-engulfing hole that annihilates all mind-bred concepts and arks, finally to subject the idea of antithetical man, the inflammable fiery dust, to a damp parody.

Conclusion

Byron's provocative and blasphemous image of the monstrous female body as the Shakespearean be-all and end-all is certainly one of the culmination points of the negative sublimity of the body in the Romantic age. What started as an uneven balance between mind and body, leaving the infirm body dwindling to almost nothing or, in Heine's grim idiom, reduced to the state of a spiritual skeleton in a vault of mattresses, turned more and more into the nightmare of overgrown philosophical minds losing control and giving monstrous birth to imps, zombies, vampires and other figurations of a sublime anti-mythology. While the descent into the hell of Bartholomew Fair and the encounter with its perverse "Parliament of Monsters" were for Wordsworth still part of a necessary dialectical process and did not hamper the growth of his philosophical mind (which ironically never surpassed the initial stage of *The Prelude*), other writers such as Lewis and Mary Shelley, however, depicted their protagonists as being fatally stuck in hell and tempted by Mephistophelean abettors to veer from their cerebral philosophies into dystopian encounters with the sensual and monstrous sublime.

As early as in Christopher Marlowe's domestic tragedy *Doctor Faustus*, the growth of the overreacher's mind is fomented by repressed sexual drives. In a gaudy pageantry, the Seven Deadly Sins parade before Faustus in lascivious shapes and underline the extent to which the over-ambitious mind seeks release in a riotous Walpurgis Night that externalizes the scholar's craving for lust. While in Marlowe's play, Lucifer is still seen as God's antagonist and the director of Faustus's illusory theatre of sensuality, in the Romantic age, the devil and his "companion prince[s] in hell" turn into the *dramatis personae* of a cerebral theater that happens in the over-heated philosophical minds. [20] It is only in this context that Romantics are reacquainted with bodies, with the corporeal that they preferred to show in a state of evanescence, pierced and obliterated as Lamia's body is by Apollonius's philosophical gaze. While in Keats's poem, the cold philosopher prevails and the serpentine body evaporates into nothing, leaving only its sartorial slough behind, in the seething sexualized minds of many other Romantics, the body defies suppression and rises to the surface in shapes of monstrous sublimity that leave their creators aghast, disgusted and terrified.

Having succumbed to the demonic whisperings of their rambling minds, Ambrosio and Frankenstein conjure up abortive figures that ruthlessly seek retaliation upon their creator, whereas in Byron's last poem cynicism has become so triumphant that Faustian man and his superhuman aspirations have undergone a process of Lilliputization, reducing him to a seafaring Gulliver on the thalassian body of a monstrous female giant. With their spectacles of a perverted sublimity of the body, the Romantics laid the foundation for a new mythology of bodily horror that, in the context of Mario Praz's idea of dark Romanticism, was to find its uncanny materializations in forms as diverse as in Swinburne's larger-than-life *femmes fatales*, in Wilde's phantasmagoric Sphinx, in the canine-teethed vampires in Stoker's *Dracula* or in H. G. Wells's humanized beasts as they spring forth from the transgressive imagination of Frankenstein's truest descendant, Dr. Moreau.[21]

NOTES

1 William Butler Yeats, "Sailing to Byzantium" (1928), line 24; quoted from *Yeats's Poems*, ed. A. Norman Jeffares, London, Macmillan, 1991, 301.

2 John Keats, "Ode on a Grecian Urn" (1819), line 5.

3 John Cleland, *Memoirs of a Woman of Pleasure*, ed. Peter Sabor, Oxford, Oxford University Press, 1986, 160, 163.

4 Johann Wolfgang von Goethe, "Elegie III" (1795), lines 90–1 (my translation).

5 Percy Bysshe Shelley, letter to John Gisborne, 22 October 1821; quoted from *The Letters of Percy Bysshe Shelley*, ed. F. L. Jones, 2 vols., Oxford, Clarendon, 1963, vol. 2, 363.

6 Friedrich Schiller, *Die Räuber* (1782), line 2 (my translation).

7 Thomas Carlyle, *Sartor Resartus* (1836), ed. Kerry McSweeney and Peter Sabor, Oxford, Oxford University Press, 2008, 82.

8 William Wordsworth, *The Prelude* (1850), Book XIV, lines 42, 55, 70–1; quoted from *The Prelude: The Four Texts*, ed. Jonathan Wordsworth, London, Penguin, 1995.

9 Compare Genesis 1:2.

10 Lord Byron, *Don Juan*, Canto II (1819), lines 598, 595–6.

11 Quoted in Nicholas Roe, *John Keats*, New Haven, CT, Yale University Press, 2012, 174; Percy Shelley, "To a Skylark" (1820), line 15.

12 Byron, *Don Juan*, Canto II, line 632.

13 Friedrich Schiller, *Don Karlos* (1805), Act 2, scene 10, line 2033 (my translation).
14 Mary Shelley, *Frankenstein*, ed. M. K. Joseph, Oxford, Oxford University Press, 1998, 48.
15 Richard C. Sha, "Mary Shelley's Monstrous Abortion," in Norbert Lennartz, ed., *The Lost Romantics*, London, Palgrave, 2020, 203–23.
16 Shelley, *Frankenstein*, 52.
17 Matthew Lewis, *The Monk*, ed. Christopher Maclachlan, London, Penguin, 1998, 60.
18 Alexander Pope, *The Dunciad* (1728), Book I, lines 37–8; quoted from *The Major Works*, ed. Pat Rogers, Oxford, Oxford University Press, 2008.
19 Caroline Franklin, "'Quiet cruising o'er the Ocean Woman': Byron's *Don Juan* and the Woman Question," *Studies in Romanticism* 29 (1990), 603–31.
20 Christopher Marlowe, *Doctor Faustus*, A-Text, Act 2, scene 3, line 87; quoted from *Doctor Faustus and Other Plays*, ed. David Bevington and Eric Rasmussen, Oxford, Oxford University Press, 1998, 159.
21 See Mario Praz, *The Romantic Agony*, trans. Angus Davidson, Oxford, Oxford University Press, 1978.

14

NINA AMSTUTZ

The Sublime in Romantic Painting

Hardly any aesthetic has become more synonymous with Romantic painting than the sublime. There is a certain irony to this historical condition, for while the sublime experienced a theoretical revival during the eighteenth century that gave the concept new meaning relative to its literary origins with Longinus, that revival did not for the most part include the visual arts. In his *Critique of the Power of Judgment* (1790), Immanuel Kant notably described the sublime as a feeling that exists not in the object but in the mind, and that while large and powerful facets of nature might occasion the experience of the sublime, nature is not the origin of that experience. Kant distanced art from the feeling of the sublime even further, on the grounds that in art "a human end determines the form as well as the magnitude" while "a pure judgment on the sublime . . . must have no end of the object as its determining ground if it is to be aesthetic and not mixed up with any judgement of the understanding or of reason" (*COPJ* §26 253–4). Kant, in other words, determined that our responses to art are rational, in that apprehending a work of art in full is generally not beyond the scope of the imagination, whereas the feeling of the sublime reflects an aesthetic response that exceeds reason. Kant did use some artistic works as potential sources of the sublime, namely, the Egyptian pyramids and St. Peter's in Rome, but these are exceptions and he qualifies his observations about them immediately after they are mentioned, redirecting the reader's attention to "raw nature" (*COPJ* §26 253).

Earlier in the eighteenth century, Burke's *Enquiry* (1757) similarly questioned the power of visual art to evoke the sublime, albeit for different reasons. Burke suggested that painting falls short of exciting ideas of the sublime, because it brings things into clarity and undermines the close relationship between the sublime and obscurity:

> It is one thing to make an idea clear, and another to make it *affecting* to the imagination. If I make a drawing of a palace, or a temple, or a landscape,

I present a very clear idea of those objects; but then ... my picture can at most affect only as the palace, temple, or landscape would have affected in the reality. (*Enquiry* II iv)

Because painting is a mimetic art, Burke insists, it is closely bound to reality. "Spirited verbal description," on the other hand, "raises a very obscure and imperfect *idea* of such objects; but then it is in my power to raise a stronger *emotion* by the description than I could do by the best painting" (*Enquiry* II iv). Whereas the vague and unfathomable are beyond painting's reach, Burke says, literature exercises a much greater force on the imagination. Burke was speaking from an understanding of art based on the aesthetics of Neoclassicism, which promoted eclectically copying the best elements of the ancients and old masters, shortly before the Romantic movement in painting took hold and disavowed these restrictive methods. The many Romantic-period paintings of landscapes shrouded in fog or darkness, of imposing mountains, waterfalls, or volcanic eruptions; of the supernatural or otherworldly; or of violence and destruction in the animal kingdom or at the hands of industrialization fall outside Burke's mimetic understanding of visual representation and approach precisely the sense of obscurity and indeterminateness that he, and others, associated with the sublime.

In the late eighteenth and early nineteenth century, many painters took up a variety of subjects that echo the descriptions of the sublime offered by Burke, Kant, and other works of philosophical aesthetics. This development was, in part, facilitated by art critics who attempted to apply the idea of the sublime to art. In Britain, Uvedale Price's *Essay on the Picturesque, as Compared with the Sublime and the Beautiful* (1794) and Richard Payne Knight's *Analytical Inquiry into the Principles of Taste* (1805) were influential for landscape painters. In Germany, the playwright and poet Friedrich Schiller published two essays about the sublime, "Of the Sublime" (1793) and "On the Sublime" (1801), which discuss how artistic representations can evoke the sublime, focusing on tragedy in theater. With respect to landscape painting, Christian August Semler's "Studies of the Highest Perfection in the Works of Landscape Painting" (1800) and Carl Ludwig Fernow's "On Landscape Painting" (1803) endeavored to apply Kant's concept of the sublime to the depiction of nature.[1] Both recognized the limitations of efforts to evoke the sublime through representation in a static and bounded medium such as painting, admitting that only nature could directly conjure the feeling, but they afforded the visual with the potential to capture the sublime through indirect means.

This essay considers a variety of responses by European Romantic-period artists to the new interest in the sublime. Specifically, I focus on artists whose work engages with three facets of the sublime that had become recurrent concerns of British and German philosophical aesthetics: (1) *vastness*, visible in the landscapes of Joseph Anton Koch and Caspar David Friedrich; (2) *power*, as it is expressed through natural catastrophes, such as Mount Vesuvius erupting in the landscapes of J. M. W. Turner and Johan Christian Dahl; and (3) *violence*, captured in paintings of animal conflict by George Stubbs and Eugène Delacroix. Although the focus of this essay is on natural phenomena, the sublime was also approached in painting through supernatural or "Gothic" themes, apocalyptic imagery of divine revelation, the French Revolutionary and Napoleonic Wars, manmade sources of power occasioned by the Industrial Revolution, and exoticism prompted by colonial conquest.

Vastness in Nature

In Romantic art, the sublime is most often associated with developments in landscape painting in Britain and Germany. Whereas landscape painters in the seventeenth century, exemplified by Claude Lorrain, preferred harmonious and self-contained compositions with idealized motifs, which would later come to be associated with the aesthetics of the beautiful, many landscape painters in the late eighteenth and early nineteenth centuries preferred formless qualities in nature that were increasingly aligned with the sublime. New tastes in landscape depiction closely relate to the emphasis on extreme facets of nature as occasions for the sublime in British and German philosophical aesthetics. Burke, for instance, mentions the ocean as a source of terror and mountains as an expression of vastness, both qualities he associated with sublime experience (*Enquiry* II ii and vii). Similarly, Kant foregrounds natural wonders in his notions of the mathematical and dynamical sublimes. The first concept refers to the feeling we experience in the face of things that are of a scale and magnitude that is beyond comparison (*COPJ* §25). The second points to our response to power in nature – to "bold, overhanging ... threatening cliffs, thunder clouds towering up into the heavens, bringing with them flashes of lightning and crashes of thunder, volcanoes with their all-destroying violence, hurricanes with the devastation they leave behind, the boundless ocean set into a rage, a lofty waterfall on a mighty river" – so long as those forces have no dominion over us (*COPJ* §28 261).

Among the first German landscape painters to take an active interest in sublime manifestations of nature was Koch: one of the so-called *Deutschrömer*, a community of German artists and writers who lived and practiced in Rome. Kant's ideas were influential in this circle, and his aesthetics were introduced to many artists by the art critic and historian Karl Ludwig Fernow.[2] During his stay in Rome, Fernow delivered a series of lectures, "Lectures on Aesthetics According to Kantian Principles" (1795–96), which were attended by many artists, including Koch.[3] Fernow's lectures do not survive in published form, but his subsequent theoretical writings on art provide insight into their content, particularly his collection of essays, *Roman Studies* (1806), which includes "On Landscape Painting." Fernow applied Kant's notion of the beautiful to the fine arts, but he ultimately agreed with the philosopher that the sublime is beyond painting's reach:

> The fine arts cannot directly awaken the feeling of the sublime through representation, as nature can; because they cannot really represent the sublime, like nature. For sense perception, the sublime is immeasurable, infinite.... Art can certainly expand and stretch the imagination through magnitude; but art can't stretch it to the point where, with the feeling of sensory incapacitation, the terror of the sublime sets in.[4]

Due to limitations of size and motion, Fernow continues, the bounded and static visual arts are left to express the sublime through indirect means, that is, through an idea that approximates the sublime or by representing natural phenomena that conjure up previous impressions of similar scenes witnessed firsthand, thereby reawakening the feeling of the sublime by tricking the imagination through the association of ideas, a key concept in eighteenth-century philosophical aesthetics (vol. 2, 70).

Fernow's reflections did not deter Koch from experimenting with the sublime in his landscapes, but the compositional strategies he employed suggest that he self-consciously grappled with the question of direct versus indirect experience. Koch's *Der Schmadribachfall* (The Schmadribach Falls) (1822; first version 1811) takes up many motifs that resonate with Kant's discussion of the mathematical sublime, including towering snow-covered mountains and the overall expansiveness of the landscape, as well as the dynamical sublime, through the mighty force of the waterfall and rushing river (see Figure 14.1).

It is not Koch's subject alone but also his compositional structure that conjures up the sublime. In Koch's time, landscapes were generally horizontal in orientation and constructed with a distinct foreground, middle ground, and background, joined by a meandering path or river that gradually guides the viewer's eye into the distance. Koch, rather, oriented his canvas vertically, exaggerating the height and immensity of the mountains. As Mark Cheetham has argued, the zigzagging diagonals of the river also lead the viewer's gaze from the bottom to the top of the canvas, rather than into

Figure 14.1 Joseph Anton Koch, *Der Schmadribachfall* (The Schmadribach Falls) (1821–2).
Neue Pinakothek, Munich.

pictorial space, as was customary in classical landscape depiction.[5] Koch
further minimized the recession of space by dramatically reducing the distance between foreground and background, so that the viewer is overwhelmed by the scale of the scene. This sensation is exacerbated by the
relative minuteness of the staffage figures in the landscape, which include a
shepherd and his flock. Kant emphasized in his discussion of the mathematical sublime that it is not simply the size of an object that generates ideas of
the sublime, but rather our relative distance from it. If positioned too far

away, the effect on the mind is obscured, in that we can no longer distinguish any details, and if positioned too close, we don't apprehend the whole in our field of vision and the sense of infinity is lost (*COPJ* §26). Koch's composition seems to consciously position the viewer in this Goldilocks zone. Every detail of the landscape is carefully articulated with botanical and geological precision, from the foreground vegetation to the snow-capped mountain peaks, so that we can apprehend nature's infinity in a single visual field.[6]

In the German context, no other landscape painter pursued the vast and infinite dimensions of nature more fully than Friedrich, but the degree to which he actively sought to represent the sublime remains contested.[7] Friedrich did not discuss the sublime in his own theoretical writings and generally did not express an interest in philosophy, but he likely absorbed the concept through Fernow's or Semler's art criticism, or visually in the choice of subjects that landscape painters such as Koch began to pursue at the turn of the century. Friedrich did receive at least one commission to paint a landscape of the sublime from the Dresden collector Johann Gottlob von Quandt in 1822, which took the form of a Northern landscape and was intended as a counterpart to a landscape of the beautiful by Johann Martin von Rohden.[8] More broadly, it is difficult to understand Friedrich's penchant for landscapes shrouded in fog, imposing mountains, and the vast sea without reference to the sublime. His *Der Mönch am Meer* (Monk by the Sea) (1808–10), for instance, situates a man, dwarfed by his surroundings, before the open ocean that, without any objects on its shore or in the water to provide the viewer with a sense of scale, stretches into the immeasurable distance. The sky also occupies three quarters of the composition, heightening the sense of nature's infinity and humanity's relative insignificance. Friedrich's contemporaries responded to the work precisely in terms of the sublime. In "Various Impressions Experienced before a Seascape with a Monk, by Caspar David Friedrich" (1810), a fictional dialogue about the painting written by Clemens Brentano and Achim von Arnim, and later revised and expanded by Heinrich von Kleist, the topic of the sublime is raised with Kantian precision. Standing before Friedrich's seascape, a man proclaims, "Infinitely deep and sublime!"[9] His female companion questions whether he is referring to the ocean or the monk standing on its shores. The man's response is neither, instead pointing to the feeling prompted by the painting: "I mean the emotion felt by the one and only Friedrich before this painting" (283). These imagined characters explain that it is not Friedrich's subject matter itself that is sublime, but rather that the artist selects immense facets of nature that conjure up ideas of the sublime in the viewer's mind. The monk – Friedrich's first example of the *Rückenfigur* motif – facilitates this experience by acting as a surrogate for the viewer and inviting us to contemplate the vastness of the sea from a safe distance. By standing in for the viewer, he serves as a reminder that our experience of nature's magnitude is at one remove and that a painting can at best offer an indirect experience of the sublime. In later manifestations of this motif, notably *Wanderer above the Sea of Fog* (1818), the *Rückenfigur* comes to dominate the composition, whereby the subject of the painting is as much the act of viewing as it is the landscape itself, asserting even more forcefully that the sublime exists in us, not the object.

Power in Nature

In addition to experimenting with the aesthetic effects of vastness, many Romantic-period landscape painters pursued power in nature as their subject, which most often manifests as an interest in natural catastrophes. As Knight explained in his *Analytical Inquiry*, "All the great and terrible convulsions of nature; such as storms, tempests, hurricanes, earthquakes, volcanos, &c. excite sublime ideas, and impress sublime sentiments by the prodigious exertions of energy and power, which they seem to display."[10] Of these "great and terrible convulsions," volcanos became particularly popular subjects. With Mount Vesuvius's somewhat regular eruptions after 1631, numerous artists were able to witness and sketch the spectacle while they were in Naples on the Grand Tour. Vesuvius's activity at this time led to significant strides in the science of geology, contributing to a shift in the scientific community's understanding of the length of the Earth's history from a few thousand years to potentially millions, in addition to yielding new theories about how the Earth's land masses formed through heat. The leap of imagination required to conceive of the Earth's long history could itself be described as a source of the sublime, and many paintings of Vesuvius express a serious interest in volcanology, notably those of Jacob Philipp Hackert. But artists were also preoccupied more directly with the phenomenon of volcanic eruption as an expression of nature's might and approached the subject by exaggerating the eruption. For instance, Joseph Wright of Derby, who took up the subject at least thirty times even though he never witnessed an eruption firsthand, painted the eruption as a cataclysmic vertical projection. Artists without their own sketches often turned to the British ambassador to the Court of Naples Sir William Hamilton's lavishly illustrated treatise, *Campi Phlegraei: Observations on the Volcanoes of the Two Sicilies* (1776).

The British Romantic painter of the sublime par excellence, Turner, completed at least three watercolors of volcanoes erupting or in repose, for which he likely consulted Hamilton's treatise, along with sketches by John Robert Cozens and James Hakewill. Although Turner visited the site in 1819, and may have witnessed some volcanic activity, his various iterations of the subject precede this trip.[11] Turner's watercolors nonetheless exhibit more geological verisimilitude than the interpretations of many of his contemporaries and were likely influenced by his acquaintances in the earth sciences, notably William Buckland, John MacCulloch, and Charles Stokes.[12] But Turner's paintings are mostly imaginative renderings that readily suggest the sublime by showcasing the power and destruction of nature. In the version now at Yale Center for British Art (1817–20), Turner scraped out accents to reveal the white of the paper beneath in order to capture the light effects of molten lava particles raining from the sky into the Bay of Naples below (see Figure 14.2). The viewer is situated on the shore near Posillipo among a group of onlookers who have narrowly escaped the explosion by boat. Mirrored in the water, the volcano's ejecting stream of lava extends into the foreground, but only through its reflection,

Figure 14.2 Joseph Mallord William Turner, *Vesuvius in Eruption* (1817–20). Yale Center for British Art, New Haven.

and the viewer is kept at a safe distance from the flames that envelop the mountain and its surroundings.

Turner also undertook a variety of strategies beyond subject matter to heighten the sense of the sublime in his paintings. He transposed his landscapes to previously unheard-of proportions, and with *Snow Storm: Hannibal and His Army Crossing the Alps* (1812) insisted that it be viewed at eye level rather than at an elevation, so that the viewer would feel enveloped by nature's might and experience the representation as if it were an unmediated storm.

Whereas Turner's paintings captured the drama of Vesuvius from afar, other artists brought viewers into much closer proximity to the eruption. The Norwegian artist Dahl painted Vesuvius from various perspectives, including several compositions staged within the caldera. Dahl traveled to Naples in 1820 at the invitation of the Danish Crown Prince Christian Frederik and he witnessed an eruption on December 20, 1820, which he sketched a few days after ascending the mountain.[13] This sketch provided the basis for a number of paintings of Vesuvius, including an 1824 commission for the Crown Prince (see Figure 14.3).[14]

Two onlookers stand right at the edge of the smoke and hot embers, while three attendants and their donkeys wait patiently at a more comfortable

Figure 14.3 Johan Christian Dahl, *An Eruption of Vesuvius* (1824). Metropolitan Museum of Art, New York.

distance. The smoke, flames, and sparks that consume the upper left register are juxtaposed with a serene view of the Bay of Naples on the right. Although Dahl opted for a less apocalyptic rendition of the geological event, he heightened the effect by setting up this juxtaposition. The immediacy of the viewer's perspective on the chaotic scene of fire and smoke prompts the terror and fear associated with the sublime, whereas the calm view of the Bay of Naples readily evokes the harmony and order associated with the beautiful in landscape depiction.[15] Aesthetic pleasure here derives from nature as a source of both great power and stability.

Animal Violence

Burke's *Enquiry* coincided with a significant shift in the representation of animals in the visual arts. Whereas portraits of domesticated animals were common in the collections of the landed gentry throughout the eighteenth century, in the 1760s a fascination with wild animals emerged. Largely initiated by the English animal painter Stubbs, this new direction in animal painting focused on wild animals at their most vulnerable and ferocious. Like many European artists in the eighteenth century, Stubbs traveled to Rome around 1754 on the Grand Tour to study the art of Greek and Roman antiquity and the Italian Renaissance. No sketchbooks survive from this trip and Stubbs claimed that his sojourn in Rome was not especially important for his artistic education, in that "nature was & is always superior to art whether Greek or Roman."[16] But it was Stubbs's encounter with a near life-size pre-Hellenistic sculpture, *Lion and Horse*, that would lead him to adopt one of his most influential themes.[17] Stubbs's *Lion Attacking a Horse* (1762) is the first of sixteen paintings by the artist on this subject (see Figure 14.4).

Staged amid a landscape subtly evoking the African savanna, a petrified horse seeks to fend off a ferocious lion that has attacked from behind. Every inch of the horse's body is in tension, which Stubbs has expressed through the horse's musculature, pulsating veins, stiff mane, and the expression of terror in its eyes. In the pre-Hellenistic sculpture, the lion stands for justice and avenges wrong-doing, represented by the horse. Stubbs's horse is far more noble and beautiful than one would expect for an embodiment of vice, and its facial expression provokes empathy much more than contempt. But his composition also makes it clear that the laws of nature do not accommodate pity. These two creatures cannot coexist peacefully in the wild: the physically stronger lion will overpower the defenseless horse, irrespective of the creature's innocence or guilt. In Stubbs's variation, there is no contest between good and evil, for nature does not distinguish.

Figure 14.4 George Stubbs, *A Lion Attacking a Horse* (1762). Yale Center for British Art, New Haven.

Stubbs's deviation from the Greek sculpture relates closely to the then growing artistic interest in the sublime.[18] And it is through the work's connection to the sublime that what otherwise might be situated squarely within the Neoclassical movement breaks away from the straightforward emulation of antiquity. Among the objects that incite ideas of terror, danger, or pain that Burke enumerates are wild animals. For an animal to stoke terror, it need not be large, Burke insists, "as serpents and poisonous animals of almost all kinds" can raise "ideas of the sublime" (*Enquiry* II ii). But most of his examples involve animals of physical stature and strength. The sublime "comes upon us in the gloomy forest, and in the howling wilderness, in the form of the lion, the tiger, the panther, or rhinoceros" (*Enquiry* II v). Strength itself is not enough, for "whenever strength is only useful, and employed for our benefit or our pleasure, then it is never sublime" (*Enquiry* II v). But wild animals whose strength we experience as pernicious, and which we cannot tame, are sources of the sublime. Stubbs's *Lion Attacking a Horse* is a showcase example of such strength and volatility in the animal kingdom. As Diana Donald has noted, the lifelike quality of Stubbs's animal paintings, in terms of both scale and attention to anatomical and zoological detail, gave eighteenth-century viewers the thrill of a real encounter with a wild and dangerous animal.[19]

Stubbs's paintings of animal conflict inspired later Romantic artists, such as Théodore Géricault and Delacroix, to depict similar scenes. Delacroix began producing images of lions and tigers in various media after 1820, with some of his largest animal paintings dating to the 1860s. The tone of these works is mixed, in that some depict wild animals at rest, engaged in play, or caring for their young, while in others they are in a predatory state, struggling with each other or with man, such as in three late versions of the *Lion Hunt* theme, painted between 1855 and 1861. The artist studied his feline subjects in animal shows, zoos, and natural history museums, which tended to present animals under the dominion of man.[20] In Delacroix's early paintings of lions, the predatory cats similarly stand in opposition to man as a rational being.[21] This dynamic is consistent with seventeenth- and eighteenth-century images of the hunt, particularly those of Peter Paul Rubens, in which rational man's conquest of the irrational forces of nature, symbolized by the savage beasts, is foregrounded.[22]

Although Delacroix drew heavily on Rubens for his *Lion Hunt* paintings, in his last version of the subject, the tension between man and brute has shifted toward the amoral scenes of animal conflict by Stubbs, and no longer expresses the belief that man holds a divinely sanctioned position of superiority in the universe (see Figure 14.5).[23] Seven Arab men, five on foot and two on horseback, wage war against a lion and lioness. Although they outnumber their prey and come armed with sabers and spears, the lions present formidable opponents, having already mauled one man on horseback and another on the ground. Who will be the victor is unclear, but there will be causalities on both sides. This antagonistic dynamic between man and lion corresponds with Delacroix's journal descriptions from the 1850s of nature as a destructive force indifferent to human life (120, 123–4). But it is noteworthy that the internecine struggle does not implicate the Western subject; it is the North African hunters who face their mortality.

Delacroix's *Lion Hunt* scenes are in line with what Marc Gotlieb has described as the "Orientalist sublime": the lure for European artists of the most inhospitable aspects of the land in the Near East, including geographic features, such as the punishing heat and blinding light of the sun, the arid desert unable to support life, or dangerous exotic animals; namely, those facets of nature that have the potential to overpower man.[24] The paintings are among Delacroix's many Orientalist works inspired by his travels to Morocco, where he accompanied a French diplomatic mission headed by Charles de Mornay in 1832. In his drawings, journals, and letters, the artist recorded countless impressions of local people, customs, topography, and

Figure 14.5 Eugène Delacroix, *Chasse au lion* (Lion Hunt) (1860–1). Art Institute of Chicago.

animals. In a journal entry from January 29, 1832, Delacroix vividly described the spectacle of two ferocious horses fighting and a bellicose soldier's intervention as "sublime," himself maintaining the detached perspective of a museum observer, even comparing the "extraordinary and fantastic" scene to something imagined by "Gros or Rubens" (52).[25] In Tangier on April 28 Delacroix also characterized Arab culture as "closer to nature" than the advanced civilization of the West (56). Lions and tigers in Delacroix's work have been shown to serve as symbols of the barbaric in man, which is exaggerated by the primal aggression of the Arab hunters in the lion hunt scenes.[26] These works, in other words, explore man's animality not only through the felines but also through a foreign body. In the 1861 version, the carnage unfolds in the foreground, with relatively little recession of space, so that the viewer observes the spectacle with a certain immediacy; however, none of the figures spill out of the frame and none implicate the implied Western observer. As in Delacroix's journal, the painting elicits ideas of the sublime by positioning us in proximity to the danger but not in its midst. The sublime here cuts across two thematic planes, nature and the exotic, which is achieved through a slippage between the "Oriental other" and the beasts.

Conclusion

The aesthetics of the sublime are among the most enduring legacies of the Romantic movement in the visual arts, arguably having never fully retreated. The motifs and compositional innovations pioneered by Romantic-period landscape painters, in particular, continued to inform the representation of nature throughout the nineteenth and twentieth centuries, visible, above all, in the Symbolist and Expressionist movements. However, even the birth of nonrepresentational art was indebted to Romantic-period images of sublime nature. The late art historian Robert Rosenblum evocatively related the placement of the spectator in front of an empty and boundless seascape in Friedrich's *Monk by the Sea* to the dematerialized expanse of color in Mark Rothko's color-field paintings from the 1950s.[27] In recent years, with the acceleration of climate change, the Romantic sublime has again been revived in the representation of nature. While such seismic environmental changes are caused by human attempts to exercise dominion over the natural world, captured, for instance, in the industrial sublime of Edward Burtynsky's monumental landscape photographs, it is once again nature's destructive forces with which humanity must contend. Contemporary artists who tackle the fast and slow violence of climate change, from Olafur Eliason to Richard Mosse, are returning to the aesthetics of Romantic painting to capture new sources of sublime experience.

NOTES

1 On the influence of Fernow and Semler on landscape painting, see Johannes Grave, *Caspar David Friedrich*, Munich, Prestel, 2012, 195.

2 Mark Cheetham, *Kant, Art, and Art History*, Cambridge, Cambridge University Press, 2001, 38–66.

3 Ibid., 44.

4 Carl Ludwig Fernow, *Römische Studien*, Zurich, H. Gessner, 1806, vol. 2, 69–70. Translation mine.

5 Cheetham, *Kant, Art*, 118.

6 Ibid., 119.

7 The most extensive analysis of the sublime in Friedrich's work surrounds his *Cross in the Mountains* (1808). See Brad Prager, "Kant in Caspar David Friedrich's Frames," *Art History* 25, 1, 2002, 66–86; Joseph Leo Koerner, *Caspar David Friedrich and the Subject of Landscape*, 2nd edition, London, Reaktion, 2009, 117–46. For arguments against reading Friedrich's work in relation to the sublime, see Grave, *Caspar David Friedrich*, 187–99, especially 196–9.

8 Grave, *Caspar David Friedrich*, 188–9.

9 Translated by Mary Whittall as "Various Impressions Experienced before a Seascape with a Monk, by Caspar David Friedrich," in Werner Hofmann, *Caspar David Friedrich*, London, Thames and Hudson, 2000, 283.

10 Richard Payne Knight, *Analytical Inquiry into the Principles of Taste*, London, 1805, 364.

11 James Hamilton, *Turner and the Scientists*, London, Tate Gallery, 1998, 124–5.

12 Ibid., 115–21.

13 Marie Lødrup Bang, *Johan Christian Dahl, 1788–1857*, Oslo, Norwegian University Press, 1987, vol. 1, 51–2.

14 Ibid., vol. 1, 176.

15 On the beautiful, see William Gilpin, *Three Essays: On Picturesque Beauty; On Picturesque Travel; and On Sketching Landscape*, London, 1792, 1–33.

16 As cited in Judy Egerton, *George Stubbs, Painter*, New Haven, CT, Yale University Press, 2007, 29.

17 Ibid., 26–7.

18 Diana Donald, *Picturing Animals in Britain, 1750–1850*, New Haven, CT, Yale University Press, 2007, 71.

19 Ibid., 73.

20 David O'Brien, *Exiled in Modernity*, University Park, Pennsylvania State University Press, 2018, 137.

21 Eva Twose Kliman, "Delacroix's Lions and Tigers: A Link between Man and Nature," *Art Bulletin*, 64, 3, 1982, 446.

22 Donald, *Picturing Animals*, 68.

23 Kliman, "Delacroix's Lions," 465. Also see Eugène Delacroix, *The Journal of Eugène Delacroix*, trans. Lucy Norton, 3rd edition, London, Phaidon, 1995, 59–60, 73.

24 Marc Gotlieb, *The Deaths of Henri Regnault*, Chicago, University of Chicago Press, 2016, 39–67.

25 "Sublime" is mistranslated as "superb" in Norton's edition.

26 O'Brien, *Exiled*, 116.

27 See Robert Rosenblum, *Modern Painting and the Northern Romantic Tradition*, London, Thames and Hudson, 1975.

15

ANDREW MCINNES

From the Sublime to the Ridiculous*

The *Oxford English Dictionary* defines the phrase 'from the sublime to the ridiculous' as 'from one extreme (esp. one characterized by lofty thoughts or noble actions) to the other' and attributes it to Napoleon in 1812, wryly facing defeat in Russia by remarking more fully (and in French, of course): 'From the sublime to the ridiculous, there is only a step.'[1] Based on Napoleon's known appreciation of the radical English philosopher Thomas Paine, the *OED* suggests that the French emperor was inspired by a similar phrase in Part II of *The Age of Reason* (1795) in which Paine critiques belief in the literal truth of the Bible: 'The sublime and the ridiculous are often so nearly related, that it is difficult to class them separately, One step above the sublime, makes the ridiculous, and one step above the ridiculous, makes the sublime again.'[2] The dictionary definition, along with Napoleon and Paine, leave the exact attributes of the ridiculous itself open to question: whereas the sublime is 'characterised by lofty thoughts or actions' – military valour, spiritual belief – the ridiculous remains the sublime's indefinite, if 'extreme', other. Placing Paine and Napoleon as originators of a phrase connecting the sublime with the ridiculous in the Romantic period is tantalizing - enabling me to flip the focus from the Romantic sublime to the Romantic ridiculous. This essay identifies the ridiculous as a counter to or flipside of the sublime, embodying transgressive and comic potential rooted in failure and finitude, and offering an alternative perspective on Romantic aesthetics.

However, the French phrase for 'from the sublime to the ridiculous' antedates Napoleon's use of it by at least thirty-five years. The miscellany *New and Philosophical Thoughts*, published in 1777, attributes the phrase to the long-lived French Enlightenment philosopher and Academician Bernard le Bovier Fontenelle. Long-lived he might have been, living as he

* The author acknowledges the support of UKRI funding in the writing of this chapter as part of the AHRC ECR leadership fellow project, The Romantic Ridiculous, 2020–2022.

did to the grand old age of 100, but Fontenelle died in 1757, rendering the 1777 attribution questionable with no exact match to be found in his written works. The closest approximation comes in his *New Dialogues of the Dead* (1683) in a discussion between Seneca and Marot (in the first edition) or Seneca and Scarron (in later editions) in which Marot/Scarron, both seventeenth-century French writers, describe a modern burlesque on *The Aeneid* to their ancient stoic interlocutor: 'the grand and the ridiculous are so close, they touch'.[3]

The grand is not quite the same as the sublime, though the first writer to bring the sublime and the ridiculous within touching distance was inspired by Fontenelle's dialogue of the dead. John Dennis, a literary critic who popularized the sublime in England and, in doing so, clashed with Alexander Pope, writes in *The Impartial Critick* (1693): 'Has not Scarron diverted all of Europe at the expense of Virgil ...? Upon which an ingenious Frenchman has made this observation, that as all human grandeur is but folly, so sublimeness and the ridiculum are very nearly related.'[4] Fontenelle and Dennis's association of the sublime and the ridiculous stems from Boileau's translation of Longinus in his *Treaty on the Sublime* (1674), which William Smith renders closely in his later 1739 translation of Longinus into English:

> *Streaming curls of flame, spewing against heaven*, and *making Boreas a piper*, with such-like expressions, are not tragical, but super-tragical. For those forced and unnatural images corrupt and debase the style, and cannot possibly adorn or raise it; and whenever carefully examined in the light, their show of being terrible gradually disappears, and they become contemptible and ridiculous. (*Longinus*, 6)

Longinus focuses on hyperbole as a problem associated with style in this passage, so 'from the sublime to the ridiculous' predates its association with Romantic-period military politics in relation to Napoleon to raise instead questions of literary taste in Fontenelle, Dennis, and their sublime interlocutors. In Smith's translation the idea that hyperbole can become 'super-tragical' and therefore 'contemptible and ridiculous' anticipates Paine's later sense that the ridiculous is in some ways an extension of the sublime into comic territory. In this essay, I review the role of the ridiculous in Longinus, Dennis, and Burke, and in Kant's theorizations of the sublime, using Dennis's literary criticism as an example of eighteenth-century cultural commentary moving from the sublime to the ridiculous, before returning to the Romantic period to explore the aesthetics of the ridiculous of Jean Paul (Johann Paul Friedrich Richter) and its influence on the life and writing of Samuel Taylor Coleridge.

Issues with Comedy: Incongruity, Superiority, Anxiety

Before turning to the role of the ridiculous in theorizations of the sublime, I will briefly review eighteenth-century cultural commentary on the ridiculous itself, contextualizing it in eighteenth-century comic theory. The first problem with eighteenth-century comic theory is that it is not very funny. For misogelast critics such as Michael Billig, the problem is really our expectation that comic theory should amuse, arguing that taking laughter and humour seriously does not require a sense of humour in the comic theorist.[5] Taking a leaf out of Longinian sublime theory, though, I argue that, as sublime theory should aim for the elevation of its subject matter, so should comic theory aim to embody the comedy of its focus. This brings us to the second problem with eighteenth-century comic theory: its seeming distance from the sublime. Laughter, humour, and the comic focus on the low rather than the elevated, from fart jokes to risqué material risking offence along sexual, gendered, and racial lines. However, many eighteenth-century cultural commentators who discuss the ethics and aesthetics of laughter also muse on the sublime, circling around the sublime and the ridiculous in a manner resembling the rise and fall in Paine's formulation of their aesthetic relationship. Shaftesbury, for example, is a key commentator on ridicule in his *Characteristicks* (1711), in which he argues that it functions as the test of truth in civilized discourse. Shaftesbury also developed his own model of the sublime, building on work by Boileau in France and Dennis in England to theorize sublimity as a manly ideal combining a rugged enthusiasm with stoical harmony.[6] Although he did not connect the sublime with the ridiculous in the manner of Fontenelle, Dennis, and Napoleon, Shaftesbury is an example of a type of eighteenth-century theorist for whom the sublime and the ridiculous were related modes of enquiry. Other critics who ranged over the sublime and the ridiculous without necessarily connecting them explicitly include Joseph Addison and Mark Akenside, two pioneering theorists of the links between imagination and the sublime. Akenside's poem *The Pleasures of the Imagination* (1744) adapts Addisonian cultural criticism in verse, ranging from the sublime as a quality of mind to the ridiculous as harmless incongruity.

'Incongruity' connects the ridiculous to a key debate within eighteenth-century comic theory. Reacting to 'superiority' models of humour running from Aristotle to Hobbes, incongruity theorists, led by Frances Hutcheson, argued that laughter arises from the comic differential between our heightened expectations and their disappointed reality. In contrast, superiority theory supposed that we laugh at the exposure of inferiority or deformity in other people (or situations). These models are more complex than they appear, with Hobbesian superiority theory including a rueful wrestling with one's own deficiencies.[7] In contrast, incongruity theory slips the superiority it appears to reject back into its evaluation of what is incongruous – judgments that might be inflected with disavowed prejudices about what is normative.

Reviewing these competing theories of humour, Laurent Berlant and Sianne Ngai open their special issue of *Critical Inquiry* on comedy with the following statement:

> Comedy's pleasure comes in part from its ability to dispel anxiety, as so many of its theoreticians have noticed, but it doesn't simply do that. As both an aesthetic mode and a form of life, its action just as likely produces anxiety: risking transgression, flirting with displeasure, or just confusing things in a way that both intensifies and impedes the pleasure.[8]

Berlant and Ngai elegantly cut through these earlier theorizations of comedy to argue that comedy's collapse of distance, its proximity, produces both discomfort and pleasure. Their extended example explores how 'an antiracist racist joke' works in Stewart Lee's 2005 set *Stand-Up Comedian*, arguing that Lee ventriloquizes 'the supremacist startle' at causing offence with 'the physicality of racialized pain' to analyse 'the inutility of explanation in explaining away the delight in comedic aggression'.[9] The white stand-up starts out by laughing at a body he racializes only to find himself subject to being laughed at himself.

Billig unearths a more straightforwardly racist joke in Schopenhauer's second edition of *The World as Will and Idea* (1844). Introducing a supposedly comic example to explain his incongruity theory, Schopenhauer cites the case of a formerly enslaved person who, he says, 'took pains to imitate whites. The man's child had died and he chose the epitaph, "Lovely, early broken lily."'[10] Billig angrily retorts: "The incongruous mirth of Schopenhauer is shocking. How can anyone, let alone a philosopher, laugh at a grieving father on account of the colour of his skin?"[11] What shocks is the lack of startle in Schopenhauer's supremacist joke, his enjoyment of racialized pain, his distance from it. Billig's 'let alone a philosopher' here waves away the history of racism undergirding Western philosophy, for example, Kant's racist quips documented in Robert Clewis's *Kant's Humorous Writings*.[12] Closer to home for me, Jean Paul, a key theorist of the ridiculous, rejects the image of a Black horse rider as insufficiently ridiculous because lacking a spiritual dimension. The ridiculous, like comic theory more generally, can be inflected with social prejudice as well as offering more progressive perspectives on nature and culture.

'Sinking from the Terrible to the Ridiculous': Longinus and Comic Theory

The classical treatise *On the Sublime*, attributed to Longinus or Pseudo-Longinus, and popularized by Boileau in France and Dennis in England, defines the sublime as 'a certain eminence of perfection of language', arguing that 'the greatest writers, both in verse and prose, have by this alone obtain'd the prize of glory, and fill'd all time with their renown. For the sublime not only persuades, but even throws an audience into transport' (*Longinus*, 3). Longinus engages with the sublime as a literary technique that provokes a transcendent response in the audience for a sublime text. For Robert Doran, Longinus's conception of the sublime as literary style is underpinned by a more thorough-going exploration of human nature, with the treatise functioning as a cultural theory connecting it to Burke and Kant's interest in human interactions with the natural sublime (see *Doran*, 9 and passim). Doran is interested in stressing the continuities between these sometimes heterogenous conceptions of the sublime. In my view, the ridiculous, as the unspecified other of the sublime, works to make the sublime seem more monolithic than it is. My review of Longinus, Dennis, Burke, and Kant's models of the sublime, especially in relation to their disparate thinking on the ridiculous, reveals fault lines in the sublime along literary, spiritual, empirical, and idealist axes.

Longinus also foreshadows the work of eighteenth-century comic theorists, by connecting his discussion of the sublime with a surprisingly in-depth exploration of the ridiculous. Developing his argument that the 'forced and unnatural images' of the 'super tragical' miss the sublime and 'gradually ... become contemptible and ridiculous', Longinus argues that the style of writers including Gorgias of Leontini, Clitarchus, and Matris, which is in 'their own opinion ... divine ... proves empty simple froth' (*Longinus*, 6, 7). Here, Longinus links ridiculousness to childishness, inauthentic inspiration aping sublime style. These authors are no longer well known, but Longinus does not spare even Homer from ridicule, arguing that *The Odyssey* represents a falling away from *The Iliad*, from epic strength to elderly frailty. The difference between these two books shows, according to Longinus, that 'in the decline of their vigour, the greatest geniuses are apt to turn aside unto trifles': in contrast to the sublimities of *Iliad*, he argues, *Odyssey* 'has in some degree the air of a comedy where the various manners of men are ingeniously and faithfully described' (*Longinus*, 26–7). Comparing the sublime Demosthenes with the smoother Hyperides, Longinus concludes that sublime style demands a risking of ridiculousness: the irregularity he celebrates as part of the sublime threatens to lower a writer as much as it elevates them.

John Dennis: Sublimeness and the Ridiculum

Dennis popularized the Longinian sublime in England by connecting the Ancient Greek literary theory to Christian spirituality, arguing that natural magnificence such as the Alps and literary innovation in, for example, *Paradise Lost* (1667) lead us to consider the supernatural power of God as the highest form of the sublime. Like Longinus, Dennis also considers the ridiculous in depth, though his discussion of what he calls the Ridiculum is separated from his exploration of the sublime. In a chapter on comic poetry in *The Advancement and Reformation of Modern Poetry* (1701), Dennis hypothesizes that 'If the end of Poetry is only to please, why then it must please by the *Ridiculum*.'[13] Dennis argues that the pleasure we receive from the ridiculous in poetry comes from surprise, concluding that 'without Surprise the *Ridiculum* cannot subsist' (224). Although Dennis does not make this connection, the surprise of the Ridiculum might be a less elevated version of the astonishment felt in sublime experience.

Embroiled in the eighteenth-century debate between the Ancients and the Moderns, which saw him satirized as Sir Tremendous Longinus in Pope, Arbuthnot, and Gay's 1717 play *Three Hours after Marriage*, Dennis celebrates the variety of style that distinguishes modern from ancient comedy, arguing that 'the Moderns seem to know Men better, and to dive into some Latent Foibles, into some ridiculous Recesses, that were utterly unknown to the Ancients' (224). As the sublime subsists in style for Longinus and Dennis, so too does the Ridiculum: its surprising variety leads us into 'ridiculous Recesses', so that ridiculousness reflects, like some renderings of the sublime, on the unconscious.

Dennis concludes his chapter on comedy by thinking about its didactic component: 'If the Design of Comedy be to instruct, it must instruct by the *Ridiculum*' (224). He argues that comic poetry shows 'Men ridiculous for their Faults' in order to 'represent them expos'd by them, or chastised for them' (224). Contrasting the 'great Passions' depicted and aroused by tragedy with 'the little Passions' of comedy which 'cause little Disquiets, and make us uneasy to ourselves, and one another' (224), Dennis's conception of comedy therefore resembles Berlant and Ngai's much more recent emphasis on the combination of anxiety and pleasure in the comic. If the sublime offers Dennis spiritual experience, the ridiculous emphasizes earthly failings, which provoke a combination of anxiety, laughter, and learning.

Ridiculing Edmund Burke

In *Enquiry* I vii, Burke defines the sublime as an encounter with uncertainty provoking strong emotion in a way that influenced the next generation of Romantic – and Gothic – writers: 'Whatever is fitted in any sort to excite the ideas of pain, and danger, that is to say, whatever is in any sort terrible, or is conversant about terrible objects, or operates in a manner analogous to terror, is a source of the sublime; that is, it is productive of the strongest emotion which the mind is capable of feeling.' In contrast to Longinus, *Enquiry* largely eschews the ridiculous, going to some lengths to avoid ridicule when it comes to exploring the olfactory sublime associated with bitters and stenches. In *Enquiry* II xxi, Burke explains that his use of classical allusion in relation to sublime smells seeks to avoid 'burlesque and ridicule' by associating the sublime with 'mean and contemptible ideas' that would 'degrade' it. This closely parallels both Longinus and Paine on the relationship between the sublime and the ridiculous, in which see-sawing between the related aesthetic categories risks humiliation.

In his account of the Burkean sublime, Philip Shaw echoes contemporary ridicule of Burke's treatment of sight (by, for example Richard Payne Knight in *An Analytical Inquiry into the Principles of Taste* [1805]) by questioning Burke's argument that the sublime might be provoked by the strain put on our eyes in trying to take in these massive views: 'It is one thing ... to claim that my feeling of lethargy is caused by the physical state of hunger and quite another to state that my idea of infinity is produced by eyestrain.'[14] Indeed, Shaw's discussion of the gendered hierarchies of the Burkean sublime, in which sublime masculinity is under threat from 'feminine languor, and the fall of heroic identity into social mediocrity' extends into a satire of Burke's 'autoeroticism': 'The man who "swells" in "contemplation" of a "power" that he has claimed for his own is protected not only from the raw, unreflective immediacy of the sublime but also from the self-destroying enthralments of erotic encounter.'[15] In spite of himself, Burke's representation of the sublime still risks a ridiculous turn inward.

Kant: From the Starry Heavens to a Ridiculous Nothing

Like Longinus before him, Kant connects sublimity with ridiculousness in a thorough-going consideration of the aesthetics and ethics of humour. Kant explored the significance of the sublime throughout his career, publishing *Observations on the Feeling of the Sublime and the Beautiful* in 1764 and developing these ideas in the *Critique of Pure Reason* (1781) and the *Critique of the Power of Judgment* (1790), which includes his 'Analytic of the Sublime'. Kant's most poetic condensation of his thoughts on the sublime comes, however, at the end of the *Critique of Practical Reason*: 'Two things fill the mind with ever new and increasing admiration and reverence the more often and more steadily one reflects on them: *the starry heavens above me and the moral law within me*.'[16] This statement combines a Burkean emphasis on the sublime in nature ('the starry heavens above me') with a distinctively Kantian emphasis on the sublimity of the human mind ('the moral law within me'). Indeed, Kant's conception of the sublime shifts the emphasis from natural objects, including the starry heavens, to the mind's ability to overcome an initial feeling of humiliation in relation to nature's power or magnitude and to acknowledge the power of reason to encompass nature and assert its own freedom.

Alongside his discussion of the sublime as *'great beyond all comparison'*, Kant develops a theory of the ridiculous as *'the sudden transformation of a heightened expectation into nothing'* (*COPJ* §25 248; §54 332; original emphases). Although the German comic novelist Jean Paul will dismiss this definition along with Aristotle's earlier account of the ridiculous as 'harmless incongruity', his own comic theory both explicitly and implicitly draws on Kant's thoughts on laughter to develop his own aesthetics of the ridiculous.[17] More fully, Kant argues:

> In everything that is to provoke a lively, uproarious laughter, there must be something nonsensical (in which, therefore, the understanding in itself can take no satisfaction). *Laughter is an affect arising from the sudden transformation of a heightened expectation into nothing.* (*COPJ* §54 332; original emphasis)

After Jean Paul, I argue, the connection between the laughable and the non-sensical offers us a sense of the ridiculous. Reviewing critical approaches to Kant that relate laughter as an affect to the sublime, Clewis argues that rather than being directly related to the sublime or the beautiful, *'the judging in laughter is analogous to the experiences of sublimity and beauty'*.[18] I argue that the ridiculous as an aesthetic experience is explicitly modelled as an alternative to the Kantian sublime by Jean Paul. More precisely, Jean Paul builds on the analogy between the sublime and the ridiculous in Kant to develop his own theory of humour as an encounter between our mortal limitations and infinity, leading not to transcendence and mastery but to a reckoning with our own littleness.

Richter's Ridiculous

In his *School for Aesthetics* (1806), Jean Paul provides a characteristically playful definition of the ridiculous as 'the eternal consequence of spiritual finitude' (87). As Jean Paul is less well known in Anglophone Romantic Studies than most of the other figures discussed in this essay, and his definition of 'ridiculous' is idiosyncratic, it is worth briefly reviewing some recent literature on him as an author with a complex relationship to Romanticism. Philippe Lacoue-Labarthe and Jean-Luc Nancy briefly imagine an alternative arrangement of Romanticism around the concept of wit that sees Jean Paul as central rather than peripheral to the development of Romantic Studies: 'if one takes *Witz* as a measure of romanticism, one is led to circumscribe it more strictly than usual (with reference only, or almost only, to Friedrich Schlegel, Jean Paul, and later Solger, along with one and only one aspect of certain texts by Novalis)'.[19] However, Lacoue-Labarthe and Nancy finally dismiss Jean Paul – in a footnote – by criticizing his *School for Aesthetics*: 'Jean Paul's text is, in fact, no longer romantic, but rather characterizes the romantics (as "nihilists": whence the fortunes of the word). But on the other hand, the charge that is always levelled at this *Introduction* is that it is only ... an auto-characterization.'[20] Jean Paul's place in conventional characterizations of Romanticism is encapsulated by his treatment in *The Literary Absolute*, from a strict circumscription that groups him with a limited range of interlocutors to 'no longer romantic', a self-regarding and auto-erotic nihilist.

Analysing Jean Paul's prefatorial strategies alongside Goethe and Hegel, Séan Williams more recently argues that Jean Paul's paratexts are self-regarding and auto-erotic, if not quite nihilist: 'To preface is therefore autopoetic and even, in its exaggerated form, autoerotic.'[21] Williams argues that Jean Paul's self-regarding self-love is satirical, connecting his preface writing with his aesthetic treatise 'through a continual humour that in its contradictoriness achieves an always incomplete state on a more abstract, yet apparently finite level, or what Jean Paul calls ... [humor as the inverted sublime]'.[22] Jean Paul's writing combines the fragmentariness of other German Romantics with his own distinctive brand of humour, which flips the focus from the sublime to the ridiculous.

Paul Fleming offers an in-depth analysis of Jean Paul's theorization of humour in relation to the ridiculous, the sublime, and the beautiful, arguing that 'Jean Paul turn[s] Kant around: the beautiful morphs into the ridiculous, the sublime into humour.'[23] Fleming distinguishes between Jean Paul's definitions of humour and of the ridiculous. For Fleming, humour is a 'trans-historical' modern aesthetic category defined against the sublime, whereas the ridiculous is only a 'necessary historical precursor' to humour as counter-sublime.[24] On the contrary, I argue that the ridiculous functions as a guiding structure in Jean Paul's aesthetics. However, Fleming offers a thought-provoking series of statements on how the ridiculous works in Jean Paul's aesthetics, which is very useful to my concern in this essay, and worth quoting in detail:

> The point of the ridiculous is not to criticize as if one knew better, but to participate in the fallenness of being – to revel in it.... If the ridiculous as an aesthetic category has a political impetus, it is in the expression of a solidarity pact between abandoned beings.... Laughter for Jean Paul does not express derision but a form of empathy or understanding, an understanding for the lack of understanding.[25]

Fleming, like Berlant and Ngai, usefully cuts through both hang-ups about humour's dark side which dogs Billig's historical overview and accusations of nihilism cast at Jean Paul by Lacoue-Labarthe and Nancy. In Fleming's view, Jean Paul's humour combines spitefulness and pleasure. Feeling ridiculous means experiencing a dark form of community with others, a communion based on failure, but failure that breeds empathy and solidarity, in contrast with the feeling of individual magnificence, even egotism, more usually associated with sublime feeling.

Richter begins his *School for Aesthetics* by dismissing the definitions of the ridiculous in both Aristotle and Kant's philosophies. In starting with Aristotle, Richter follows an eighteenth-century tradition of grounding theories of humour and comedy in classical territory. Aristotle defines the ridiculous in a brief discussion of comedy prefacing his fuller exploration of tragedy: 'The Ridiculous may be defined as a mistake or deformity not productive of pain or harm to others; the mask, for instance, that excites laughter, is something ugly and distorted without causing pain.'[26] For Aristotle, the comic is associated with lowness and the ridiculous with ugliness. It is worth noting that the 'harmless incongruity' here is only harmless to others – the mistake, deformity, or ugliness may well be painful to the supposedly ridiculous individuals themselves.

For Jean Paul, Aristotle's definition of the ridiculous as 'harmless incongruity' is 'on the right road to the goal' but fails to explain its comic dimension, listing examples of unfunny incongruousness that challenge Aristotelean poetics (71). Moreover, for Jean Paul, Aristotle's definition does not explain the humorous dimension of the ridiculous, contesting: 'such incongruity in animals or in the insane is not comic', and criticizing later uses of Aristotle as missing a 'spiritual meaning' within the ridiculous (71–2). Jean Paul similarly dismisses the Kantian definition of the ridiculous as arising from 'a sudden resolution of expectation into nothing', archly noting that 'Kant's explanation is just as indefinite and hence just as true as if I said the ridiculous consists in the sudden resolution of the expectation of something serious into a ridiculous nothing' (71). Against these earlier definitions of the ridiculous, Jean Paul argues that it functions as a counter-sublime, emphasizing smallness where the sublime seeks infinity, further connecting the ridiculous to a lack of understanding between subject, object, and situation. Like Dennis before him, Jean Paul asks how the ridiculous leads to pleasure in poetry, concluding that the laughter it provokes distinguishes the ridiculous from the '*Derision, or moral indignation*' available through the sublime (73). He argues that the ridiculous is 'the hereditary enemy of the *sublime*' rather than the converse of either tragedy or the sentimental 'as the very expressions "tragicomic" or "sentimental comedy" prove', concluding that 'the ridiculous consequently is the infinitely small' (73). Linked to his earlier dismissal of Kant's definition of the ridiculous, Jean Paul is again reacting to Kant's definition of the sublime here as 'the absolutely great'; otherwise, 'the infinitely small' could be categorized in at least the Burkean understanding of the microscopic sublime. Jean Paul will go on to explore how humour stems from a conflict in our finite experience with our conception of infinity.

'So Says Jean Paul': Coleridge Translates

Coleridge read and reread Jean Paul's writing over the course of at least ten years, freely translating jokes, aphorisms, and longer passages, as well as drawing on the German writer's works for his lectures on comedy and humour. Coleridge's biographer Richard Holmes characterizes the English poet's relationship with Jean Paul as a communion with a 'brother spirit'.[27] Kathleen Coburn, the editor of Coleridge's *Notebooks*, suggests that Coleridge's position was more 'negatively critical' than his repeated returns to Jean Paul suggest.[28] I argue that Coleridge looked on Jean Paul as a kind of literary double, useful to reflect upon in the safe space of his life writing.

Jean Paul helps Coleridge grapple with the subject of humour in two lectures on comedy given in 1818 and 1819. In a complex passage from *School for Aesthetics* that Coleridge alludes to in his 1818 lecture, Jean Paul argues that when our subjective experience of the finitude of our experience contrasts negatively with an objective idea of infinity, 'Then we would have *humour* [Jean Paul uses the English word], or the romantic-comic.'[29] Building on the juxtaposition of perspectives experienced in a ridiculous situation, Jean Paul universalizes this sensation into an encounter between infinity and our finite appreciation of it, which he describes as a negative sublime leading to 'humour'. Given that Jean Paul is self-consciously building on eighteenth-century theories of the comic from Hobbes to Kant, I find it especially interesting that he uses the English term 'humour' to express his sense of the ridiculous.

Coleridge echoes Jean Paul in his lecture of 1818 focusing on Sterne: 'when we contemplate a finite in reference to the Infinite, consciously or unconsciously, *Humor*. (So says Jean Paul Richter).'[30] Humour, for both Coleridge and Jean Paul, is intimately tied up with sublime experience, but humour adheres to experience that emphasizes our finitude. Coleridge builds on his engagement with Jean Paul's comic theory in his lecture of 1819, asking whether humour is 'manifold' or if there is 'some one *humorific* point common to all that can be called *humorous*'.[31] Coleridge's lecture also attests to the influence of Kantian aesthetics on his own – and Jean

Paul's – thoughts on humour, arguing that 'it consists in a certain reference to the General, and the Universal, by which the ~~infinite~~ finite great is brought into identity with the Little, or the Little with the <Finite> Great, so as to make both *nothing* by comparison with the Infinite' (vol. 3, 4503 29.192). The crossings-out and lack of clarity surrounding infinity and the finite suggest Coleridge's struggle with these arguments, but the relationship between littleness, greatness, infinity, and nothing suggests he is bringing together Jean Paul and Kant's thinking on humour and sublimity here. Coleridge concludes that in 'the highest humour at least' there is something 'ridiculously disproportionate in our feelings' about the relationship between infinity and our own subjective experience of finitude (vol. 3, 4503 29.192).

Conclusion

In the first of the second series of British Association of Romantic Studies digital events, 'Zany Romanticism', Rebecca Schneider spoke of the difficulty of aligning ideas of the sublime and the beautiful with the zany.[32] Mapping Sianne Ngai's concept of the zany as a postmodern aesthetic category onto Romantic aesthetics allowed Schneider and her interlocutors to consider both the forced pleasure in work of consumer capitalism as a Romantic affect as well as the lack of relationship between the sublime and the zany. Having failed to formulate a response in the virtual seminar ('Hey! The ridiculous is right here!' did not feel suitably academic), I conclude that the ridiculous as an aesthetic rooted in failure and misunderstanding, laughter and play, is allied with Lacoue-Labarthe and Nancy's understanding of wit as 'non-work, sub-work, or anti-work'.[33] The ridiculous can be glimpsed in seminal Romantic-period literary engagements with the sublime, including Wordsworth's disappointment at having crossed the Alps without realizing it in *The Prelude* (1805), Keats's anxieties about his 'smokeable' poetry, and Elizabeth Bennet's wild and witty perspective on the world in Jane Austen's *Pride and Prejudice* (1813). Through the ridiculous, Romantic writers and their creations can laugh at the world, at each other, and at themselves.

NOTES

1 'sublime, adj. and n. Phrases', *OED Online*, Oxford University Press, December 2021, www.oed.com/view/Entry/192766. Accessed 20 December 2021. OED translation.
2 Thomas Paine, *The Age of Reason, Part the Second*, 2nd edition, London, 1795, 20.
3 Fontenelle, quoted in Michael Silk et al., *The Classical Tradition*, Hoboken, NJ, Wiley Blackwell, 2017, 371. Silk et al. attribute the Fontenelle quotation solely to

Scarron and discuss the English writer John Dennis's retooling of it, which I also explore later in this essay.

4 John Dennis, *The Impartial Critick*, in *The Critical Works of John Dennis*, ed. Edward Niles Hooker, 2 vols., Baltimore, MD, Johns Hopkins University Press, 1939, vol. 1, 11–41, 16.

5 In an 1877 lecture, George Meredith coiled the term 'misogelast' to refer to people who dislike humour. Michael Billig begins *Laughter and Ridicule* (London, Sage, 2005) by arguing against the need for funniness in theorizing the comic.

6 For a discussion of Shaftesbury's contribution to the theory of the sublime, see Philip Shaw, *The Sublime*, 2nd edition, London, Routledge, 2017, 57–60; in the same chapter, Shaw considers Addison and Akenside's cultural theory, along with that of Dennis and John Baillie (41–66).

7 See Billig, *Laughter*, 51.

8 Lauren Berlant and Sianne Ngai, 'Comedy Has Issues', *Critical Inquiry*, 43, 2017, 233–49 (233).

9 Ibid., 247–8.

10 Quoted from Billig, *Laughter*, 79.

11 Ibid., 80.

12 See Robert Clewis for Kant's 'ethnic and sexist quips and jokes' and for a reckoning with Kant's racism (*Kant's Humourous Writings*, London, Bloomsbury, 2021, 133–4 and 97–101).

13 John Dennis, *The Advancement and Refinement of Modern Poetry*, in *The Critical Works of John Dennis*, ed. Edward Niles Hooker, 2 vols., Baltimore, MD, Johns Hopkins University Press, 1939, vol. 2, 127–278, 224.

14 Shaw, *The Sublime*, 69.

15 Ibid., 83, 76.

16 Immanuel Kant, *Critique of Practical Reason*, trans. Mary Gregor in *Kant, Practical Philosophy*, ed. Mary Gregor, Cambridge, Cambridge University Press, 1999, 5:161, original emphasis.

17 Jean Paul Richter characterizes Aristotle's definition of the ridiculous as 'harmless incongruity' in his *School for Aesthetics*; see Jean Paul Richter, *Horn of Oberon: John Paul Richter's School for Aesthetics*, trans. Margaret Hale, Detroit, MI, Wayne State University Press, 1973, 71.

18 Clevis, *Kant's Humourous Writings*, 54; original emphasis.

19 Philippe Lacoue-Labarthe and Jean-Luc Nancy, *The Literary Absolute*, Albany, SUNY Press, 1988, 52, original emphasis.

20 Ibid., 148.

21 Sean Williams, *Pretexts for Writing: German Romantic Prefaces, Literature, and Philosophy*, Lewisburg, PA, Bucknell University Press, 2019, 36.

22 Ibid., 132.

23 Paul Fleming, *The Pleasures of Abandonment: Jean Paul and the Life of Humor*, Würzburg, Königshausen and Neumann, 2006, 44.

24 Ibid.

25 Ibid., 46.

26 Aristotle, *Poetics*, quoted from *Philosophies of Art and Beauty*, ed. Albert Hofstadter and Richard Kuhns, New York, Random House, 1964, 103.

27 Richard Holmes, *Coleridge: Darker Reflections*, London, Flamingo, 1999, 252.

28 Kathleen Coburn, ed., *The Notebooks of S. T. Coleridge*, vol. 3, Princeton, NJ, Princeton University Press, 1974, n3684.

29 Jean Paul Richter, quoted in Samuel Taylor Coleridge, *Lectures 1808–1819 on Literature*, ed. R. A. Foakes, Princeton, NJ, Princeton University Press, 1987, 172.

30 Samuel Taylor Coleridge, '1818 Lectures on European Literature', 'Lecture 9', in Foakes, *Lectures*, 172.

31 Coburn, ed., *Notebooks*, vol. 3, 4503 29.192. Thanks to Edge Hill University's MA Nineteenth Century Studies 'Romantic Movements' students who helped me work through the complexities of Coleridge's notes for his 1819 lecture.

32 Rebecca Schneider, 'Zany Jack Jingle', online presentation at 'Zany Romanticism' BARS Digital Event, 18 November 2021.

33 Lacoue-Labarthe and Nancy, *Literary Absolute*, 54.

16

CASSANDRA FALKE

The Sublime in American Romanticism

Roderick Nash's classic study *Wilderness and the American Mind* (1967) tells the story of the United States' transition from a frontier mindset, in which "taming the wilderness gave meaning and purpose to the frontiersman's life," to a pervasive "Romantic mood" in which "Sublimity suggested the association of God and wild nature."[1] "Nature," as Ralph Waldo Emerson phrases it, offers "sanctity that shames our religions ... and judges like a god all men who come to her."[2] The influence of English Romantic poets, especially Byron and Coleridge, on this shift is well documented. Less well known is the converse influence of American naturalism on English and European Romantic writers. In 1791, William Bartram published an account of traveling through the American southeast that enchanted Wordsworth, Coleridge, and Chateaubriand. Coleridge was reading Bartram's *Travels through North and South Carolina, Georgia, East and West Florida, the Cherokee Country, the Extensive Territories of the Muscogulges, or Creek Confederacy, and the Country of the Chactaws* (1791) when he composed "Kubla Khan" (1816) in 1797–8 as was William Wordsworth when writing "Ruth" (1802) in Germany in 1799.[3]

In his book-length argument that America "favors more drastic sublimities than Europe," Harold Bloom draws on the work of Emerson, Nathaniel Hawthorne, Emily Dickinson, Walt Whitman, and Herman Melville.[4] Compared with these more well-known American authors, Bartram's sublime evokes less drastic imagery and greater continuity between human life and the ecosystems we inhabit. His focus is not on the subjective experience of being imperiled or unable to cognitively subsume all of a view, but rather on the fecundity of the land he moves through. Bartram's intervention in the discourse of the sublime, however quiet compared with Melville or Whitman, is important because it preserves "ecocentric principles" latent in the natural sublime in a less anthropocentric model.[5] This chapter discusses Bartram's description of the sublime in his *Travels*, both as a historical influence on later Romantic representations of the sublime and as a philosophically distinctive model of experiences in wild ecosystems. It unfolds in three parts. I begin by introducing Bartram and positioning him in reference to the longer history of eighteenth- and early nineteenth-century conceptions of the sublime in America. I then articulate what is unique in Bartram's understanding of sublimity. Finally, I consider Bartram's influence on and differences from Coleridge and Wordsworth.

Bartram and the American Context

In the words of his biographer, Thomas Slaughter, Bartram was "the first American to devote his life to the study of nature."[6] Bartram grew up under the shadow of his father, John, a prominent early American naturalist, friend of Benjamin Franklin and Royal Botanist to King George III. Born and raised in Kingsessing, now a neighborhood of Philadelphia, William traveled with his father as a boy and followed him into botany after failing in several other ventures. In 1768, he obtained the patronage of John Fothergill, a doctor and medical researcher in London. He had apparently written to the doctor implying a desire to travel in Florida collecting seeds and documenting plants and animals; Fothergill found it "a 'pity that such a genius should sink under distress.'"[7] He agreed to support him for two years at fifty pounds per year beginning in 1773. Almost two decades later, the report that Bartram sent to Fothergill became the basis for his revised and published *Travels*. After his travels, Bartram settled into a quiet life out of the public eye. A contemporary satire portrays him wandering up and down the banks of the Schuylkill River, grumbling, in Rousseau-esque fashion, about the "unnatural state of civilization" that "continues to corrupt the natural innocence and cramp the native freedom of man."[8] He was invited to teach at the University of Pennsylvania, but declined. He even declined an invitation to travel with Lewis and Clark on their expedition to explore the lands west of the Mississippi River. He preferred to devote his time to maintaining the eight acres around his home, which John Bartram had converted into the United States' first botanical garden in 1728. An accomplished botanical illustrator, William gained some recognition for drawings in Benjamin Barton's *Elements of Botany* in 1803, but for the most part, he settled into gardening. As Slaughter writes, if he went "more than a day's journey" from his house between his return from Georgia and Florida in 1777 and his death in 1823, "there is no record of the trip."[9]

It is hard to know which philosophical explorations of the sublime Bartram had read when he departed on his journey south in 1773. He attended the recently founded Philadelphia Academy from age twelve to seventeen. Benjamin Franklin, the Academy's first president, designed the curriculum and specified that students should read in "History, Rhetoric, Logic, Moral and Natural Philosophy" in Latin, as well as "the best English Authors ... Tillotson, Milton, Locke, Addison, Pope, Swift, [and] the higher Papers in the *Spectator* and *Guardian*."[10] As a schoolboy, then, Bartram would have mused on Joseph Addison's description of that "rude kind of magnificence which appears in many of these stupendous works of nature." Writing in *The Spectator* (1712), Addison suggests that "We are flung into a pleasing astonishment at such unbounded views, and feel a delightful stillness and amazement in the soul at the apprehension of them."[11] That stillness and amazement comes through in the pace of Bartram's writing, as he lingers over the diversity of species in a forest or an expanse of mountaintops. He would certainly have known Longinus and probably also Burke's *Enquiry* (1757), which was published just as Bartram was finishing school. Because it was offered for sale at a book auction in 1769, we know *Enquiry* was being read in Bartram's milieu at the time.[12] Immanuel Kant's *Critique of the Power of Judgment* (1790) reached the United States too late to influence Bartram's *Travels*, but it remains significant for the discourse shaping the reception of the book.

The vocabulary shaping Bartram's perception of the natural world reflects the scientific and aesthetic thinking of his age, but the overall relationship between humans, nonhuman nature, and the sublime implied by the *Travels* is unique. In both Europe and America, there is a shift in the late eighteenth century away from a focus on *producing* the sublime through art or rhetoric and toward a *discernment* of the sublime as it already exists in nature. In her history, *The Sublime in Modern Philosophy*, Emily Brady coins the term "empirical sublime" to describe the growing assumption that sublimity exceeds human perception because it preexists the perceiving act.[13] Bartram participates in this shift, but he finds sublimity in unexpected places – not only in the "unbounded views" Addison and others, including Burke in *Enquiry* II vii, praised but also in the bounded richness of the forest. The loamy soil, birdsong, and plant life astounded him. "[S]portive vegetables," he exclaims on finding a Venus flytrap; "Astonishing production!"[14] Whereas for Burke, the sublime is associated with terror and terror with death (see *Enquiry* II ii), for Bartram it is life in its infinite variety that expresses boundlessness. The diversity of living things speaks to him of more-than-human creativity. "This world, as a glorious apartment of the boundless palace of the sovereign Creator, is furnished with an infinite variety of animated scenes, inexpressibly beautiful and pleasing, equally free to the inspection and enjoyment of all his creatures" (13). Readers who are not botanists may become frustrated with Bartram's lists of plants and animals, usually noted by their Latin names in the recently created Linnean system (he names forty-seven plants in his first three pages) but Bartram's lists reinforce his wonder at the plentitude and connectedness of life. Life in the "self-moving" bodies of plants, he argues, partakes of the same "vivific principle of life" as animals (19). And nonhuman animals are not as different from humans as "the general opinion of philosophers" implies (xxv). When a hunter he is traveling with shoots a mother bear, Bartram records that the cub "approached the dead body, smelled, and pawed it, and appearing in agony, fell to weeping and looking upwards, then towards us, and cried out like a child" (xxvi). This is evidence, for him, that the "filial affections ... sensibility and attachment" are as "active and faithful" in nonhuman animals "as those observed to be in human nature" (20). Bartram's portrayal of ursine sensibility could hardly differ more from Burke's presentation of predators as the instruments and image of sublime terror, which "comes upon us in the gloomy forest, in the howling wilderness, in the form of the lion, the tiger, the panther, or rhinoceros" (*Enquiry* II v). Whereas Burke's focus on terror implies the innate goodness of protecting human life, Bartram's fondness for "sportive" vegetables and sensible cubs points toward what Christopher Hitt calls an "ecological sublime," characterized by humility and responsibility toward all forms of life.[15]

Bartram's writing is situated near the beginning of a long tradition of American writing on sublimity. Chandos Michael Brown breaks early American contributions into three categories. The "ideological sublime," which corresponds with the post-1700 provincial era, arises from the merging of English empiricism, especially the writings of John Locke, and North American Protestantism. The epistemological underpinnings of the ideological sublime support the possibility of discovering a nation in its geology and fauna. Unique and spectacular, American nature foreshadows the newness of a great nation-to-be. Between the revolutionary decades of the 1760s and 1770s and the early years of the republic, Brown suggests a new "nationalist sublime" emerged. The success of the American Revolution meant that the new nation could be more of a cause, less of an effect of the remarkable landscape. The "first American sublime," a category subsuming and exceeding the other two, lasts, according to Brown, until the mid-1800s.[16] By that point, he argues, the sublime was retreating, spatially westward, temporally into an imagined past. Bartram's *Travels*, written in the 1770s but published in 1791, straddles Brown's first two periods. He shares an intellectual heritage with the ideological sublime, although, as a Quaker, he believed in direct revelation more than the New England Protestants Brown has in mind. Chronologically, Bartram might fit in the frame of a nationalist sublime, but *Travels* attends to local politics and ecosystems much more than a national political imaginary, which makes his concept of the sublime politically and epistemologically unique. His account of the Treaty of Augusta in 1773 reveals this well. The treaty ceded two million acres of Cherokee and Creek land to pay off debts to "the merchants of Georgia" (52). Bartram participates in the survey to determine the boundaries of the land to be transferred. He recounts "a remarkable instance of Indian sagacity" in which a Cherokee chief and a colonial surveyor argue over the best course for reaching a particular confluence of the Savannah River seventy miles away (57). The surveyor relies on his compass, the Chief on prior knowledge of the land. The Chief, being proven correct, is granted leadership of the surveying party forthwith. He insists the compass be thrown away. The epistemological tension here is not between empiricism and either theology or rationalism, but between a machine-dependent empiricism current among the colonial upper classes and know-ledge reliant on emplaced and embodied lived experience. Bartram favors the latter. In consequence, his writings on sublimity do not struggle with the bounds of quantifiability so central in Kant, but as primarily empirical, neither do they rely on an assessment of affect like Burke.

The nationalism underlying many US accounts of sublimity reads "American" greatness into specific landscapes while ignoring others. In his widely cited "Essay on American Scenery" (1836), painter Thomas Cole implies that affection for the wilderness is a national duty:

> [Scenery] is a subject that to every American ought to be of surpassing interest; for, whether he beholds the Hudson mingling waters with the Atlantic, explores the central wilds of this vast continent, or stands on the margin of the distant Oregon, he is still in the midst of American scenery – it is his own land; its beauty, its magnificence, its sublimity – all are his; and how undeserving of such a birthright, if he can turn towards it an unobserving eye, an unaffected heart![17]

Note the regions Cole equates with American scenery: New York, the "central wilds" of the inland west, and Oregon in the Pacific Northwest. By the time Romanticism really took hold of American letters in the 1830s and 1840s, the rural South Bartram enthuses about posed a problem. In travel literature depicting the areas Bartram had walked, local populations were portrayed as incapable of achieving the expansionist ideal of taming the wilderness, but their habitations sprawled across the mountains in a way that interfered with the pure wilderness increasingly associated with *American* sublimity. "Wildness" is identified by Cole and others as "the most distinctive, and perhaps the most impressive, characteristic of American scenery" because "in civilized Europe the primitive features of scenery have long since been destroyed" (30). The consolidation of

American ideas about the sublime around the dichotomy of wild versus civilized worked to exclude the forms of ecologically attuned living that Bartram admired. For him, the sublime bears witness to the creativity and universal provision of God, not a national "birthright." Ignoring the US national framework other writers were quick to impose, he writes of moving through the Cherokee, Creek, and Seminole nations, of visiting a Quaker village and "the Floridas." The only discernible moment of pride in *Travels* that could be called nationalistic is a paean to "our turkey of America," which are "exceedingly splendid" and three times as big as those in Europe or Asia (36).

Bartram's Sublime Descriptions

Bartram's first description of the sublime begins fairly typically. It is April of 1773, and he has just departed from Cape Henlopen in Delaware on his way to Charleston. After beginning with a "prosperous gale," he encounters two days of severe storms. Bartram reflects that "There are few objects out at sea to attract the notice of the traveller, but what are sublime, awful, and majestic: the seas themselves, in a tempest, exhibit a tremendous scene, where the winds assert their power, and, in furious conflict, seem to set the ocean on fire" (28). When describing terror as "the ruling principle of the sublime," Burke, too, turns to the ocean and also credits "raging storms" with sublime magnitude (see *Enquiry* II ii and II xvii). But unlike Burke, Bartram's attention does not remain on the ocean tempest or the terror it caused. Already in the next sentence, he finds the moon, animals, colors, even smells that strike him as competing with the storm in sublimity:

> On the other hand, nothing can be more sublime than the view of the encircling horizon, after the turbulent winds have taken their flight, ... the gentle moon rising in dignity from the east, ... the prodigious bands of porpoises foreboding tempest, that appear to cover the ocean; the mighty whale, sovereign of the watery realms, who cleaves the seas in his course; ... the water suddenly-alive with its scaly inhabitants; squadrons of sea-fowl sweeping through the air, impregnated with the breath of fragrant aromatic trees and flowers; the amplitude and magnificence of these scenes are great indeed, and may present to the imagination, an idea of the first appearance of the earth to man at the creation.   (28)

What Bartram sees, when he sees himself at the center of a perceptual act at all, is its horizon. The sea may be boundless, but it returns him to his finitude. Mortal finitude, which limits us spatially and temporally, provides the basis for sublime experience. The trees, flowers, and porpoises to him are not only "magnificent" as an aesthetic experience, but also meaningful in appearing ontologically miraculous. The sublime, for him, is to perceive something as though neither he nor anyone else has ever seen it before.

There is one other description of sublimity in *Travels* that reflects a commonplace of aesthetic discourse, but here too Bartram's approach is unique. In the eighteenth and nineteenth centuries, mountains, along with storms at sea, become so closely associated with the aesthetic of sublimity that their appearance in poetry, novels, and paintings functions as a symbolic reference to sublimity itself. Cian Duffy suggests that mountains consolidate "a variety of ostensibly unrelated forms of elevation: moral, political, epistemological, aesthetic – as well as religious" in what he calls a "discourse of ascent" (*Landscapes*, 30). It is therefore not surprising to find Bartram ascending a peak in the Jore (Nantahala) mountains to find "with rapture and astonishment, a sublimely awful scene of power and magnificence, a world of mountains piled upon mountains" (362). However, comparing Bartram's mountain descriptions with those of his contemporaries is telling. Describing the White Mountains in New Hampshire, Jeremy Belknap wrote in 1793 that here "A poetic fancy may find full gratification amid these wild and rugged scenes" because "Almost everything in nature, which can be supposed capable of inspiring ideas of the sublime and beautiful is here realized."[18] There is a category of natural objects that equate sublimity, and he finds them, ergo the view is sublime. For Thomas Cole, whose writing and paintings become a foundational part of what Andrew Wilton calls "an indigenous American pictorial language," writing about mountains requires the comparison with previously approved sublime landscapes in Europe: "It is true that in the eastern part of this continent there are no mountains that vie in altitude with the snow-crowned Alps," but "Snowdon in Wales, and Ben-Nevis in Scotland, are not more lofty," and New Hampshire has "been called the Switzerland of the United States."[19] Bartram's writing simply does not reveal this anxiety to justify his perception of sublimity in terms of preordained categories of objects or paradigmatic landscapes.

More than any other natural feature, it is the forest Bartram regards as sublime.[20] Eighteenth-century engagements with the sublime often associate forests with unseen threats: mountains or ocean storms achieve sublimity through their indifference to human fates, but forests seethe with hostility. For Burke, as noted, the sublime "comes upon us in the gloomy forest" (*Enquiry* II v). Individual oaks or elms are "awful and majestic," but an ecosystem of "darkest woods" connotes obscurity and death (*Enquiry* II xvi, iii). The association of forests with primeval threats was preserved in American nineteenth-century discourse because the wildness that uncut forests represented was seen as a distinguishing feature of the new world.

Cole portrays forests as "primeval," their gloom peopled by "savage beasts, and scarcely less savage men" (30). Bartram, in contrast, discovers in their variety a purposiveness almost resembling the "form of purposiveness of an object ... without representation of an end" that Kant associates with beauty (*COPJ* §17 236). He describes entering a "sublime forest" that has been "thinly planted by nature with the most stately forest trees" (55). It is not sublime because of what hides from knowledge or threatens him but because it has been "planted by nature" with "mighty trunks" of "seemingly of an equal height," which together create the impression of "superb columns" (55). The orderliness suggested by the forest does not cancel out its sublimity because it does not suggest the possibility of human understanding, only human appreciation. The order is itself superfluous, a gift.

Foregrounding the forest as sublime, as opposed to fields of ice or sea or desert, affects the perceptual orientation implied by Bartram's descriptions. Many travel writers during the period compose in painterly scenes with landscape features described at a distance from the viewer.[21] Bartram tends to write from within a scene. This implies a significant shift in the human relation to sublime experience because it does not position the human viewer as the organizing perceptual angle. Like Burke, Bartram contemplates sound, touch, and smell, rather than just vision, and this too has a tendency to decenter human perceptual control since we cannot direct these senses in the way sighted people direct vision. Bartram hears "the plunging and roaring of the crocodiles, and the croaking of the frogs" on all sides of him (92). He records turkeys, which he describes as "social sentinels," "saluting each other ... in an universal shout" (88). Bartram perceives animals and plants as communal creatures, whose sociality can beneficially instruct humankind. "How cheerful and social," he writes, "is the rural converse of the various tribes of tree frogs" (162). Sighting clouds of Ephemera mayfly, Bartram begs "the reader's patience whilst we behold the closing scene of the short-lived Ephemera, and communicate to each other the reflections which so singular an exhibition might rationally suggest to an inquisitive mind" (88). The community that begins with mayflies extends to include not only Bartram but also the reader. Their number is "greater than the whole race of mankind that have ever existed since the creation"; their "frame and organization is equally wonderful, more delicate, and perhaps as complicated as that of the most perfect human being" (82). Bartram feels small in relation to the possibility of discovery on every side of him. He writes as though the community of nature takes him in, rather than positioning himself on the edge of a precipice taking in a sublime view. Nature itself has "a pulse," a "universal vibration of life insensibly and irresistibly" moving, which fills "the high lonesome forests with an awful·reverential harmony, inexpressibly sublime" (161–2). The sense of sublimity arising out of pervasive life is awe inspiring, but not terrifying.

Bartram and the English Romantics

Bartram was not, like Burke or Kant, a theorist of the sublime so much as a promoter. His occasional conflation of the beautiful with the sublime is just the sort of indiscriminate enthusiasm that would frustrate a Kantian like Samuel Taylor Coleridge, but his enthusiastic descriptions of sublime encounters fired the imaginations of English Romantic poets.[22] Viewing Salt Springs in central Florida, Bartram describes "the enchanting and amazing crystal fountain, which incessantly threw up, from dark, rocky caverns below, tons of water every minute" (150). As Lowes points out, not only the image, but even the language appears in "Kubla Khan":

> A mighty fountain momently was forced:
> Amid whose swift half-intermitted burst
> Huge fragments vaulted like rebounding hail,
> Or chaffy grain beneath the thresher's flail:
> And 'mid these dancing rocks at once and ever
> It flung up momently the sacred river.[23]

Similarly, Wordsworth draws on Bartram when writing "Ruth." The narrator describes the young man Ruth marries as pining for Georgia woods he has left behind. The landscape has given him "So much of earth – so much of Heaven." In constructing an exoticized wilderness with dolphins, panthers, strawberry fields, savannahs, and magnolias, Wordsworth merges ecosystems that the scientific Bartram documents as distinct, but as Lowes notes all the imagery comes straight from Bartram.[24] Wordsworth even credits him in a footnote.

What Coleridge and Wordsworth do with Bartram's imagery is interesting. Where Bartram finds life and food and beauty in the seasonal changes of southern wilds, Wordsworth imagines danger. The uncontrolled ecosystem communicates its tendency toward undisciplined extremes to Ruth's future husband:

> Whatever in those Climes I found
> Irregular in sight or sound
> Did to my mind impart
> A kindred impulse, seem'd allied
> To my own powers, and justified
> The workings of my heart.

Nor less to feed unhallow'd thought
The beauteous forms of nature wrought,
Fair trees and lovely flowers ...[25]

Why the orchards and "houseless woods" around Tintern Abbey would impart to the poetic speaker "that blessed mood" in which we "become a living" and harmonious "soul," but the "fair trees and lovely flowers" of the South would promote "irregular" impulses and "unhallow'd thought," is quite mysterious. It has to do not with the trees or flowers but with what Duffy calls the "classic ground" of the sublime. The Alps, the desert, polar expanses, and the groves of antiquity (Italy and Greece) were all already colored by the discourse of sublimity, "the essential claim" of which, as Thomas Weiskel writes, "is that man can, in feeling and in speech, transcend the human" (*Weiskel*, 3). Tintern Abbey was hallowed ground, and Wordsworth's reception of that blessed mood or sublime gift repeats an act of receiving more than human inspiration ritualized by the Abbey's late residents. Wordsworth treats the American South as unhallowed. The "cultural blankness" of Carolina and Georgia veil the area in the obscurity associated with sublimity, but not with blessing (for the concept, see *Landscapes*, 10).

Coleridge stays closer to Bartram in the precision of description. He also preserves the sense of the sacred, but in "Kubla Khan" measurement (five miles) is associated with circumscription and enclosure and placed in contrast to the "measureless" sublime. Following Kant, Coleridge equates the sublime with "a standard ... which is not usable for any logical (mathematically determinate) judging of magnitude, but only for an aesthetic one" (*COPJ* §25 249) In contrast, Bartram combines the scientific rigor of measurement and species designation with the language of wonder and mystery with no sense of tension between them. Being "struck with a kind of awe" at cypresses does not prevent him noting the depth of water in which they grow or the height and diameter of cypress knees (93–4). Foregrounding an emphasis on objectivity, Bartram rejects rhetoric that might foster in readers the kind of awe he describes feeling himself. "To keep within the bounds of truth and reality, in describing the magnitude and grandeur of these trees, would, I fear, fail of credibility; yet, I think I can assert, that many of the black oaks measured eight, nine, ten, and eleven feet diameter five feet above the ground" (55). Being measurable does not make the trees less amazing. To return to the example of the Cherokee Chief and white surveyor, Bartram values tools of empirical measurement for describing lived experience, but makes no claim that measurements or concepts could capture experience. For Bartram, the South is not unhallowed. He blithely declares sublimity where he finds it with little regard for what counts as sublime for others. There is so much of the universe for him that we can never see and yet remains sublime: "If then the visible, the mechanical part of the animal creation, the mere material part is so admirably beautiful, harmonious and incomprehensible, what must be the intellectual system? that inexpressibly more essential principle, which secretly operates within?" (19).

Conclusion

Late twentieth- and twenty-first-century conceptions of the American sublime have turned away from nature, toward capital and technology. Rob Wilson argues that many Americans experience "large-scale displacements of the natural sublime by megastructures of capital."[26] According to David Nye, Americans have a penchant for a "technological sublime" that "sees new structures and inventions as continuations of nature," and they "experience the dislocations and perceptual disorientations caused by this reconstruction in terms of awe and wonder."[27] Bartram's forest wanderings may seem quite removed from these more recent understandings of sublimity. But Bartram's willingness to marvel at the complexity of what is not human-made continues to be important, not just for aesthetic history but for epistemology and environmental ethics because it is not predicated on a sense of mastery. William Spanos argues for the ongoing value of the concept of sublimity on the basis of its ability to counter "the spectacle's reduction of the fully human being to a mere spectator." He associates sublimity, in contrast, with "an active wonder, the alienated (ek-sistent) faculty of the human that, in humility before its immensity, mobility, and variety asks questions about being rather than, as in the Western tradition, imposes answers on its ontological indeterminacy."[28] Bartram's early American sublime joyfully resigns certainty and express-ability as a goal, in favor of "an active wonder."

NOTES

1 Roderick Nash, *Wilderness and the American Mind*, New Haven, CT, Yale University Press, 1982, 40, 60, 46.

2 Ralph Waldo Emerson, "Nature," in *Essays and English Traits*, ed. Charles W. Eliot, New York, Collier and Son, 1937, 223.

3 John Livingston Lowes documents Coleridge's reading of Bartram in detail in *The Road to Xanadu*, Princeton, NJ, Princeton University Press, 1927, 367–70.

4 Harold Bloom, *The Daemon Knows: Literary Greatness and the American Sublime*, Oxford, Oxford University Press, 2015, 6.

5 Christopher Hitt, "Toward an Ecological Sublime," *New Literary History* 3, 30, 1999, 603–23 (607).

6 Thomas P. Slaughter, "The Nature of William Bartram," *Pennsylvania History* 62, 1995, 429–51 (429).

7 Frances Harper and William Bartram, "Travels in Georgia and Florida, 1773–74: A Report to Dr. John Fothergill," *Transactions of the American Philosophical Society* 33, 1943, 121–242 (126).

8 Benjamin Silliman, *Letters of Shahcoolen*, Russell and Cutler, 1802, 139.

9 Slaughter, "Nature of William Bartram," 429.

10 Benjamin Franklin, "Idea of the English School, [January 7, 1751]," Founders Online: National Archives , https://founders.archives.gov/documents/Franklin/01-04-02-0030.

11 Joseph Addison, *The Spectator*, vol. 3, ed. Donald F. Bond, Oxford, Oxford University Press, 1965, 540 (No. 412, June 23, 1712).

12 Michael Chandos Brown, "The First American Sublime," in Timothy Costelloe, ed., *The Sublime: From Antiquity to the Present*, Cambridge, Cambridge University Press, 2015, 147–70 (148n.4).

13 Emily Brady, *The Sublime in Modern Philosophy: Aesthetics, Ethics, and Nature*. Cambridge, Cambridge University Press, 2013, 13.

14 Bartram, *Travels through North and South Carolina, Georgia, East and West Florida, the Cherokee Country, the Extensive Territories of the Muscogulges, or Creek Confederacy, and the Country of the Chactaws*, in *Travels and Other Writings*, ed. Thomas Slaughter, New York, Library of America, 1996, 3–426 (17).

15 Hitt, "Toward an Ecological Sublime," 607.

16 Brown, "First American Sublime," 148.

17 Thomas Cole, "Essay on American Scenery," *American Monthly Magazine* (January 1836). Reprinted in Robert E. Grese, ed., *The Native Landscape Reader*, Amherst, University of Massachusetts Press, 2011, 27–36.

18 Jeremy Belknap. *The History of New-Hampshire*, 3 vols., Boston, 1792, vol. 3, 51.

19 Andrew Wilton and Tim Barringer, *American Sublime: Landscape Painting in the United States, 1820–1880*, Princeton, NJ, Princeton University Press, 2002, 11; Cole, "Essay on American Scenery," 30.

20 See, for example, Bartram, "Travels," 55, 162, 165, 193, 256, 28, 309, 316, 341, 368–9.

21 Edward Cahill, *Liberty of the Imagination*, Philadelphia, University of Pennsylvania Press, 2012, 106–7.

22 See Dorothy Wordsworth's account of Coleridge growing frustrated at a tourist's imprecise use of "majestic," "beautiful," and "sublime" in *Journals of Dorothy Wordsworth*, ed. Ernest de Selincourt, 2 vols., New York, Macmillan, 1952, vol. 1, 223–4.

23 Samuel Taylor Coleridge, "Kubla Khan, or a Vision in a Dream," lines 19–24. See Lowes, *Road to Xanadu*, 368–70.

24 See Lowes, *Road to Xanadu*, 455 n.28.

25 William Wordsworth, "Ruth" (1802), lines 73–80; quoted from Fiona Stafford, ed., *Lyrical Ballads 1798 and 1802*, Oxford, Oxford University Press, 2013, 244–5.

26 Rob Wilson, "The Postmodern Sublime: Local Definitions, Global Deformations of the US National Imaginary," *Amerikastudien/American Studies* 43, 1998, 517–27 (519).

27 David E. Nye, *American Technological Sublime*, Cambridge, MA, MIT Press, 1994, 282.

28 William Spanos, *Redeemer Nation in the Interregnum*, New York, Fordham University Press, 2016, 10, 7.

PART III

Legacies

17

TATJANA JUKIĆ

The Victorian Chthonic Sublime

A certain disregard for the sublime may be that which most pointedly distinguishes Victorian culture from Romanticism: the Victorians seem to have defined themselves against Romanticism by neglecting the sublime as a linchpin of the Romantic conceptual apparatus. What was at stake, however, may have been a sustained redistribution of the sublime rather than its neglect or even repression – a redistribution anticipated by Thomas Carlyle in 1827 when he writes about "inverse sublimity."[1] In Carlyle's words, inverse sublimity is that "true humor" which "issues not in laughter but in still smiles, which lie far deeper": it exalts, "as it were, into our affections what is below us, while sublimity draws down into our affections what is above us" (189).

Drawing on Jean Paul Richter, Carlyle clearly begins by adopting a Kantian explanation of the sublime. For Carlyle, as for Kant, the sublime serves to exact a rupture between affect and reason whereby reason is emancipated and, with it, the Enlightenment humanity; it is as such that sublimity then draws down into our affections what is above us. Yet, by insisting on inverse sublimity, Carlyle unpacks the Kantian sublime, from a concept into a relation whereby the sublime is dismantled into a busy metonymy, one that claims a truth on its own terms (true humor, says Carlyle). Insofar as this relation implies an extra below that the Kantian sublime does not accommodate, Carlyle evidently shapes his metonymy around the geological sublime that will find its ultimate template in Charles Lyell's *Principles of Geology* (1830–3): not only because the Earth's vast underbelly, closely studied, exceeds the fascination with the planetary mass that is instrumental to the sublime, but because the geological study has revealed the planetary mass itself to be an open-ended, metonymic structure, to which such ruptures are secondary. The Earth, fundamentally unfinished, entails "the immensity of time," says Lyell, which is "too vast to awaken ideas of sublimity unmixed with a painful sense of our incapacity to conceive a plan of such infinite extent."[2] Indeed, historians cite geology as "one of Carlyle's original passions" and insist that "Carlyle's interest in learning German was first aroused not by the German Romantics whose work he did so much to popularise in Britain, but by a desire to read the geologist Abraham Gottlob Werner."[3] John Burrow references Carlyle's "apocalyptic sublime," to be reached "through lurid geological metaphors," especially in his 1837 history of the French Revolution.[4] Even so, a case could be made that Carlyle's apocalyptic sublime is inflected in his earlier inversion of sublimity, just as his preference for metaphor is inflected in metonymic thinking.

The geological sublime, therefore, may well be a misnomer in the wake of Lyell, one anticipated by Carlyle when he speaks of inverse sublimity: one is, rather, invited to mourn for the sublime, in a structure of feeling where affect, once bound in awe, terror and rupture, is reclaimed for melancholia. In short, the Victorian sublime begins as a function of mourning; this, again, is anticipated by Carlyle when he identifies inverse sublimity as a humor that issues not in laughter but in still smiles, which lie far deeper.

It is a structure fully revealed in the Industrial Revolution, when the planetary mass, chiefly coal and iron ore, was engaged for a relentless metonymic traffic beyond the Earth's surface, as if to complete, and accelerate, Lyell's argument about the Earth as a vector of transformation. Massive emissions of industrial smoke, along with dross, were how the metonymic redistribution of the planetary mass in fact continued; it was only that no less than humanity was now perceived to be reconceived in this transformation. Because work increasingly became a function of coal and iron, industrial modernity meant that the idea of work could be divorced from the human condition, and reconfigured as detachment and loss. The human condition thus stood to be reconsidered as one of the melancholy relation to the world, whose truth, like work, was contiguous with humanity but not identical to it.

Thus emancipated from human self-definition and reassembled into an alienating spectacle, it was work that took on a sublime aspect in Victorian culture. Yet, rather than replacing the planetary mass as a placeholder of the sublime, work was how humanity itself was unpacked into a relation of radical proximity to the planet. It was a proximity whose conclusive index was the soot that spread everywhere, inside and across different flows, cavities, passageways and membranes, in human bodies too, so much so that accounts of subjectivation were inflected in the language of pathology, even extinction. In the 1880s, John Ruskin wrote about the climate-altering storm cloud of the nineteenth century, which affects the constitution of sensations and senses, especially of vision; Ruskin's is "blinded man."[5] For Ruskin, this storm cloud, as well as the sense change in its wake, is expressly how the sublime stands to be renegotiated. One meets, he writes, with "deep, high, *filthiness* of lurid, yet not sublimely lurid, smoke-cloud; dense manu-facturing mist" (26). Lewis Mumford called Ruskin a "paleotect," only to call attention to a "paleotechnic regime" in the 1850s, dominated by "the soot and cinders" whose "color spread everywhere, from grey to black: the black boots, the black stove-pipe hat, the black coach or carriage, the black iron frame of the hearth."[6] Like Ruskin, Mumford responds to pervasive planetary particles by cultivating a metonymic language, and suggests it was in metonymy that the mid-Victorian education of affect was decided: "Was it mourning?" asks Mumford, "Was it protective coloration? Was it mere depression of the senses?"[7]

The Victorian novel takes on a sublime aspect insofar as its privileged relation is to work, to the point of becoming a narrative machine – a condition aptly described by Caroline Levine as the "narratively networked sublime."[8] The industrial novel seems to have been designed to address this issue; tellingly, Victorian industrial novels do not coincide with great Victorian Bildungsromane, whose narration peaks on functional subjectiva-tion. Charlotte Brontë, for instance, first published *Jane Eyre* in 1847 as an exemplary Victorian Bildungsroman, to be followed in 1849 by *Shirley*, an industrial novel whose two heroines read as Jane Eyre split in two as the novel itself is unpacked into a narrative machine, to match the industrial labor it aspires to describe and contain.

Elizabeth Gaskell contributed *North and South* (1854) to this network, an industrial novel that patently invokes *Shirley*, and Brontë's biography, as if to suggest that Brontë's biography conforms to the template of the industrial novel. In *North and South* Brontë's place-names (e.g., Thornton) are claimed for persons, and personal names (e.g., Helstone) for places, in support of a language that captures subjectivation in territorial terms, in an industrial world, however, in which the terra is given over to metonymy. Gaskell's is a world in which factory chimneys "are constantly sending out one-third of their coal," and the industrial dust is how this world is brought together.[9] Affect is engaged for mourning rather than for the sublime: Margaret Hale, the focalizing consciousness in Gaskell's novel, coheres around losing her parents to this terra, as dust to dust, and it is only her excellence at the work of mourning that elevates her to a sublime figure, in what anticipates Freud's explanation of mourning as work (*Trauerarbeit*). If this is how Margaret comes to reciprocate Antigone, it is also how the Victorian sublime is shown to be moored in different chthonic structures, to which the work of mourning is key. Like Antigone, Margaret commits her own self to dust at the end, and the novel suggests that her consistency as the focalizing con-sciousness derives from steady mourning, whose closure coincides with Margaret's decision to hand over herself, for life, to Mancunian soot.

That chthonic humanity is thus invoked can be inferred from the fact that Gaskell renames Manchester to Milton, in another instance of a personal name being claimed for a place. The reference is clearly to John Milton and *Paradise Lost* (1667), an epic account of Genesis whose chthonic geography is unpacked by Gaskell into expansive industrial particles and surfaces, as Milton's puritan sublime is inverted. It is a humanity eventually captured in Charles Darwin's evolutionary theory. In the words of Gillian Beer, "instead of descent from a lofty deity" Darwin's history of humanity "shows the difficult ascent from swamp, from an unknown progenitor, but asserts the nobility of this story"; this is why "there is an 'umgekehrte Erhabene' or 'inverted sublime'" in Darwin's theory, writes Beer, as if echoing Carlyle.[10] What Beer also underlines, more than once, is Darwin's intimate "contact with Milton, the one book he never left behind when he set out on his isolated land-journeys from the *Beagle*."[11]

Paleotecture

Ruskin was instrumental to subliming work in Victorian culture, not least by privileging architecture as a portal to an aesthetics that took its cue from the Industrial Revolution. It was an aesthetics based in vision, to which light was both rationale and rationality, as if heralding the role that cinema was to play in the twentieth century. In this aesthetics, "positive shade is a more necessary and more sublime thing in an architect's hand than in a painter's," and "as light, with the architect, is nearly always liable to become full and untempered sunshine seen upon solid surface, his only rests, and his chief means of sublimity, are definite shades": thus Ruskin in 1849.[12] Ruskin's alignment of architecture with the sublime, which recalls Burke and Kant, proceeds perhaps from his previous decision to exclude architecture (and aesthetics!) from art theory, even as the intelligence of architecture is of the same order. For Ruskin, "essential utility ... as in architecture, invariably degrades, because then the theoretic part of the art is comparatively lost sight of; and thus architecture takes a level below that of sculpture or painting, even when the powers of mind developed in it are of the same high order."[13]

Hence Ruskin's fascination with stone, in *The Stones of Venice* (1851–3) and elsewhere: not because stone holds light, or shade, but because – subjected to the work of an architect – stone unholds them. This is why work is as sublime to Ruskin as stone, if not more so: stone receives its sublimity from work, as stonework and a scene of transformation. Moreover, Ruskin perceives stonework to be contiguous with the operation of environmental forces, through which architectural work is exceeded, as it is lost; hence his interest in the work of lichen on diverse rock formations, even on pieces of brick, as Kate Flint has convincingly shown.[14] In *Seven Lamps*, Ruskin signals the "sublimity of the rents, or the fractures, or stains, or vegetation, which assimilate the architecture with the work of Nature," only to argue that "a building cannot be considered as in its prime until four or five centuries have passed over it" (202–3). Robert Browning adopts a similar view of architecture in "Love among the Ruins" (1855), a poem whose climax – human and sexual – is staged in "the single little turret that remains / ... By the caper overrooted, by the gourd / Overscored," that "[m]arks the basement whence a tower in ancient time / Sprang sublime" (lines 37–44).[15] In a poem pointedly divided into long and short lines, Browning references sublimity in a short line, and the short lines, as Isobel Armstrong has noted, merely disrupt the "flow of the long lines" that "make perfect sense without them."[16] Like the short lines, Browning's sublime points to work as assimilable loss: the short lines being a Ruskinian rent, fracture or stain, now in the architecture of a Browning poem.

If this means that, for Ruskin as for Browning, the idea of work fails to coincide with the idea of humanity, except as loss, it also means that architecture preempts other formats of mourning, as perfect mourning. It is a mourning tasked, also, with redistributing the sublime, which is why there is no unified theory of sublimity in Ruskin, even as he steadily invokes the concept. George Landow detailed Ruskin's different uses of the concept; Armstrong calls Ruskin's "a distorted form of the sublime," whose dismantling serves to usher a theory of the grotesque.[17] Rather than being retained as a concept, the sublime in his writings tends to be claimed for relations. If anything, Ruskin's is an empiricist, Humean sublime, in "a world where the conjunction 'and' dethrones the interiority of the verb 'is.'"[18]

This particular sublime shows acutely in Ruskin's discussion of Tintoretto in volume two of *Modern Painters* (1846) – a volume noted for its impact on the formation of the Pre-Raphaelite Brotherhood in 1848, whose paintings then led Ruskin to outline a theory of realism. Tintoretto is praised for "the most sublime instances" of "sympathies in every minor detail," sympathy being Ruskin's term for the intensity of relations (vol. 2, 186). Ruskin singles out *The Entombment of Christ*: a painting in which the body of Christ is given over to "the rocks of the sepulchre" in "a desert place, where the foxes have holes, and the birds of the air have nests, and against the barred twilight of the melancholy sky are seen the mouldering beams and shattered roofing of a ruined *cattle-shed*, the canopy of the Nativity" (vol. 2, 187). It is when entombed, that is, that the body of Tintoretto's Christ fully reveals the world to be a juncture of sympathies, and the sublime resides not with his body so much as with the sympathies thus revealed. His sepulcher is perfect architecture: a dwelling that coincides with mourning, it shows architecture being decided in the work claimed for humanity as detachment or loss – in the moldering of beams, in foxholes being dug. Of course, an architecture that is essentially sepulchral, as Ruskin's is, entails chthonic humanity. (Equally so for Browning, whose human geography in "Love among the Ruins" receives its coherence from the mark of a basement.)

Ruskin's aesthetics received its philology in volume three of *Modern Painters* (1856), in his discussion of pathetic fallacy. Meant as a critique of the Romantic tendency to solicit the natural world for human subjectivation, Ruskin's discussion of pathetic fallacy entails a grasp of language to which affect management is key, at a remove, however, from the sublime. Instead, Ruskin argues for a language so invested in relations – sympathies in every minor detail – that they can hardly support personification, identity, even functional subjectivation. As Ruskin puts it, "[t]he foam is not cruel, neither does it crawl" (vol. 3, 170). What is fallacious in pathetic fallacy, in other words, is the self reinforced through pursuing the sublime, or not, which is how the world is lost to hysterical narcissism. Ruskin seems to anticipate Freud when he relates mismanaged affect to grief as its true destination; we can pardon the fallacy, says Ruskin, if "we see that the *feeling* is true," and are pleased with the quoted lines "not because they fallaciously describe foam, but because they faithfully describe sorrow" (vol. 3, 175). A Freudian equation is at stake: Ruskin associates narcissism with pathetic fallacy, and its truth with melancholia – a truth to be arrived at only by an impoverished self.

That a critique of pathetic fallacy was Ruskin's way of engaging, also, a theory of realism can be evinced from his involvement with the Pre-Raphaelites, whose microscopic *truth to Nature* he championed in the early 1850s precisely as a laborious, self-absorbing visual record of sympathies in every minor detail. Impressed with the Pre-Raphaelite work on the minutiae of the natural world, Ruskin argued that "the mere labor bestowed on those works, and their fidelity to a certain order of truth . . ., ought at once to have placed them above the level of mere contempt" (vol. 24, 59).

His portrait painted by John Everett Millais in 1853–4 at Glenfinlas in Scotland (see Figure 17.1) reveals Ruskin himself to be one such realist subject. Produced "under Ruskin's strict supervision" and with a plan "to revolutionise British landscape painting and portraiture," Millais's Ruskin is a portrait as much as it is a self-portrait, which is to say that a self – a concept that underlies both portraiture and self-portraiture – is detached from the prerogatives of identity, substitution and authorship.[19] Instead, Ruskin and Millais are engaged for a metonymic assemblage where a self is given over to the fullness of detail, which is why the (self-)portrait cannot but entail a landscape, itself a network of metonymic relations. The Pre-

Figure 17.1 John Everett Millais, *John Ruskin* (1853–4). Ashmolean Museum, Oxford.

Raphaelite Ruskin, dressed in the color of soot, is portrayed against different rock formations as they are worked upon by a rushing mountain stream and the vegetation. His figure is a juncture of sympathies exactly like Tintoretto's dead Christ about to be entombed, down to the fact that the placement of Ruskin against whitish rocks corresponds to the rocks of the sepulcher of Tintoretto's Christ. This suggests that Ruskin's *portrait* coincides, also, with a study of ultimate *architecture* – of sublime stone*work*, just as the self in this dwelling is taken apart into a chthonic grouping, whose order of truth is one of radical, unresolved mourning.

A study of gneiss rock at Glenfinlas (see Figure 17.2) that Ruskin produced at the time is in many ways a companion piece to the portrait. By sketching closely the gneiss that defines his figure in the Millais portrait, Ruskin reinforces a chthonic undoing of self, which is why this sketch is, also, Ruskin's self-portrait, and as much so as Millais's portrait of Ruskin. Worked upon by the torrent, honeysuckle and mountain ash, the gneiss exemplifies paleotecture, and the sharp lines in the stone, which testify to form only in terms of transformation, demand that a human face – a rationale of a portrait – be understood along similar lines. Observe the rock's

Figure 17.2 John Ruskin, *Study of Gneiss Rock, Glenfinlas* (1853). Ashmolean Museum, Oxford.

two cavernous holes just below the foliage in the top, and a gaping recess in the rock's lower half: they seem to be Ruskin's caveat against mistaking the caverns for eyes, the foliage for hair, and the recess for a gasping mouth.

Touchstones: Poetry and Criticism

It is in Matthew Arnold's criticism, especially in the 1860s, that Victorian culture appears to have found that foothold which foreshadows the renewed interest in the sublime in the twentieth century – not least because Arnold seems to have recreated the Kantian concept against its Carlylean inversion. In *Culture and Anarchy* (1869), Arnold argues for the sublime to be relished against man's "natural taste for the bathos," an argument so important to him that he repeats it six times, nearly verbatim.[20] When he calls for a "perversion of us by custom or example as might compel us to relish the sublime," perversion is not only an apt anticipation of what perversion is to mean in psychoanalysis but also, apparently, an attempt to go back on Carlyle's inverse sublimity as *true humor* (82). (Catherine Maxwell will associate the sublime with masochism in Victorian poetry, specifically with A. C. Swinburne; Yopie Prins writes of Swinburne's "Sapphic sublime," with Sappho as "his dominatrix").[21]

Yet, rather than yielding a functional concept, the six-times sublime to relish points to a stutter in Arnold's language. It is as if the intensity of relations that Carlyle and Ruskin associate with the inverse sublime could not be fully suppressed in Arnold's language, leaving in their wake a stutter as intense as the relations Arnold wanted to suppress. That the sublime is relative to Arnold can further be evinced from his contention, in the essay on Heinrich Heine, that "the Hebrew spirit" reaches the infinite "by sublimity" and "the Greek spirit by beauty."[22] By divorcing the Greeks from the imperative of sublimity, Arnold in fact disengages the sublime from the domain of the imperative, while the Greeks – Arnold's preferred index of modernity – are how the affect that would otherwise be engaged for the sublime is fundamentally unbound: a condition not unlike Freudian melancholia.

Arnold's poetry in the 1850s, notably "Empedocles on Etna" (1852), is an early indication of affect thus unbound and realigned. A dramatic poem, it shows Empedocles, an exemplary pre-Socratic poet-philosopher, climbing Etna with a view to committing suicide in its crater, his voice – like his natural philosophy – caught between the voices of Pausanias, a physician, and Callicles, a poet. The scene is thus set for the sublime to receive its perfect notation, as Mount Etna is to undo Empedocles. Yet his suicide in Etna is of the order of the Victorian inverse, chthonic sublime, because Empedocles's last words, to Etna, are "Receive me, save me!," as he is being undone into the very relations of his natural philosophy (Act II, line 416).[23] As if echoing, also, Lyell's geology, Etna's active crater about to receive Empedocles reverses his earlier frustration with "the unallied unopening earth," and releases him into "our individual human state," which is to "at last be true / To our own only true, deep-buried selves, / Being one with which we are one with the whole world" (Act II, lines 360–72). Etna is to Empedocles what the rock of the sepulcher is to Ruskin's Christ in the

Tintoretto painting: a dwelling where the (Romantic mountaintop) sublime gives way to chthonic humanity.

To Arnold this dwelling is melancholy, not sublime. The summit of Etna is "this charr'd, blacken'd, melancholy waste," where stars "slowly begin to marshall" their "distant, melancholy lines," having "survived" themselves (Act II, lines 2, 279–80). The lines of poetry in "Empedocles" reflect the same condition: they are of unequal length, and their stanzaic forms and rhyming schemes are inconsistent, as if having survived themselves – as if having survived the idea of meter. These charred remains of meter stutter, as Arnold's sublimity to relish stutters: a stutter that now amounts to a poetic condition. Arnold himself relates this stutter to a poetic condition when, in 1853, he goes back on his choice of Empedocles as a poetic subject, because Empedocles exemplifies a "mental distress" that is "prolonged, unrelieved" and whose description is, therefore, "monotonous" – monotony an apt name for charred poetry.[24] Arnold finally excluded "Empedocles" from the 1853 *Poems*, a crisis after which, as Kenneth Allott notes, he found it increasingly difficult to write poetry. Allot further notes that Arnold attributed to Empedocles the melancholia he found "stamped" on the atomism of Lucretius, and that he described both these poet-philosophers, and himself, as "over-tasked" – a word Freud would use to describe a melancholiac.[25]

Arnold's crisis over "Empedocles" is symptomatic of Victorian poetry in general, insofar as it defined itself against Romantic sublimity. Christina Rossetti may be an unlikely but matchless example, invested as she was in negotiating religious poetry against melancholy excess. Tellingly, Rossetti's poetry often reads like a metonymic network of chthonic minutiae (stones, gems, moss, grass, things being buried or planted), whose short lines, frequent anaphors and syncopated meter intimate stutter.

After all, Arnold's "Dover Beach," one of the definitive Victorian poems, published in 1867 but written probably in 1851, reads in many ways as "Empedocles" redux. It is a dramatic monologue with an emphasis on "glimmering and vast" cliffs, "the moon-blanch'd sand," and on "the vast edges drear / And naked shingles of the world" (lines 5, 8, 27–8); they cradle the poem and are the speaker's true dwelling. Yet the response this world elicits from the speaker is pointedly not in the sublime register. Rather, "the grating roar / Of pebbles which the waves suck back, and fling" (lines 9–10) entails a cadence and a note of sadness that the speaker explicitly engages for melancholy, and for Sophocles, particularly perhaps for the corresponding lines (636–41) from the *Antigone*.[26] The cadence implies the monotonous poetry that has survived itself, whose rhythm admits stutter, just as the language of Antigone, with her commitment to the chthonic gods, admits stutter, with the many "negations that riddle her speech."[27] Like

Empedocles, Antigone coincides with her true self only in relation to being buried alive; like Empedocles, Antigone is rejected by Arnold in 1853 as a flawed poetic subject.[28] Yet, retained as charred poetry, lines from the *Antigone* riddle Arnold's speech in "Dover Beach" to the point that Arnold's own voice is revealed to be Antigonic: because his English voice, in its obstinate chthonic dwelling, addresses the silent listener as much as it addresses a Creon – the French just across the Channel, in line three, with their flickering (post)revolutionary lights and violence. A foil for Empedocles and his volcanic *burial*, Arnold's Antigone reverses the conditions of Percy Bysshe Shelley's revolutionary sublime, notably in *Prometheus Unbound*, whose privileged image is one of "volcanic *eruption*."[29]

A Victorian idea of criticism was decided in this constellation. In "The Function of Criticism at the Present Time" (1864), Arnold argues for a criticism profiled against concepts, not against – political – relations, only to engage in an analysis of the English and French Revolutions. In Arnold's words from *Essays*, "1789 asked of a thing, Is it rational?" whereas "1642 asked of a thing, Is it legal? or, when it went furthest, Is it according to conscience?" (10). To Arnold, this implies that English modernity is not likely to favor criticism over literature, its revolution indebted to great literature (Shakespeare), and to political relations, over concepts. This also implies that English modernity, with its stress on law and conscience, is remarkably in line with the *Antigone*, which is why the sublime as a kind of concept-trigger is suspended in unresolved mourning and the political excess this entails.

Arnold's central critical concept, touchstone, outlined in "The Study of Poetry" (1880), betrays the same excess. Meant to indicate fragments of great literature that steer thinking, touchstones are not merely an entrenched geological metaphor, which derives from "a way of telling whether a given lump was a genuine piece of gold, because it would make a mark on the touchstone."[30] They actually describe poetry that has survived itself *and* the idea of meter, and on whose charred fragments the critics make their stuttering mark as the speaker in "Dover Beach" makes his mark on the lines from the *Antigone*. J. Hillis Miller observes that, interestingly, "[a]ll of Arnold's examples are of suffering and loss"; Stefan Collini that nearly all "express a melancholy or stoic mood."[31] What touchstones suggest, therefore, is not only an Antigonic hold on Victorian criticism but also a radical displacement of the sublime onto the work of mourning.

In an 1856 essay about Antigone, George Eliot singled her out for her capacity to act on what she thought right even as she knew that that was, also, wrong. This is why Antigone, according to Eliot, cannot truly aspire to martyrdom and sacrifice, even as she compares to a modern-day "reformer" and "revolutionist."[32] When Neil Hertz attributes "the end-of-the-line sub-limities" to the suicide scenes in Eliot's fiction, the same seems to apply to her Antigone; suspended from sacrifice, however, Eliot's Antigone suggests that the opposite may be the case – that her suicide marks the end of the line for sublimity.[33] Like Arnold, Eliot signals that the sublime has been suspended in Victorian modernity, and that modernity perhaps begins in truth only once the sublime has been suspended.

NOTES

1 Thomas Carlyle, "Jean Paul F. Richter," *The Edinburgh Review* 91, June 1827, 176–95 (189).
2 Charles Lyell, *Principles of Geology*, 3 vols., London, 1830, vol. 1, 63.
3 See Gareth Stedman Jones, "The Redemptive Power of Violence? Carlyle, Marx and Dickens," *History Workshop Journal* 65, 1, 2008, 1–22 (20); John Burrow, "Images of Time: From Carlylean Vulcanism to Sedimentary Gradualism," in Stefan Collini, Richard Whatmore and Brian Young, eds., *History, Religion, and Culture: British Intellectual History 1750–1950*, Cambridge, Cambridge University Press, 2000, 198–223 (207); and John M. Ulrich, "Thomas Carlyle, Richard Owen, and the Paleontological Articulation of the Past," *Journal of Victorian Culture* 11, 1, 2006, 30–58. For the popularization of geology in the nineteenth century, see Ralph O'Connor, *The Earth on Show: Fossils and the Poetics of Popular Science, 1802–1856*, Chicago, University of Chicago Press, 2007.
4 Burrow, "Images of Time," 219, 209.
5 John Ruskin, *The Complete Works*, 30 vols., New York, Kelmscott Society, 1900, vol. 24, 27.
6 Lewis Mumford, *Technics and Civilization*, London, Routledge & Kegan Paul, 1934, 185, 165, 163.
7 Ibid., 163.
8 Caroline Levine, *Forms: Whole, Rhythm, Hierarchy, Network*, Princeton, NJ, Princeton University Press, 2015, 130.
9 Elizabeth Gaskell, *North and South*, New York, Norton, 2005, 76.
10 Gillian Beer, *Darwin's Plots*, Cambridge, Cambridge University Press, 2009, 106. See also Paul White, "Darwin, Concepción, and the Geological Sublime," *Science in Context* 25:1, 2012, 49–71.
11 Ibid., 27.
12 John Ruskin, *The Seven Lamps of Architecture*, London, George Routledge & Sons, 1907, 86–7.
13 John Ruskin, *Modern Painters*, 5 vols., London, George Allen, 1906, vol. 2, 11.
14 Kate Flint, "Ruskin and Lichen," in Kelly Freeman and Thomas Hughes, eds., *Ruskin's Ecologies*, London, The Courtauld, 2021, 35–53.
15 Quoted from Robert Browning, *Selected Poems*, ed. John Woolford, Daniel Karlin and Joseph Phelan, London, Routledge, 2013, 536.
16 Isobel Armstrong, *Victorian Poetry*, London, Routledge, 1993, 17.

17 George P. Landow, *The Aesthetic and Critical Theories of John Ruskin*, Princeton, NJ, Princeton University Press, 1971, 2015, 183–221; Armstrong, *Victorian Poetry*, 233.

18 Gilles Deleuze, *Desert Islands and Other Texts 1953–1974*, Los Angeles, CA, Semiotext(e), 2004, 163.

19 Alastair Grieve, "Ruskin and Millais at Glenfinlas," *The Burlington Magazine* 138, 1117, 1996, 228–34 (228).

20 Matthew Arnold, *Culture and Anarchy*, Oxford, Oxford University Press, 2006, 84.

21 Catherine Maxwell, *The Female Sublime from Milton to Swinburne*, Manchester, Manchester University Press, 2001, 8, 187–93; Yopie Prins, *Victorian Sappho*, Princeton, NJ, Princeton University Press, 1999, 112, 123.

22 Matthew Arnold, *Essays in Criticism*, London, Macmillan, 1865, 179.

23 Quoted from *The Poems of Matthew Arnold*, ed. Kenneth Allott, London, Longmans, 1965, 192.

24 Matthew Arnold, "Preface" to first edition of *Poems* (1853); quoted from Allott, ed., *Poems*, 592.

25 Kenneth Allott, "A Background for 'Empedocles on Etna,'" in David. J. DeLaura, ed., *Matthew Arnold: A Collection of Critical Essays*, Englewood Cliffs, NJ, Prentice-Hall, 1973, 55–70 (68, 63, 65).

26 Sophocles, *Antigone*, Oxford, Oxford University Press, 2003, 79–80. For more on Arnold and *Antigone*, see Gerhard Joseph, "The *Antigone* as Cultural Touchstone: Matthew Arnold, Hegel, George Eliot, Virginia Woolf, and Margaret Drabble," *PMLA* 96, 1, 1981, 22–35.

27 Judith Butler, *Antigone's Claim*, New York, Columbia University Press, 2000, 68.

28 Arnold, "Preface" to *Poems*; quoted from Allott, ed., *Poems*, 603.

29 Cian Duffy, *Shelley and the Revolutionary Sublime*, Cambridge, Cambridge University Press, 2005, 154, 183, 185.

30 Christopher D. Morris and J. Hillis Miller, "An Interview with J. Hillis Miller," *Derrida Today* 8, 1, 2015, 77–109 (105).

31 Ibid.; Stefan Collini, *Matthew Arnold: A Critical Portrait*, Oxford, Clarendon Press, 1994, 65.

32 George Eliot, "The Antigone and Its Moral," *Leader* 7, March 29, 1856, 306.

33 Neil Hertz, *George Eliot's Pulse*, Stanford, CA, Stanford University Press, 2003, 10.

18

JOANNA E. TAYLOR, CHRISTOPHER DONALDSON AND
IAN N. GREGORY

Mapping the Nineteenth-Century Sublime

'Every word is a dead metaphor.'[1] Borges attributed this idea to Leopoldo
Lugones. The paraphrase is a loose one. Lugones only wrote that 'each word
is a metaphor'.[2] Yet the point Borges was attempting to make stands. What
is the history of words but the study of the afterlife of so many metaphors?
The history of 'sublime' is a case in point. The word's origins are obscure.[3] It
seems, though, that saying something went up to the lintel (*sub limen*)
became a way of describing something eminent or immense. In time, the
word was used to mean supreme as well. It certainly meant as much by the
end of the nineteenth century. Dip into the *Oxford English Dictionary*, and
you will discover two sample uses of the word from the 1890s. Both, in fact,
date to 1897. The first is a line from a Lloyd Mifflin poem, which describes
'beetling cliffs that loomed sublime'. The second is from an advertisement in
the *Daily News* for a bottle of 'Sublime Salad Oil'.[4] The bathos of the latter
example amuses, but both uses of the word affirm Borges's observation.
Both, moreover, illustrate an important point about the vicissitudes of
'sublime'. By the end of the nineteenth century the word had become
ubiquitous. It was as much a part of literary as of commercial language,
and it was generally used unsparingly. The appearance of the word in fin de
siècle guidebooks (where literary and commercial language tended to mix) is
especially noteworthy.

You will find 'sublime' scattered throughout the pages of popular tourist
'handbooks' – such as the ones published by Thomas Cook and John
Murray – which advised tourists not only where to go, but what to say
when they got there. Sabine Baring-Gould poked fun at this aspect of tourist
print culture in his novel *The Pennycomequicks* (1889). Having placed his
protagonist, Mrs. Sidebottom, at Lucerne, Baring-Gould implied that people
who used the word 'sublime' were merely parroting the clichéd language of
popular guidebooks: '"This," said Mrs. Sidebottom, dipping into "Murray's
Handbook" to ascertain what it was proper to say, "this is distinguished
above every lake in Switzerland, and perhaps in Europe, by the beauty and

sublime grandeur of its scenery." Then past her drifted a party of English tourists, also with "Murray" in their hands and on their lips.'[5]

As in the advert for 'Sublime Salad Oil', the sublime here is reduced to little more than dressing for a stock experience. A parallel might be drawn with James Plumptre's comic opera, *The Lakers* (1798). Like the exclamations of Plumptre's puffed-up heroine Miss Beccabunga Veronique, Mrs. Sidebottom's statements remind us that the taste for the sublime was an affectation of polite society. But the satire of this passage from *The Pennycomequicks* goes further than that. In mechanically reaching for Murray's handbook, Mrs. Sidebottom and the passing 'party of English tourists' parodically reveal their anxiety not to appear improper. What is more, their prescribed use of 'sublime' hints at how the word's use shifted over the course of the nineteenth century. In Plumptre's day, 'sublime' was part of the vocabulary of the educated elite. By Baring-Gould's time, the word had become a commonplace expression. Its meaning had largely loosened from the philosophical and psychological contexts in which it had been used in the mid-eighteenth century. Instead, the word had become an intensifier: a label for promoting the quality of commercial goods, whether those goods were salad oils or the experiences of tourists on packaged holidays.[6]

In what follows, we examine the use of 'sublime' in late nineteenth-century literature at scale, drawing on a methodology devised in a previous spatial study of the historical use of the word, in which we analysed how it was used in a corpus of eighty texts describing the English Lake District between the seventeenth and nineteenth centuries. Our aim was to ascertain which places in the Lake District had been described as 'sublime' in order to determine how the word was used in landscape descriptions.[7] Here, we turn to a much larger corpus: the British Library's Nineteenth-Century Books Corpus, which comprises over 60,000 titles – approximately 25 million pages – published over the course the 'long' nineteenth century. Originating in a digitization partnership between the British Library and Microsoft, this multi-genre corpus includes novels, poetry, travel writing, scientific treatises, philosophy, histories, and geographical studies.[8] The size and complexity of this corpus means that bringing it into a format that is suitable for applying digital humanities methods is very labour and resource intensive. Consequently, for this study, we focused on a single decade, the 1890s, and to explore how uses of the word 'sublime' at the end of the nineteenth century either corresponded with or deviated from its use in earlier landscape writing. Extracting this portion of the corpus resulted in a sub-corpus of around 10,000 texts, which, collectively, contain about 900 million words.

We needed to transform this sub-corpus into machine-readable text in order to work with it in a digital environment. The British Library and Microsoft had scanned the books included in the corpus, and they then used Optical Character Recognition (OCR) to translate the scanned images into digital texts. The OCRed scans of this corpus were downloaded from the British Library (https://data.bl.uk/digbks/), and read into Lexi.Db, a corpus analysis software package, for processing and tagging.[9] This process enabled us to ask questions such as: What words co-occur with 'sublime'? Do particular categories – certain place types, for instance – recur more frequently? And what do these co-occurrences suggest, at a large scale, about the ways the sublime was used and thought about in written works from the 1890s?

These are valuable starting points, but we can go further by translating these texts into mappable data for use in a geographical text analysis (GTA). Geographical text analysis is a set of techniques that attempt to ask the deceptively simple question, 'What is a corpus saying about where?' The 'what' part of this question needs to be answered using approaches from corpus linguistics, such as concordances (which allow qualitative reading of the text surrounding a particular search term or set of search terms) or collocation (which identifies what words occur near to a search term).[10] The 'where' part needs geographical information systems (GIS) approaches that allow the mapping and spatial analysis of geographical data.[11] These two approaches come from very different subject areas – linguistics and geography, respectively – and draw on very different types of data. Corpus linguistics requires textual sources usually with mark-up such as XML to embed additional information, while GIS uses tables of usually quantitative data where each row of data is linked to map-based locations.

Crossing the divide between these approaches requires the corpus to be *geoparsed*. This is an automated, two-stage process in which a computer program first identifies words that are likely to be place names. These candidate names are then compared with a place name gazetteer, effectively a database table that lists place names and their coordinates, which both verifies whether the word is likely to be a place name and provides a coordinate for it.[12] Although simple in theory, geoparsing is an error-prone process, since place names are often ambiguous in terms of whether they refer to a place or another entity (for example, London might be the city or refer to the author Jack London) or the fact that multiple places may have the same name (London, UK, or London, Ontario) and spellings may also vary significantly. To mitigate these errors in our large and complex corpus, we used an interactive process known as concordance geoparsing, in which only a set number of words to the left and right of a search term are geoparsed. The relatively small number of results from this process can be checked and manually updated as required, and the results of these updates fed into the geoparsing of subsequent search terms.[13] Once the required parts of the corpus have been geoparsed, the coordinates can be used to map the data. For this chapter, we concordance geoparsed the text around the search-term 'sublime'. This provides what we term the place name co-occurrences (PNCs) of the search term, which shows the place names that occur within ten words of 'sublime'. By identifying where 'sublime' co-occurs near to a place name, we can start to ascertain the sorts of spatial qualities with which the word was associated, and begin to ask how space and place affected the ways 'sublime' was used and understood.

Simplified example of a place name co-occurrence (PNC) for 'sublime'

The place name 'London' has been identified by the geoparser. It is enclosed within the XML tags '<enamex>...</enamex>.' The longitude, latitude, and a standardized spelling of the place name are also included as XML attributes. It is found within ten words of the search term ('sublime'), so we assume the two are linked.

A: Original text fragment

Ridoser had intended to return to London at once, but this sublime effrontery changed his determination. At least, he thought, he could make the blackguard uneasy ...

B: Geoparsed text fragment

Ridoser had intended to return to <enamex long="-0.125" lat="51.509" name="London">London</enamex> at once, but this sublime effrontery changed his determination. At least, he thought, he could make the blackguard uneasy ...

Digital approaches like GTA provide a means of uncovering historical and literary trends at unprecedented scales, but this automated process is not without its flaws.[14] For example, when we search for PNCs within ten words of 'sublime' in our 1890s sub-corpus, we find that only two continents have been labelled as such through this automatic process: Europe and Asia. The geoparser has erroneously labelled three additional continents as 'countries': America, Australia, and Africa. This oversight is less problematic for the first two, since, when we read the individual examples, it is clear that the individual instance for America and the three for Australia refer to the countries. For the Australian poet Percy Russell, for example, Australia (apparently unironically) 'Forth stands ... in her birth sublime / The only nation from the womb of Peace', while the New South Wales poet Alphonsus W. Webster finds that 'Of all Australia can produce / Of soft or grand, sweet or sublime, / Is Botany the most profuse / In what can wake the Poet's rhyme / Or stimulate his Muse.'[15] In both cases, Australia's sublimity is imbricated in the country's nationhood. The mislabelling of Africa as a country is more serious. Not only is it geographically erroneous, but it also occludes the continent's complex social, cultural, and political milieux – not to mention its hugely diverse environments. There are two PNCs for 'Africa', both from Roden Berkeley Wriothesley Noël's epic poem *Livingstone in Africa* (1874, reprinted 1895). In one instance, Noël describes how one of Livingstone's companions expressed 'sublime surprise' at the sight of a ship. (Noël imagines the same character believing, despite all evidence to the contrary, that 'the English have good hearts for Africa!') From a methodological point of view, the second PNC is more problematic; it describes the 'honourable trade in all the wealth of Ethiopia; Ebony, amber, gold, and ivory'.[16] Yet Ethiopia is not recognized as a country. This example highlights the importance of closely reading the results produced by digital methods, such as GTA: computer-led analysis is not foolproof, and instances like this highlight the inherent biases that remain encoded into our toolkits.[17]

Nevertheless, in utilizing methods like GTA we can learn from the historical texts we seek to analyse: we have seen users of the term 'sublime' mocked for their inattention and lack of specificity, but we can benefit from this lesson, too. So long as we remain attentive to closely reading even our large-scale datasets, methods like GTA can refine our understanding of concepts like the sublime, allowing us to test assumptions about the way the word was used and how its meaning adapted and changed. As we will see throughout the remainder of this chapter, this approach incorporates lesser-known texts, and overlooked voices, alongside canonical and well-known examples. Studying the sublime on this scale allows us to ascertain how precisely – or not – the word was being used during this period, and to do so more comprehensively than is otherwise possible. Doing so highlights the extent to which debates about the sublime still mattered, even in an age that seemed to have disregarded it.

'Sublime' Collocates

In our 1890s selection from the Nineteenth-Century Books Corpus, the word 'sublime' appears 8,213 times. We can start to get a sense of how 'sublime' was being used in this period by examining the sorts of place names

Table 18.1. *Terms that collocate with sublime (within four words on either side)*

Collocates in the Nineteenth-Century Books Corpus	Log-likelihood score	Collocates in the Newspapers dataset	Log-likelihood score
Porte	8092.233	Porte	2799.471
Ridiculous	1852.511	Ridiculous	455.756
Beautiful	1689.311	Constantinople	196.155
Time	1628.478	Time	186.638
One	1592.955	Great	185.055
Scenery	1499.088	Beautiful	160.706
Grand	1392.32	Poet	146.864
Faith	1281.621	Powers	144.723
Spectacle	1117.159	Suffer	137.429

alongside which the word was used in close proximity or, to put it another way, by determining what its collocates are. Table 18.1 shows terms that collocate with sublime within four words on either side. The reason for using a smaller bandwidth here is that we tend to be looking for terms that are being described by the adjective 'sublime', and these tend to be closer than place names that are described in this way. We have removed common stop words (terms that are used so frequently in English, like 'the' or 'and', that their presence is not statistically significant) to leave the terms that suggest nuances about how the sublime was understood. To develop this further, we have compared our dataset from the Nineteenth-Century Books Corpus with the same years (1890–1900) from the British Library's digitized collection of newspapers to give us a more comprehensive idea of what the sublime meant to writers and readers across genres and print forms in this period. The Newspapers dataset contains 1,008 examples of 'sublime' across 897 documents.

These collocates indicate the extent to which the appearance of 'sublime' was, to a large extent, simply the result of geographical terminology: the strong collocations with 'Porte' in both corpora, and 'Constantinople' in the Newspapers collection, are a result of references to the Ottoman seat of power, the Sublime Porte (the name is a French translation from the Turkish Bâbıâli for 'High Gate' or 'Gate of the Eminent').[18] Ongoing discussions and territory disputes meant that this gateway between Europe and Asia remained topical throughout the last quarter of the nineteenth century. Of the twenty-seven collocations of 'sublime' with Europe or Asia, ten reference the Sublime Porte.

The collocation with 'ridiculous', moreover, reveals that the word 'sublime' frequently appeared in quotations: specifically, in quotations of the comment attributed to Napoleon on his return from Russia, that there is 'but a step from the sublime to the ridiculous'.[19] That expression evidently occurred to several travel writers when they found themselves in unusual or uncomfortable situations. Arthur Campbell discovered that 'in Rome as elsewhere, from the sublime to the ridiculous is but a step'.[20] Similarly, a new edition of Dora Quillinan's *Journal of a Few Months' Residence in Portugal and Glimpses of the South of Spain* (1895) recalled one moment from her travels when the sublime seemed to tip into the ridiculous, in the village of Caldas on the night of 6 June 1845. Having spent the day before musing on Portugal's impressive mountain scenery, she found that 'the croaking of the frogs all night made it impossible to sleep'; she surmises that the frogs must leave when visitors arrive in the bathing town: 'unless deafness be part of the complaint', she writes, the 'hapless invalids' could derive no benefits from taking the waters. Even if their deafness was cured, she thinks, 'one night's concert of frogs would … make the patient wish himself deaf again'.[21] Before dawn, Quillinan was once again riding in the shadow of the mountains – although, thanks to a temperamental mule, the ridiculousness of the situation constantly threatens to overwhelm the sublimity of the mountains. Throughout this episode, Quillinan foregrounds the potential to slip between the sublime and the ridiculous in ways that exaggerate the close connection between the two states, particularly as the sublime's meaning became increasingly diffuse.

Even by 1803, Samuel Taylor Coleridge noticed that tourists to Scotland seemed to use terms like 'sublime' indiscriminately. Standing beneath Cora Linn, the highest of the Falls of Clyde, Coleridge was musing on 'the precise meaning of the words … majestic, sublime, etc' when a couple fell into conversation with him. It was a 'majestic waterfall,' the gentleman declared. His wife agreed, adding that it was 'sublime and beautiful', too.[22] Coleridge's mockery of his interlocutors anticipates Baring-Gould's frustration with English tourists abroad: both groups of people typify a much-mocked aspect of the Picturesque movement, which saw tourists employ words like 'sublime' without a clear understanding of their meaning and philosophical histories.[23] This looseness of definition, already notable by the Romantic period, had within a century become a characteristic feature of the word's use. In both the Nineteenth-Century Books Corpus and the British Library Newspapers collection, 'sublime' collocates closely with 'beautiful'. Although seven of the thirty-eight collocations between these terms in our geoparsed dataset are references to Edmund Burke's *Enquiry* (1757), in the remaining instances the sublime and beautiful are treated synonymously. An imagined visit to the same waterfall that Coleridge had admired is a case in point: in J. Gordon Phillips's historical novel, *Cora Linn*, the hero-hermit

Kentigern exclaims: 'How beautiful … how grand, how sublime! Glorious Clyde, what river can equal thee?'[24] For this novel's narrator, though, the river's sublimity derives from more than just its appearance: if Kentigern 'could have looked down the centuries and seen the huge leviathans of the deep floating in the stream that rushes from the Lanark Hills; if he could have heard, if only for a minute, the rush and the roar and the swirl of human life which that stream has been the means of creating upon its banks – could he have seen that, he would have stood in awe, though he might perhaps have loved it less' (174). For the narrator, the immense changes to the region that have occurred over time – not least the massive increase in human population that transformed the river – are equally as sublime as any static sight. Time, for this narrator, as for writers across our corpora, has the potential to be as sublime as space. Nevertheless, the locations with which the sublime co-occurs perhaps indicate the most cohesive understanding of what 'sublime' was understood to mean in this period.

Mapping the Sublime at the End of the Nineteenth Century

Of the 8,213 instances of 'sublime' in the 1890s sub-corpus, just 370 (or 4.5%) occur within ten words of a place name (see Figure 18.1). This low figure suggests that, by the 1890s, the sublime had become a concept that was only loosely related to geography: 234 of these 370 PNCs for 'sublime' (63.2%) refer to entire countries or continents, rather than to particular landmarks. Where the sublime is used directly to describe a place, it is often as a hyperbole: several locations, including the Aberglaslyn Pass in north

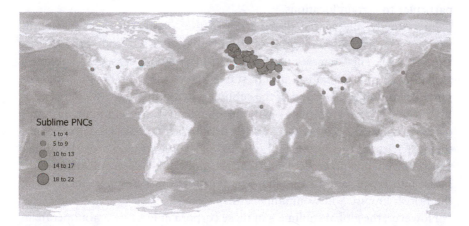

Figure 18.1 Place name collocates for 'sublime', where 'sublime' occurs within ten words of a place name, in the 1890s selection from the British Library's Nineteenth-Century Books Corpus.

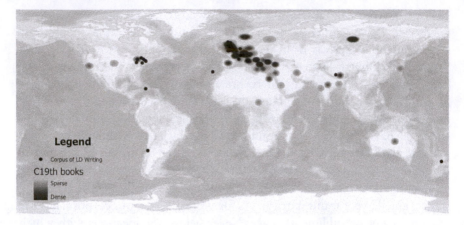

Figure 18.2 Point data for 'sublime' PNCs in the Corpus of Lake District Writing, compared with heat map data for the PNCs for 'sublime' from the Nineteenth-Century Books Corpus.

Wales and the Naero Fjord in Norway, are claimed as being among the most sublime sights in Europe. This phenomena complements a pattern noticed at the smaller scale of the Corpus of Lake District Writing (CLDW). Here, locations across the Lake District were declared to be 'sublime', yet the word was used most often as a way of describing locations where the mountains seemed to coalesce into what one writer called 'sublime confusion'.[25] In both corpora, a diffuse geographical footprint underscores a problem with the term: that nineteenth-century writers were not always – in fact, were not often – very specific about its usage. By the end of the nineteenth century, the sublime served as an intensifier of experience, rather than an aesthetic particular to certain locations.

Interestingly, the spatial distribution of the sublime in the Nineteenth-Century Books Corpus correlates with that seen in the CLDW (see Figure 18.2). This suggests that, for British writers at least, the sublime's global geography remained largely stable across the century. In both corpora, Britain is the heartland of the sublime – it accounts for 15.4 per cent of PNCs in the 1890s corpus – but the global PNCs also mimic Britain's overseas concerns: they echo a trade corridor leading across Europe, into the near East via the Suez Canal (opened in 1869), and towards the Indian subcontinent. It is no coincidence that the global PNCs – from Australia to India, into Egypt, and to Canada – map closely onto countries included in the British Empire and Commonwealth.

However, the global sublime – in these corpora at least – do not operate in the same way as the picturesque did. Mary-Anne Stevens has demonstrated that, in the early nineteenth century, the picturesque had played a significant role in encouraging British travellers to document unfamiliar places, but global references to the sublime tended instead to reinforce British centrality.[26] In both the CLDW and the 1890s sub-corpus, global PNCs often indicate comparisons for domestic features in ways that situate Britain's comparatively modest sights alongside significant international phenomena. In the CLDW, for instance, John Robinson finds that the cataract at Lodore in the northern Lake District 'presents a singularly harmonious assemblage of the sublime and beautiful', making it 'the Niagara of Derwentwater', while the clergyman Samuel Barber optimistically compared the Lakeland fells with the Andes and the Himalayas:

> These characteristics belong more or less to every mountain, from the glorious peaks of the Andes and Himalayas to the fern-clad slopes and mossy peaks of our own varied Lake district. The sublime aspects of every mountain range, the world over, speak to the human race like an abiding voice with an ever-enduring lesson, to tell the vastness of the Divine plan, the perfection of the Divine architecture and the insignificance of man.[27]

In this version of the sublime, what Robert Macfarlane, drawing on Gerard Manley Hopkins, calls the 'mountains of the mind' matter much more than the physical terrain. The sublime, here, encapsulates a sense of human insignificance in the face of environmental and spiritual vastness – and the experience is comparable whether the viewer is at the foot of the Andes, the Himalayas, or in the Lake District. Barber's hyperbolic comparisons emphasize his feeling that a sublime sense of individual insignificance in the face of natural phenomena could be found as much at home as anywhere else. The sublime, Barber implies, is in the eye of the beholder.

Barber was by no means alone in comparing British mountains to their global counterparts. Just as the Lake District fells were popularly known as 'the British Alps', so were the Highlands referred to – after Byron – as the 'Caledonian Alps'.[28] However, one local poet, Robert Ford, admitted that these mountains 'are nought to the towering height / Of the Himalayahs sublime; / Nor can they compare with the hoary Alps / We saw in the Switzer's clime.'[29] Nevertheless, for this poet their association with his earliest memories means that these mountains, though less physically impressive, possess as much sublimity as any of their loftier cousins. Similarly, one traveller to Yorkshire writes that a visitor 'will not here find the weird wildness of the grim fiords and defiles of Norway, or the sublime grandeur of the Alps of Switzerland, Savoy, and the Tyrol', but will still find themselves surrounded by pleasant scenery.[30]

In fact, of the seven references to the Alps in the Nineteenth-Century Books sub-corpus, three refer to the Highlands, and another sees the Poet Laureate

George Meredith suggest that Britain contains more sublime sights than the Alps. Only one of these PNCs refers directly to the Alps: James Smith, in his *Pilgrimage to Italy* (1899), exclaims that 'not while I live shall I forget the sublime grandeur of the Alps, the soft beauty of the lakes, the weird skirting or crossing of yawning chasms, the sombre threading of the many tortuous and pitch-dark tunnels, or the stirring sight of the sky-piercing and snow-capt peaks'.[31] Unlike his fictional compatriot in Baring-Gould's novel, Smith is able to determine precisely what makes the Alps sublime: the deep chasms, high peaks, and the terrifying yet invigorating experience of navigating both impress his imagination with a sense of sublime awe. Yet, even here, Smith understands the sublime predominantly as a means of intensifying his description of the overwhelming grandeur to which he bore witness.

As these examples indicate, then, in this corpus the sublime's apparently global geography is more usually thanks to descriptions of British scenery, which borrows the fabled sublimity of faraway places to enhance the domestic landscape, than to the aesthetic's global exportation. Another way in which reading these maps requires some caution was anticipated by what we have seen with the collocates of 'sublime': not all the PNCs refer directly to location. Istanbul, for instance, appears as a significant location largely because it was the location of the Sublime Porte. PNCs for 'sublime' across the Ottoman Empire territories ceded during the 1870s – Austria, Bulgaria, Montenegro, Persia, Turkey, and Russia – all refer to imperial administration, rather than to the sublime as an aesthetic, apart from one, which describes Russia as a country of 'sublime sadness'.[32] One example that maps to Jerusalem proves the necessity of combining a distant reading with close attention to individual sources. A mention of the sublime in a reprint of Robert Smith Surtees's popular novel *Handley Cross; or, Mr. Jorrocks's Hunt* (1854, reprinted 1892) erroneously maps to Jerusalem because the eponymous hero wears a 'grand order of Jerusalem' – a gold and enamel collar modelled after the lord mayor's – to signify his presidency of the Sublime Society.[33] When Jorrocks finds himself in legal trouble, his associate, Bill Bowker, explains the Sublime Society's rules to the judge: 'Fundamental rules of the "Sublime Society" are, that members eat nothing but chops and Welsh rabbits; drink nothing but port wine, porter, or punch, and never take offence at what each other say or do' (500). In addition to this sublime quantity of alcohol, other rules include that 'no member shall be considered drunk or liable to the pains and penalties contingent upon intoxication, if he can lie without holding' – that is, if he can lie down without holding on to the floor (502).

Surtees's tale is slyly indicative of the globalization of the sublime imaginary throughout the Victorian period. This PNC, for instance, is part of a small yet notable cluster – comprising three PNCs at Jerusalem and one each at Mecca and Cairo – suggestive of the new influence of Near Eastern travel on the sublime. Simon Coleman has explained that the so-called 'Holy Land loomed large in the Victorian imagination'; a boom in travel literature to the region in the 1830s was followed by the opening of the Suez Canal in 1869, and the establishment of the British Protectorate of Egypt in 1882.[34] By this latter date, over 5,000 people had travelled with Thomas Cook's package tours of the Near East, and the area had become a crucial bridge – politically and economically, as well as geographically – to the Indian sub-continent. As Coleman also argues, thanks to its deep religious histories (and the fact that it was the closest place to Britain where Christianity was not the dominant faith), this region 'occupied a liminal position in Western thought, between the known and the unknown'.[35]

How that liminal positionality contributes to the sublime at the end of the nineteenth century is, perhaps, clearest with the PNC at Mecca. This example derives from H. F. Fairbanks's influential travel narrative, *A Visit to Europe and the Holy Land* – but the reference is not to Mecca itself. Rather, Fairbanks notes that the Lake District of Killarney, in the southwest of Ireland, has 'not inaptly been entitled "the Mecca of every pilgrim in search of the sublime and beautiful in nature"'.[36] In Fairbanks's view, the 'craggy rocks and silver islands', coupled with the 'green, blue, and purple mountains' found both 'near at hand and stretching away in the distance,' create at Killarney 'the mountain Paradise of the West' (457). Fairbanks's comparison of Killarney with Mecca puts one in mind of Samuel Barber's description of Helvellyn. Both appeal to 'sublime' in order to transcend local reference points. It indicates, too, a sense that this western landscape might be as unfamiliar and unknowable as the Holy Land itself will prove. What makes it so is the sense that the mountains stretch away out of knowledge, becoming something bigger than an individual can comfortably comprehend.

Conclusion

One trait links these multifarious uses of the 'sublime': in each, whether describing scenery or alcohol intake, the sublime indicates a sense of indescribable excess. One fin-de-siècle novelist, Alfred Henry Wall, neatly summarizes what the sublime had become by this period: 'in vastness, whatsoever its nature, there dwells sublimity'.[37] Wall encapsulates what we have seen throughout this chapter: that, by the 1890s, the sublime no longer relied on geographical specificity, but had instead become an intensifier: a word for labelling any experience or phenomena that defied description. Using a massive corpus of texts helps us to replicate something of this quality of the sublime: through it, we have charted the major uses of, and locations for, the sublime in the final decade of the nineteenth century. There are, undoubtedly, limitations to this approach. Another study might, for instance, identify PNCs based not on the syntactical relationships on which we rely here but on semantic connections that might allow different conclusions to be drawn from the same datasets. In time, moreover, it may be possible to conduct a more comprehensive analysis of the use of the word 'sublime' in the entire British Library Nineteenth-Century Books corpus. For now, though, the patterns we have traced prove how digital methods can aid us in mapping what, to return to Borges, we might call the afterlives of metaphors.

NOTES

1 Jorge Luis Borges, *This Craft of Verse*, Cambridge, MA, Harvard University Press, 2000, 22.

2 Leopoldo Lugones, *Lunario sentimental*, Buenos Aires, Moen, 1909, 6: 'una metáfora cada vocablo'.

3 Friedrich Ritschl, *Opuscula philologica*, 5 vols., Leipzig, Teubner, 1866–79, vol. 2 (1868), 462–9.

4 'sublime, adj. and n.', *Oxford English Dictionary*, www.oed.com (accessed 25 January 2022).

5 Sabine Baring-Gould, *The Pennycomequicks*, London, Spencer Blackett & Hallam, 1889, vol. 3, 51.

6 See Ann Colley, *Victorians in the Mountains: Sinking the Sublime*, Farnham, Ashgate, 2010, 1.

7 See Christopher Donaldson, Ian N. Gregory, and Joanna E. Taylor, 'Locating the Beautiful, Picturesque, Sublime and Majestic: Spatially Analysing the Application of Aesthetic Terminology in Descriptions of the English Lake District', *Journal of Historical Geography* 56, 2017, 43–60.

8 British Library, 'Digitised Printed Books', www.bl.uk/collection-guides/digitised-printed-books# (accessed 7 December 2021).

9 See Matthew Coole, Paul Rayson, and John Mariani, 'LexiDB: Patterns & Methods for Corpus Linguistic Database Management', *Proceedings of the 12th Language Resources and Evaluation Conference*, Paris, European Language Resources Association, 2020, 3128–35.

10 See, for example, Senja Adolphs, *Introducing Electronic Text Analysis*, London, Routledge, 2006; and Tony McEnery and Andrew Hardie, *Corpus Linguistics*, Cambridge, Cambridge University Press, 2011.

11 See, for example, Paul Bolstad, *GIS Fundamentals: A First Text on Geographic Information Systems*, 6th edition, Ann Arbor, MI, XanEdu, 2019; and Ian Heywood, Sarah Cornelius, and Steve Carver, *An Introduction to Geographical Information Systems*, 4th edition, Harlow, Prentice Hall, 2011.

12 Geonames (www.geonames.org/) provides a good example of a gazetteer. See also Humphrey Southall, Ruth Mostern, and Merrick Lex Berman, 'On Historical Gazetteers', *International Journal of Humanities and Arts Computing*, 5, 2011, 127–45; Claire Grover, Richard Tobin, Kate Byrne, Matthew Woollard, James Reid, Stuart Dunn, and Julian Ball, 'Use of the Edinburgh Geoparser for Georeferencing Digitized Historical Collections', *Philosophical Transactions of the Royal Society*, 368, 2010, 3875–89.

13 See C. J. Rupp, Paul Rayson, Ian N. Gregory, Andrew Hardie, Amelia Joulain, and Daniel Hartmann, 'Dealing with Heterogeneous Big Data When Geoparsing Historical Corpora', *Proceedings of the 2014 IEEE Conference on Big Data*, Washington, DC, IEEE, 2014, 80–3.

14 For more examples of GTA in action, see Catherine Porter, Paul Atkinson, and Ian Gregory, 'Geographical Text Analysis: A New Key to Nineteenth-Century Mortality', *Health and Place* 36, 2015, 25–34; Laura Paterson and Ian N. Gregory, *Representations of Poverty and Place*, Basingstoke, Palgrave, 2019; and Joanna E. Taylor and Ian N. Gregory, *Deep Mapping the Literary Lake District: A Geographical Text Analysis*, Lewisburg, PA, Bucknell University Press, 2022.

15 Hezekiah Butterworth, *Zigzag Journeys in Australia*, Boston, Estes & Lauriat, 1891, 299; Alphonsus W. Webster, *Fragments of Coloured Glass: Poems and Ballads, Historical, Religious, Australian and Miscellaneous*, London, Digby, 1894, 203.

16 Roden Berkeley Wriothesley Noël, *Livingstone in Africa*, London, Sampson Low, Marston, Low and Searle, 1874, 101.

17 See Katie Roscoe, 'Radical Changes: Decolonising, Not Just Diversifying, Digital Crime Archives', *Journal of Victorian Culture Digital Forum*, 27, 1, January 2022, 167–73. Attempts to address such biases are ongoing: see, for example, Maryam Bahojb Imani, Swarup Chandra, Samuel Ma, Latifur Khan, and Bhavani Thuraisingham, 'Focus Location Extraction from Political News Reports with Bias Correction', *IEEE International Conference on Big Data (Big Data)*, Paris, IEEE, 2017, 1956–64.

18 Rachel Finnegan, *English Explorers in the East (1738–1745): The Travels of Thomas Shaw*, Leiden, Brill, 2019, 18.

19 'Origin of a World-Wide Saying', *The Blackburn Standard & Weekly Express*, 7 November 1891, 7.

20 Arthur Campbell, *A Ride in Morocco, and Other Sketches*, Toronto, W. Briggs, 1897, 109.

21 Dorothy Quillinan, *Journal of a Few Months' Residence in Portugal and Glimpses of the South of Spain*, ed. E. Lee, London, Longman, 1895, 94.

22 Dorothy Wordsworth, *Recollections of a Tour Made in Scotland*, ed. J. C. Sharp, Edinburgh, James Thin, 1874, 37.

23 Donaldson et al., 'Locating the Beautiful, Picturesque', 44.

24 J. Gordon Phillips, *Cora Linn: A Romance of the Clyde*, Paisley, A. Gardner, 1895, 174.

25 Charles Mackay, *The Scenery and Poetry of the English Lakes*, London, 1846, 97.

26 Mary-Anne Stevens, 'Western Art and Its Encounter with the Islamic World 1798–1914', in Mary-Anne Stevens, ed., *The Orientalists: Delacroix to Matisse. European Painters in North Africa and the Near East*, London, Royal Academy of Arts, 1984, 15–23 (16).

27 Samuel Barber, *Beneath Helvellyn's Shade*, London, Elliot Stock, 1892, 159.

28 Byron coins the phrase in a footnote to the title of his 1807 poem 'Lachin y Gair'.

29 Robert Ford, *The Harp of Perthshire*, Paisley, A. Gardner, 1893, 233.

30 William Wheater, *Handbook for Tourists in Yorkshire*, Leeds, R Jackson 1891, 408.

31 James Smith, *A Pilgrimage to Italy*, Aberdeen, John Avery & Co., 1899, 494.

32 Joyce Emmerson Preston-Muddock, *For God and the Czar! A Tale*, London, George Newnes, 1892, 12.

33 Robert Smith Surtees, *Handley Cross; or, Mr. Jorrocks's Hunt*, London, Bradbury & Evans, 1854, 501.

34 Simon Coleman, 'From the Sublime to the Meticulous: Art, Anthropology and Victorian Ppilgrimage to Palestine', *History and Anthropology* 13, 4, 2002, 275–90 (275).

35 Ibid.

36 H. F. Fairbanks, *A Visit to Europe and the Holy Land*, 4th edition, New York: Benziger Brothers, 1896, 457.

37 Alfred Henry Wall, *A Princess of Chalco*, London, Chapman & Hall, 1892, 16.

19

TESS SOMERVELL

The Romantic Sublime and Environmental Crisis

The current environmental crisis is a product of the Romantic period in several ways. Not only does it have geophysical and social roots in eighteenth- and early nineteenth-century Europe, but its cultural mediation has a significant Romantic heritage too. One of the major aesthetic and philosophical frameworks that has been used to represent and think about the environmental crisis is the sublime. A sublime aesthetic has been used in representations of and responses to natural disasters, climate change, pollution, biodiversity loss, and other attributes of what is often called the Anthropocene, the new proposed epoch of geologic history characterized by massive human impacts on Earth systems. The sublime is present in media about the environmental crisis including art, literature, film, television, news reporting, advertising, environmentalist campaigning, and critical theory. It is used to present both the forms of nature that we should cherish and the forms of nature that we should shrink from. We value and are therefore more likely to protect particular landscapes and creatures because they inspire a sense of sublimity; at the same time, the danger of the environmental crisis is most often represented in sublime images or narratives of nature turning on us, in the form of natural disasters like extreme weather events, or through sublime narratives of apocalypse. Both of these tendencies, love and terror, are the two sides of the same sublime coin, not opposing poles but facets of a continuous affective response to the nonhuman world. In the Anthropocene we respond to the nonhuman world as William Wordsworth did in *The Prelude* (1805), 'Fostered alike by beauty and by fear' (Book I, line 306).

But in the twenty-first century, the sublime has been criticized as a framework for thinking about the environment, whether in terms of conservation or catastrophe. Or, to be more specific, a particular conceptualization of the sublime has been criticized, one that is often generalized as 'the Romantic sublime' but is based mainly on Kant's theory of the sublime process, in which awe in the face of nature's power and scale is followed by the transcendence of the human mind, its sense of its own 'superiority over nature' (*COPJ* §28 261). This Kantian sublime has been persistently associated, in academic critiques of the sublime, with Romanticism more widely, and with various Romantic authors, particularly William Wordsworth and Percy Shelley. This version of the sublime may be either impossible or undesirable in the face of environmental crisis. First, it depends on a distance between human and nonhuman that the environmental crisis has shown to be false – humans are intimately entangled with and inseparable from the nonhuman environment. We cannot stand back from the environmental crisis to observe and aestheticize it, because we are in it and of it. Second, a sublime perspective on the environment creates the false impression that we can transcend the crisis that we have created, control its effects, and even solve it through the same technological ingenuity that contributed to the problem in the first place.

Attempts have recently been made to reclaim the sublime for environmentalism, to articulate an eco-sublime that is frequently defined against the so-called Romantic. Attempts have also been made to find alternative forms of Romantic nature writing that do not depend so heavily on the sublime and which therefore might speak more usefully to the current environmental crisis. In other words: defenders of the green credentials of the sublime argue that the sublime does not have to be 'Romantic' (in the sense defined by Kant's 'Analytic'), while defenders of the green credentials of Romanticism argue that Romanticism does not have to be sublime. But do Romantic-period engagements with the sublime still have a role in helping us to think about the nonhuman world and our relationship to it in a time of crisis?

Valuing Sublime Landscapes

In 1872, an area of land in the Territories of Montana and Wyoming became the United States' first national park (although Bogd Khan Uul in Mongolia claims to have been the world's first, legally preserved from development in 1783). Yellowstone National Park was legally 'dedicated and set apart as a public park or pleasuring-ground for the benefit and enjoyment of the people' and preserved 'from injury or spoliation, of all timber, mineral deposits, natural curiosities, or wonders within said park, and their retention in their natural condition'; also forbidden were 'the wanton destruction of the fish and game found within said park, and ... their capture or destruction for the purposes of merchandise or profit'.[1] A wide cultural interest in the 'wonders' of nature, and a belief that humans benefitted from seeing these wonders in 'their natural condition', enabled the legal protection of landscapes like Yellowstone and the national parks that followed across the world, such as the Royal National Park in Australia, Banff in Canada, Sarek in Sweden, Virunga National Park in the Democratic Republic of the Congo, and the Lake District in England. This interest and belief is traceable directly to Romantic literature and culture, and is sometimes linked specifically to Wordsworth's remark in his *Guide to the Lakes* (1810–35) that visitors of taste to the Lake District 'deem the district a sort of national property, in which every man has a right and interest who has an eye to perceive and a heart to enjoy'.[2] Wordsworth's writings influenced John Muir, nineteenth-century America's most prominent advocate for protecting natural areas, who wrote in *Our National Parks* (1901) of the joys of 'sublime wilderness'.[3] One area protected by the US National Park Service is the Canyon of Lodore, named in 1869 after 'The Cataract of Lodore' (1820), Robert Southey's poem about a waterfall in Cumbria. The national park movement is one of the clearest examples of the influence of Romantic-period engagements with the sublime in shaping modern environmental conservation. This preference for particular kinds of landscape permeates environmental media too. The grand vistas of the conventional nature documentary, for example, which locate the implied human observer at a distance from a pristine nonhuman world, are another inheritance of those same Romantic engagements with the sublime.

Thanks to the Romantic celebration of sublime landscapes, the world has a significant legal precedent for the preservation of natural spaces 'from injury or spoliation'. But in the late twentieth and early twenty-first century this emphasis in conservation on sublime natural 'wonders' and spectacular landscapes has been questioned. William Cronon's influential 1996 essay 'The Trouble with Wilderness: Or, Getting Back to the Wrong Nature' complained of the American tendency to 'fetishize sublime places', arguing that the selection of particular areas for protection 'had nothing to do with nature and everything with the cultural traditions of the sublime' inherited from European Romanticism.[4] Furthermore, these places were not really wild at all, but constructed through the forced removal of their indigenous human inhabitants, or in some cases the disturbing dehumanization of those inhabitants. These areas were then further altered by the tourism infrastructure that arose within and around them. Cronon distinguishes this American 'domesticated sublime' from its ancestor, the earlier Romantic sublime of Wordsworth, which, he suggests, entailed fear more than pleasure; but arguably the Romantic poets wrote about false wildernesses too, omitting or sentimentally naturalizing the humans who lived and worked in these landscapes.[5] The Romantic sublime, in this critique, is both obsessed with a fictional and unhelpful ideal of uninhabited nature and also profoundly anthropocentric, concerned with what that uninhabited nature can do for its single, isolated, usually white male human observer. It celebrates a non-human world that is fictional or at best distorted, and then instrumentalizes it, not just for humans but for a small privileged group of humans.

The environmental crisis means that not only the carefully delimited and curated national parks, but even the most plausibly wild places on Earth – the desert, the rainforest, the ocean floor – are not free from human influence. Does this mean that the first stage in the Kantian paradigm of the Romantic sublime – the encounter with 'raw nature' as Kant puts it – is no longer available? (*COPJ* §26 253). In his 2011 lecture 'Waiting for Gaia', Bruno Latour declared that 'the sublime has evaporated', because 'we are no longer taken as those puny humans overpowered by "nature"' and have become instead 'the main geological force shaping the Earth'.[6] (The 'we' here is still, of course, a particular, privileged group: neither all present-day nor historical humans and human societies have contributed, or certainly not equally or with equal agency, to the current environmental crisis, an inequality not always reflected in the blanket use of the term 'Anthropocene'.) Latour looks to Percy Bysshe Shelley to illustrate this lost way of relating to the world: 'how could you still want to feel the sublime while watching the "everlasting" waterfalls sung by Shelley when, one, you simultaneously feel that they might disappear; when, two, you might be responsible for their disappearance'?'[7] Arguably, of course, this is a new version, rather than a rejection, of the Kantian analytic of the sublime, in which human power is ultimately endorsed. But the conventional Romantic sublime depends, as Schiller writes, on cognitive independence from nature rather than 'physical superiority over natural forces': physical power over the object 'weakens or completely destroys the sublimity of the object'.[8] In the Anthropocene, humans achieve not only imaginative transcendence but physical influence over the nonhuman world, a different kind of transcendence than that articulated by Kant or by Shelley in 'Mont Blanc' (1816), from which Latour quotes. In 'Mont Blanc', Shelley may ask what the mountain would be 'If to the human mind's imaginings / Silence and solitude were vacancy', but he is also emphatic that 'the power is there', there in the nonhuman world (lines 143–4, 127).

Romantic ecocriticism has responded to such green critiques of the sublime by seeking other Romantic environments and other kinds of Romantic nature writing. Louise Economides has argued for the importance of 'wonder' as an alternative category in Romanticism, characterized by 'nature's de-centering force' rather than 'qualities associated with the [Kantian] sublime (privation, anthropocentric empowerment, narcissistic identification)'.[9] Rousseauian 'reverie' has been offered as another potentially more ecocentric and sustainable Romantic aesthetic response to nonhuman nature.[10] And whereas William Wordsworth and Henry David Thoreau were the darlings of first-wave ecocriticism in the 1990s, they were overtaken in the twenty-first century by John Clare, with his sensitive, detailed poetry of small things like bird nests, insects, and flowers. In Romantic ecocriticism, the sublime has been displaced by the humble and the local, the lone observer by the community, the mountain by the molehill.

Fearing Sublime Catastrophe

If the Romantic sublime is a questionable tool for encouraging humans to value and protect the nonhuman world, is it better suited to reminding us that nature can be dangerous and terrifying, even or especially when humans have interfered with it? Is there still space for the Romantic sublime in representations of environmental catastrophe? Climate change, for example, gains most public and political attention, at least in privileged countries in the global North, when it manifests in particular extreme weather events like hurricanes, floods, or forest fires. Sublime renderings of such events may help to catalyze personal, public, and political action. This kind of sublime may not appear so obviously Romantic as the wild landscapes that Wordsworth, the Shelleys, Jean-Jacques Rousseau, Giacomo Leopardi, and myriad other Romantic-period writers around Europe actively celebrated. But sublime environmental catastrophes appear frequently in Romantic art and litera-ture, such as in paintings by John Martin, Thomas Cole, J. M. W. Turner, Caspar David Friedrich, and Knud Baade; Wordsworth's dream of the world destroyed by deluge in Book 5 of *The Prelude* (1805); Mary Shelley's plague novel *The Last Man* (1823); and Byron's vision of the sun's death in his poem 'Darkness' (1816), and his Cuvier-inspired, catastrophist vision of earth history in *Cain* (1821). Such representations of environmental catas-trophe have gained increased attention in Romantic ecocriticism, as readers consider the parallels that may be drawn with the current climate crisis.[11]

There are several potential problems with thinking about environmental crisis through Romantic-period formulations of the sublimity of nature's dangerous power. One is that although the sublime object causes fear, it must not pose real danger. Burke's discussion in *Enquiry* I viii is of course the best known of such arguments about the role of vicarious terror in the experience of the sublime. Schiller similarly insists that 'where we actually find ourselves in danger', 'where we ourselves are the object of an inimical natural power, aesthetic judgment is finished. As sublime as a storm at sea may be when viewed from the shore, those who find themselves on the ship devastated by the storm are just as little disposed to pass this aesthetic judgment on it' (29–30). If we truly understand that we are in the storm – that the environmental crisis is here, now, not somewhere else or in the future – then our experience will not be one of sublimity, which requires a certain distance from the sublime object: 'one must neither come too close to them nor be too far away' (*COPJ* §26 136). Sublime mediations, then, might diminish rather than enhance our sense of danger. They create the impression that the crisis is elsewhere. Another related problem is that the sublime might imply that the crisis is under control. Disaster movies and even some news coverage about natural disasters are examples of this mode of the sublime, in which the power of humans to aestheticize catastrophe translates subtly into the power of humans to solve the problem. The intended audience gasps at the destructive power of nature, and perhaps feels a tinge of guilt at their own contribution towards the climate crisis. But they also enjoy the spectacle from a safe distance, comforted that humans are clever enough to capture all this on film and shape it into a satisfying story or neat report; everything is under the artist's control, and therefore humanity's. To confirm this comforting implication, most popular fictional treatments of environmental catastrophe conclude with a technocratic solution or at least some kind of positive narrative resolution. Perhaps the audience enjoys a tinge of virtuousness that they've thought about the climate crisis at all.

As well as potentially unethical and unhelpful, sublime renderings of environmental catastrophe might also give an inaccurate portrait of the larger crisis, presenting it as a phenomenon composed of individual, comprehensible events like floods and oil spills, rather than as a vast process or number of processes, distributed across space and time. The environmental crisis is a form of 'slow violence' rather than a single apocalyptic climax or series of sublime catastrophes.[12] David Collings coins the term 'the melting sublime' to describe the experience of seeing the diminished glaciers near Mont Blanc, but adds that this isn't really sublimity, because 'thanks to climate change' this quintessential scene of the Romantic sublime 'now bristle[s] with implicit references to quotidian functions within the earth's biodynamic systems'.[13] That is, the glacier invites us to calculate human impact on the environment, not in Latour's terms of our huge collective geological force, which might itself be sublime, but in terms of tiny impacts that accumulate. Alpine glaciers – landscapes that Romantic-period engagements with the sublime taught us to love and fear – won't be destroyed by cataclysm – which Romantic-period engagements with the sublime taught us to fear and love – but by complex, continuous, and mostly invisible processes.

Post-Romantic Eco-Sublimes

For some thinkers in the environmental humanities, apparent problems with the sublime are really problems with what they understand to be the 'Romantic sublime', rather than inherent in the sublime itself. There have been several attempts to articulate new sublimes that might recover the advantages of the sublime aesthetic but shake off its perceived shortcomings. The late twentieth and early twenty-first centuries have produced categories including the environmental sublime, ecological sublime, eco-sublime, toxic sublime, nuclear sublime, apocalyptic sublime, technological sublime, hysterical sublime, postmodern sublime, and posthuman sublime. Broadly, attempts to reclaim the sublime for environmentalism take one or both of two related avenues: they argue that the sublime usefully articulates the unknowability of the environment and environmental change, and/or that it usefully shocks us into recognizing our entanglement with and within the vast system of nonhuman nature. These eco-sublimes are frequently defined against the so-called Romantic. In the standard two stages of this 'Romantic' sublime, 'A sublime subject matter gives us in the first place a feeling of our dependency as natural beings, because in the second place it makes us aware of the independence that, as rational beings, we assert over nature.'[14] An eco-sublime must retain the first and discard, or at least radically alter, the second of these stages.

If the dynamical sublime (Kant's term for the sublime inspired by the physically threatening power of nonhuman nature, such as in storms and volcanos) is no longer possible or desirable, as the above critiques suggest, perhaps the incomprehensible complexity of the Anthropocene could be expressed in the mathematical sublime: Kant's term for the sublimity of nature's 'appearances the intuition of which brings with them the idea of its infinity' (*COPJ* §26 255). But if this sublime is not going to lead to Kant's sense of 'our imagination in all its boundlessness' and 'nature ... paling into insignificance beside the ideas of reason', and thus the hubristic notion that we can solve the environmental crisis through our technological ingenuity, then the final stage of transcendence must be omitted (*COPJ* §26 257). The best-known version of this reconstituted mathematical sublime is Timothy Morton's theory of hyperobjects, 'things that are massively distributed in time and space relative to humans' including the biosphere and global warming.[15] Although he explicitly draws on Kant's theory of the sublime to help articulate the hyperobject, Morton claims that confronting the hyperobject destroys that second stage of transcendence: 'When hyperobjects are fully exposed to human being, the power and freedom of the Romantic sublime inverts itself into contemporary lameness.'[16]

The 'postmodern sublime' offers a potential environmentalist alternative to Kant's mathematical sublime, particularly in its theorization by Jean-François Lyotard.[17] Both the environmental crisis and the environment itself are too complex for humans to comprehend in their entirety, and an environmental sublime must capture this destabilizing recognition without the subsequent Kantian step of re-asserting the human power to comprehend. The Lyotardian sublime emphasizes the differend, the gap between imagination and reason, perception and idea, which the sublime encounter shocks us into recognizing but does not then resolve. Sensory perception and the objects that create it are not subsumed by a more powerful reason in this sublime, but remain as troubling contradictions to reason. It is easy to see why scholars in the environmental humanities have turned to the Lyotardian sublime to find a post-Romantic alternative for the Anthropocene.[18] We cannot grasp or comprehend nature, but neither can we forget it or pretend to be independent of it.

The hope is not only that the postmodern sublime appropriately expresses the unknowability and unrepresentability of the environment and the environmental crisis, but that this aesthetic might open the way to a posthumanist ethic of human-nonhuman respectful reciprocity. Such a sublime would not depend on the human-nature binary, as Kant's does, but would reveal our participation in a mesh of human-nonhuman interconnection. Nature would be allowed to retain its otherness, but our powerful affective response to it entailed in the experience of the sublime would become a symptom and reminder of our ecological embeddedness.

A Romantic Eco-Sublime

Eco-sublimes are almost always framed in opposition to the egocentric Kantian sublime. But could they still be Romantic? Critics such as Christopher Hitt, Emily Brady, and Byron Williston have defended the environmentalist credentials not just of the sublime but of Romantic-period engagements with (and even the Kantian analytic of) the sublime.[19] They remind us that Romantic-period encounters with the sublime frequently retain a sense of humility, of nature's centrality to the experience, and of moral agency and responsibility. Many cultural critics still draw on Romantic philosophy and literature of the sublime in order to illustrate what an eco-sublime can offer. Morton, though sceptical of the Kantian sublime because it requires a distance from the object that is not possible now that we are inside the environmental crisis, repeatedly quotes Romantic poetry in order to articulate his theory of hyperobjects: the hyperobject is like the mountain looming after Wordsworth in the boat-stealing episode in Book

1 of *The Prelude*; it is like Shelley's Mont Blanc, 'The awful shadow of some unseen power'.[20] When Frances Ferguson developed her theory of the 'nuclear sublime' in 1984, she used *Frankenstein* (1818) to articulate a sublime that could enable us to 'think the unthinkable and to exist in one's own nonexistence'.[21] Ferguson shows how useful it can be to think with Romantic literature, even when theorizing 'new' sublimes for the Anthropocene.

Any effective environmental aesthetic, including an eco-sublime, must somehow acknowledge both nature's unknowable otherness and our inseparable entanglement with it; must display the urgent danger of the environmental crisis but also its slow, disturbing banality; must reveal our responsibility towards, but not our power over, nature. Romantic-period engagements with the sublime might help us to think through these paradoxes. Wordsworth's 'Lines Composed a Few Miles above Tintern Abbey' (1798), for example, describes several different kinds of sublime, subtly distinguished. First is the youthful sublime in which 'nature ... To me was all in all', and waterfalls, mountains, and woods inspire 'dizzy raptures' (lines 76–86). This naïve sublime, a capitulation to sense without thought, has been lost in adulthood, but was 'followed' by something more paradoxical and ethical (line 88). Wordsworth uses the adjective 'sublime' for this latter experience (line 96). Now he has 'elevated thoughts' inspired by nature, but these are not of human superiority; they are 'a sense sublime / Of something far more deeply interfused' (lines 96–7). This is a sublime that binds human and nonhuman, not in animal 'appetite' but in 'moral being' (lines 81, 112). The nonhuman world has been infused with the 'still sad music of humanity', with the word 'humanity' working in both its moral and species senses (line 92). This sublime 'something' dwells in sunlight, ocean, air, sky, 'and in the mind of man': this sublimity is a quality of both the observer and the observed, and closes rather than opens the gap between 'thinking things' and 'objects of ... thought' (lines 97–100, 102). This sublime is able to 'chasten and subdue' but also 'disturb' with 'joy' (lines 94–5). 'Tintern Abbey' by no means resolves all the potential environmentalist concerns with the Romantic sublime. It is perhaps too egocentric, too reposeful, and too optimistic that human-nonhuman interactions will be harmonious, to serve as a poem for the environmental crisis. But it does demonstrate the complexity of engagements with the sublime during the Romantic period and the capacity of those engagements to relate to the environment in multiple ways. It expresses both a longing for and a slight dissatisfaction with a sublime that is emptied of complicating ethics, and a recognition that a more challenging sublime has the potential to reveal our ecological interfusion with our nonhuman environments, although the revelation is both joyful and disturbing. The paradoxes of the eco-sublime are postmodern, but they are also Romantic.

The sublime aesthetic has shaped the global response to our environmental crisis, influencing both conservation efforts to protect nature and influential representations of the dangers we face. Whether we collectively embrace the sublime or reject it, or whether and how we adapt the sublime for the Anthropocene, is a matter of life and death. Scholars of Romantic literature, art, and philosophy, whose subjects of study explored the sublime and its environmental implications in depth and detail, are well placed to contribute to the ongoing discussion of the role of the sublime in the environmental crisis.

NOTES

1 Congress of the United States of America, 'An Act to Set Apart a Certain Tract of Land Lying Near the Headwaters of the Yellowstone River as a Public Park', National Park Service, www.nps.gov/yell/learn/management/yellowstoneprotectionact1872.htm, n.p.

2 William Wordsworth, *A Guide through the District of the Lakes*, 5th edition, Kendal, 1835, 88.

3 John Muir, *Our National Parks*, San Francisco, CA, Sierra Club Books, 1991, 226.

4 William Cronon, 'The Trouble with Wilderness: Or, Getting Back to the Wrong Nature', *Environmental History* 1, 1, 1996, 7–28 (22).

5 Ibid., 11.

6 Bruno Latour, 'Waiting for Gaia: Composing the Common World through Arts and Politics', 2011, www.bruno-latour.fr/sites/default/files/124-GAIA-LONDON-SPEAP_0.pdf (3).

7 Ibid., 4.

8 Friedrich Schiller, 'On the Sublime (Toward the Further Development of Some Kantian Ideas)', trans. Daniel O. Dahlstrom, in *Essays*, ed. Walter Hinderer and Daniel O. Dahlstrom, New York, Continuum, 2005, 22–44 (29).

9 Louise Economides, *The Ecology of Wonder in Romantic and Postmodern Literature*, Basingstoke, Palgrave Macmillan, 2016, 52.

10 See, for example, Joseph H. Lane, Jr., 'Reverie and the Return to Nature: Rousseau's Experience of Convergence', *The Review of Politics* 68, 2006, 474–99; and David E. Cooper, 'Nature, Aesthetic Engagement, and Reverie', *The Nordic Journal of Aesthetics* 18, 2006, 96–106.

11 See, for example, David Higgins, *British Romanticism, Climate Change, and the Anthropocene: Writing Tambora*, Basingstoke, Palgrave Macmillan, 2017; and Anne Collett and Olivia Murphy, eds., *Romantic Climates: Literature and Science in an Age of Catastrophe*, Basingstoke, Palgrave Macmillan, 2019.

12 Rob Nixon, *Slow Violence and the Environmentalism of the Poor*, Cambridge, MA, Harvard University Press, 2011.

13 David Collings, *Disastrous Subjectivities: Romanticism, Modernity, and the Real*, Toronto, University of Toronto Press, 2019, 174.

14 Schiller, 'On the Sublime', 22.
15 Timothy Morton, *Hyperobjects: Philosophy and Ecology after the End of the World*, Minneapolis, University of Minnesota Press, 2013, 1.
16 Ibid., 196.
17 Jean-François Lyotard, *Leçons sur l'analytique du sublime*, Paris, Galilée, 1991.
18 See, for example, Maggie Kainulainen, 'Saying Climate Change', *symplokē* 21, 2013, 109–23; and Jana María Giles, 'Can the Sublime Be Postcolonial? Aesthetics, Politics, and Environment in Amitav Ghosh's *The Hungry Tide*', *Cambridge Journal of Postcolonial Literary Inquiry* 1, 2, 2014, 223–42.
19 See Christopher Hitt, 'Toward an Ecological Sublime', *New Literary History* 30, 3, 1999, 603–23; Emily Brady, 'The Environmental Sublime', in Timothy M. Costelloe, ed., *The Sublime: From Antiquity to the Present*, Cambridge, Cambridge University Press, 2012, 171–82; and Byron Williston, 'The Sublime Anthropocene', *Environmental Philosophy* 13, 2, 2016, 155–74.
20 Morton, *Hyperobjects*, 51, 72.
21 Ferguson, 'The Nuclear Sublime', *Diacritics* 14, 2, 1984, 4–10 (7).

FURTHER READING

The increasing prospects tire our wandering eyes,

Hills peep o'er hills, and Alps on Alps arise!
    —Alexander Pope, *Essay on Criticism* (1711), lines 231-2

Alexander Pope's well-known use of the Alps as a metaphor for the unattainable horizon of knowledge is an especially apt figure for the task of compiling a bibliography, even a highly selective bibliography, of scholarly studies of the place of the sublime in the cultural history of the eighteenth century and Romantic period in Europe and America. The sheer volume of such scholarship, which crosses the boundaries of genre, language and national traditions, is almost itself, to adapt another well-known aphorism from Pope's *Essay on Criticism*, that great sublime it draws. With those caveats in mind, the following list should be considered only broadly representative of historical and recent trends in scholarship, comprising general surveys as well as studies of specific authors, themes and types of sublimity. Primarily Anglophone scholarship has been included, although a range of national traditions and cultural contexts are covered.

General Studies, Histories and Anthologies

Albrecht, William, *The Sublime Pleasures of Tragedy: A Study of Critical Theory from Dennis to Keats*, Lawrence, University of Kansas Press, 1975.

Ashfield, Andrew, and Peter De Bolla (eds.), *The Sublime: A Reader in British Eighteenth-Century Aesthetic Theory*, Cambridge, Cambridge University Press, 1996.

Axelson, Karl, *The Sublime: Precursors and British Eighteenth-Century Conceptions*, Oxford, Peter Lang, 2007.

Bevis, R. W., *The Road to Egdon Heath: The Aesthetics of the Great in Nature*, Montreal, McGill-Queen's University Press, 1999.

Bloom, Harold, *The Daemon Knows: Literary Greatness and the American Sublime*, Oxford, Oxford University Press, 2015.

Brady, Emily, *The Sublime in Modern Philosophy: Aesthetics, Ethics, and Nature*, Cambridge, Cambridge University Press, 2013.

Brillenburg Wurth, Kiene, *Musically Sublime: Indeterminacy, Infinity, Irresolvability*, New York, Fordham University Press, 2009.

Brown, Chandos Michael, 'The First American Sublime', in Timothy M. Costelloe, ed., *The Sublime: From Antiquity to the Present*, Cambridge, Cambridge University Press, 2015, 147–70.

Burgard, Chrystèle, and Baldine Saint Girons (eds.), *Le paysage et la question du sublime*, Paris, Réunion des musées nationaux, 1997.

Canuel, Mark, *Justice, Dissent, and the Sublime*, Baltimore, MD, Johns Hopkins University Press, 2012.

Carboni, Massimo, *Il sublime è ora: Saggio sulle estetiche contemporanee*, Rome, Castelvecchi, 1993.

Clewis, Robert (ed.), *The Sublime Reader*, London, Bloomsbury, 2018.

Costelloe, Timothy M. (ed.), *The Sublime: From Antiquity to the Present*, Cambridge, Cambridge University Press, 2015.

De Bolla, Peter, *The Discourse of the Sublime: Readings in History, Aesthetics and the Subject*, Oxford, Blackwell, 1989.

Donaldson, Christopher, Ian N. Gregory and Joanna E. Taylor, 'Locating the Beautiful, Picturesque, Sublime and Majestic: Spatially Analysing the Application of Aesthetic Terminology in Descriptions of the English Lake District', *Journal of Historical Geography* 56, 2017, 43–60.

Doran, Robert, *The Theory of the Sublime from Longinus to Kant*, Cambridge, Cambridge University Press, 2015.

Duffy, Cian, *The Landscapes of the Sublime, 1700–1830: 'Classic Ground'*, London, Palgrave, 2013.

'The Romantic Sublime', in Patrick Vincent, ed., *The Cambridge History of European Romantic Literature*, Cambridge, Cambridge University Press, forthcoming.

Duffy, Cian, and Peter Howell (eds.), *Cultures of the Sublime: Selected Readings, 1700–1830*, London, Palgrave, 2011.

Ferguson, Frances, *Solitude and the Sublime: Romanticism and the Aesthetics of Individuation*, London, Routledge, 1992.

Freeman, Barbara, *The Feminine Sublime: Gender and Excess in Women's Fiction*, Berkeley, University of California Press, 1995.

Fry, Paul, 'The Possession of the Sublime', *Studies in Romanticism* 26.2, 1987, 187–207.

Giacomoni, Paola, *Il laboratorio della natura: Paesaggio montano e sublime naturale in età moderna*, Milan, Franco Angeli, 2001.

Gottlieb, Marc, 'Figures of Sublimity in Orientalist Painting', *Studies in the History of Art* 74, 2009, 316–41.

Hancock, Stephen, *The Romantic Sublime and Middle-Class Subjectivity in the Victorian Novel*, London, Routledge, 2005.

Hertz, Neil, *The End of the Line: Essays on Psychoanalysis and the Sublime*, New York, Columbia University Press, 1985.

Hibberd, Sarah, and Miranda Stanyon (eds.), *Music and the Sonorous Sublime in European Culture, 1680–1880*, Cambridge, Cambridge University Press, 2020.

Hipple, Walter John, *The Beautiful, the Sublime, and the Picturesque in Eighteenth-Century British Aesthetic Theory*, Carbondale, Southern Illinois University Press, 1959.

Hollis, D. L. 'Aesthetic Experience, Investigation and Classic Ground: Responses to Etna from the First Century CE to 1773', *Journal of the Warburg and Courtauld Institutes*, 83, 2020, 299–325.

'The "Authority of the Ancients"? Seventeenth-Century Natural Philosophy and Aesthetic Responses to Mountains', in Dawn Hollis and Jason König, eds., *Mountain Dialogues from Antiquity to Modernity*, London, Bloomsbury Academic, 2021, 55–73.

'Mountain Gloom and Mountain Glory: The Genealogy of an Idea', *ISLE: Interdisciplinary Studies in Literature and Environment*, 26.4, 2019, 1038–61.

Ibata, Hélène, *The Challenge of the Sublime: from Burke's Philosophical Enquiry to British Romantic Art*, Manchester, Manchester University Press, 2018.

Knapp, Stephen, *Personification and the Sublime: Milton to Coleridge*, Cambridge, MA, Harvard University Press, 1985.

Le Scanff, Yvon, *Le paysage romantique et l'expérience du sublime*, Seyssel, Champs Vallon, 2017.

Lombardo, Giovanni, *Tra poesia e physiologia: Il sublime e la scienza della natura*, Modena, Mucchi, 2011.

Lombardo, Giovanni, and Francesco Finocchiaro (eds.), *Sublime antico e moderno: Una bibliografia*, Palermo, Centro internazionale di studi di estetica, 1993.

Maxwell, Catherine, *The Female Sublime from Milton to Swinburne: Bearing Blindness*, Manchester, Manchester University Press, 2001.

Mazzocut-Mis, Maddalena, and Pietro Giordanetti (eds.), *I luoghi del sublime moderno: Percorso antologico-critico*, Milano, LED, 2005.

McCarthy, Anne C., *Awful Parenthesis: Suspension and the Sublime in Romantic and Victorian Poetry*, Toronto, University of Toronto Press, 2018.

Monk, Samuel Holt, *The Sublime: A Study of Critical Theories in XVIII-Century England*, Ann Arbor, University of Michigan Press, 1960.

Moreno, Beatriz González, *Lo sublime, lo gótico y lo romántico: La experiencia estética en el romanticismo inglés*, Ciudad Real, Universidad de Castilla La Mancha, 2007.

Nicolson, Marjorie Hope, *Mountain Gloom and Mountain Glory: The Development of the Aesthetics of the Infinite*, Ithaca, NY, Cornell University Press, 1959.

Paley, Morton D, *The Apocalyptic Sublime*, New Haven, CT, Yale University Press, 1986.

Pipkin, John G., 'The Material Sublime of Women Romantic Poets', *Studies in English Literature, 1500–1900* 38.4, Autumn 1998, 597–619.

Porter, James, *The Sublime in Antiquity*, Cambridge, Cambridge University Press, 2016.

Potkay, Adam, 'The British Romantic Sublime', in Timothy M. Costelloe, ed., *The Sublime: From Antiquity to the Present*, Cambridge, Cambridge University Press, 2015, 203–16.

Price, Fiona L., and Scott Masson (eds.), *Silence, Sublimity and Suppression in the Romantic Period*, Lampeter, Edward Mellen Press, 2002.

Richardson, Alan, *The Neural Sublime: Cognitive Theories and Romantic Texts*, Baltimore, MD, Johns Hopkins University Press, 2010.

Saint Girons, Baldine, *Le sublime: De l'antiquité a nos jours*, Paris, Desjonquères, 2005.

Shaw, Philip, *The Sublime*, 2nd edition, London, Routledge, 2017.

Simpson, David, 'Commentary: Updating the Sublime', *Studies in Romanticism* 26.2, 1987, 245–58.

Stanyon, Miranda, *Resounding the Sublime: Music in English and German Literature and Aesthetic Theory, 1670–1850*, Philadelphia, University of Pennsylvania Press, 2021.

Stevenson, Warren, *Romanticism and the Androgynous Sublime*, Madison, NJ, Fairleigh Dickinson University Press, 1996.

Tuveson, Ernest, 'Space, Deity, and the "Natural Sublime"', *Modern Language Quarterly*, 12.1, March 1951, 20–38.

Twitchell, James B., *Romantic Horizons: Aspects of the Sublime in English Poetry and Painting, 1770–1850*, Columbia, University of Missouri Press, 1983.

Viëtor, Karl, 'Die Idee des Erhabenen in der deutschen Literaturgeschichte', in *Geist und Form: Aufsätze zur deutschen Literaturgeschichte*, Bern, Francke, 1952, 234–66.

Weiskel, Thomas, *The Romantic Sublime: Studies in the Structure and Psychology of Transcendence*, Baltimore, MD, Johns Hopkins University Press, 1976.

Wilton, Andrew, and Tim Barringer, *American Sublime: Landscape Painting in the United States, 1820–1880*, Princeton, NJ, Princeton University Press, 2002.

Wood, Theodore, *The Word 'Sublime' and Its Context, 1650–1760*, The Hague, Mouton, 1972.

Individuals

Albrecht, William, 'Hazlitt and the Romantic Sublime', *The Wordsworth Circle* 10.1, 1979, 59–68.

'Tragedy and Wordsworth's Sublime', *The Wordsworth Circle* 8.1, 1977, 83–94.

'The Tragic Sublime of Hazlitt and Keats', *Studies in Romanticism* 20.2, 1981, 185–201.

Bode, Christoph, 'A Kantian Sublime in Shelley: "Respect for our Own Vocation" in an Indifferent Universe', *1650–1850: Ideas, Aesthetics, and Inquiries in the Early Modern Era*, 3, 1997, 329–58.

Brose, Margaret, 'Leopardi's "L'Infinito" and the Language of the Romantic Sublime', *Poetics Today* 4.1, 1983, 47–71.

Clarke, Bruce, 'Wordsworth's Departed Swans: Sublimation and Sublimity in "Home at Grasmere"', *Studies in Romanticism* 19.3, 1980, 355–74.

Clewis, Robert, *The Kantian Sublime and the Revelation of Freedom*, Cambridge, Cambridge University Press, 2009.

Crawford, Joseph, *Raising Milton's Ghost: John Milton and the Sublime of Terror in the Early Romantic Period*, London, Bloomsbury, 2011.

Crowther, Paul, *The Kantian Sublime: From Morality to Art*, Oxford, Clarendon, 1989.

Duffy, Cian, '"My purpose was humbler, but also higher": Thomas De Quincey's "System of the Heavens", popular science and the sublime', *Romanticism* 20.1, 2014, 1–14.

Shelley and the Revolutionary Sublime, Cambridge, Cambridge University Press, 2005.

Ende, Stuart, *Keats and the Sublime*, New Haven, CT, Yale University Press, 1976.

Evans, M., *Sublime Coleridge: The Opus Maximum*, London, Palgrave, 2012.

Ferri, S., 'Vittorio Alfieri's Nature Sublime: The Physiology of Poetic Inspiration', *European Romantic Review* 23.5, 2012, 555–74.

Fulford, Tim, 'The Politics of the Sublime: Coleridge and Wordsworth in Germany', *Modern Language Review* 91.4, October 1996, 817–32.

Furniss, Tom, *Edmund Burke's Aesthetic Ideology: Language, Gender and Political Economy in Revolution*, Cambridge, Cambridge University Press, 2008.

Gaetano, Raffaele, *Giacomo Leopardi e il sublime: Archeologia e percorsi di una idea estetica*, preface by Giovanni Lombardo, Soveria Mannelli, Rubbettino, 2002.

Grave, Johannes, *Caspar David Friedrich und die Theorie des Erhabenen: Friedrichs Eismeer als Antwort auf einen zentralen Begriff der zeitgenössischen Ästhetik*, Weimar, VDG, 2001.

Halliwell, Stephen (ed.), *Pseudo-Longinus: On the Sublime*, Oxford, Oxford University Press, 2022

Hardie, Philip, *Lucretian Receptions*, Cambridge, Cambridge University Press, 2016.

Hinnant, Charles H., 'Schiller and the Political Sublime: Two Perspectives', *Criticism*, 44.2, 2002, 121–38.

Ibata, Hélène, 'William Blake's Visual Sublime: The "Eternal Labours"', *European Romantic Review* 21.1, 2010, 29–48.

Janowitz, Anne, 'Adam Smith's Campaign against the Sublime', *The Wordsworth Circle* 35.1, 2004, 11–16.

Leighton, Angela, *Shelley and the Sublime: An Interpretation of the Major Poems*, Cambridge, Cambridge University Press, 1984.

Meisel, Martin, 'The Material Sublime: John Martin, Bryon and Turner', in *Realizations: Narrative, Pictorial, and Theatrical Arts in Nineteenth-Century England*, Princeton, NJ, Princeton University Press, 2014, 166–88.

Merritt, Melissa M., *The Sublime*, Elements in the Philosophy of Immanuel Kant, Cambridge, Cambridge University Press, 2018.

Modiano, Raimonda, 'Coleridge's Conception of the Sublime', in *Coleridge and the Concept of Nature*, London, Palgrave, 1985, 101–37.

Rzepka, Charles J, *Sacramental Commodities: Gift, Text, and the Sublime in De Quincey*, Amherst, University of Massachusetts Press, 1995.

Ryan, Vanessa L, 'The Physiological Sublime: Burke's Critique of Reason', *Journal of the History of Ideas*, 62.2, 2001, 265–79.

Speitz, Michele, 'The Infrastructural Sublime and Imperial Landscape Aesthetics: Robert Southey, Poet Laureate, and Thomas Telford, Father of Civil Engineering', *European Romantic Review* 32.1, 2021, 41–63.

Stafford, Fiona, *The Sublime Savage: A Study of James Macpherson and the Poems of Ossian*, Edinburgh, Edinburgh University Press, 1988.

Stokes, Christopher, *Coleridge, Language and the Sublime: From Transcendence to Finitude*, London, Palgrave, 2010.

Strickland, Edward, 'John Clare and the Sublime', *Criticism* 29.2, 1987, 141–61.

Veliki, Martina Domines, 'The Capital and the Romantic Sublime: The Case of Thomas De Quincey', *CounterText* 2.1, 2016, 55–65.

Vine, Steve, 'Blake's Material Sublime', *Studies in Romanticism* 41.2, 2002, 237–57.

Wallace, A. D., 'Picturesque Fossils, Sublime Geology? The Crisis of Authority in Charlotte Smith's *Beachy Head*', *European Romantic Review* 13.1, 2002, 77–94.

White, Paul, "Darwin, Concepción, and the Geological Sublime," *Science in Context* 25.1, 2012, 49–71.

Wilson, Eric, *Emerson's Sublime Science*, London, Palgrave, 1999.

Wilton, Andrew, *Turner and the Sublime*, London, British Museum Publications, 1980.

Wlecke, Albert O., *Wordsworth and the Sublime: An Essay of Wordsworth's Imagination*, East Lansing, Michigan State University Press, 1969.

Themes

Altick, Richard, *The Shows of London*, Cambridge MA, Harvard University Press, 1978.

Bainbridge, Simon, *Mountaineering and British Romanticism: The Literary Cultures of Climbing, 1770–1836*, Oxford, Oxford University Press, 2021.

Bohls, Elizabeth, *Women Travel Writers and the Language of Aesthetics, 1716–1818*, Cambridge, Cambridge University Press, 1995.

Bowers, Katherine, 'Haunted Ice, Fearful Sounds, and the Arctic Sublime: Exploring Nineteenth-Century Polar Gothic Space', *Gothic Studies* 19.2, 2017, 71–84.

Brady, Emily, 'The Environmental Sublime', in Timothy M. Costelloe, ed., *The Sublime: From Antiquity to the Present*, Cambridge, Cambridge University Press, 2012, 171–82.

Collett, Anne, and Olivia Murphy (eds.), *Romantic Climates: Literature and Science in an Age of Catastrophe*, Basingstoke, Palgrave Macmillan, 2019.

Colley, Ann C., *Victorians in the Mountains: Sinking the Sublime*, London, Ashgate, 2010.

Doak, Robert, 'The Natural Sublime and American Nationalism, 1800–1850', *Studies in Popular Culture* 25.2, 2002, 13–22.

Ellis, Markman, '"Spectacles within doors": Panoramas of London in the 1790s', *Romanticism*, 14, 2, 2008, 133–48.

Ferguson, Frances, 'The Nuclear Sublime', *Diacritics*, 14.2, 1984, 4–10.

Freeman, Michael, 'Early Tourists in Wales: 18th and 19th Century Tourists' Comments about Wales', https://sublimewales.wordpress.com.

Garda, Michela, *Musica sublime: Metamorfosi di un'idea nel Settecento musicale*, Milan, Ricordi, 1995.

Hamilton, Paul, 'Romantic Economies and the Sublimation of Money', *The Wordsworth Circle*, 25.2, 1994, 79–81.

Hansen, Peter H, *Summits of Modern Man: Mountaineering after the Enlightenment*, Cambridge, MA, Harvard University Press, 2013.

Heringman, Noah, *Romantic Rocks, Aesthetic Geology*, Ithaca, NY, Cornell University Press, 2004.

  Romantic Science: The Literary Forms of Natural History, Albany, State University of New York Press, 2013.

Higgins, David, *British Romanticism, Climate Change, and the Anthropocene: Writing Tambora*, Basingstoke, Palgrave Macmillan, 2017.

Hitt, Christopher, 'Toward an Ecological Sublime', *New Literary History*, 30.3, 1999, 603–23.

Holmes, Richard, *The Age of Wonder: How the Romantic Generation Discovered the Beauty and Terror of Science*, London, Harper, 2008.

Janowitz, Anne, *England's Ruins: Poetic Purpose and the National Landscape*, Oxford, Blackwell, 1990.

Lennartz, Norbert, *Tears, Fluids and Porous Bodies in Literature across the Ages: Niobe's Siblings*. London, Bloomsbury, 2022.

Loomis, Chauncey C. 'The Arctic Sublime', in U. C. Knoepflmacher and G. B. Tennyson, eds., *Nature and the Victorian Imagination*, Berkeley, University of California Press, 1977, 95–112.

Macfarlane, Robert, *Mountains of the Mind: A History of a Fascination*, London, Granta, 2003.

Modiano, Raimonda, 'Humanism and the Comic Sublime: From Kant to Friedrich Theodor Vischer', *Studies in Romanticism* 26.2, 1987, 231–44.

Morris, David B., 'Gothic Sublimity', *New Literary History*, 16.2, 1985, 229–319.

Potter, Russell A., *Arctic Spectacles: The Frozen North in Visual Culture, 1818–1875*. Seattle, University of Washington Press, 2007.

Powell, Cecilia, and Stephen Hebron, *Savage Grandeur and Noble Thoughts: Discovering the Lake District 1750–1820*, Grasmere, Wordsworth Trust, 2010.

Sha, Richard C., *Imagination and Science in Romanticism*, Baltimore, MD, Johns Hopkins University Press, 2018.

  Perverse Romanticism: Aesthetics and Sexuality in Britain, 1750–1832, Baltimore, MD, Johns Hopkins University Press, 2009.

Smith, Andrew, 'The Gothic and the Sublime', in *Gothic Radicalism*, London, Palgrave, 2000, 11–37.

Springer, Carolyn, *The Marble Wilderness: Ruins and Representation in Italian Romanticism*, Cambridge, Cambridge University Press, 1987.

Stafford, Barbara Maria, *Voyage into Substance: Art, Science, Nature, and the Illustrated Travel Account, 1760–1840*, Cambridge, MA, MIT Press, 1984.

Williston, Byron, 'The Sublime Anthropocene', *Environmental Philosophy* 13.2, 2016, 155–74.

INDEX

Cambridge Companions To ...

AUTHORS

Edward Albee edited by Stephen J. Bottoms
Margaret Atwood edited by Coral Ann Howells (second edition)
W. H. Auden edited by Stan Smith
Jane Austen edited by Edward Copeland and Juliet McMaster (second edition)
James Baldwin edited by Michele Elam
Balzac edited by Owen Heathcote and Andrew Watts
Beckett edited by John Pilling
Bede edited by Scott DeGregorio
Aphra Behn edited by Derek Hughes and Janet Todd
Saul Bellow edited by Victoria Aarons
Walter Benjamin edited by David S. Ferris
William Blake edited by Morris Eaves
Boccaccio edited by Guyda Armstrong, Rhiannon Daniels, and Stephen J. Milner
Jorge Luis Borges edited by Edwin Williamson
Brecht edited by Peter Thomson and Glendyr Sacks (second edition)
The Brontës edited by Heather Glen
Bunyan edited by Anne Dunan-Page
Frances Burney edited by Peter Sabor
Byron edited by Drummond Bone
Albert Camus edited by Edward J. Hughes
Willa Cather edited by Marilee Lindemann
Catullus edited by Ian Du Quesnay and Tony Woodman
Cervantes edited by Anthony J. Cascardi
Chaucer edited by Piero Boitani and Jill Mann (second edition)
Chekhov edited by Vera Gottlieb and Paul Allain
Kate Chopin edited by Janet Beer
Caryl Churchill edited by Elaine Aston and Elin Diamond
Cicero edited by Catherine Steel
J. M. Coetzee edited by Jarad Zimbler
Coleridge edited by Lucy Newlyn
Coleridge edited by Tim Fulford (new edition)
Wilkie Collins edited by Jenny Bourne Taylor
Joseph Conrad edited by J. H. Stape
H. D. edited by Nephie J. Christodoulides and Polina Mackay
Dante edited by Rachel Jacoff (second edition)
Daniel Defoe edited by John Richetti
Don DeLillo edited by John N. Duvall
Charles Dickens edited by John O. Jordan
Emily Dickinson edited by Wendy Martin
John Donne edited by Achsah Guibbory

Dostoevskii edited by W. J. Leatherbarrow
Theodore Dreiser edited by Leonard Cassuto and Claire Virginia Eby
John Dryden edited by Steven N. Zwicker
W. E. B. Du Bois edited by Shamoon Zamir
George Eliot edited by George Levine and Nancy Henry (second edition)
T. S. Eliot edited by A. David Moody
Ralph Ellison edited by Ross Posnock
Ralph Waldo Emerson edited by Joel Porte and Saundra Morris
William Faulkner edited by Philip M. Weinstein
Henry Fielding edited by Claude Rawson
F. Scott Fitzgerald edited by Ruth Prigozy
F. Scott Fitzgerald edited by Michael Nowlin (second edition)
Flaubert edited by Timothy Unwin
E. M. Forster edited by David Bradshaw
Benjamin Franklin edited by Carla Mulford
Brian Friel edited by Anthony Roche
Robert Frost edited by Robert Faggen
Gabriel García Márquez edited by Philip Swanson
Elizabeth Gaskell edited by Jill L. Matus
Edward Gibbon edited by Karen O'Brien and Brian Young
Goethe edited by Lesley Sharpe
Günter Grass edited by Stuart Taberner
Thomas Hardy edited by Dale Kramer
David Hare edited by Richard Boon
Nathaniel Hawthorne edited by Richard Millington
Seamus Heaney edited by Bernard O'Donoghue
Ernest Hemingway edited by Scott Donaldson
Hildegard of Bingen edited by Jennifer Bain
Homer edited by Robert Fowler
Horace edited by Stephen Harrison
Ted Hughes edited by Terry Gifford
Ibsen edited by James McFarlane
Henry James edited by Jonathan Freedman
Samuel Johnson edited by Greg Clingham
Ben Jonson edited by Richard Harp and Stanley Stewart
James Joyce edited by Derek Attridge (second edition)
Kafka edited by Julian Preece
Kazuo Ishiguro edited by Andrew Bennett
Keats edited by Susan J. Wolfson
Rudyard Kipling edited by Howard J. Booth
Lacan edited by Jean-Michel Rabaté
D. H. Lawrence edited by Anne Fernihough

TOPICS

Printed in the USA
CPSIA information can be obtained
at www.ICGtesting.com
LVHW011743151123
764000LV00001B/50

9 781009 013055